BETTY GRABLE

THE GIRL
WITH THE
MILLION
DOLLAR LEGS

by

Tom McGee

Foreword by Alice Faye

The Vestal Press, Ltd.
Vestal, New York

DEDICATION

For my mother, MAMIE, whose love of the
Hollywood musical has never deserted her.

Printed in the United States of America
Library of Congress Cataloging-in-Publication Data
McGee, Tom.

Betty Grable: the girl with the million dollar legs / by Tom McGee.
           p.   cm.
      Includes bibliographical references (p. -) and index.
      ISBN 1-879511-15-0 (cloth) :
      ISBN 1-879511-18-5 (pbk.)
      1. Grable, Betty, 1916-1973. 2. Motion pictures actors and
actresses--United States--Biography. I. Title
PN2287.G66M35   1995
791.43'028'092--dc20
[B]   94-31145
CIP
Published by The Vestal Press, Ltd.
PO Box 97
Vestal, NY 13851-0097

Cover and book design by Don Bell

TABLE OF CONTENTS

FOREWORD

When I think of Betty Grable, I think of happier times.

During the Forties she was the biggest star around and I had the double pleasure of knowing her and working with her.

She and I both started in the chorus and we both married band-leaders. We were both blondes and she danced where I sang.

Betty's big movie break came when I was rushed to the hospital with appendicitis and Twentieth Century Fox gave her my part in *Down Argentine Way*. She was a hit and we both starred as a sister act in *Tin Pan Alley*, which I still fondly remember. Of course, the studio tried to concoct a feud between us . . . it was good publicity for them . . . but no one was fooled and Betty and I got along well.

After I retired from movies to bring up my daughters — and Phil —we stayed in touch and I saw her whenever I was in Las Vegas, where Betty lived and both our husbands worked. She loved to golf and gamble and was always a fun person to be with.

When I last saw her she knew she was dying of cancer, but still put on that beautiful, brave, optimistic face and cracked jokes.

As long as there are movie theatres and movies to run in them, Betty Grable will never die —- for the marvellous thing about film is that it preserves talent, truth, and beauty like hers for ever more.

God bless you, Betty.

Alice Faye
Rancho Mirage, California
5 September, 1993

PREFACE

To understand my admiration for Betty Grable — the woman and her movies — you would have to imagine a dull, gray Glasgow during the years of World War II.

Like every city in the United Kingdom (indeed all of Europe) there was total blackout. Nobody traveled, and the main entertainment outlet was the local cinema. I was lucky; I had three local cinemas in my district — the Paragon, the Crown, and the Palace. All were within comparatively safe walking distance, as long as you carried the all-important flashlight!

One evening, my mother took my brother, Pat, and me to the Paragon. The film was *Coney Island*. From the moment Betty Grable appeared, the screen lit up and my world changed forever.

As they would say today, she was something else! Such sparkle, such gaiety, such color — she set the screen alight with her beautiful blue eyes, blonde hair, and warm smile. We, in Britain, had never seen anything like her.

Of course there were other stars I loved at the time: Alice Faye, Deanna Durbin, Rita Hayworth, Betty Hutton, Dorothy Lamour. Later there would be Doris Day, Marilyn Monroe, and Goldie Hawn. But for me, no one could touch Betty Grable when it came to sheer entertainment.

Thanks to the shortage of new films in the U.K. during the war, the distribution companies constantly reissued movies, so I was able to catch up on the ones I had missed, from *Down Argentine Way* onward.

As I grew up and began to visit the cinema on my own, I traveled quite some distances to see a Grable film that had eluded me. Fortunately I didn't have to travel all that often, as Glasgow was regarded as the most cinema-conscious city in Britain, except for London. So there was always a Grable film showing in one or more of the hundred-plus cinemas around the city.

Betty seemed to be a perennial favorite among Glaswegians, for her films were constantly breaking box office records in the city. Her film *Springtime in the Rockies* held that honor in one cinema — the Picture House (later Gaumont) — for 17 years, until it was overtaken by the road-showing of *South Pacific* in 1960. A plaque noting her record was displayed proudly in the foyer until the cinema was demolished in the early 1970s.

When Betty abandoned her screen career in 1955, we British fans were at a loss. Apart from the occasional TV appearance, she all but disappeared from British and European screens.

Then came her huge success with *Hello, Dolly!* which, to us Grable fans, was like the phoenix rising from the ashes. She was a star again — although for her true fans, there had never been any question of her status.

Of course, I had written to her over the years and in reply always received an autographed photograph which I treasured. When she was on Broadway in *Hello, Dolly!* she wrote me saying that her chances of taking the show into London were nil. How disappointing.

However, two years later, our paths were finally to cross when she arrived in Glasgow to headline *Belle Starr. Belle* may have been an ill-conceived show and a bad career move on Grable's part, but it gave the United Kingdom its first in-the-flesh glimpse of Hollywood's greatest musical star — and it gave me the chance to meet the legend who had enchanted me all those years with her gay, carefree films. I met her at the press call, and waited till almost the end of the conference before I plucked up the courage to speak to her. I handed her the letter she had written me, she scanned it then exclaimed, "McGee!" then that warm smile came over her face and we were instant friends. The reference to McGee came from a line she uttered in *Sweet Rosie O'Grady* in which Betty is plagued by a journalist named McGee, played by Robert Young.

The Girl With the Million Dollar Legs

During her four-month stay in Britain, we had many long conversations about her life, loves, and career, the result of which unfolds on the following pages. I joked with her just before she was to return to the U. S. A. that I had enough material to write her biography. Betty laughed, "Honey, not until I'm dead and buried!" She certainly did not mean it that way, but sadly, that's the way things turned out.

A warm, outgoing woman, she made friends easily and always treated her fans with the utmost respect. It is my intention to make this book a living testament to that.

Tom McGee,
Glasgow, Scotland, 1994

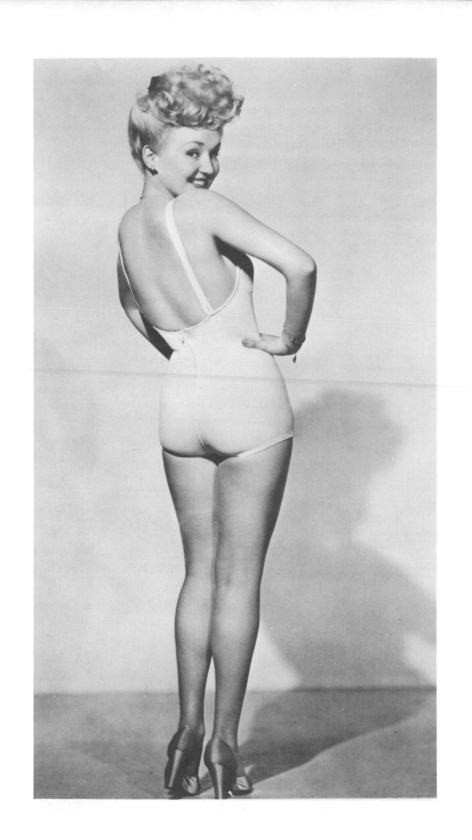

ACKNOWLEDGEMENTS

The bulk of my gratitude for this biography must go to the late Betty Grable, who spent many hours with me backstage, in hotel lobbies, hotel rooms, her apartment in London, and the occasional function suite, answering questions she must have answered a thousand times before.

From February until May, 1969, she encouraged my questioning by her straightforward answers and, indeed, prompted me to ask questions she felt would further enhance my research.

Our friendship blossomed not only from our interest in show business, but from our mutual fondness for animals, particularly dogs. I found Miss Grable a charming, honest, down-to-earth woman. Like most true greats, she displayed none of the star trappings or affectations typical of many show business personalities I've met — particularly those who don't possess an ounce of talent.

To me, Betty Grable was immensely talented and in my years of intense research, it became abundantly clear that this was also the opinion of her peers.

Secondly, I'd like to offer my sincere thanks to Bob Remick, Miss Grable's lover and constant companion in her final years, who assisted me in every way possible during Betty's 1969 stay in Great Britain.

I am also indebted to Betty Grable's friends and co-workers who spent much time talking to me in person, by telephone, and by patiently answering my letters. They include Harry James, Marjorie Grable Arnold, Alice Faye, Jack Lemmon, Mitzi Gaynor, Dick Haymes, Diana Dors, Bette Davis, Betty Ritz Baez, Dan Dailey, Cesar Romero, John Payne, Rory Calhoun, Robert Wagner,

Natalie Wood, Tom Jones, Danny La Rue, Valerie Walsh, Blayne Barrington, Jeanine Basinger, Ray Chiarella, Warren Douglas, Jack Card, Dick Shane, Marc Urquhart, Frank Rainbow, Freddie Carpenter, Linda M. Schreiber, Gordon Reed, Norman Macdonald, Richard Marohn, M. D., Millie De Palmer, Billy Sloan, Michael Hawkins, Andrew McDonald, Len Scumaci, Bob Isoz, John Hickey, George McGhee, Robert Johnson, Dorothy Purdy, Tina Scott, Gene Yusem, Mike Thomas, Ms. Terrel Frey, and Eric Trovinger of Fox Video.

For help with my research in this venture, my thanks go to the following individuals and organizations: The Margaret Herrick Library, Academy of Motion Picture Arts and Sciences; the British Film Institute; Chris Moor of New Zealand; Aldo Triballi, Toronto, Canada; Keith Raistrick, Melbourne, Australia. Special appreciation is due to my friends John Purdy, Manchester, England, and Bernie Freedman, Toronto, Canada, for allowing me access to their huge collections of stills and clippings, film magazines, videos, recordings, books, and pressbooks. These superfan/collectors form the foundation of this tribute to their beloved Betty Grable.

Thank you to my agent, Robert Kendall, to Grace L. Houghton, to Elaine Stuart and Courtney Erdman at Vestal Press, to Michon Stuart and Sam Mairs for indexing assistance, to my friends, colleagues, and library staff at the *Scottish Daily Record*, Glasgow, for their patience and understanding in my quest to have this book published. Particular thanks go to my brother Bernard for sharing his knowledge of computer technology with me, to Rosemary Apartopoulos for her help with proofreading, and to my former colleagues Anthony Nesbit and Donald McMillan, who encouraged me right from the outset.

My deep gratitude goes to Michael Levitt of Chicago who so generously shared with me many of the precious moments of his special relationship with Betty Grable. Without his help, cooperation, and friendship, this book would not have been possible.

My only is regret that my letters to Betty's daughters, Victoria and Jessica, went unanswered. Through Mike Levitt I understand they had had enough of inquiring biographers anxious to uncover another side of Betty Grable. I hope my book will help dispel any unpleasantness they may have suffered in the past.

Finally, I must pay tribute to the late Len (Leonard) Scumaci, whose Chicago home was a treasure of Grable memorabilia. Len had collected many notes and anecdotes on Grable, to which he allowed me full access.

BETTY GRABLE

THE GIRL
WITH THE
MILLION DOLLAR LEGS

PROLOGUE

There was magic in the air on that warm spring evening.

The stars twinkled brightly high above the Hollywood Hills. Below, at the Dorothy Chandler Pavilion, crowds of fans eagerly awaited the arrival of other stars — earthly beings, but just as sparkling as their heavenly counterparts.

It was the night of the 1972 Academy Awards presentation, and the motion picture industry had put on its most glamorous face. Limousines rolled up to the entrance, rewarding the public with glimpses of their all-time favorites.

Jack Lemmon was there. So, too, were Ann Miller, Jack Nicholson, Jane Russell, Natalie Wood, Robert Wagner, Martha Raye . . . the line-up seemed endless.

One of the last to arrive drew a special cheer, for she really was Hollywood. With her blonde curls piled high on her head, Betty Grable didn't seem much changed from the days when she was Hollywood's golden girl, and she cheerily acknowledged the warm applause.

It looked as though 1972 was going to be a good year for the former pin-up queen. Apart from her highly successful American stage tour with *Born Yesterday*, she had just signed for the lead in the Australian national production of *No, No, Nanette* — which would also give her the chance to meet thousands of her faithful fans in the Southern Hemisphere.

The opening of the stage show was pure nostalgia — and, in a way, a tribute to Betty. Entitled "Lights, Camera, Action," it featured a Grable lookalike, which pleased Betty immensely. Escorted by Bob Remick, Betty went backstage to check her make-up and await her "on stage" call. She was to accompany her old pal and co-star Dick Haymes in the presentation ceremony.

She stood chatting with some of her co-presenters while waiting her cue. Typically, Betty — a heavy smoker — felt the need of a cigarette, and left her backstage companions to light up in the smoking area.

Now that the excitement of her arrival had worn off, Betty felt strangely uneasy. She put it down to "nerves," although she confided to Haymes that she hadn't been feeling too well for the past few weeks. He asked her if she wanted to see a doctor, but Betty said she felt well enough to go on with the show.

Master of ceremonies Jack Lemmon introduced Betty and Dick, who strode onstage to a tremendous reception from the star-studded audience. Indeed, if she was suffering from any ailment it certainly didn't show.

Betty Grable looked every inch the movie queen as she made her way to the podium — a blonde, slim beauty in a shimmering turquoise evening gown with a thigh-high slit to reveal her still-perfect legs. She glowed happily in the warm applause from an audience whose appetite for the real Grable had been whetted by the lookalike earlier.

The presentation — an award to composer Michel Legrand — went over smoothly, and Betty made her way to her table in the auditorium. She settled down with a large vodka to watch the rest of the show with Bob and their table companions.

The following day the couple returned home to Las Vegas for a few weeks' respite before Betty was to embark on her forthcoming Australian tour.

On arrival at the desert city airport Betty suddenly felt very queasy, and complained to Bob she had a pain in her chest. When she began gasping for breath, Bob became alarmed. He seated her on the edge of a nearby luggage carousel in the arrivals hall. "Something isn't right," she told him. "I know I had a healthy belt of vodka last night, but I've never felt this bad before."

Bob suggested they call the airport's emergency medical services, but Betty refused. "Let's just get home. I don't want a big fuss made over what might be just a bad hangover."

She knew that whatever ailed her it certainly wasn't a hangover, but she couldn't bear the thought of being examined in the airport's impersonal medical section by an equally impersonal doctor.

Once home in her Tropicana Road mansion, Betty felt so ill that she went immediately to bed. Despite Bob's protestations, she said there was no need to call a doctor. Bob left her to rest in her bedroom, but Betty was too frightened to sleep. She hadn't felt really well for some time, but had kept it to herself. But in all her life, she had never felt as sick as she did now. Betty knew she would have to seek medical advice — and she feared the worst. [1]

The nausea passed, but she still had difficulty breathing and the nagging chest pain continued. In the morning Betty made an appointment with her doctor. After a preliminary examination, he was noncommittal, but advised her to see a specialist in Los Angeles as soon as possible — "just to be on the safe side," he added reassuringly. Betty wasn't reassured. Apart from childbirth and a recurring back ailment, she hadn't had to see any doctors.

A few days later Betty underwent exploratory surgery at St. John's Hospital, Santa Monica. She called her sister, Marjorie, who lived in nearby Beverly Hills, telling her of the tests (for a suspected ulcer, she lied) and not to be worried by any newspaper reports. "I'm feeling fine and hope to be out and about in a day or two," she said in her usual chipper fashion. [2]

That afternoon the consulting physician spoke with Bob Remick. The young man was stunned by the doctor's diagnosis. Asked if Betty would be able to take the news, Bob assured the doctor that Betty was a very brave person.

A short while later the physician visited Betty in her flower-filled room. His news was grim. As gently as he could he told her she was suffering from lung cancer.

Betty appeared to take the news calmly, but his voice hardly registered in her ear. Shortly after the doctor left Bob tried to comfort her. She knew she was dying.

Once she had got over the initial shock of the news, Betty quickly regained her composure. She asked Bob to call her agent, telling him to cancel the tour of Australia, and notify Betty's two daughters and ex-husband Harry James of the "ulcer." She insisted that no one be told she was suffering from cancer; she couldn't stand the pitying looks from relatives and friends if they knew the truth. Bob agreed to her wish. Betty had taken the news like the trouper she was, but as Bob walked down the quiet hospital corridor, he was close to tears.

Alone in her room, Betty phoned Marjorie, joking about the inconvenience of having an ulcer. "Just remember — don't offer me a vodka martini when I come visit you next week," she laughed as she hung up.

She turned on her side and lay against the pillow. Previously, the future had never worried her. Betty's maxim had always been that tomorrow would take care of itself.

But now, was there any tomorrow left?

CHAPTER ONE

Elizabeth Ruth Grable was a child of fate. She hadn't been planned for, and the circumstances surrounding her entry into the world would tax the imagination of a Hollywood writer. Yet those circumstances would haunt her for the rest of her life — a life she always felt she was given by default.

She was born to John C. Grable (known as Conn) and Lillian Hoffman, on December 18, 1916. She was their third and last child.

The Grables were married in 1910 when Lillian was nineteen years old and fresh out of school. She had desperately wanted to become a dancer, and often had tried to persuade her parents to allow her to go on the stage. However, the Hoffmans were very respectable middle-class Americans, and it was not quite proper to have a daughter in show business in those days.

Instead, the small dark-haired vivacious girl had married Conn. She hoped to persuade her husband to allow her to concentrate on a career. He listened to her theatrical notions all during their courtship, and while he didn't condemn her ambition for the theatre, he didn't exactly encourage her.

Once married, however, he proved to be the old-fashioned type of husband — he wanted a wife at home when he was, and said so in no uncertain terms.

Conn Grable's parents had settled in St. Louis from Europe; his mother was Dutch and his father German. [3] He was a typical son of European stock — ambitious to improve his lot in his adopted country, but not at the expense of his European heritage. His parents had brought him in up the traditional ways of young European gentlemen, and after marriage, he retained many of the habits of his forebears.

7

His socializing tastes ran to the simple things of life; he loved to make the rounds of the local speakeasies with his many friends, where he could indulge himself in European-style beer and reminisce about his homeland — a homeland that he knew only from his grandfather's sentimental recollections.

Conn was, however, a hard-working young man, holding a post as a clerk with the Board of Trade in St. Louis, Missouri. Anxious to succeed in business, his first goal was to provide a decent home for his young bride. The couple took a house at 3955 Lafayette Avenue, on the inexpensive South Side of the city. It was to be a temporary home for them, and once Conn had gained his due promotion they intended to move to a more fashionable district.

Lillian Grable, of Dutch, Irish, and English heritage, was by far the stronger partner, and while outwardly resigned to her husband's lifestyle, she secretly vowed that any children of the marriage would be steered into show business. Years later, Betty Grable would admit she could never understand her mother's driving ambition, perhaps because she herself lacked Lillian's pushiness. But she respected — and feared — her mother's powerful influence.

Lillian Grable was a force to be reckoned with, as Conn soon found out. The highlight of an otherwise dull week for Lillian was to visit the local vaudeville theatre. She practically had to drag Conn with her, for he was not in the least interested in the entertainment world. Once there, Mrs. Grable would live all her dreams and ambitions, if only for a couple of hours. It was her only escape from her humdrum married life.

While Conn was at work, Lillian continually played the phonograph to keep up with all the latest dance steps. It helped her pass away the boring afternoons. According to Betty and sister Marjorie, she wasn't a particularly good dancer in a technical sense, and lacked discipline. "But," said Marjorie, "she had a certain style and way with her that you really believed that what you were watching was actually a young woman who had had training as a dancer. Only when you compared her to a professional dancer at the theatre, did you realize that Lillian was no more than a gifted amateur."

After the birth of first daughter Marjorie, Lillian could hardly wait until the child was walking so that she could pass on her artistic skills to her. By the time Marjorie was eighteen months old, she was frequently whisked away from play periods with her friends to be taught the basics of dance.

Around three years of age, however, Marjorie began to rebel against her mother's wishes, throwing a tantrum to avoid being taken to dancing classes. She also refused to practice at home, no matter how much Lillian tried to persuade her. Lillian could not accept that her daughter had a mind of her own — or that any child of hers could be more interested in playing with her dolls and toys than performing.

When Lillian again found herself pregnant, some of her attention was deflected from her daughter, and Marjorie at last was allowed to lead a normal life with her friends. She was a very bright child and looked forward to learning something new each day at kindergarten.

In 1913, Lillian gave birth to a boy, John Carl. Conn Grable was ecstatic. At last he had the son he always wanted. The Grable family was complete; both Conn and Lillian agreed not to have any more children.

Unfortunately, the couple's only son was very delicate, and was on constant medication for cold and chest infections almost from the moment of his birth. He was only twenty-one months old when he contracted bronchial pneumonia from which he never recovered. [4]

Conn felt cheated that his son had been taken from him, and Lillian was completely crushed. The pregnancy had been fraught with difficulties and the delivery painful, and John's illness and death left her in a state of physical and mental exhaustion. The couple decided to stand by their pact: no more children.

But for Lillian, that also seemed to mean no more Conn. After the bereavement, Lillian would often go into a mood of deep depression which could last up to several weeks at a time. A bewildered Conn found himself being shut out of her life more and more each day until the couple barely spoke to one another.

Eventually, with the help of her mother and close family friends, Lillian began taking an interest in life again. She resumed her visits to the theatre (a sure sign that she was feeling more like her old self) — sometimes with Conn, at other times with neighbors or friends.

In May, 1916, Lillian Grable visited her doctor. She had been having dizzy spells and nausea. After a brief examination, the doctor informed her she was pregnant. Lillian was worried. Her two previous confinements were difficult, and after the last birth she had been warned to think carefully before having any more children.

That night she told her husband the news. Despite their prior agreement, Conn was delighted. He was especially insistent that Lillian follow the doctor's advice and instructions to the letter, so the forthcoming birth would be as easy as possible.

She had been carrying the baby for just over ten weeks when fate took a cruel turn. Lillian, always an excellent housekeeper, was waxing the kitchen floor. Walking across the highly polished surface to reach the stove, she slipped, lost her balance, and fell heavily to the floor with a resounding crack. When she came to, Lillian did not know how long she had lain there, but she found she was unable to move.

Minutes later, young Marjorie arrived home from a friend's house. Lillian sent her next door to summon help from their neighbor.

Within half an hour Lillian was on an examination table at the local hospital. Conn was summoned at work and sped to her side.

The hospital physician diagnosed a fracture to her right hip. A plaster cast was fitted and she was detained in the hospital for several days to make sure she had not miscarried.

Before leaving for home, the doctor in charge of Lillian's case told the couple that they had two choices. One was to terminate the pregnancy as soon as possible, thus enabling Mrs. Grable to have an immediate operation on her hip. The alternative was to allow the pregnancy to progress normally, which would entail Mrs. Grable's being confined to bed until after the birth. If she agreed to the latter, Lillian would be left with a permanent limp but the birth would, in all probability, be quite normal.

The doctor strongly advised Lillian to terminate the pregnancy, thereby allowing treatment to her hip. He emphasized there would almost certainly be no risk of her not being able to have any more children. Conn was inclined to agree with the doctor, and asked for time to talk the matter over in privacy with his wife.

Lillian silenced them both. "I'm going to have my baby. We've already lost a son; perhaps this time we will have better luck. I want us to have another son."

The normally energetic Mrs. Grable took life very easy for the next seven months, running the household as best she could from her bed. She spent much time with Marjorie discussing names for the new baby. It was decided he would be named Thomas Carl John, after Conn's grandfather and as a mark of respect to their dead son. However, should it be a girl she would be named Elizabeth Ruth, after Lillian's mother.

Although he could ill afford it, Conn hired a woman to act as maid/cook/nanny — looking after the daily housekeeping chores and attending to Mrs. Grable and Marjorie. Lillian recalled the summer and fall of 1916 as the only inactive period of her life.

The long wait came to a climax on the evening of December 17, 1916, when Lillian's water broke. The doctor was called, and Marjorie was dispatched to a neighbor's house for the night.

The doctor advised that she should be removed to the hospital in case there might be complications, and, after a struggle carrying Lillian downstairs, he drove the Grables there in his own car.

There were no complications, and in the early hours of the next morning, Lillian safely delivered a seven-pound, nine-ounce daughter. A nurse emerged from the hospital room to relay the good news to Conn, and he was allowed a short visit. Lillian smiled contentedly, her hour-old daughter laying on the bed beside her.

"Look at her, Conn," beamed Lillian. "Isn't she the prettiest little lady?"

Conn Grable swelled with pride as he lifted the baby into his arms. "Hello, Betty Grable," he said softly.

Despite her infirmity, Lillian Grable said the delivery was quite painless, "the easiest of my three children."

Five weeks after leaving the hospital, the new arrival was baptized Elizabeth Ruth Grable, although her father, still celebrating the birth of his new daughter, had recorded her birth with the town's registrar as Ruth Elizabeth. (Betty herself never knew this until years later when she applied to her home town for details of the registration for a passport application.)

The baptism service was conducted by the local Episcopalian minister, both parents being of that persuasion, though they were not regular churchgoers.

Marjorie remembered her little sister as "a dolly who slept a lot and smiled often."

Elizabeth (as Lillian preferred to call her) appeared to be a healthy and contented child, hardly ever crying. At an early age she showed a marked preference for cuddly animal toys rather than dolls. At five months she was crawling, and took her first faltering steps on her own a couple of weeks after her first birthday.

About this time, Conn Grable earned a promotion, and was able to put down a deposit on a large apartment at the Forrest Park Apartment Hotel in a more upscale area of St. Louis.

The Grables enjoyed their new home. They had three bedrooms, two bathrooms, a huge living room, and an adjoining den for the children. The smallest bedroom was decorated as a nursery for the youngest Grable, and Marjorie enjoyed the luxury of a bedroom of her own.

Young Betty fell in love with the huge German Shepherd dog next door. It was the beginning of a lifelong love affair with all kinds of animals. She would own and care for many dogs throughout her life, from expensive toy poodles (usually gifts from admirers) to stray mutts she found on the street. Their pedigrees didn't matter to Betty; she loved them all equally.

With Marjorie now in grade school, Mrs. Grable spent most of her day attending to young Betty. She was a fair-haired, placid child who showed no signs of temperament. And best of all, she showed unmistakable signs of an interest in dancing. One day, Mrs. Grable recalled, she was playing some ragtime music on her phonograph as she went about her chores in the kitchen. She could no longer dance properly because of her limp, but she always liked to have music around the house. As she worked, she heard a thump-thump-thump coming from the den area. She went to investigate and found Betty jumping up and down in time to the music.

Lillian Grable was overjoyed. She hardly dared believe her own "dancing madness" (as her husband so often called it) had been inherited by little Betty. Thereafter, most afternoons Mrs. Grable set aside a couple of hours to teach Betty all the latest dance steps she knew, despite her disability.

If the doting mother is to be believed, Betty could repeat simple routines without much effort. However, as in the case of Marjorie, the novelty soon began to wear off; Betty wanted to spend more time with the neighbor's dog who was as docile as a lamb even though she teased it unmercifully. It was a big thrill for Betty when she managed to teach the dog to sit and beg for scraps of meat she had taken from the kitchen table while her mother's attention was elsewhere.

Besides dogs, Betty was also captivated by horses. In the dawn of the 1920s, there were plenty of stables around, and horse-drawn brewery floats abounded on the streets of St. Louis. Lillian noted this equestrian passion and kept it in mind, feeling sure that one day she could use the information to her own benefit.

As soon as she could, Lillian enrolled Betty in dance classes — tap, ballet, classical, and acrobatic. Initially, the child was enthusiastic, and the arrangement worked smoothly. The only part of the routine Betty rebelled against was the acrobatic dance, but after much tear-spilling this segment of the curriculum was dropped. Lillian Grable simply substituted an extra tap lesson for the acrobatics. As far as she was concerned, Betty could never get enough practice.

Mrs. Grable also signed Betty up for music classes where the child learned to play the saxophone, ukulele, and drums. Conn Grable often protested the cost, but Lillian never bothered with such mundane matters, and left her husband to worry about paying the bills. And when he protested about the toll it was taking on young Betty, that too was ignored. It was all part of Lillian's grand plan.

At the age of six, Betty's school years began at the Mary Institute, a fashionable St. Louis establishment which provided an education program geared to the needs of children from well-to-do homes. She claimed her earliest memory of school life was "playing a piece of coral[in the underwater ballet sequence for the school's annual Christmas show] — which just goes to show where my mind was when it came to formal lessons!"

Conn Grable continued his protestations about the escalating fees for her music and dance lessons, feeling Lillian was pushing young Betty too far. However, the youngster seldom complained, and as she appeared a normal, healthy child, Mrs. Grable ignored her husband's threats to stop allowances for the lessons. She reckoned that if he could afford his nights out in the local speakeasies, he could afford a few extra dollars for Betty's dance and music lessons.

Interestingly, movies, which would become the cornerstone of Betty's future success, were not one of her great childhood passions. Her visits to the local cinemas were usually confined to the Saturday afternoon matinee. Like most children, Betty enjoyed Westerns (mainly because of the horses), and Rin Tin Tin was another of her favorites.

However, as Betty grew older, Lillian took her to see more sophisticated films, pointing out the acting techniques of the various stars. Betty was frankly bored with love stories, and much preferred an evening at the local vaudeville theatre. She said, "To me, actors on the screen were merely shadows. They moved, but they didn't speak. It was all rather unreal."

But vaudeville was different. "There was always something exciting about being in a live theatre — the crowds, the fancy decor, the orchestra tuning up. There was something magical and wonderful in waiting for the curtain to go up. I always remember my feeling of anticipation at what delights lay in store on that colorful stage. It is an excitement that I never got over. And I don't think I ever will."

When Betty was seven years old, Lillian entered her in a local amateur talent show. These contests were a highly popular form of entertainment throughout America in the twenties. Comedian and vaudeville headliner Frank Fay was auditioning amateur talent at the local theatre and Lillian took Betty along. Mr. Fay was impressed with the pretty, curly-haired youngster as she sang and tapped her way through a popular song of the period. He told Mrs. Grable to bring Betty along to compete in the first heat on the following Monday.

Excitedly, Lillian rushed home to tell Conn the good news. He was less than thrilled. He told his wife that he wasn't having any of his daughters paraded around a vaudeville stage for all the world to gape at.

Undeterred, Lillian coaxed, pleaded, and even threatened to leave him if he didn't allow Betty to appear in the show. "I gave up the chance of a career to marry you," she sobbed dramatically. "Now I'd like one of my children to have a shot at a stage career."

Conn Grable scoffed, "You had no career when I married you."

Lillian Grable was angry about her husband's attitude and made a determined stand to get Betty to the theatre on Monday for the contest. Nothing was going to stop her, not even her husband. Least of all her husband!

In an effort to stop his wife's continual nagging, Conn relented. Although Lillian was overjoyed at what she considered a major victory over her husband's Victorian attitude about show business, it was the beginning of the end of their marriage.

Mrs. Grable spent most of the weekend at her trusty Singer treadle machine, running up an outfit for Betty to wear on stage. Although her mother was bursting with excitement, Betty was quite unconcerned and went horseback riding as usual on Sunday afternoon. All she could think about was her mother's promise that she would be able to spend two days at the riding stables if she did well in the contest.

Betty did remember arriving at the theatre:

> Mother was in a state of agitation. Strangely enough, I didn't suffer as she did. In fact, I felt no emotion at all. Perhaps that was because I was too young and didn't realize what was ahead of me. I just kept thinking about those horses!
>
> We were shown into a dressing room, a dungeon beneath the stage which we shared with several other girls competing in the show. And, of course, their mothers were there, too!
>
> I got a big thrill out of being made up. And when I was dressed in my costume — a bright blue outfit made of satin — I felt my first real tinge of excitement. It didn't worry me though; it was a nice warm feeling. I had always enjoyed dressing up in mother's long dresses and fancy hats — Marjorie and I were always in trouble over that!

The competitors, accompanied by their doting mothers, made their way upstairs to the stage area, and the contest, introduced by Mr. Fay, was soon under way.

It was then that Betty got her first real taste of how determined (and malevolent) stage mothers could be. Just before she heard her name being announced, a woman delivered a hefty kick to Betty's shinbone. She yelped in pain. Her mother turned to ask what was wrong, but before Betty could explain, the woman had moved away from the side of the stage.

> I quickly forgot my pain when I heard the M. C. announce my

name. My mother was behind me now, fussing over my hair and my costume. Suddenly, I found myself being propelled to the center of the stage with an almighty push from my mother. The pianist went into my song and I heard this little voice singing. It didn't sound like me; it was as if I was just opening and shutting my mouth while someone else was doing the vocals. I caught glimpses of the upturned faces of the audience — it hadn't occurred to me until that moment that there would be people out there in the darkness watching me — and everything I did. Once or twice I dried up for a few seconds, but a look from my mother was enough to get me going again. After a brief tap dance it was all over.

My mother was hugging and kissing me — a rare display of affection from her. She kept telling me how well I'd done and that I was sure to win. Win or not, I had done my share and earned an extra afternoon with those precious horses!

Neither Betty nor her mother could recall the song she sang, but Betty had a vague idea that it was "Tea for Two." After the last competitor had left the stage, the children were reassembled in a line in front of the audience. As the M.C. touched each child on the head, the audience applauded. The contestant who received the loudest applause would be the winner for the night, and asked back to the grand final contest on Saturday night.

Happily Betty won the first heat. She remembered her mother giving her a congratulatory hug and showing her the twenty dollar bill she had earned for her night's work.

"Mama," asked Betty thoughtfully, eyeing the money, "how many dollars would we need to buy me a horse of my very own?"

Mrs. Grable smiled. She had found the key to keep Betty going. "Just win a few more of these competitions, baby, and soon you'll have a whole stable full of horses."

Little did Lillian realize what a prophetic statement she had just made.

When the ecstatic mother and tired (but happy) youngster arrived home that night, Conn Grable appeared less than excited to hear that his daughter had won her way through to the finals. Instead of congratulating Betty on her triumph, Conn reached for his coat and headed for the door. He made his way to the local speakeasy to escape his wife's non-stop commentary on the evening's events.

Lillian couldn't understand her husband's apparent lack of enthusiasm. Betty felt later that her father was secretly as proud of her as Lillian was — only he knew that if he showed any enthusiasm at all, his wife would embark on even more ambitious plans for their young star. At best, he hoped that Lillian's enthusiasm would wane if he did not give her (or Betty) any encouragement at all.

Mrs. Grable was quick to let relatives and neighbors know that Betty had made it to the finals on Saturday night, thereby making sure that the theatre would be packed with people rooting for her talented daughter.

The child wore the same outfit for the final night. Her father had adamantly refused to allow Lillian to buy a "flashy" red outfit, complete with feather boa, which Mrs. Grable thought would look sensational on Betty.

On the big night, Betty sang the same song, danced the same routine, and received about the same applause as she had in her winning heat.

Mrs. Grable stood expectantly in the wings as the judges, including Mr. Fay, considered their verdict. Unlike the earlier heats, the final night's judging was left to the professionals appearing on the bill and a civic dignitary or two, and was not based on audience applause.

Eventually, the star of the show announced the winner. Lillian Grable could hardly believe her ears. Betty had been placed third and was to be awarded $50 for her efforts. Marjorie, who was not allowed to attend, later learned from Grandma Hoffman that Lillian had to be restrained from marching on to the stage in protest.

Betty retreated to the wings, expecting congratulations (or at least condolences) from her mother. Instead, she was greeted by the palm of Lillian's hand flat across her face. Tears sprang from the bewildered child's eyes, and her jaw stung with the force of the blow. Relatives, including Grandma Hoffman, protested. But Mrs. Grable felt Betty hadn't put as much pep into her act as she had on the first night.

Angrily pointing to her hip, she told a sobbing Betty, "I suffered agonies bringing you into this world. Don't you ever dare to let me down again!" It was a childhood memory Betty never forgot. It was the first time her mother had ever hit her in anger. The child was completely bewildered, but she realized — even at her tender years — that no matter what she did, she would always have to do her best to please her mother. And she had better not do anything to incur her wrath.

It was the first of many physical and mental "slaps" Betty would endure right up until she was a woman in her twenties. Years later, Betty admitted that she was always aware of her mother on the edge of the set as she was filming a dance sequence. "My mother knew every lyric, dance step, turn, and camera angle, and I could see her going through my routine at the back of the set. I'm sure that had she been given the chance, she would have been a much better performer than I was . . . she was the one who wanted a career — not me!"

The ambitious mother made a promise to herself. Elizabeth Ruth Grable was going to be number one all over the country — no more third place for her. All that was needed was a guiding hand and the opportunities Lillian herself had been denied. Betty Grable was a "lucky" child; she had the ambitious Lillian to pilot her through to stardom!

And so Betty's course was plotted with all the navigational skill of a sea captain steering his precious cargo through perilous waters. Lillian knew she could mould Betty into the glamorous image she had envisaged for herself all those long years ago in her youth — and nothing was going to stop her.

It was as simple as that.

CHAPTER TWO

Betty returned to the Mary Institute the following Monday, regarded by her fellow-pupils as something of a celebrity. Her teachers paid not the slightest bit of attention to the adulation the other children paid the young Miss Grable, and the "show business" side of her life was totally ignored by them.

"That was good for me," recalled Betty. "It could have turned my head and goodness knows where I would have ended up. Instead of getting any preferential treatment, I was plunged into the familiar routine of daily lessons."

She proved to be an average pupil, good at English and recitation, but much less than average at addition and subtraction. She found she had to work much harder than the other children in her class in order to make her grades.

"My favorite teacher was Mrs. Minton who was kind enough to take the time to explain some of the scholarly problems I had difficulty with. Some of the [other] teachers were less than helpful. I think they must have resented my being a personality of sorts — even at that early age."

Betty was popular among the other pupils, and though she had to attend dance and music classes every other day, she still found time to play with children her own age. She loved skipping, and she remembered engaging in all the usual schoolyard games — softball, hopscotch, etc.

"At one period I even roughed it with some of the boys in our neighborhood — often playing against them at football. Mother tried to put a stop to that whenever I returned home with bruised shins or a bloodied knee. My father was delighted, though, and we often had a game of catch on the lawn in front of the apartments.

But I don't think I was ever regarded as a tomboy."

Sister Marjorie had her own circle of friends and was not particularly interested in the cinema or theatre. She was a studious child with a much quieter disposition than Betty. She preferred to stay home with a good book or spend hours browsing at the local library.

Mrs. Grable, still very much against her husband's wishes, hammered on the doors of local theatrical booking agents in her efforts to get Betty a spot in vaudeville. Occasionally she was able to persuade otherwise disinterested agents to book Betty at local theatres on a semi-regular basis, should some down-the-bill act fail to turn up for an engagement.

Betty's dance lessons continued and she still attended music school. By now she was adept at the ukulele, sax, and drums. The lessons cut deeply into the child's leisure time, but Betty never complained. She was afraid to, knowing full well the outburst she would receive from her mother.

Through Mrs. Grable's determined efforts, Betty was also heard regularly on a local radio station, for which she was paid five dollars a broadcast. As she became more proficient on the ukulele, she was soon in demand on a radio show featuring hillbilly music. Betty claimed that it was during the recording of these shows that she took a great dislike to country and western music. But in a good week she could earn up to $50, and by the age of ten, Betty had come to be regarded as a sort of local "wunderkind," often written up in local newspapers. Her income helped to pay for her music and dance lessons, and Mrs. Grable was farsighted enough to put some money in an account for Betty, ready for the day when her daughter would embark on a full-time show business career.

On family vacations, Mrs. Grable encouraged Betty to entertain hotel residents in the lobby. Betty complied, but not willingly. "I hated the idea of getting up in front of a group of strangers and dancing for them," she said later. "My mother could never understand this. I tried to explain to her that it was different when I was on stage or in a radio station. With make up and bright lights, I was another person. Just to go out there in the hotel lobby and go through my act (such as it was) was completely alien to me. I loathed those holidays."

However, the management at the various resorts where the Grables vacationed were always pleased to have young Betty perform for the other guests. It saved them hiring professional entertainers and kept the residents — mainly middle-aged to elderly people — occupied. (A scene in one of Betty's best films, *Mother Wore Tights*, was very reminiscent of those early family holidays.)

Mrs. Grable insisted that the management pay her for her daughter's performances, but this amounted to very little — sometimes as little as two dollars a night. However, money was money, reasoned Mrs. Grable, and it was faithfully put into the account for the official launch of Betty Grable.

It was on one such vacation that Lillian Grable should have first recognized the toll Betty's "career" was taking on the child. Mrs. Grable checked on her daughters before she and Conn retired for the night. She found Betty's bed empty. Quickly she roused Marjorie and together they searched the corridors, but Betty was nowhere in the building. Eventually, the hotel's night porter found Betty sitting on a wall in an ornamental garden in front of the hotel. He called Mrs. Grable to the scene and told her that the child was "in some kind of a trance."

Sensing something was wrong, Mrs. Grable gently steered Betty back to her room and tucked her safely in bed, locking the door, and checking that the windows were secure before she left.

The next day, Lillian consulted the hotel's doctor, and related the events of the previous evening. He examined Betty and found her physically fit but a little high strung. He said that in his opinion she appeared to be a sleepwalker, a common problem among children who are pushed too far — mentally and physically — or are psychologically disturbed by domestic problems. He advised Mrs. Grable to be careful of pushing Betty, and warned her that if she ignored this advice, the consequences could be dire.

Much to Betty's relief, the hotel entertaining ceased, and she and Marjorie were able to enjoy a normal holiday "for the first time in years." However, the sleepwalking continued, and resurfaced in her adult life, particularly in times of stress. [5]

When Betty was twelve, the family decided to visit Hollywood for their annual vacation. Rather, Lillian decided; Conn would have preferred the quiet Ozark mountain resorts nearer home, but as usual, he didn't get a choice. The Grable family arrived in Hollywood in 1928.

It was a year all Hollywood would remember, but not for the arrival of the Grables. Al Jolson had successfully made the transition from Broadway to the "film city" as the star of the world's first talking picture, *The Jazz Singer* (1927). The film was successful beyond all expectations and the studios were in turmoil.

The major film companies scrapped their current production schedules in an effort to convert quickly to the new "talkies." An influx of stage-trained British and continental actors (who were suddenly in great demand for dramatic films) swelled the population and changed the face of small-town California. It was the start of Hollywood's golden period which would last for the next twenty-five years. Betty Grable had arrived just at the right time.

Metro-Goldwyn-Mayer was busy on its first all-talking, all-singing, all-dancing extravaganza, *Broadway Melody* (1929), starring Anita Page, Charles King, and Bessie Love. This film heralded the advent of the musical which became the mainstay of the film industry for the next three decades. Singers and dancers from New York and other major entertainment areas found rich pickings around the sound stages, as the other studios fell over each other to better the Warner-M-G-M confections which had been so successful at the box office.

The youthful Miss Grable was absolutely fascinated by Hollywood. "I shall never forget my first glimpse of the town," she said. "It was just exactly as I had pictured it. Orange trees on the wide boulevards, actors and extras everywhere you looked — and all those different accents and cultures coming together in one small town made it all so exciting."

After a guided tour of one of the studios where Betty remembered seeing the legendary Mary Pickford filming a scene in a muddy swamp, she begged her parents to stay on in the city. "I knew even then that my future lay in films. And I was determined to try my luck."

However, at the insistence of Conn Grable, the family returned to St. Louis where he had to report back to work. The Midwest was no longer exciting to Betty. She didn't want to go back to the long, hard grind of radio and theatre work. She argued with her father, "Who will ever discover me this far from Hollywood?"

Mrs. Grable, delighted she had instilled some ambition in her daughter, suggested to her husband that it might be a good idea to move permanently to Hollywood. Conn, for once, was adamant; he was forty-two years old, progressing steadily in his job, and did not feel up to any major domestic upheavals. Besides, he reasoned, they had a comfortable home in one of the better districts of St. Louis, and he and Marjorie were quite content with their lives.

Lillian Grable thought long and hard, torn between family loyalty and ambition. She loved both her children dearly, so Marjorie must also be considered — but she desperately wanted Betty to have a career in show business. After many long arguments with herself, ambition finally won. Lillian and Betty would return to Hollywood in the spring of 1929. Marjorie elected to stay at home and prepare for her entrance to the state university. She would also keep house for her father.

It wasn't a tearful family farewell as Mrs. Grable and Betty boarded the train for California. Conn Grable was in a huff, sure that they would return when their money ran out. But Lillian knew, as the train pulled out of the station, that she would never return to live in St. Louis.

Betty remembered her first night in her newly adopted city. After they had found modest accommodations in a rooming house just off Sunset Boulevard, mother and daughter decided to take in the town. Their trip consisted mainly of streetcar rides through the main thoroughfares. Mrs. Grable was just as excited as Betty at their new environment, if not more so. Betty recalled, "I kept looking into people's faces desperately trying to recognize them. I was so sure everybody in Hollywood was a movie star."

Hollywood. The city of dreams. It was the mecca for beautiful and talented girls who came from all over the world to seek fame and fortune. Mrs. Grable and her aspiring daughter were duplicated countless times in the city.

Unfortunately most of the hopefuls didn't make it. Many took jobs as waitresses, receptionists, hotel domestics, and other less glamorous occupations to eke out their modest budgets while waiting for the big break that always seemed to be so tantalizingly out of reach. Some girls with office skills managed to secure work as secretaries or typists in the studios, but that was the nearest they would ever get to a sound stage. Others, not so fortunate, drifted into prostitution as a means to earn money while still hoping for that elusive lucky break. The lucky ones were those who realized they didn't have that "extra something" required of them for film stardom, and took the first bus back to their home towns.

Left to her own devices, the teenage Betty Grable probably would have headed back to St. Louis after the initial excitement had worn off. Even at the tender age of thirteen, she was well aware of her shortcomings and never regarded herself as something special.

It was her mother who did all the groundwork. If Mrs. Grable had any trepidation about embarking on such an ambitious project — the making of Betty Grable, film star — she didn't let it show. She said, "Promoting Betty was like a poker game. I knew I held all the aces."

Betty was immediately enrolled at the Hollywood Professional School to continue her education. A teacher there remembered the young Miss Grable as a better-than-average pupil, but lacking in concentration.

After school, she attended the Albertina Rasch Dance Academy — one of many similar establishments springing up all over the city to meet the studios' demand for trained dancers. Although Betty excelled in tap and ballroom dancing, she was a rather poor student of ballet (ironically, her favorite dance form). "Briefly I thought I'd like to be a leading ballerina with sleek black hair, change my name to a Russian-sounding one, and dance with the Ballets Russes," she recalled.

One evening she was put through her paces in ballet class. Betty had all but completed the intricate movement when she stumbled and fell. Blushing with embarrassment, she asked if she could begin again. The ballet master agreed. Nervously, Betty recommenced the movement. Once again she tripped.

The ballet master stood up. He faced Betty and said quietly, "Enough." In front of the assembled pupils, he added, "Miss Grable, if I were you I would give up the idea of ever becoming a dancer. You are a very pretty and intelligent girl. Take my advice — give up dancing. You will never make it."

The teenager was mortified. She ran from the room crying, packed up her practice clothes ,and went directly home, where she unfolded the unfortunate incident to her mother.

After hearing Betty's story, Mrs. Grable calmed her down. At first she was disappointed, but she realized that as much as she hated to admit it, there must be some things her daughter wasn't good at. And in any case, it was never a part of Mrs. Grable's plans to have Betty become a ballerina (even though, years later, she told a fan magazine that it was). Who would ever hear of her in the chorus of the Ballets Russes?

Instead of the usual slap in the face and the by-now automatic pointing to the injured hip — as Betty had feared — Mrs. Grable consoled her daughter. She told the trembling Betty, "It's not the end of the world. There are plenty of good dance schools. We'll just have to find another one. No — a better one. You'll make out all right."

The following week Betty joined the Ernest Belcher Dance School. Mr. Belcher, father of dancer Marge Champion, remembered Betty as a willing pupil who picked up the most demanding routines with seemingly effortless ease. "She was a fair-haired, happy-go-lucky kid, always popular with the other girls. Not too pretty, but she had an attractive winning smile. She was a pupil who appeared not to take any notice of instruction, yet when called to repeat a routine she had apparently shown no interest in, she would be step-perfect."[6]

School work still remained her biggest problem, though. In later years, she recalled struggling through a math test at Hollywood Professional. Each question she faced seemed tougher than the one before it, and some of the questions had been so difficult that she gave no answer at all. When she did eventually manage to answer, it was only after several fumbled tries and much erasing. She was only about halfway through it when she noticed other students holding up their hands to signal they had finished. Betty knew she was in trouble.

When the bell rang to signify the end of the test period, she was relieved that the ordeal was over, but worried about the outcome. It was several days before the results were announced. Betty sighed with relief when she heard her mark was 65 — the lowest possible passing mark.

Later she spoke to her teacher and told him that she was concerned about her grade. He told her, "You haven't a thing to worry about. First of all, you've passed the test. And secondly, I doubt that a girl as pretty as you will have to get by in this world on her ability as a mathematician." Her teacher was flirting with her, and she knew it. But she was immensely flattered.

Although Betty had continued her dance studies, she hadn't had any professional engagements since arriving in Hollywood. "It appeared to me at the time," she said, "that I was destined to remain a student of the dance for the rest of my life. And that wasn't going to be any help to the family budget which, at that time, was at its lowest."

A former school friend from St. Louis arrived in the city and began studying at the same dance school as Betty. She was Emeline Pique (later to gain Broadway and film fame under the name of Mitzi Mayfair). Under the critical eye of Mrs. Grable, they put together a musical act in which they sang a duet, then Emeline tap-danced to a tune Betty played on a saxophone almost as big as she was.

Once satisfied with their competence, Mrs. Grable hammered on the doors of booking agents to get the youngsters a spot in local theatres and variety cinemas.

The girls were not too popular with sophisticated Los Angeles cinema audiences and had only moderate success. Mrs. Grable watched their every performance, adding bits here and there in an effort to put some pep into what was really a poorly constructed act. She often chided the girls for not playing it as it had been rehearsed. Mercifully, the act broke up after only a few weeks when Emeline got a lucky break and was cast in a Broadway-bound show. Betty continued as a solo — singing, dancing, and playing the sax and drums. This act, however, found even less favor with booking agents and theatre-goers than her duet with Emeline had.

A visit to the dentist soon put an end to the sax playing; the dentist warned Mrs. Grable that Betty's front teeth could loosen with the activity of dancing and playing the instrument simultaneously. If she were to grow up with perfect teeth, the saxophone would have to go.

Mrs. Grable reluctantly agreed, to Betty's great relief. Maybe now her mother would give up this crazy notion of playing second-rate theatres and concentrate on the movies. No such luck. Mrs. Grable merely replaced the saxophone with the ukulele, and continued in her efforts to get bookings for her teenage protégée.

Betty despaired of ever getting a break in the movies. They had been in Hollywood for six months (a long time to a thirteen-year-old) and she hadn't even set foot inside the magical world of a film studio.

Then fate took a hand. Mrs. Grable unexpectedly called at the dance school one night to take Betty home. She overheard one mother remind her youngster to "get to bed early so that you can be at your best for tomorrow's audition."

Lillian Grable wasted no time in finding out that Fox Studios had put out a casting call for chorines for a musical entitled *Happy Days*. She told an excited Betty on the way home, "No school for you tomorrow, young lady. You're going to audition at Fox."

That night Betty sat patiently as her mother brushed her hair and gave her advice on how to behave, and what to say if she were asked any awkward questions.

Early the next day, Betty lined up with scores of other young hopefuls waiting to audition. To her amazement, the chorus master gave her the thumbs up after she had danced for only a few minutes. She was told to leave the line and give her name to the assistant director. As she left the line-up he called to her, "How old are you, kid?"

"Sixteen," she lied glibly.

The director nodded his approval. Betty couldn't believe her good fortune. She raced home to tell her mother the news.

The following Monday Betty was at work on her very first film. It was the last day of Betty Grable's childhood, such as it was.

Her chorus work in the film lasted only two weeks. She appeared in several shots in the film, disguised in blackface, as part of a line of forty dancers. Her father claimed he, along with Marjorie, saw the film several times in St. Louis, but they both failed to recognize Betty.[7]

The dance director must have been satisfied with her work, for a week or so after she completed her first film, she was selected for the chorus of another musical, *Let's Go Places*, and then straight into *New Movietone Follies* at the same studio.

(*Let's Go Places* has often been listed as Betty's first film, perhaps because it went on general release before *Happy Days*, since the latter had a limited showing. In the 1940s Fox publicity always maintained that *Let's Go Places* was her debut movie. The publicity line ran, "Betty's first film was '*Let's Go Places*'. . . and she did!").

By the time Betty had completed another two or three weeks' work in the chorus for the princely sum of fifty dollars a week,

The Girl With the Million Dollar Legs

Lillian Grable was on top of the world. Her investment was getting off the ground at last. There was no doubt at all in her mind that her daughter would make it to stardom.

She reasoned that after a year or so in the chorus, followed by a period where Betty would be promoted to featured roles, she would then be ready for the big time. The sky was the limit as far as Mrs. Grable was concerned. Her plan was being realized. On the strength of Betty's earnings, Lillian took a lease on a more upscale apartment at the Canterbury Apartment Hotel in Hollywood.

Then the blow fell. The city authorities tightened up on child labor laws; too many children were being exploited, not only in the studios, but also in almost every industry in the Los Angeles area. Before the studio came under investigation by the authorities, Fox dropped Grable and several other girls after they were quizzed by a suspicious administrative assistant. Under the cross-examination, Betty had admitted she was only thirteen.

Undaunted by this latest setback, Lillian simply touted her daughter around to different casting offices. She had Betty's hair lightened to a bright blonde and officially stepped her age up to sixteen, telling the child: "If you have to tell a lie, make it a big one!"

She padded out Betty's brassieres (she was still rather under-developed), instructed her in the use of make-up, and, despairing of the child's skinny legs, bought her high-heels and silk stockings.

One evening after going through the lengthy process of "dressing older," Betty finally rebelled. "I look ridiculous," she cried, as she viewed herself in the full-length mirror. "I look like a freak in this get-up." She started to tear off the print dress she was wearing.

Mrs. Grable rose from her chair and slapped Betty hard across the face. "Don't you ever say that again, young lady! Why do you think I am going through all this? Didn't I maim myself to bring you into this world? You're an ungrateful little wretch. Stop

sniveling! Don't you realize I am doing this for you? Not for anyone else. FOR YOU!" she screamed at the sobbing child.

But Lillian wasn't doing it for Betty. She was doing it for herself
— to satisfy a deep-rooted urge that demanded some claim to
fame in her life. She was reliving her fantasies through her
daughter. There was never a time in Betty Grable's childhood that
she was allowed to speak for herself about how she would have
liked to live. She was a child of ambition — not her own, but her
mother's. Even when Betty expressed the usual childish ideas
about becoming a nurse, a sales clerk, or a secretary, Mrs. Grable
would quickly silence her. "Stop these fanciful notions. You are
going to be a great actress. You were born to it."

Nobody (except possibly Conn) ever thought to ask Lillian if her
ambitions to make Betty an actress weren't too fanciful. Failure
just wasn't in Mrs. Grable's vocabulary as far as Betty's career was
concerned — and she wouldn't let Betty mention the word either.

For six months or so, Betty alternated between school and
studio. This led to problems with the Education Authority which
was worried about the child's low academic ability.

However, whenever possible, Betty did attend school. She realized her education was sadly lacking and was ashamed at her lack
of knowledge. A teacher advised her to read everything and
anything to improve her general knowledge, and introduced her
to crossword puzzles to improve her vocabulary and spelling.

Crosswords became an addiction for Betty, and any spare
moments on the set would find her holed up in a quiet corner
scanning the newspapers for puzzles. She also became an avid
reader — anything from Agatha Christie to Truman Capote, as she
stated years later. Even at the height of her career, she still
managed to get through two to three books a week.

Later, in the 1950s, when she met Marilyn Monroe, she passed
on this advice when Monroe complained about her lack of education. Marilyn also became an enthusiastic reader, but never
managed to master crossword puzzles.

In truth, Mrs. Grable wasn't all that concerned about her

daughter's lack of education. She religiously made Betty complete her rounds of the casting offices whenever possible, and encouraged her to take time off from her school studies to do so.

Betty had grown into a quiet, shy, and slightly awkward girl in company, and she would often be too tongue-tied to speak. This trait made her stand out from the other more pushy types who made the same daily rounds. Casting directors came to know her and talk to her, and gradually she felt at ease with them. Their acceptance of her made her more self-confident and gave her a new belief in her own ability to make the grade in movies.

Nevertheless, business was business, and if you didn't have much film footage to your credit, it was difficult to break out from the chorus line and into feature work.

Many times she was invited on to the "casting couch." Her fresh, dewy looks, slender figure, and becoming personality made her a target for many of the casting-office wolves. She would pretend complete innocence of such goings-on and usually managed to flee the office before events became too serious. She knew from the other girls on the rounds that it was more or less expected of them to dispense their charms for favors, but Mrs. Grable insisted it was wrong. Not from a moral point of view — simply, Lillian felt that "any girl who gives in that easily will never get anywhere. You have the talent, Betty," Lillian would add. "I know you have — and that will separate you from the others."

On one of her daily rounds, Betty just missed a call for chorus girls for Eddie Cantor's new musical about to go into production at Goldwyn Studios. She arrived home disconsolate, but her mother had an idea. She telephoned the studio and managed to get through to Cantor's office. Loftily, she informed his secretary that Betty had once appeared on the bill with Mr. Cantor in St. Louis. "And," she continued, "Eddie said I was to look him up when we got to Hollywood. So here we are!"

Mr. Cantor had no recollection of Betty or of his offer of help. (Betty had appeared in her school's annual Christmas musical program in which Cantor had made a guest appearance.) But in order to get the insistent Mrs. Grable off the line, Cantor instructed his secretary to set up an appointment. Mrs. Grable was told to report to the Goldwyn Studios in the morning.

Betty and her mother arrived at the studio at the appointed time. Dressed in a smart rehearsal outfit which showed her padded-out figure to full advantage, her blonde curls carefully arranged atop her head, Betty gathered wolf whistles as she made her way past the sound stages to the administration building.

Her arrival, and the commotion it caused among the male population at the studio, was witnessed by film director Thornton Freeland. After watching Betty go through the stock rehearsal routine, Freeland instructed that Betty be signed to a contract as a Goldwyn Girl. He knew that Sam Goldwyn was always on the look-out for pretty young fillies to add to his stable of stunning chorines.

She became the youngest-ever member of the famous troupe which was destined to become world-famous throughout the next two decades of Hollywood musicals. The troupe included such future stars as Paulette Goddard and Jane Wyman. Jane and Betty were regarded as "ponies" — being the smallest of the chorines!

Betty said later, "I signed the contract which stated that I was 16 years old. It simply meant that when I did reach sixteen, I would have to stand still for two years until my real age caught up with me."

Betty started work on the new film, *Whoopee*, which starred Cantor and Sally Morgan. In the film's first number, young Betty was given plenty of footage, some flattering medium/close shots, teased the chorus boys with a lasso, and generally made her presence felt. Later in the film Betty was seen briefly as a brides-maid at a wedding ceremony. She looked quite beautiful in the early two-strip Technicolor process. In addition, she led the chorus into the film's opening musical number, "Cowboys" — and the youthful Grable voice was heard for the first time on the screen.

During rehearsals, she was promoted to line captain by chore-ographer Busby Berkeley, due to her expert knowledge of dance routines. A sixteen-year-old line captain was just too much for the older chorus girls to bear and the promotion caused a certain amount of jealousy on the set. They would have been even more resentful if they had realized their captain was actually only fourteen! But Betty, if she was aware of the other girls' feelings at all, didn't let it show. She was enjoying her status as line captain.

The title of the film summed up just what Lillian Grable felt like shouting when she saw the finished product. She managed to secure the services of an agent to help her promote Betty. Expensive as these services were, the ambitious mother knew it was the best way to bring her daughter to the attention of influential film producers.

And what did the expense matter anyway?! Betty Grable was on her way to stardom!

CHAPTER THREE

While Betty's star was rising in Hollywood, the Wall Street crash of 1929 ushered in the worst depression the country had ever known. Like millions of others, Conn Grable found himself out of a job. With no means of keeping up the mortgage payments, he and Marjorie reluctantly decided to sell their home and head West to California in the hope that he would find employment there. [8]

Mrs. Grable's financial burden had lessened as Betty began to bring home regular paychecks, thanks to her Goldwyn contract. With her film work and the occasional theatrical engagement, she could earn over $100 a week.

The Grables' new-found security was thrown to the wind with the arrival of Conn and Marjorie, who appeared unannounced on the doorstep. While Betty was delighted that her family was reunited, she quickly realized that her father, who was overweight and suffered a mild heart condition, would have difficulty in finding employment. Although he was brilliant with figures, he wasn't a trained accountant. Perhaps, she thought optimistically, he would be able to find a post at one of the studios. But for now, Betty was the sole support of her family — and she was not yet fifteen years old!

To accommodate their enlarged family, the Grables took an apartment at the Knickerbocker Hotel in Hollywood.

Betty was now at work on her second Goldwyn film, *Kiki*, starring America's sweetheart, Mary Pickford. On its completion, the Goldwyn Girls went into yet another Cantor epic — this one entitled *Palmy Days*.

It was a milestone for the young Grable who got to speak a few lines. She was seen briefly as a receptionist at a "futuristic" bakery. In the following scene, Betty led the chorus during a typical Charlotte Greenwood high-kicking routine.

Betty had gained immense popularity around the studio and was fast making new friends. Miss Greenwood, then at the height of her career, encouraged Betty in every way possible, and, despite their age gap, the two became firm friends. Charlotte became her surrogate mother during Betty's spell at the Goldwyn Studios.

Another friendship also developed on the set of *Palmy Days* — this time a romantic one. George Raft, who was playing Joe the Frog, became interested in the cute chorus captain. Betty was flattered, but at fourteen didn't know how to handle the situation. It was the first time an adult male had shown any more than a passing interest in her as a person in her own right.

Excitedly, she told her mother that George wanted to take her to the famed Hollywood Six-Day Cycle event. Mrs. Grable was suspicious of Raft's intentions towards her little girl. She didn't like or trust him. It was well known around Hollywood that he had gangster connections. Still, she reasoned, it would do Betty no great harm to be seen around with up-and-coming heartthrob Raft, provided she was properly chaperoned. Lillian decided Betty could go on the date; she and Marjorie would chaperone.

It soon dawned on George that Betty was indeed much younger than sixteen or seventeen, or whatever she now claimed she was. After several frustrating dates, Raft decided to wait a few years until she had really grown up. Lillian was relieved Betty had come to no harm, and had quickly gotten over her crush on Raft.

Talking about those youthful years spent on the sound stages, Betty said:

It was an education in itself. From a young age, thanks to my earlier experiences on the theatre circuit in Missouri, I learned how to handle would-be child molesters. A good old-fashioned hat pin (which no respectable girl was ever without!) or a high kick aimed at the right part of the anatomy soon put them off. Actually, compared to some cities, Hollywood was a very moral town in many ways. Working on a film was like being part of a family. We all had to look out for each other. There was a comradeship on a sound stage that you don't find anywhere else in the world, except possibly among men at war. We shared each other's triumphs and heartaches, fell in love with some boy during the making of a picture — and completely forgot about him once the film was in the can.

The chorus boys and girls were a particularly clannish lot. We jealously guarded ourselves — and each other — from a 'star' who threatened our existence in any way, either privately or professionally. We would teach each other the newest dance steps, but we would never pass on any trade secrets to the principals on a picture. The only weapon we had was our dancing talent, and we guarded it zealously.

Throughout her career, Betty always maintained a good relationship with the dancers in any film or show she was working on. It was a move that always paid off. The "gypsies" were very protective of Betty.

On the home front, the Grable family reunion didn't last long. Marjorie decided to go back to the university and continue her studies. She didn't particularly like Hollywood and opted to return to St. Louis, boarding at the university. [9]

Conn was in and out of work. He had no great success in Hollywood and had to accept some very low-paying jobs. To augment the family income (and further her screen exposure) Betty appeared in several "shorts" directed by Fatty Arbuckle who, because of a scandalous court case some years earlier, was now out of favor in the Hollywood mainstream and was working under the name of William Goodrich. When appearing in Arbuckle's films, Betty used the name Frances Dean in order to cover herself with the Goldwyn contract. She also hoped it would bring her a new image; Frances Dean sounded much more glamorous than Betty Grable!

The films were none too successful and didn't receive a wide distribution, but Betty realized the experience was good for her, providing a touch of needed dramatic training.

It was during this spell as Frances Dean that Betty began getting mentioned in the fan magazines; her mother began clipping magazine articles and newspapers items on her famous daughter and pasting them in scrapbooks. By the time Betty's film career ended, the scrapbooks amounted to several volumes.

Betty also made shorts for Astor Films. One of these, entitled *Spirit of '76*, cast her in a dramatic tale concerning an America of the future where work had been abolished. The characters in the story didn't have names — only numbers! It was a highly original (if slightly corny) concept of life in the future. But it did have a ring of truth about it, rather reminiscent of an early *1984* without the malice.

Betty played a "number" in love with the president, who is, of course, "Number 1." Matters come to a head when the president finds his Utopia crumbling and the population fed up with all play and no work.

Betty's screen father is discovered with gardening tools and is sentenced to death for his "crime." In the final scene Betty rushes up to the president and makes a stirring plea for her father's life. She confesses that she too has been "working" . . . knitting a sweater for Number 1. The president is so touched by her devotion that he immediately rescinds the order of play, not work, and America gets back into its working clothes. Of course the father's life is spared as well.

Spirit of '76 remains a real curio among the history of short films being made at that time; its theme did not endear it to the American public in general, still in the throes of the Depression.

Astor reissued a compilation of Betty's shorts in the early 1940s, attempting to cash in on Grable's name by giving her top billing. It didn't seem to matter; the fans still stayed away.

At the time, though, the film was good exposure for Betty. It showed the Hollywood moguls that she could deliver her lines with an amazing clarity, yet still come across as soft and feminine.

Another short Betty made in those early days was *A Quiet Fourth*, purported to be a comedy surrounding the holiday weekend. A comedy it wasn't, but it was certainly full of errors. This fiasco had Betty on a Fourth of July picnic, involved with a youngster who had a talent for creating explosions. She was badly photographed, her voice suffered from a terrible soundtrack, and the film was a disaster for her. Other shorts she made during this period included *Hollywood Luck*; *Lady! Please!*; *Crashing Hollywood*; *Over the Counter*; *Air Tonic*, and *The Love Detectives.*

Fortunately, Goldwyn kept her busy on more substantial fare. Betty's first film of 1932 was *The Greeks Had a Word for Them* (a classy comedy of gold-diggers which would be remade several times over the years with Betty starring in two versions). Again Betty was cast as a Goldwyn Girl, with little to do but look pretty — no great problem for her! This would be her busiest year to date, with no less than five feature films being completed, including other shorts (some in the early Technicolor process).

Sister Marjorie regularly came West to visit during university vacations. She was still unimpressed by the glamour and fast pace of life. Betty took her around the Goldwyn lot . . . "showing off," she laughed. The girls double-dated with some of Betty's work pals, though after a couple of weeks in town, Marjorie was only too happy to return to St. Louis and her quieter lifestyle.

Betty recalled:

> It was when I was with Marjorie that I realized just how much of my childhood I had missed — party dresses, class dances, football games, boyfriends, and all the teenage excitement of growing up. To me I had been grown up since I arrived in Hollywood, playing at being a sixteen-year old from the age of thirteen. When I think back on it, I don't know how I had the nerve to carry it off! Working all day at the studio, I was usually too tired to go out at night. It was a 6 a.m. call when I was work-ing, and we didn't get through until 8 or 9 p.m., depending on what was shooting. Occasionally, one of the boys on the crew might ask me out for a coffee and a doughnut after the day's work — but you'd hardly call that a date!"

With Marjorie gone, Betty started work on *The Kid from Spain*, again with Eddie Cantor. Once again the choreographer assigned to the film was Busby Berkeley. He was pleased with Betty's clever footwork and her easy understanding of complex routines. He gave the young Grable lots of encouragement and promised he would be using her in his next picture. Betty was thrilled at being singled out by the famed Berkeley.

Sad to say, Betty's contract was not renewed on the completion of this picture. For no particular reason, she was dropped by Sam Goldwyn. Years later, the movie mogul was to say, "Betty Grable . . . I had that girl under contract once. Why didn't I do something with her?"

Her departure from the Goldwyn Studio also meant that she wouldn't get the chance to work with the legendary Berkeley for almost two decades.

Her work for Goldwyn came to the notice of Edward Buzzell who was casting a drama entitled *Child of Manhattan* over at Columbia. He contacted Betty's agent, offering her a featured role as Lucy, the first time she ever had a "name" character. Betty willingly accepted. It gave her her best screen exposure yet in a full-length feature, but despite the star names of Nancy Carroll and John Boles, the dreary drama went nowhere.

Next came an offer from Chesterfield Films, a small independent production company. They offered her a role in yet another drama, *Probation*, playing a character called Ruth Jarrett. Once again Betty was happy at work on a sound stage, adding to her knowledge of filmcraft. But her part in this one was whittled away in the cutting-room and the finished product left Betty with what amounted to a walk-on, even though she was prominently billed. It gave her even less exposure than her Goldwyn Girl films. She felt she was making little or no progress in the film business.

Offers of new film assignments weren't forthcoming, and the Grables' financial position, to put it mildly, was perilous. Rather than sit around and wait for a studio call, Betty decided to audition for the chorus of the new Frank Fay-Barbara Stanwyck revue, *Tattle Tales*. She was accepted, and after two weeks' rehearsal she was promoted to a solo spot, introducing a couple of numbers. The show opened in Anaheim, near Los Angeles, then moved up to San Francisco for a six-week engagement. After that, if all went well, the show could head east to Broadway.

It was Betty's first trip to the Golden Gate city and she loved it. Naturally, Mrs. Grable went along too, leaving Conn to look after their rented apartment in Hollywood.

Although Betty was featured in the show and, as such, had a couple of routines, she was very dissatisfied with the set-up. The routines were changed daily, and Betty found the behavior of Frank Fay bewildering. He was often drunk, sometimes too drunk to go on stage. In general, there was a complete lack of professionalism among the leading players.

The exception to this was Miss Stanwyck, who, in response to a desperate plea from husband Fay, had temporarily abandoned her blossoming film career and joined *Tattle Tales* to bolster the show. "Poor Barbara," Betty recalled. "She was stuck with a turkey that would fold at any minute, but out of loyalty to her husband she stayed with it."

Bandleader Ted Fiorito, an old boozing buddy of Fay's, was also appearing in San Francisco. He had been to see the show several times and noticed Betty. It is said that when he learned that Betty had given her notice to the show's producer and would be leaving it at the end of the San Francisco run, he invited her to audition as a singer with his dance band.

It is not known whether Mr. Fiorito — a renowned womanizer — had designs on the youthful Betty, but when she turned up at his suite at the St. Francis Hotel with her mother in tow, he had no alternative but to go through with the audition. To Betty's amazement, she was engaged on the spot.

But it wasn't her singing talents that got her the job. It was Mrs. Grable's steely appraisal of Ted that scared the bandleader into engaging the teenager.

I had fancied myself as a dancer, but Ted decided I was good enough to front his band as a singer — and he did prove to be a wonderful teacher. I travelled with the outfit for several weeks all over the Western states. The experience was good for me; it helped me get over my nervousness about appearing before large audiences. More importantly, though, through these appearances I was heard by millions of radio listeners on Ted's regular broadcasts. Slowly but surely, my name was becoming known.

The bandleader was quite happy with Betty's work. She looked quite glamorous fronting the band, and always had a crowd around the stage when she was singing.

Much to Mrs. Grable's disapproval, Betty also became romantically involved with a young drummer in the band. Any young man who showed more than a passing interest in her peaches-and-cream daughter was sure to fall foul of an otherwise amiable Lillian Grable. Betty wasn't allowed real dates, and if she had to appear at any after-show social function with the band, her mother was always on hand to chaperone her. Betty found this a very frustrating period of her young life.

Working regularly with Ted Fiorito gave her (and the family) financial stability, and also gave her the opportunity to think well before jumping off at any offer which might come along. But while appearing with the band at the Miramar, Santa Monica, Betty got another movie call. RKO beckoned with the female lead in a Wheeler and Woolsey comedy, *Hold 'Em Jail*. She replaced the duo's regular leading lady, Dorothy Lee, who had been holding out for more money. Instead of putting it down to her talent or good luck, Betty maintained once again that she was there by default.

Wheeler and Woolsey were at the peak of their career and their films were huge box office successes, enabling Betty to be seen by millions of cinemagoers throughout the country. Otherwise, her latest role didn't advance her career any better than her Goldwyn contract had. The film did, however, temporarily end her association with Fiorito's band, and that finished her romantic interlude. Again she got prominent billing — placed third.

Looking back on her first three years in Hollywood, Betty admitted she had fared a lot better than some of her contemporaries. It was all too easy to fall into the clutches of the wrong people. Betty was somewhat sexually naive and, she would later admit, was forever grateful that she had her mother around most of the time. Chorus girls were often propositioned by promoters of stag films, and Betty was horrified when she was approached by an assistant director on the set of a film one day, offering her good money if she would work on one of these. Betty had regarded the assistant as a good friend, but that friendship came to a sudden end when she refused him.

"It's sad to admit," said Betty, "but some of the girls did accept these offers — usually because they were broke and needed the money to pay the rent or whatever — but they were seldom hired by a reputable studio afterwards and faded from the film scene." Even at the time, Betty added, she had no second thoughts about refusing such offers. "It wasn't anything moralistic on my part. I was just too scared of what my parents would say if they found out!" Throughout her career, Grable firmly maintained that any girl who got into movies via the "casting couch" would quickly be forgotten.

Betty's next film assignment was at Fox, where it had all begun. This time she was cast in Noel Coward's screen adaptation of his stage hit, *Cavalcade*. The cast was supposedly all British and it was to be Fox's movie of the year (it did win an Oscar as best picture). But even Betty's most ardent fan would have a hard time spotting her as "the girl on a couch." However, Betty was always proud of her association of working on an Oscar-winning picture — though she would be first to admit she did nothing to contribute to the film's status. [10]

With her ten days' stint in the Coward film behind her, Betty was once more asked to join Fiorito's orchestra on a series of dates around the California area. Betty agreed, providing she would be able to be released from her contract should any new film work come her way.

The band stint proved fortuitous for Betty. On completion of the short tour, they were signed up by Monogram to supply the music for its forthcoming *Sweetheart of Sigma Chi*. Betty was prominent in the film, fronting the band with their new male singer, the handsome Leif Erikson.

This Mary Carlisle-Buster Crabbe starrer again brought Betty to the notice of RKO which promptly cast her in its next musical, *Melody Cruise*. In this, Betty was cast as a stewardess on a cruise liner. It was one of the studio's minor musicals, and at the end of it she was once more out of work.

Her next two films during the year were both dramas. *What Price Innocence* at Columbia featured her as Jean Parker's good-natured girlfriend in a lightweight teenage problem picture.

The other sent her back to RKO (by now she and the gatemen were on nodding terms) for *By Your Leave* with Frank Morgan. Betty was one of a group of girls enlisted to help the star overcome the pangs of middle-age. She played the teenager next door and had two showy scenes in the picture.

New Year, 1934, started promisingly enough for Betty. She was selected for the chorus of M-G-M in a college caper entitled *Student Tour*. It was the first time she had worked at Metro (although a couple of her short films as Frances Dean were released by M-G-M, they were filmed at an independent studio) and she was overawed by the sheer professionalism she found there.

Apart from her chorus duties, Betty was featured in a classroom scene, given a couple of smart lines to say, and had a very flattering medium close-up. She was also assigned a song to sing, "The Snake Dance," but just as she started the number, the plot got in the way and Betty's best showing in the film was lost. However, the film was a dud and is only remembered today as being the one that introduced Nelson Eddy to the screen.

Betty was very disappointed when she was dropped at the end

of the film. Of the five or so studios where she had worked, Metro had been by far her favorite in many ways. She badly wanted to be signed by them and felt that she could advance more quickly under their banner. But it wasn't to be.

By now, Betty was represented by a new agent, Vic Orsatti, who regarded her as the most promising youngster he had on his books. Vic was instrumental in booking Betty into various night spots around the Southern California area. He also landed her a contract with the Jay Whiddon Orchestra, with whom Betty had great success — particularly as a blues singer. This surprised Betty greatly, as she never believed she had much of a voice, but her appearances with the Fiorito outfit had given her a measure of confidence when fronting a band.

While appearing with Whiddon, Betty got a call for another film musical. Once more, it was her old standby, RKO. While not one of the major studios, RKO had a massive success on its hands with the release of *Flying Down to Rio*. It had also discovered the ideal screen dance partnership in Fred Astaire and Ginger Rogers.

Head of production Pandro S. Berman planned to star the couple in a series of big budget musicals, starting with Astaire's stage hit, *The Gay Divorcee*. Director Mark Sandrich was assigned to the production and no expense was to be spared to make it the year's biggest box office success.

Luckily for Betty, she was spotted on the lot by the film's choreographer, Hermes Pan. He remembered her from her earlier films (and shorts) at RKO and knew how good she was. He introduced her to Sandrich, telling him Betty would be ideal for a specialty spot in the film.

She was tested, and on viewing the results, the director agreed with Pan — the specialty spot was Betty's. Immediately she set to work with the talented dance director, rehearsing "Let's K-knock K-knees," the routine which she would perform with comedy actor, Edward Everett Horton. Pan found her easy to choreograph and remembered she had a "natural and graceful" dancing style. Sandrich liked her work, and noted that she photographed well. The scene was filmed without any problems and Betty's singing voice would be heard in a major production number.

At the end of the routine, Fred Astaire strolls casually into view and exchanges a few caustic comments with Horton. Grable and Astaire exchange the merest of nods. Betty is seen in the background, framed between the two stars. There is a sweet, yet wistful look on her young face as if she is thinking, "Well, that's it. I've given it my best shot; let's hope someone will take notice."

People did sit up and take notice on the film's release, particularly the critics. She was mentioned in several reviews as a "promising youngster." To be mentioned, however briefly, in an Astaire-Rogers movie was indeed a step up. The favorable notices led to several local radio spots which further helped to exploit her name. Mrs. Grable was delighted. She was sure Betty was on her way at last.

From this movie, Betty came away with three things — two new friends (Hermes Pan and E. E. Horton) and a film contract with RKO, with the usual six-month options.

Wasting no time with its newest acquisition, RKO gave Betty the glamour treatment. They turned her into a platinum Jean Harlow blonde, and the publicity department sent out a batch of photographs to fan magazines, labeling her "The Quicksilver Blonde." With all this attention, Betty felt sure the studio had big plans for her.

She could hardly hide her disappointment when she was slotted into yet another Wheeler and Woolsey vehicle, entitled *The Nitwits*. She was even more dejected when the film's director George Stevens insisted Betty's hair be restored to its natural color. A despondent Betty was dispatched to the studio's hairdressing department to have her "Quicksilver Blonde" tresses dyed back to their original shade.

The madcap comedy had Betty playing a secretary suspected of murdering her boss. Boyfriend Bert Wheeler sets about to prove her innocence, and in the mayhem that follows, he and his partner run the gamut of screen slapstick.

Betty handles the part quite well, and the film did her no harm — although it wasn't the kind of vehicle that would boost her stock. She and Wheeler sing a duet together — "Music in My Heart," written by Dorothy Fields and Jimmy McHugh — followed by a rather clumsy and unimaginative dance routine. Then Betty gets arrested and is thrown in jail, and little more is seen of her until the all-revealing climax.

To coincide with the release of the film, Betty accompanied the comedy team on a short vaudeville tour. She was well received. The film's song was given saturation treatment on the tour.

Betty returned to the studio and started work on *Old Man Rhythm*, a low-budget musical starring Charles "Buddy" Rogers, in which she played a co-ed.

With no new roles on the horizon for Betty, RKO loaned her out to Paramount for yet another college caper, *Collegiate*, which featured her with Joe Penner and Jack Oakie.

She finished her work at Paramount in time to be assigned to RKO's latest Ginger and Fred epic, *Follow the Fleet*. It has been said that Lela Rogers, mother of Ginger, jealously guarded her daughter against any usurper, and that Betty's role in this new film was kept to a minimum, even though she was fourth-billed. Her work consisted of a few walk-on scenes, no dialogue, and accompanying Miss Rogers in the number "Let Yourself Go" as a member of a trio of singers in the background. But she did look very decorative — her star quality was beginning to show.

Another leggy young newcomer also appeared in *Follow the Fleet* — Lucille Ball. However, redheaded Lucy fared much better than Betty in that she actually had several lines of wisecracking dialogue and consequently came to the attention of fans and critics as a name worthy of note. (Poor Lela Rogers — if it wasn't one starlet, it was another!) During the making of *Follow the Fleet*, Betty and Lucy became firm friends — a friendship that lasted more than forty years.

Betty was fortunate in her facility for striking (and retaining) friendships. Her easygoing style, sense of humor, and seeming lack of pushiness endeared her to many of her female co-stars over the years . . . such greats as Alice Faye, Dorothy Lamour, Lauren Bacall, Lucille Ball, Mitzi Gaynor, and Marilyn Monroe.

Her present predicament, though, had nothing to do with making friends. On the completion of *Follow the Fleet*, the studio did not renew Betty's option. Down, but certainly not out, she gathered her things from the dressing room and resumed her rounds of the casting agencies.

Although in later years Betty claimed it was her mother who wanted her to have a career, by this time she must have had some ambition of her own. Now truthfully eighteen years old, she could quite easily have stood up to her mother and opted for another career. She was certainly not unintelligent and could have taken a course of business studies, or even realized her childhood dream of becoming a nurse. [11]

But no. She had become enchanted with the magic of the movies and the excitement she felt at the first day on the set of a new film. And, most importantly, she had developed a determined streak in her that told her that her future lay in film-making. This time it was her own choice — not her mother's.

CHAPTER FOUR

Around this time, romance came back into Betty Grable's life in the shape of handsome former child-star Jackie Coogan.

It has been widely reported that they met on a cruise ship to Catalina Island — not according to Betty. She remembered:

> I had seen Jackie at a few parties in Hollywood, but the first time we spoke to each other was at a beach outing in Santa Monica. He joined our crowd which included Lucille Ball and many of the boys and girls from the RKO chorus.
>
> Well, he didn't actually join in the fun, but stood around, looking a little lost. I remember thinking he was acting rather stand-offish, but later, when I got to know him better, I found he was really quite a shy person despite all the fame that had gone before him. Nothing very exciting happened on that occasion. I think we exchanged a few words with each other. But I do remember noting that he had beautiful eyes!

It was weeks later on that fateful trip to Catalina that Jackie formally introduced himself to Mrs. Grable, who was accompanying Betty, as usual. Jackie had learned that Betty would be on the Catalina trip and had arranged to be on board.

"He was extremely polite and courteous; mother loved him for that," recalled Betty. "They got on famously. I think she was more impressed with him than I was. I liked him. But then I liked lots of young men at the time — I was always falling in love!"

Jackie asked Mrs. Grable's permission to date Betty, and Lillian agreed. "Such a pleasant young man," she remarked as he excused himself, "and very wealthy too, I believe."

At the time, that would have been a natural assumption but an inaccurate one. Jackie Coogan had indeed been one of the highest-paid child actors in the business. Starting in films when he was six years old, he had became an overnight sensation in Charlie Chaplin's *The Kid* in 1920. He then went on to make a series of money-spinning films, including *Little Robinson Crusoe, Oliver Twist, Tom Sawyer,* and *Huckleberry Finn.*

By 1931, however, he was 17 years old — and out of work. At six feet two inches tall and weighing around 190 pounds, he was physically too mature for the roles he had excelled in, and producers didn't want to take a chance with him in expensive sound films. His father, who had been his business manager and banked most of young Jackie's earnings (a sum reputed to be around $4 million), was killed in a road accident. When the father's will was read, it was revealed that everything had been left to Jackie's mother, Lillian, who promised Jackie his earnings when he reached the age of 21.

However, Lillian Coogan fell into the clutches of businessman Arthur Bernstein, whom she married. Once the knot was tied, Bernstein made sure that Jackie would never get his hands on his legal entitlement. Jackie had passed the age of majority when he met Betty and he was beginning legal proceedings against his mother and Bernstein to recover his cash. One legal wrangle after another ended in a stalemate, with no resolution in sight.

While all this was going on, Jackie continued to date Betty, and the relationship began to turn serious. Regarded as a "hot item," Jackie and Betty regularly appeared in the gossip columns. Jackie had completed a small-budget Western entitled *Home on the Range* just prior to meeting her, so for the moment he was solvent. He loved to spend money and enjoyed treating friends and hangers-on to sprees on the town. Betty sometimes accompanied him on such bashes, but more often than not she was in bed early, getting her much-needed rest for the next day's work at the studio.

Jackie was signed by M-G-M to feature in one of its Technicolor musical shorts entitled *Sunkist Stars at Palm Springs.* He suggested that producer Louis Llewlyn use Betty in the film. The M-G-M bosses saw it as a good publicity angle and signed Betty to appear with Coogan in a dance sequence. It was their first screen appearance together.

Betty was freelancing at Fox (now Twentieth Century-Fox). She had won a leading role in *Pigskin Parade*, co-starring opposite Johnny Downs, Stuart Erwin, and Patsy Kelly. Betty played Laura Watson who is romanced by Downs, the local football team's star player. Arline Judge, Dixie Dunbar, and handsome newcomer Tony Martin rounded out the cast. Once again, Betty was given a solo number to sing —"It's Love I'm After." Betty thought it was her best part to date and felt sure she would really click with the audiences after this one. She was very disappointed to find her number was deleted in the final cut of the film.

Fourteen-year-old singing sensation Judy Garland — in what was her only loan-out from M-G-M and her first full-length feature film — stole the show. *Pigskin Parade* would go down as her film, and deservedly so. Judy wore pigtails and freckles and she looked distinctly homely, but that magical voice was unmistakable.

Even though Betty was eclipsed from the limelight for *Pigskin Parade*, the gossip-mongers still hounded her for the latest on her romance — and Jackie's court battles. Some suggested that Betty was a blonde gold digger who was only after the Coogan millions. This hurt her. She was by no means wealthy, but she earned her living honestly and felt she didn't merit this treatment.

One columnist put out a story that Betty had been living with a 64-year-old British aristocrat named Sir Guy Standing, who was well-known around the movie scene. Handsome, distinguished-looking Standing (father of British actress Kay Hammond) was knighted for his services in the British Royal Navy during World War I, retiring from the service with a combat disability. He resumed his acting career in Hollywood, appearing in supporting roles in such films as *The Lives of a Bengal Lancer* (1934, Paramount), in which he was billed under Gary Cooper and Franchot Tone.

Sir Guy was more renowned for his socializing on the Hollywood scene than for his dedication to an acting career. He had a string of girlfriends and spent many happy evenings touring the Hollywood night spots, but there is no record of his ever being involved with Grable.

Betty was angry at the rumors but dismissed them as nonsense, saying she hardly knew the titled gentleman. She thought the story had been fed maliciously to the press by Jackie's mother, who was determined to go to any lengths to put an end to the romance. Apparently not only the press men thought she was after the "Kid's" cash. Lillian Grable received several telephone calls from Lillian Bernstein, warning her that Betty had better back off from her son. "He's a pauper," Mrs. Bernstein is reported to have said. "He has no money, and he never will have!"

Despite the enormous personal pressures put on the young couple, their romance continued to flourish. Betty was head over heels in love with Jackie and he was similarly smitten. They talked of marriage, and Jackie asked her parents' permission. To the young couple's dismay, he was refused. Lillian and Conn Grable maintained that Betty had her career to think of, and while she was still a minor and under their care, marriage now was out of the question.

Betty and Jackie were two very unhappy — and star-crossed — young lovers. They both came from ambitious parents, both had been child performers, and neither had had a normal childhood upbringing. Now that they were grasping at the chance to live as normal a life as was possible in Hollywood, they were being denied this privilege. On top of all this, Jackie's legal battles with his mother and stepfather continued, and the young couple were often so broke they could hardly afford to go out on dates.

Betty had returned to RKO for *Don't Turn 'Em Loose*, a dismal story about the prison parole system. And on the film's completion, Betty and Jackie decided to capitalize on the public's interest in their romance — and make some fast money — by touring the United States together with a slickly packaged vaudeville act. Tantalizingly titled *Hollywood Secrets*, the revue purported to let the audiences into the secrets of filmmaking.

The couple played to packed houses; it seemed all of America wanted to see Hollywood's newest twosome in the flesh. They were warmly welcomed and made front page news in every city where they appeared, with Betty getting good personal notices.

Then Lady Luck smiled on Betty. Her good press notices on the recent tour had brought her to the attention of the Marathon Street studio bosses, and she was offered the lead female role in Paramount's *This Way Please*. The role had originally been scheduled for Shirley Ross, but she walked out on the film, claiming Mary Livingstone's part was being fattened up at Shirley's expense. Therefore, Betty was in by default — again.

This Way Please, which introduced the comedy team of Fibber McGee and Molly to the screen, was fundamentally a vehicle created to bolster the sagging career of Charles "Buddy" Rogers. Betty played an aspiring actress who turns up for an audition, but through a series of misunderstandings, is engaged as a cinema usherette. She stays with the job, hoping for her big break, and takes a fancy to crooner/orchestra leader Rogers.

Unfortunately, the film did nothing to rescue Buddy Rogers' career. *This Way Please* should have seen Betty Grable emerge as a top-flight star. In her role as a young woman eager to further her stage career, she acted the part with great style and her legs were well displayed in the short usherette uniform. She had a very clever musical number in which she sang "Is It Love or Infatuation?" in front of a blank screen which suddenly filled up with multiple images of herself, all singing in harmony. Betty also handled her love scenes with a new maturity, and her whole presentation was highly commendable.

Paramount also must have been pleased with Betty, for she was offered a contract, starting at a salary of $500 a week. Betty was delighted to sign. Surely this time, she reasoned, she would make it to the top of the heap — Paramount was in the big league as a major moneymaker.

At the same time, another source of income opened up to Betty as well. She was signed by CBS for a series of fifteen-minute radio programs entitled "Song Time." She was featured with a darkly handsome Hollywood newcomer who would figure large in Betty's future career — John Payne. The program ran for several months. Betty even managed to get Jackie a guest spot on the bill.

Betty worked hard for her new bosses, and for the first time, she was making significant money. She decided it was time to start a savings account for herself. Amazingly, Lillian Grable was still handling her youngest daughter's finances; she had Betty's salary paid into her own bank account and doled out pocket money to Betty if and when she felt like it. All that was about to change.

Betty arranged with her agent to deduct a sum from her weekly pay and deposit it in her own account. One way or another, Betty Grable was determined to gain her freedom — and marry Jackie.

Marjorie, who visited Hollywood at regular intervals, knew of Betty's intention to marry Coogan and promised to help in any way she could, despite her parents' objections. [12] And the Grables were not the only ones opposed to Jackie's and Betty's marrying. Gossip columns, which continued to run blow-by-blow accounts of the youngsters' romance, had been fed a few juicy, spiteful items by Jackie's mother who was just as determined as Mrs. Grable that the two would never marry. In comparison to Lillian Bernstein, Lillian Grable was a saint!

Tensions ran high in the Grable household, and seldom a day went by without some kind of argument involving Betty's relationship with Jackie, particularly when Lillian learned that much of Betty's hard-earned cash was going toward Jackie's legal bills. More often than not, Betty backed down, always fearful of her mother's vicious temper. Conn Grable was caught in the middle. He had been accustomed to Betty's bringing home the household cash, and pondered the family's future should Betty do something hasty — like elope. Eventually the Grables reached a compromise. Betty and Jackie could marry on her 21st birthday — a little over a year away.

The lovers discussed this latest move and agreed their love could wait that long. In any case, reasoned Jackie, his court case would be well out of the way by that time, and they could settle down to happy wedded bliss in financial comfort. Jackie would also have had more time by then to resume his career and become the breadwinner of the family.

Now that the way was cleared for their wedding, Jackie and Betty began to relax and have fun. They loved partying, and were on everyone's invitation list, the life and soul of many a Beverly Hills soirée. Although the couple's financial woes were scarcely behind them, they appeared to be happy and carefree. Particularly Betty. For one thing, her dates were no longer chaperoned by her mother, and this freedom was a new experience for Betty. Not that her mother needed to worry; teenage Betty was as clean as her screen image. She disliked alcohol and abhorred smoking.

"I tried drinking once when I was about fifteen, on a night out with some of the girls at Goldwyn," she explained in an interview some years later. "We devoured a fifth of bourbon between us and I was so sick, I vowed that I would never touch alcohol again. As for smoking, I was warned that to be a really fit dancer and singer I would need full control of my breathing at all times and that cigarettes would be harmful. So I never started the habit." (Sad to say Betty developed both habits later in life — with dire consequences, at least as far as smoking was concerned.)

Paramount was happy with Betty's progress and kept her hard at work. She had become known as Betty Co-Ed because almost every film she made there cast her as a pretty campus queen — and not much else! The storylines didn't matter very much, so long as there was plenty of singing and dancing, and any excuse to show off the Grable torso. Her fan mail was rising, too, by a much higher percentage than any of the other young stars currently under contract.

Lillian kept pushing and prodding Betty to lobby the studio for better roles, better billing, and more and more press layouts. Betty tried, but her requests fell on deaf ears at the studio — all except the publicity angles. The publicity boys were only too happy to promote Betty. She was highly photogenic and had quickly become a pet of the lot's photographers.

> At one time I would pose all day without a complaint. I realized it was one way of getting people to sit up and take notice. So if the layouts kept my name in front of Joe Public and his wife, I willingly co-operated.
>
> I did have my hard core of fans, however, who wrote me after every picture release. One was Matt Erlich, of Philadelphia, who wrote me my first fan letter when I was about sixteen. He wrote to me faithfully throughout my film career.
>
> I always remember with a thrill receiving my first fan letter from England. I found it hard to believe that people in a foreign country had heard of me and seen my pictures. The letters from the British fans multiplied. They were among my most loyal fans, and I vowed that someday I would take a trip over there and visit them. Many sent me picture postcards of their home towns. They looked so pretty that I suggested to Jackie that we should honeymoon in Britain and Europe — if we could afford it!

But the trip Betty longed for wasn't to be realized for at least another thirty years. In fact, she realized that unless there was a turnabout in Jackie's financial wrangles with his mother and stepfather, there would be no cash left over for a honeymoon. Jackie had developed an expensive habit of changing lawyers midstream, and Betty was paying out more and more money to retain their services.

Many of Betty's friends found her rather crotchety during this period. But she found it hard to stay continually cheerful with so much seemingly going against her. Her romance with Jackie was solid enough and they were counting the days until she was 21. It was her career —and her parents — that made Betty testy. On one hand she had her mother urging her on to bigger and better roles, and on the other, the all-powerful Paramount chiefs, who were quite happy with the returns of her college pictures.

She also had nagging doubts about her own ability to make it as a full-fledged screen actress. Her money at Paramount was great — $500 a week in the mid-thirties was a fortune in anyone's eyes, particularly for one so young. (In 1994's terms, this would amount to approximately $8,000 a week.) But artistically, she felt she was not progressing fast enough. She often cast her eyes towards Twentieth Century-Fox, where Alice Faye — a virtual newcomer to Hollywood in comparison to Betty — was their leading musical star. (Alice, a Broadway import, had achieved success after only one film, *George White's Scandals of 1934*, and was now a top star with her latest release, *Sing, Baby, Sing*.)

Financially, Betty was stretched to the limit. She had the upkeep of the family house they had recently purchased in Brentwood, her parents, and her car. (She'd learned to drive when she was sixteen and found her car a necessity to get to work each morning.) She was also concerned about Jackie's extravagant tastes; at the end of an evening out, he almost always had to borrow money from her. And she was still helping to pay off Jackie's legal bills.

Jackie still believed he would inherit his millions. As long as he was paying the lawyers their fat fees, they encouraged him to believe this, but Betty never counted on it for a moment. For one thing, she was a realist. She often warned Jackie to be very wary of lawyers. Retaining them was costing the young couple more and more each month — and Betty had yet to see any concrete results.

A few months before her wedding, Betty made a trip home to St. Louis in connection with a film première. The local press made a big fuss over the local girl who was making good in Hollywood and gave her the full star treatment.

Conn and Lillian, who accompanied her on the trip, dismissed questions about the forthcoming marriage. "Betty won't marry until she is at least twenty-one," repeated Lillian Grable. "It's in her contract, so there is not much she can do about it. She realizes her career comes first and has worked hard to get where she is. But this is just the beginning — soon Betty will be a household name all over the world."

It seems odd that Mrs. Grable kept trotting out the old "won't marry till she's at least twenty-one" spiel, as she and Conn had already agreed to the wedding which was to be held almost a month before Betty's birthday in December. Perhaps the ambitious mother kept hoping that Betty and Jackie would become bored with each other and split up. Lillian certainly did nothing to keep the young couple's spirits up when things weren't going well for Jackie in court. Clearly Lillian saw Jackie as a threat to Betty's career. She regarded him as a has-been and felt that if he and Betty married, Betty would surely end up the same.

While Betty enjoyed her trip back home, she was anxious to get back to Hollywood and Jackie. She had a lot of planning to do for the wedding, a dress to be made, outfits for her bridesmaids to be chosen. The minister had to be booked, as well as a place for the reception. Betty was busy, but happy, as she made her wedding preparations. Lillian did nothing to help her, still hoping the marriage would not take place.

Invitations were sent out, and most of the cream of Hollywood accepted. It was to be the biggest day in Betty Grable's young life, and not even Lillian was going to be allowed to spoil it. Conn had been much more malleable of late and willingly agreed to give his daughter away. This pleased Betty. Even though she fought constantly with her parents, she loved them dearly and wanted both of them to be present on her big day.

(Obviously, Betty didn't get on at all with Jackie's mother and stepfather. When they did meet by chance on an evening in town, Arthur Bernstein called Betty "a conniving little bitch" to her face, and Betty had to be restrained by Jackie from a physical attack on Bernstein.) [13]

In the end, Jackie and Betty had their way. The wedding took place on November 20, 1937, a few weeks before Betty's twenty-first birthday. It was widely publicized, and beautiful bride Betty was photographed from every conceivable angle by Paramount's top photographers. Bob and Dolores Hope were among the guests. Said Dolores, "Betty was a beautiful bride and we were so happy for her. She was a lovely sweet girl and Bob and I were both very fond of her." [14] However, there was no time for a honeymoon. Apart from the fact that they couldn't afford such a luxury, Paramount wanted Betty to start immediately on a new film, *College Swing*.

As a wedding present, the studio offered Jackie a role in the film as well. *College Swing* had a top-drawer cast in Bob Hope, Burns and Allen, and Martha Raye. Betty's radio partner John Payne, recently put under contract by Paramount, played a romantic young student. Her old RKO dancing pal, Edward Everett Horton, was also in the line-up, as was newcomer Robert Cummings.

Following completion of the role, Betty went straight into *Give Me a Sailor*, again partnering Hope and Raye. Although the top roles in this crazy romantic comedy went to Bob and Martha, Betty more than held her own against these two scene stealers, getting to sing a couple of numbers with the Jack Whiting Orchestra. Yet Betty played a strangely unsympathetic, sometimes bitchy character — a million miles removed from her usual sunny image. Perhaps she saw this as a step towards serious acting!

All in all, Betty had fond memories of this film:

> It gave me the chance to prove myself in a modern comedy with music. And I think it came off pretty well. Bob and Martha didn't have as much filming experience as I had, and I often helped them out with little bits of business they were unfamiliar with. I was happy to do this for them, particularly so for Bob who, I seem to recall, was a terrible worrier despite his wonderful ability to make us laugh between scenes. He was full of nervous energy. He was also quite a wolf in his younger days and Martha and I spent a lot of time repelling his amorous advances. But I think a lot of it was just ego-boosting for Bob. Basically he was a shy man.

Viewed today, the film emerges no better — although certainly no worse — than many of the madcap romantic comedies churned out by most of the studios in the late thirties. Grable looked more grown-up, more alluring, especially on the dance floor. One Grable devotee noted, "This film gave us Grable, the woman, for the first time on screen. She had matured immensely and was blossoming into the beauty she was later to become."

It was another success for Betty, so much so that Paramount decided to give her top billing in her next college caper, *Campus Confessions*. During the making of *Confessions*, however, it became obvious to those around Betty that her marriage was in deep trouble.

Betty and Jackie had rented a house on Montana Street in Brentwood, acquired a couple of dogs, and generally lived the high life. At least Jackie did. While Betty was busy at the studio, he was reverting to his bachelor days, living it up with his cronies. If he ran short of money, no problem — Jackie simply sold off a few wedding presents to tide him over. One night Betty arrived home from work to find Jackie missing and her car gone. Jackie didn't show up for two or three days. After all the trouble Betty had gone to to become Mrs. Coogan, the strain was beginning to tell on her. She was irritable, often foul-mouthed to her co-workers, and generally unhappy with her lot. Already she imagined she could hear the know-it-alls whispering behind her back, "I told you so."

After telling her mother of her marriage difficulties, she decided to confront Jackie and tell him it was over. Jackie moved out to stay with a buddy, and Betty remained in the Brentwood house. Although sad about her daughter's unhappiness, this state of affairs did not altogether displease Mrs. Grable. She felt that once the marriage was over, Betty could really concentrate her attention on her slightly dipping career.

Following the artistically disappointing *Campus Confessions*, Betty was offered the lead female role in a new Jack Benny starrer, *Man About Town*, a romantic musical comedy tailored specially for the talents of the great Benny. Just before production got under way, Betty suffered a cruel blow. For several days she had been complaining of stomach pains, constipation and nausea. Eventually she sought out her doctor. He diagnosed acute appendicitis, and she was operated on immediately. Her starring part went to friend Dorothy Lamour.

Jackie, now sober and trying to get his career back on course, was on a personal appearance tour of Texas when he heard of Betty's hospitalization and rushed back to be at her side. The couple was reconciled.

Two weeks later Betty was declared fit and ready for any work that would come her way. Paramount recalled her to the *Man About Town* set, adding a couple of lines for her and even briefly showcasing her wearing a black wig. The studio also gave her a specialty number to sing, "Fidgety Joe," which became the smash hit of the film. Her energetic dancing and singing style contrasted with Miss Lamour's more sultry approach, and once again the critics predicted a bright future for Betty.

After the rave notices for *Man About Town,* ever-optimistic Betty looked forward to bigger and better roles. Jackie was back in her life, and the couple was genuine in its efforts to secure a lasting reconciliation.

Disappointingly, Paramount cast them in yet another college musical, this one entitled *Million Dollar Legs.* (The title referred to a college rowing team and not the Grable underpinnings.) Betty was once again top billed, with her husband in fourth place. (A youthful Donald O'Connor was also in the cast.) The film did little to boost their careers, and it certainly did not help them resolve their matrimonial problems. Soon after the film was in the can, they again separated.

Deciding the marriage was over this time, Betty confronted Jackie and told him so. She blamed herself for the failure. Jackie was equally upset at the way things had turned out. Despite everything, they were still in love with each other. He had reached a settlement with his mother and was paid around $200,000. It was all there was left of the Coogan fortune, and it barely covered his debts. Columnists suggested Betty had left Jackie because he didn't come into his fortune, although Betty had signed a prenuptial agreement forfeiting any claim on the money.

A few weeks later Betty sued Coogan for divorce, but before the action could be heard Betty instructed her lawyer to abandon the plan. They were going to try again.

This was to be the start of almost a year of on-again, off-again headline-hitting items which kept the gossip columnists busy. Betty avoided being seen in public as much as possible. At one time she would have given anything to have her name on everyone's lips, but this was publicity she didn't need — or want.

To add to her troubles, Paramount called her to the studio. They told her they were anxious about her future, and as they had nothing new to offer her in the way of film work, they had reluctantly decided to release her. To Betty, this seemed like the straw that would break her dangerously fragile career. Her mother was also alarmed at this turn of events. The Paramount bosses had dealt Betty a critical blow.

Betty later told the press that she was not pleased with the way her career was being handled at Paramount and had asked for her release. The studio countered the actress's statement by saying that Betty's sex appeal did not come across on the screen. Hurt, Betty dismissed this by saying that she would never do another college musical: "They were blah films, and I acted blah in them."

Whatever the reason, Betty was brokenhearted. At the age of twenty-two, she had an unsuccessful marriage and a career that was going nowhere. On top of all this, Lillian Grable had decided to divorce Conn. Mrs. Grable and Betty appeared in court on May 31, 1939. Lillian charged that her husband abused and berated her constantly until she suffered a nervous breakdown. She said that her husband said he was going back to live in St. Louis, as soon as he got his share of Betty's earnings.

Mrs. Grable added that she had been bedridden for the past six weeks from a nervous ailment aggravated by her husband's constant quarreling, abuse, and threats. Stating that she had been threatened many times by Conn, Mrs. Grable sought an order to restrain Conn from harming or molesting her. She also sought clear title to the deed of their home at 250 Chadbourne Avenue,

Brentwood. Mrs. Grable was granted the divorce. Conn Grable moved out of the house, but stayed in the area, visiting Betty whenever he could.

Betty was very unhappy over her parents' divorce and did everything she could to get them back together. She was equally fond of both, but closer to her mother through the latter's involvement in her career.

Shortly afterwards, Betty filed suit for her divorce from Coogan. She paid all the expenses. Her attorney, Joseph P. Kelly, applied to the court for a hearing, but there was a backlog of cases.

Betty firmly believed that her career in films was finished. While her friend Dorothy Lamour was going from strength to strength, Betty was slipping out of the film scene. Her agent managed to secure the female lead in a Joe Penner comedy at RKO. The film, *The Day the Bookies Wept*, was a vehicle designed to showcase the talents of Mr. Penner. One critic commented that she was merely decoration, which was rather unfair. She was top female lead with several good scenes and displayed a gift for comedy. But it was still a disappointing film.

In a period of reflection, Betty did much soul-searching, trying to discover the reasons for her career coming to a standstill. For the past ten years she had worked for all the major studios, only to discover she was no longer in demand. She said, "The avenues to fame were fast closing for me. It looked as though I was going to be a promising youngster until I was a grey-haired grandmother."

Her mother, always active on Betty's behalf, tried all the tricks she knew to get some attention from the studios. She fed stories to fan magazines and newspapers, but despite a healthy press on her marriage problems, Betty's career problem was largely ignored by the columnists during this period. They were still very interested in Betty's private life, though. Especially the new man in her life — Artie Shaw, a thirty-year-old twice-married jazz clarinetist.

The darkly handsome ladies' man was sophisticated, well-read and worldly, despite his humble New York upbringing. Lillian

Grable was quite happy about Betty being seen out on the town with Shaw. It kept Betty in the limelight, but mother made sure there was no romance.

Betty gave serious thought to quitting show business. "At one point, I thought of taking up nursing, but I realized I didn't have the necessary formal education. In fact, I had no training whatsoever for any profession outside the film world."

Her agent eventually came up with an offer of a vaudeville tour on the East Coast with Eddie "Rochester" Anderson and company. Betty wasn't keen on returning to the stage. "Films were hard work, but two [shows] a day was murder. I discussed the offer with my mother. She was all for it. But I kept asking myself where would it lead. It all seemed so pointless." On her mother's insistence, she accepted the six-week engagement at $1500 a week — three times her Paramount salary.

It was the wisest decision she ever made. *Variety* caught her act in Baltimore and was enthusiastic about the performance of the ex-film actress, as she was now being described by the press — a sure sign that her film career was truly over.

Her divorce petition was finally heard on October 11. The first decree was granted by Judge John Beardsley. It was an interlocutory decree, which would take a year to become final and would give both parties time to attempt reconciliation.

Betty's last stop on her vaudeville tour was Chicago. Now that she was making it in a stage career and earning good money, she was a much happier person. After her show one evening, she was introduced to young crooner Dick Haymes, and with Haymes and another couple, she went out to a nightclub to hear a new band that was all the rage of the Windy City — Harry James and his Music Makers.

The foursome sat at a ringside table and enjoyed the music. During the floorshow, Harry came to their table. He had recently signed Haymes as a singer, but he was most anxious to meet the beautiful blonde at Haymes' side. [15]

Betty remembered the occasion well. "I was fascinated by

his light blue eyes. He was so quiet that I found I was doing all the talking. He looked so thin — I felt I just wanted to feed him huge nourishing meals! As for instant romance? Nothing doing! I was still legally married to Jackie."

Betty returned to Los Angeles the following weekend, and immediately signed on with Jack Haley as a singer, dancer, and general comedy feed in a show he was presenting at the Treasure Island Music Hall, as part of the San Francisco Golden Gate Exposition. She took the offer principally because none of the studios was blazing a trail to her door with film offers, and there was nothing else on the horizon.

She enjoyed her stint with the comedian. Betty had learned how to handle herself on stage and how to milk an audience for all it was worth. And she was no mean ad-libber when the occasion called for it. She received excellent notices for the show and was again sought by various San Francisco columnists for interviews, though they were much more interested in her private life and her entanglement with Shaw.

Then fate took a hand once again. In his offices at Twentieth Century-Fox, on West Pico Boulevard, Darryl F. Zanuck got down to his first chore of the day — reading the newspapers.

His secretary had laid the papers on his desk, with items that might interest him circled in red crayon. Thumbing through the papers, he came upon a stunning picture of Betty Grable with a story alongside that told of her huge success in San Francisco. He went on to read other items, but kept coming back to the Grable photograph. The story goes that he reasoned with himself, "If I keep returning to the Grable shot, other folks might be doing the same!"

He telephoned his casting director, Lew Schreiber. "What about Betty Grable? Is she under contract to anyone?" Schreiber informed his boss that Grable had recently been dropped by Paramount and was now freelancing. Zanuck didn't hesitate. "Sign her," he ordered and hung up.

Schreiber got word to Betty's agent that she was required in

Zanuck's office the following Monday. Betty couldn't believe it. Twentieth Century-Fox — the studio where it had all begun so many years ago — wanted to sign her, just when she was sure that the movies had abandoned her. She spent the rest of the week, she said, "pinching myself to make sure I wasn't dreaming. It was more than I had ever hoped for. My mother took it more calmly than me. She simply said she knew it was bound to happen sooner or later."

Twentieth Century-Fox, in the four years of its existence, was indeed regarded as one of the major studios. The company had been set up in 1935 when the Fox Film Corporation merged with Twentieth Century Pictures, and was headed by Joseph M. Schenck. Zanuck, a producer at Warner Brothers, had been brought in to the company as vice-president in charge of production. It was a position he was to hold for the next twenty years, running the studio with complete autonomy.

The studio had moved into top gear with a series of films starring Shirley Temple, then at the height of her popularity; and Zanuck was personally responsible for promoting Alice Faye's career. He took a chance with Faye, a New York chorus girl who made a big impact in the famous New York review, *George White's Scandals*. Her vocal talent so impressed Rudy Vallee that he offered her regular work on his weekly radio show. A couple of years later, when leading lady Lillian Harvey walked off the set of *Scandals*, the film's star, Vallee, suggested Alice as Harvey's replacement. Zanuck handed the lead to Faye.

The rest is history. She was by now one of the studio's top money-makers on a par with Tyrone Power and Don Ameche and had enjoyed successes such films as *Alexander's Ragtime Band* and *In Old Chicago*.

It was Zanuck's policy to keep his stars in line by signing newer talent just in case his top attractions got temperamental. The studio was always bigger than its stars — that was his personal motto, and he stuck by it throughout his term at Twentieth.

On October 25, 1939, Betty arrived at the studio with her agent and mother in tow. After a few preliminaries, Betty signed a seven-year contract, starting at $750 dollars a week. Mrs. Grable stood proudly beside Betty as she signed the deal. She was happy in the knowledge that at last she had helped her daughter get to the top. Mrs. Grable said later, "I always knew Betty was going to make it. It was all a matter of timing. And now the time was right."

Betty's hopes of instant stardom were short-lived. The ink was hardly dry on the contract when Zanuck told her point-blank that he had no roles lined up for her at the moment. "Go back to the Haley show and keep up the good work in learning your craft," he told her.

Alice Faye was reigning queen of the Fox lot, and Zanuck saw no reason to upset her or the studio's prepared schedules by slotting Grable into any of the current productions.

Disappointed, Betty returned to San Francisco. On the strength of her new film contract, Haley cashed in by giving her bigger billing and more time on the show. Betty didn't mind in the least, just as long as her name was prominent.

Several days later, Broadway agent Louis Schur and composer Buddy DeSylva were in the audience. They were bowled over by the gorgeous blonde and went backstage to meet her after the performance. They told Betty they were casting a new musical for Broadway starring Ethel Merman. They suggested she would be ideal for the ingenue role. Flattered, Betty was reported to have said, "I've never been in a Broadway show." DeSylva is reported to have replied, "That's Broadway's loss."

Betty was sorely tempted by the chance for Broadway fame, but at the same time she was terrified at the prospect. In truth, Betty Grable was terrified of the stage itself; she had never gotten over stage fright and suffered agonies during those few minutes before she appeared in front of a live audience. She phoned Zanuck next morning, telling him of Schur's offer. He strongly advised her to accept; the publicity value alone would be good for her.

Grable wasn't so sure of the move. Her new contract with Twentieth carried the usual options. If the Broadway show flopped, Zanuck could quite easily exercise the option clause and drop her like a hot potato, and her career would be back in limbo. It was a big decision.

Schur and DeSylva stayed on in San Franciso for a few more days, hoping to persuade the reluctant Betty to accept their offer. She had read the script, and while there was obviously little for her to do, she would get to sing two songs and dance several numbers with Phil Regan and Bert Lahr. Besides, she would be performing with Ethel Merman, the toast of Broadway, who had never been associated with a flop in her life — certainly not in any show she was headlining.

Betty and her mother discussed the Broadway offer at great length. For the first time, her mother told Betty, "It's time you took charge of your own career. I won't always be around to advise you, and I certainly can't always be on the road with you. Some day you will have to make all the major decisions for yourself. Now is as good a time as any. What do you think, Betty?"

Betty was thinking hard. If only Zanuck would come up with a film, then all her problems would be resolved. She would have accepted any film except a college musical. Artie was all for Betty moving East, but Betty's self-confidence was at a low ebb. She checked once more with Zanuck who wasn't available. His secretary said she had no word of any new film being prepared for Miss Grable. Betty took a deep breath and rang her agent, Vic Orsatti, telling him to inform Louis Schur that she would do the play.

After her final performance in San Francisco, Jack Haley threw a good-luck party for Betty. He had always been in favor of Betty's accepting the Broadway offer. "I knew she had what it takes; the audiences in San Francisco proved it with the amount of applause she received after each performance," said the actor. Betty remembered the occasion as a happy, yet sad time. "I knew my life would never be the same again — one way or another. It was a crossroads I had reached and, for better or worse, I had stepped over it into the unknown."

As Betty and and her mother boarded the train for the four-day rail trip to New York, Betty bemoaned wasting all those years. "They were not wasted years, Betty," Mrs Grable told her. "One day you'll be able to put it all to good use." Betty smiled. "At least you still have faith in me, Mom, even if no one else has." Quietly Lillian Grable faced her despondent daughter. "If you don't have faith in your own ability, no one else will. Up there on the screen, if the public senses that you're not believing in what you're doing, they will quickly forget you."

Looking out the train window, Betty knew that her mother was right. Her final Hollywood film didn't help matters. One critic had described her performance as "ineffective," which didn't do much for Betty's frame of mind. She was sure that Hollywood had dismissed her as a mere flash-in-the-pan, despite the lucrative Fox contract she had just signed.

The problems regarding her future seemed insurmountable. Supposing the new show was a flop. Where would she be then? Would Zanuck still have faith in her? After all, she was an untried commodity on the Broadway stage. Could she go back to vaudeville? No; it was a dying institution, and established vaudevillians were finding it difficult to secure work for even six months of the year.

And there was Alice Faye. Only a few years Betty's senior, she was at the pinnacle of success and showed no signs of abdicating.

Betty certainly didn't want to go back to dance band singing and felt that she didn't have the special talents required of radio performers. She also knew that her welcome as a guest star on radio shows would quickly wear out if she didn't have a major film to back her appearances.

All these thoughts churned through the pretty blonde's mind as the train rattled eastward. Fingers crossed, she hoped and prayed that this time she would finally make good.

F542-S154

CHAPTER FIVE

New York was freezing cold and frosty as the *Du Barry Was a Lady* company rehearsed in drafty rehearsal rooms off Broadway. America had come out of its crippling Depression and the city, gearing up for a boom Christmas shopping spree, sparkled in the winter sunshine.

The company moved to the Shubert Theatre, New Haven, for its final try-out. The out-of-town show had all the ingredients for success. One or two changes were made; Phil Regan, who was to play Betty's love interest, left the show after it was discovered his voice couldn't be heard beyond the first dozen rows of the orchestra. He was replaced by Charles Walters. And some costuming improvements were made after Betty complained to the show's producers about her lack of colorful outfits. *Du Barry Was a Lady* opened on schedule on December 6, 1939, at the 46th Street Theatre. The show was an instant success — practically a foregone conclusion with Merman heading the cast.

While Ethel was undoubtedly the star, Betty's big number was "Well Did You Ever," and she came in for a generous share of press compliments. Brooks Atkinson of *The New York Times* wrote, "The performers supply more pleasure than the authors and composer. Betty Grable and Charles Walters dance and sing with remarkable dash." *Daily News* writer Burns Mantle said, "Miss Grable is a graceful and spirited dancer," while John Mason Brown of the *New York Post* thought she had "much grace and charm."

She found herself being sought out for interviews, and for the first time in her career was accorded the full star treatment. Asked about her time spent as Betty Co-ed, she said:

I know I have knocked those collegiate films. But the truth is that if it wasn't for them, I might not have made it to Broadway at all! My mother, realizing how unhappy I was at being assigned to yet another college epic, encouraged me. She constantly reminded me it was my apprenticeship. True enough, it was a long, hard grind. Up each morning at 4 a.m. six days a week, then home to bed at around 9 p.m.

There was very little social life, and even though the end product nearly always turned out something of a disappointment, I came away from each film feeling I had gained a little more experience. There was always so much to remember while making a picture — make-up, lighting, shadows, angles — it was all so interesting and the more films I made, the easier it became. Everything gradually fitted into place. My biggest problem then was [trying not to] appear 'mechanical' — [I needed] to approach each new assignment as though it was something new. I suppose you could say movie people are a world apart from the rest of show business.[16]

Life magazine also interviewed Betty, and featured her on the cover of their December 12, 1939 issue. To their staff man, she said, "Hollywood has a way of letting you down that is rather discouraging. I guess the only reason I am in a Broadway show is because the studios didn't want me. It comes as something of a shock after you've worked in several studios and been publicized around the country for years, only to find there are no suitable roles for you."

Betty settled in for what promised to be a lengthy New York run. Miss Merman, although kindly disposed to Betty, led a separate life from the rest of the cast, although she and Betty went nightclubbing together whenever Artie Shaw visited. Betty was noted for her high spirits and good humor. She was very popular with the cast and also with the stagehands, with whom she'd play card games between scenes. "But not gin rummy," said Betty. "I always lose at that game — and I can be a sore loser!"

Co-star Bert Lahr said that he was entranced with this lovely girl "who had the face of an angel, but nightly, while we were dancing on stage, she would whisper the naughtiest suggestions in my ear — she nearly broke me up with laughter many times." [17]

Betty loved New York. She would often be seen in the wintry afternoon sunshine skating at the Rockefeller Center. She proved herself quite an adept skater and more than once referred to herself as "Zanuck's secret weapon against Sonja Henie." (Henie, a Norwegian-born Olympic ice-skater, had also been signed by Twentieth Century-Fox, and was enjoying considerable success in a series of lightweight musicals.) She was happy with the show, and had her collection of stage-door Johnnies, including Scots-American chain store heir Alex Thompson. Almost every night after the show, she could be seen at 21 or El Morocco, dancing the night away with most of the eligible young men around town.

A frequent dance partner was young bandleader Desi Arnaz who was believed to be completely besotted with Grable. The arrival of Lucille Ball in town soon put an end to that budding romance. Redheaded Lucy had been dating him for some time. Of course, there was always Artie, who visited regularly in the first couple of months.

Just before she had left for New York, Shaw and Grable had one last date at the Coconut Grove. Betty had fallen deeply in love with Shaw and told him so. She wanted to marry him as soon as she was free. The more worldly Shaw hedged his bets. He advised her to concentrate on her career, and once she had settled down on Broadway, they would talk about marriage. Betty saw the sense in this, and happily declared herself unofficially engaged, telling her sister Marjorie that she was deeply in love with the musician and planned to marry him. Betty knew that he was also seeing the youthful Judy Garland on his trips back to California, but she never regarded Judy as a serious competitor.

Unknown to both ladies, Shaw had met Lana Turner and they set Hollywood back on its heels when they married on a trip to Las Vegas after a whirlwind romance. A report of their elopement hit the national press on February 9, 1940. Judy Garland reportedly broke down in tears and was inconsolable for days.

Not Betty. She put a call through to Artie's friend, Phil Silvers, who remembered that she was plenty mad. "The son of a bitch," she screamed down the line. "How dare he do this to me!" [18]

After that, Betty Grable refused to talk to anyone about the Shaw romance. However, she didn't waste time moping about it, either. She threw herself into the New York social scene, and Marjorie, who visited her sister regularly, said she didn't remember Betty ever having as much fun as she did during that period. "She had all the men at her feet, and she knew it. She very quickly got over her feelings for Artie Shaw." [19]

Proof that she had finally arrived — as far as Broadway was concerned — was the hanging of her portrait in the Gallery of Fame at Sardi's Restaurant, the most popular dining place for the Broadway theater set. Betty enjoyed her new status as a Broadway personality, with some reservations. It surprised and embarrassed her to be asked to sign autographs; she could never understand why people wanted them!

The New York press corps, quite interested in the exploits of its newest acquisition, loved it when Jackie Coogan came to town. His visits kept the Coogan-Grable marriage on the boil and added fuel to the rumors that the couple were on the point of kissing and making up. Buddy DeSylva was also spotted wining and dining his new ingenue, and he admitted to close friends that he had fallen in love with her. Although he was married, he had separated from his wife years earlier. DeSylva was not without influence in Hollywood. Since he had broken up with his song-writing partners, Brown and Henderson, he had worked at several major studios, including Fox. Delighted with his new find in Betty, he had big plans for her. He was about to take up an offer at Paramount as a freelance producer and had considered buying up Betty's new contract from Twentieth and returning with her to Paramount for his new film project.

When he told Betty of his plans for her, she made it clear she wasn't very enthusiastic. Paramount, she felt, had let her down in the past, and she wasn't about to give that studio the chance to do it again. Despite her seven-year contract with Twentieth Century-Fox, she was sure that Hollywood was finished with her and now believed that her future career was as a stage actress. Zanuck came to the rescue. He wouldn't even put a price on Betty's head. Her contract was not for sale, and so DeSylva's plan was abandoned.

Betty's mother traveled to New York several times over the next few months, delighting in the fact that her daughter was "the toast of Broadway." She kept Betty up to date on what was or wasn't happening in Hollywood, but had nothing to report by way of any film projects for the future. [20]

Europe was by now well into World War II and the prospect of American involvement grew daily. All eyes were focused across the Pacific on the Land of the Rising Sun. Most Americans, however, felt the distance between the the U. S. and Japan afforded them a measure of safety.

In Hollywood, the shrewd Mr. Zanuck noted the public's preference for escapist musicals, preferably with exotic backgrounds. With film markets in Europe closing due to the war, he adopted a policy of film-making that would make big inroads in the vast South American markets.

Alice Faye had recently completed filming a highly fictionalized biography of Lillian Russell and was scheduled to go straight into an expensively mounted Technicolor production called *Down Argentine Way*, to be directed by Irving Cummings. A second unit team had already returned to Hollywood with useable footage for the projected film. A couple of weeks before the scheduled start date, however, Alice was hospitalized. According to a studio statement, she underwent an emergency appendectomy and would be convalescing for approximately four to six weeks. The cast and crew of *Down Argentine Way* were all set to go into production, and Zanuck knew he couldn't hold up such an expensive film to wait for Alice's recovery. He had no choice but to recall Grable from the Broadway show and cast her in Alice's role.

After speaking with her agent, Betty excitedly sought out

DeSylva to tell him the news. DeSylva, who had recently asked her to sign for another six months as well as tour with the show when the Broadway run ended, was delighted for her, but disappointed she was leaving the show. Although Ethel Merman was top-billed, perky Betty's name on the marquee and her girl-about-town image helped sell tickets; she was regarded as a rare Broadway draw. In fact, DeSylva had been toying with the idea of writing a show especially for her. Reluctantly, he gave her his blessing and wished her well.

Betty returned to Hollywood on June 5, 1940, to find that her Broadway fame had traveled ahead of her. The press and fan magazines were dubbing her "Hollywood's hottest property." Betty was thrilled. "It was so exciting. Suddenly I knew it was all happening for me, and this would be my last chance in a bid for film stardom. If I flopped this time, I would have no one to blame but myself — so I grabbed at the opportunity with both hands."

Vaudeville success, Broadway acclaim, and now what she had always hoped, worked, and prayed for: the lead in a major musical film. Betty knew her film record to date had been mediocre to say the least. Only *The Gay Divorcee* and *Man About Town* had given any boost to her career. The rest of her movie work had been lost in a surfeit of college musicals.

It is interesting to note that Betty's return to Hollywood was regarded as a comeback by most columnists. She told one reporter, "I feel I wasn't ready until now for really important work on the screen. And no matter how bad those earlier films were, they gave me the experience to be able to handle what's before me now."[21]

Betty reported for work at Twentieth Century-Fox for costume and color tests. The studio make-up men experimented with various cosmetics to show Betty to her best advantage. In each case, she appeared to be overly made-up. The studio's head of make-up, Guy Pearce, came down on the floor to try and solve the problem. After several minutes studying the new star's complexion, he ordered all the make-up removed and only the lightest foundation applied, with loads of mascara and just a little coloring to highlight her cheekbones. The result was perfect. The lighter make-up helped to enhance her natural peaches-and-cream complexion. Mack Gordon, who had written the songs for the film, watched the first few days' rushes of the new star at work. He spread the word all over town: "Wait till you see Betty Grable in Technicolor. She is an absolute knockout. You wouldn't believe it was the same girl!" [22]

Her charms were not lost on co-star Don Ameche who was at the height of his popularity as a leading man, and had several years of experience behind him in both musicals and dramas. Betty knew Ameche had a reputation as a ladies' man and, at first, treated him warily. When he realized she was not interested in him, however, their friendship got on to a much happier footing. Although Betty appeared calm and assured on the surface, he sensed she was nervous. He also knew how much this break meant to her. Don treated her well and put her at ease with his warm sincerity and sense of humor. He was also a well-known practical joker and Betty was often on the receiving end. She didn't mind; to her it meant she was accepted as one of the gang.

The studio announced that Don would dance for the first time in this film and stated that he had spent hours rehearsing the steps. In the final film, Mr. Ameche is indeed seen dancing with Betty, but his feet are always kept hidden. In long shots, the back of someone's head was strategically placed to hide his "neat footwork." Years later, Betty remembered Don as a sweet man, but a very poor dancer. Today, anyone reviewing *Down Argentine Way* could only regard it as a mindless curio of songs and sketches strung together by a limp script involving horse racing. Its main attraction was the sensational screen debut of the "Brazilian Bombshell," Carmen Miranda.

Betty had very few comedy lines to speak (Charlotte Greenwood, who played her aunt, had the bulk of them) and Carmen's numbers were much more extravagant than Betty's, though her duet with Ameche, "Two Dreams Met," was a big hit.

However, it says much for her personal magnetism that she managed to win audience (and studio) approval in the end. At a sneak preview, the film was hailed as a success. The public raved over the studio's new Golden Girl. After ten years of hard, often unrewarding work, Betty Grable had finally made the big time.

With her success in movies now assured, Betty began to enjoy her new status. New boyfriend Victor Mature was her constant escort, and she was often seen at various night spots with him. But she would always deny any attachment. "I'm not the least bit in love with anyone right now," she reported laughingly. "It doesn't seem to matter whom I go out with, just so long as they are pleasant and can dance." [23] She was also seen about in public with Jackie Coogan. "There won't be any reconciliation," she told a columnist. "Our divorce is final on October 9 and that's final!" [24]

Zanuck, anxious to get Betty into another hit and solidify her position, cast her opposite his top star, Alice Faye, in *Tin Pan Alley*. The move was Zanuck's way of keeping Faye on her toes, but he did feel slightly afraid that Alice would balk at starring opposite her new "rival." He had no cause to worry; Alice, a charming and unaffected girl, quickly befriended the newcomer and they remained friends until Betty's death.

All this chumminess didn't please the gossip columnists one little bit. They had hoped for some juicy stories of sniping from the two most glamorous blondes in the movie musical business, but it just didn't happen. Alice Faye was much too wise and too much of a lady to fall into the gossip mongers' traps, and Betty was a level-headed young woman who always believed there was plenty of room at the top. In addition, both had been around the film scene long enough to realize what Zanuck was up to, and they were usually one step ahead of him. They were genuine in their praise of each other. There was no rivalry. Said Betty, "That was all studio publicity. Alice and I wouldn't play their game. Zanuck would have loved us to have a feud — anything that would have brought in a few more bucks at the box office."

Alice, who had a quiet disposition, enjoyed Betty's clowning around and general high spirits on the set. She also admired Betty's enthusiastic approach to the dance sequences. Prior to meeting Betty, Alice had always had to work hard at her dance routines and never found them much fun, but Betty's lifelong training and vast knowledge of dance helped her enormously. It was Betty who privately coached Alice in some of the more intricate steps. Alice quite freely admitted that she wasn't up to Grable's standard as a dancer, while Betty conceded that she couldn't sell a song as well as Alice. Such modesty was most becoming from two of Hollywood's top musical queens!

Alice and Betty duetted on "Lovely Hawaii" and "The Sheik of Araby" (This ran into censorship problems because of the brevity of their costumes, but Billy Gilbert's clowning helped to save it from the censor's scissors.) During filming Betty had three songs of her own. In the final cut of the film only one of them remained— "Honeysuckle Rose." Miss Faye's hit solo numbers, "You Say the Sweetest Things, Baby", and "America I Love You", remained intact. Another big production number missing from the final cut was "Get Out and Get Under" which Alice and Betty performed with Jack Oakie, although stills from it survive to this day. [25]

Despite its bustling verve and vitality, there were some moments of pathos in *Tin Pan Alley*, particularly in the London dockyard scene where Alice bids a tearful farewell to John Payne. It took all the comic ability of Jack Oakie to lighten the proceedings by missing the gangway and plunging into the water. It was a clever scene and, of course, it gave a shivering Jack the opportunity to come up with the "problem" song of the film, "K-K-K- Katy," (songwriters Payne and Oakie could never find the right lyrics!) which immortalized Alice's character in the film. After a few brief scenes at the war front comes the victory parade down Broadway, with a smiling Alice and John happily reunited — but flirty Betty (who has no intention of winding up with Oakie) is seen casting a wandering eye over the officers on parade. It was a wonderful ending to an epic musical.

Today, *Tin Pan Alley* is regarded as much more than a cavalcade of songs and dances. It was a good reliable story — a sister act, a struggling young songwriter (Payne), and separation by love and war — and with stars like Faye and Grable, who could blame Twentieth Century-Fox for continually resurrecting the storyline? Its predictability notwithstanding, the film proved a massive box office winner for the studio, and it won musical director Alfred Newman an Oscar for best scoring of a musical picture. The film was particularly praised for its sets and costumes and fine screenplay by Robert Ellis and Helen Logan. Director Walter Lang steered the girls through a cavalcade of song, dance, and drama with his usual skill. He understood the Grable/Faye charms perfectly and exposed them to full advantage.

Betty's fan mail was still pouring in from the general release of *Down Argentine Way,* and two secretaries were assigned to deal with it. Her mother was also put on the payroll to help with Betty's mail. (Though Mrs. Grable thought she could be better utilized in the studio's drama school!)

Betty finally made the list of Hollywood's promising newcomers and the trade papers enthused over the "overnight" discovery. Betty quipped, "After eleven years' hard work — from chorus girl to leading lady — suddenly I'm an overnight discovery? That sure was a long night!"

Her relationship with DeSylva had fizzled out, though they had met several times in the past year. She felt much safer playing the field and had no shortage of escorts: Victor Mature, Tyrone Power, and old flame George Raft who was back in her life. She was very enthusiastic about Tyrone Power and said she'd love to do a film with him. Zanuck said he would keep her request in mind. (The handsome Power enjoyed Betty's company, but he was also seeing Lana Turner at the same time, her brief marriage with Shaw having ended in disaster.)

Betty was whisked off to New York to help promote *Tin Pan Alley* which had opened to excellent business in the city. Alice Faye was top-billed, but Betty received great notices for her performance. She traveled east with Victor Mature, who was to appear in a play on the New York stage. They stopped over briefly in Chicago, where Betty once again danced to the music of Harry James and his band.

Mature and Grable heading for New York together? This led to stories that the couple were eloping — or at the very least, were engaged. They both denied the rumors.

Betty was treated to full celebrity status on her first trip back to New York since her sensational Broadway debut. She received the big-star treatment wherever she went and was mobbed by autograph hunters in the lobby of her hotel, having to be rescued several times when the crowds reached an alarming scale. "It was the first time I had ever been mobbed, and I found it very frightening. In stores, the clerks were very courteous and nobody bothered me too much — once I had gotten used to being stared at. But outside on the sidewalk was another matter. Sometimes I feared for my life," she recalled.

Betty and friend Paula Stone attended the opening night of Vic's play and went backstage to offer him their congratulations. But Betty made a hasty retreat when she realized she was unwittingly stealing the limelight on what should have been Mature's big night.

Grable soon returned to Hollywood , where she continued to keep gossip columnists busy trying to keep track of her beaux.

The Shaw affair had left Betty a little wary when it came to romance. She'd felt betrayed. She wasn't the type of girl who slept around, but when she fell in love, she gave her all. She still hadn't gotten Artie Shaw totally out of her system; the affair had left a bitter taste in her mouth. Now that he was free again, would she fall once more for his charms? Once again fate stepped in.

George Raft, who claimed he had put Betty on hold years ago, saved the situation when he began an old-fashioned courtship of the star. He sent flowers, furs, jewelry — and something he knew would melt her heart: a loveable miniature poodle puppy which she promptly named Punky. Later there was a gift of a racehorse. To keep himself in favor with the family, mother Lillian and sister Marjorie were also recipients of expensive pieces of jewelry.

Betty was far too busy at the studio to spend much time on the town. She started work on *Moon Over Miami*, re-teaming with Ameche and receiving solid support from Carole Landis, Bob Cummings, and Charlotte Greenwood. Jack Haley was also added to the starry line-up, much to Grable's pleasure. She always regarded Jack as a true friend and felt he was instrumental in her career reaching these heights.

Miami was the second of six highly successful films she made with director Walter Lang. Another bonus was that Hermes Pan who had just been signed by the studio was to choreograph the film. The story, which had previously been filmed as *The Greeks Had a Word for Them* and *Three Blind Mice*, cast Betty as a gold-digger on the lookout for a millionaire husband in Florida's playground resort. As the only female dancing star in the film, Betty had several numbers assigned to her, and she worked long and hard with Hermes Pan to perfect the routines.

One sequence, "Conga to a Nursery Rhyme," was a show stopper. Partnered by Pan on screen, Betty was in her element as she swirled and tapped her way around the huge mixed chorus. (Hermes Pan danced with Betty in several films. He disliked appearing in front of the camera, but he made an exception for Betty. Another star he partnered was Rita Hayworth; Pan regarded Betty and Rita as the two top female dancers on the screen.)

Moon Over Miami has often been regarded as a forerunner to Gene Kelly's *On The Town*, as the musical numbers were woven into the storyline instead of the usual staged numbers typical of Grable's later musicals. Everything appeared spontaneous, particularly when Grable, Landis, and Greenwood, on arrival at their Miami hotel, go into the "Miami" number, utilizing the confines of their suite for their high-spirited production number. Most critics agreed it was a musical way ahead of its time.

Perhaps the most striking feature of the film is how much it is ahead of its time, predating *On The Town* which, in many ways, resembles it in its use of free dancing through sets and locations.

...The songs flow naturally out of the action, expertly wedded to the dialogue... this is a film of irresistible American energy and verve, orchestrated to perfection by Alfred Newman, electrifyingly recorded, especially in the 'Conga to a Nursery Rhyme' number, expertly danced by Betty Grable and the chorus in an hotel lounge." [26]

Director Lang was delighted with Betty's work, and it turned out to be a happy business partnership. He claimed he had more satisfaction directing a Grable movie than any other he had done up to that time — though he also made the same statement when discussing the films he made with Alice Faye!

The studio's publicity department was kept busy feeding information to the fan magazines. One publicist got so carried away that she organized a beautiful legs competition. She fed information to newspapers that Betty had been voted as "the girl with the world's most perfect legs." Betty, who was once voted Miss Hollywood in a phony competition in the thirties, complained bitterly to the boss, but her pleas were ignored. Instead, Twentieth Century-Fox announced that they had insured her legs with Lloyds of London for a staggering $1,250,000.

So the seal was set on future Grable publicity — plenty of leg show. No one particularly disagreed with the studio, least of all Betty's growing legion of fans. Her 7-inch ankle, 12-inch calf, and 19-inch thigh were indeed perfection. Soon the letters started arriving requesting pictures of Betty in leggy poses.

Still Grable protested. She told one reporter, "The leg publicity was all right when I was in my teens. It was good for me, but it didn't mean very much. You can convince the public of almost anything if you talk about it long enough, but there are lots of girls in movies with just as good-looking legs as mine. Besides I'd like people to forget my legs and remember that I am an actress. It's time my face got a little attention!" [27] She said she thought an actress's face was her fortune — and much more important than a good figure.

At about the time Betty finished *Moon Over Miami* and Alice Faye was busy with the latest South American extravaganza, *That Night In Rio*, Zanuck was on to his next project. He fancied himself a writer (often quite successfully) and had penned a short story entitled "Eagle Squadron" under the pseudonym Melville Crossman. The story was about an American airman who volunteers for action in Europe and is killed in battle at the end. It was his own personal tribute to the Royal Air Force for the magnificent job they were doing in the war in Europe. The working title was changed from "Eagle Squadron" to *A Yank in the RAF*. He thought it an ideal vehicle for his top male star, Tyrone Power, but in the pre-production stages, the British War Office learned of the project and was horrified that the hero would die in the film. The Brits thought it would be very demoralizing to audiences when the film would be shown in their nation, now in the throes of a horrific war. [28]

Zanuck conceded and allowed the character to come through unscathed at the end of the film. Moreover, to add some cheer to war-torn British audiences, he decided to cast his top female star, Grable, as the airman's girlfriend. Although Betty wasn't too keen on the project, she accepted it for two reasons — she still had a crush on Power, and she was to be given two musical numbers which, she felt, would help her overcome her acting limitations.

Power played a pilot who joins up with Britain at the beginning of the war. Betty was a showgirl based in London entertaining at a West End night club. The film also featured John Sutton and Reginald Gardiner, two supporting actors who came to be included among Betty's best friends. They appeared in several films together over the next few years — particularly Reggie Gardiner, whose work at Fox continued until the 1950s. Betty's blondeness was toned down for the black-and-white film. She didn't have any highly dramatic scenes, but her sexuality came through, particularly in her scenes with Power. They created a fine screen chemistry between them.

Director Henry King did well to pull Betty through her first dramatic role, although she was generally unhappy with her work in this film. The storyline was slight; Betty had little to do but fall in and out of love with the devastatingly handsome Power — no great acting feat for any girl, on or off the screen. In *The Secret Life of Tyrone Power*, director King is quoted as saying, ". . . I feel certain that Betty Grable has talents for straight dramas. Give her three dramatic roles in a row and she will surprise Hollywood. She can do what Ginger Rogers, Myrna Loy, Joan Crawford and many other stars who began as dancers have done." [29]

The highlights of the film were the magnificent aerial sequences with authentic battle scenes woven into the film. Zanuck's only disappointment was that *Yank* didn't share in the Academy Awards spoils, though he could hardly complain as the studio's other blockbuster that year, *How Green Was My Valley*, scooped no less than six Oscars.

Yank was the first Hollywood film dealing with World War II and it was given a splashy Hollywood première in aid of the British War Relief Fund. Most of the major stars of the time attended, and Betty arrived on George Raft's arm — much to Zanuck's displeasure. He did not approve of her association with Raft, mainly because he was married, but also because it was widely believed he had underworld connections.

Zanuck was in good company. Lillian Grable also disapproved of Betty's dates with Raft, although it must be said that George treated Betty like a lady at all times. His generosity was often an embarrassment to Betty, but she was enjoying being spoiled for a change. They went to all the major fights, the race tracks, and ended up in the top night clubs. Neither of them touched alcohol; Raft was a complete teetotaler.

When Betty had an early shooting schedule, he always made sure she was home on time, and when Marjorie visited, she was taken along on all their dates. It was a fairy-tale romance. Unfortunately, it wasn't to have a happily-ever-after ending.

While most critics approved the film, a few blasted Betty over her performance in *A Yank In The RAF*. She pleaded with her boss never to assign her to another drama. She said she felt much safer doing what she did best — singing and dancing. One trade magazine of the time stated that Grable came across quite well, considering she wasn't noted as a dramatic actress. The writer continued: "There were no complaints about Grable's lack of acting ability from the men in the audience!" [30]

However Betty regarded the film, *A Yank In The RAF* was very popular with British audiences, and the Royal Air Force honored Betty by naming one of its squadrons after her.

Unfortunately, Zanuck still had no musical vehicle for Betty. He summoned her to his office when he learned how unhappy she was over her drama outing. He began, "I know how you feel about *Yank in the RAF* but the notices you got weren't at all bad. Remember it was your first dramatic role. And who cares about the critics? The film is doing excellent business."

Before Grable could interrupt, he continued, "I want you to take this script home with you and study its possibilities. You'll have a great cast backing you and I am assigning it to Bruce Humberstone, who thinks you would be ideal for the role." Betty relented and took the script home with her. It was *I Wake Up Screaming*, a murder mystery based on the best-selling book by Steve Fisher.

Over dinner, she discussed it with her mother. Mrs. Grable was full of enthusiasm. "Take it, Betty," she advised. "You can't get too many experiences in this business. Besides, it only has a six-week shooting schedule. Perhaps by the time it is finished, they will come up with a musical." Her mother had a secret longing to see Betty's name up there with Joan Crawford and Bette Davis who were in the drama major league. Betty wasn't so sure. She was well aware of her acting limitations. And so were the critics!

However, the film's producer, Milton Sperling, had a meeting with Betty, urging her to take the role. He told her he had viewed her earlier work and thought she had the makings of a fine dramatic actress, a statement which stunned Betty. Sperling reassured her he was serious, and claimed he was her Number

One Fan . . . after her mother, of course! Victor Mature was also instrumental in cajoling Betty into taking the role. He persuaded her that he needed her in this picture — his big break in a top-budget movie — and Betty was never one to let a pal down.

A week later she joined Mature, Carole Landis, and Laird Cregar in the new film. The story wove around Carole (playing a character named Vicky) as Betty's sister, who heads for the big-time society bunch in New York City, and is murdered. Mature is the prime suspect, but Betty believes in his innocence and stands by him. Naturally, they fall in love.

Cregar walked off with the acting honors. As for Betty, she held up well and displayed her dramatic talents without resorting to histrionics. The fabled legs were not much in evidence in this film, except for a scene filmed in a city swimming pool. It was the only phony part in the film and Betty hated it. "The scene could just as easily have taken place in a drug store or bar, but Zanuck would have me and Victor strip down. I loathed that scene," she said.

Betty found another champion in director Humberstone who later claimed he discovered Betty in the chorus at RKO in the early thirties and had helped get her career started there. He enjoyed working with her, and said she showed much promise as a dramatic actress. "With a little coaching and a lot more self-confidence, Betty could become one of our top dramatic stars," he enthused. [31]

Zanuck was most pleased with Betty's performance. However, most critics thought she could do with a lot more dramatic coaching. Nevertheless, the film was a healthy box-office winner. Her mother was particularly pleased with Betty's showing. Singing and dancing were all very well, but Mrs. Grable wanted her daughter up there alongside the drama queens.

I Wake Up Screaming became a favorite late-night TV offering in later years and Grable's performance stands up well, showing a lot more dramatic talent than some of her drama sisters of the time and even some of today's. It became a highly-regarded "film noir" by latter-day critics, boasting Edward Cronjager's magnificently low-key black-and- white photography.

At a sneak preview, Zanuck was perturbed that the audience filled in their preview cards stating that they had expected a musical. They generally expressed disappointment in the film, which was to be released under the title *Hot Spot*. Back at the studio, Zanuck instructed the publicity department to add "Grable — as you've NEVER seen her before!" to the posters. He also instructed that the original title, *I Wake Up Screaming* be reinstated. [32]

Zanuck's idea worked and on release the film brought a positive response from Betty's fans who were delighted with their favorite star's change of pace. (Many film buffs and Grable fans insist that Betty originally sang a number in the final scene while she is dancing with Mature, claiming it was cut from the final print. However, no facts could be found to substantiate this claim.)

Betty was earning $1,500 a week by now and was worth every penny. Her first five films for Twentieth had all been box-office successes. Instead of cashing in on Betty's new-found dramatic abilities, Zanuck returned her to the musical. This was possibly the studio chief's major tactical error in handling Grable's career. Despite requests from Sperling and several other producers at Twentieth Century-Fox to use Grable's services in future dramas they were planning, he decided on another splashy musical. As a reward — and to keep her happy — Zanuck cast her in *Song of the Islands*, again with Vic Mature and Jack Oakie.

Betty was happiest when she was among her favorite co-workers. Initially, she was nervous about the man who was playing her father, Academy Award-winner Thomas Mitchell. But they got on well together and she often sought out his advice on how to play scenes with him. He was only too happy to oblige, as long as it was out of earshot of director Lang! It was Mitchell's first film musical and he was thoroughly enjoying the experience. Hermes Pan was again in charge of the dance routines, and Betty was stunning in a grass skirt. The film took five months to complete and the end result was well worthwhile. It was just the kind of escapist entertainment needed in a world darkened by war.

Although *Song* didn't receive any critical acclaim, the public loved it. It gave them Grable as they wanted her, and played to capacity audiences. The film, which had cost just over a million dollars to make, took in over four million dollars in the U.S. alone, and put Betty among the top-ten moneymakers at American box offices. It also determined Grable's future as a musical star.

At the end of shooting, world events took a serious turn. On December 7, 1941, the Japanese bombed Pearl Harbor in Hawaii. America was stunned. President Roosevelt announced on radio that his great country was now at war with Japan and would support its British allies in the war in Europe. When Betty heard the news about Pearl Harbor she was devastated without really knowing why — apart from the fact that war was a dreadful business. Man against Man. How inhumane, she thought.

Until she received a phone call from Jackie Coogan, the true impact of the war did not hit home. Though Betty and Jackie hadn't met in months, he wanted to tell her he had enlisted in the Army. The news stunned her. It had been only four short years since Betty had become Mrs. Coogan, and so much had happened in that time. Jackie hadn't worked in a movie since *Million Dollar Legs*, and had found the going tough. He was getting out of Hollywood to fight for his country. Before Jackie hung up he said, "I've seen all your movies and you are one helluva star. Keep up the good work." The couple had long since realized that their romance, while genuine at the time, was a childhood affair, much like the youthful marriage of Elizabeth Taylor and Nicky Hilton. There was no animosity between them, and Betty wished him a speedy and safe homecoming. Jackie went to war and distinguished himself admirably, particularly in Burma. He was the first of many Hollywood stars to volunteer his services for the country he loved so much.

At that time, little did Betty Grable realize how valuable her own contribution to the war effort would become in the next few years. But with different weapons — beauty, talent, and, above all, gaiety.

CHAPTER SIX

Betty Grable's career was now well in orbit. In the past eighteen months, she had completed six major films and every one of them was a box-office success. As far as the motion picture industry was concerned, she could do no wrong. Exhibitors were delighted with the lines outside theatres showing her films and were eager for more films featuring her. She was a breath of fresh air to the industry.

It pleased Grable enormously to have at last proved to the world that she had "what it takes" to be a successful film actress. She never considered herself a star. In fact, she loathed the word.

While her career was progressing extremely well, her personal life wasn't. To all outward appearances, her romance with George Raft was exciting and glamorous, but to Betty it was another story.

George had proposed marriage, and Betty accepted. He had been a major star for the past decade, he was wealthy, charming, physically attractive, and considerate — in other words, just about everything Betty wanted in a lover. But he was also very much married. Although he and his wife Grayce had separated years before his involvement with Betty, divorce was out of the question. Grayce, a devout Catholic, would never consent to a divorce, and the situation would remain that way until her death many years later.

Raft, born in the Hell's Kitchen section of Manhattan in 1905, started his screen career in 1929 in *Queen of the Night Clubs*, starring Texas Guinan. But it was the 1932 version of *Scarface*, in which he played a coin-flipping gangster, that set him on the road to stardom. During the thirties and forties, he was one of Warner Bros.' top box-office stars, along with Cagney, Bogart, and Pat

O'Brien. He was also an accomplished dancer (and Betty loved dancers), proving his prowess in such films as *Bolero* and *Rumba*.

His affair with Betty was great fodder for the gossip columnists and fan magazines. The fans loved reading about the romantic entanglements of their favorite stars, and Grable and Raft were big stars — and big news.

George was about to end his contract with Warner Bros. and had high hopes for a musical drama script he had commissioned. It was to be a vehicle for Betty and himself, and he hoped it would be filmed at Fox and released by them. Betty knew of his plan and went along with it. She also knew Zanuck didn't like Raft and didn't approve of her association with him, particularly when she and Raft were seen in the company of notorious gangster Bugsy Siegal. The studio boss ordered that a closer watch be kept on Grable and wanted her romance with the shady Raft discouraged at all costs.

Grable was pretty sure Raft's ambitious idea would never get off the ground. Whenever he discussed the project with her, which was often, she quickly changed the subject, causing a certain amount of tension between them. He was sure Betty loved him, but he seemed to feel he had to keep proving his love. Instead of further endearing himself to Betty, he irritated her. She was in love with him. She wanted to marry him, but she was beginning to realize the marriage would never take place. The stalemate brought even more friction to their perilous romance.

Most of Betty's girlfriends — Hayworth, Turner, Lamour — were by now married, and Betty feared she would end up on the shelf. She confided to one columnist, "I'd marry George in a minute . . . if he was free." [33]

But he never would be. Deep down, Betty knew this and she felt trapped. It was a strange situation. She was Hollywood's newest and brightest sex symbol with fans all over the world lusting after her, leading men like Vic Mature trying to romance her offscreen as well as on, and countless eligible Hollywood wolves desperately trying to get into her little black book — but she was trapped in a romance that was going nowhere. It was the most frustrating period of her life so far. Throughout her life, Betty was a great believer in Fate, and Fate was about to smile on her once more.

Reporting for dance rehearsals at the studio, she heard that Harry James was coming to town for a series of concerts at the Palladium. Betty was intrigued. It had been two years since they had last met. By now Harry had become the top bandleader and trumpeter in the States and was the idol of bobbysoxers. Betty asked George to take her to see the show. He agreed and even escorted her backstage afterward to congratulate James and renew their acquaintance.

Betty had been easing off on her dates with Raft and spent most of her free nights at the Hollywood Canteen, entertaining and dancing with the servicemen. Soldiers and sailors stood in line for over an hour just to be able to whirl her around the dance floor for a few minutes. She was one of the most popular attractions at the Canteen. Many young men went into battle with a signed photograph of Betty, reminding them of the night they danced with the world's most glamorous blonde.

Harry and his band also began playing after hours at the Canteen, and it was during these late-night sessions that the two really got to know each other.

Harry Haag James was born on March 15, 1916, in Albany, Georgia, under the canvas of the Mighty Haag Circus. His mother, an aerialist who doubled as a singer and elephant rider, performed until a month before he was born. His father, Everette James, played trumpet and led the circus band. Almost before he could toddle, Harry was being tutored by the circus contortionist and by the time he was five years old, he was tying himself in knots in an act with his 70-year-old teacher. They were billed as the youngest and oldest contortionists in the world. At six, mastoid trouble forced him to give up his back bends. But everyone who travels with a circus has to earn his living, so Harry's father enrolled him in the band as a trainee drummer.

The boy was a born showman and quickly realized that the

drummer never got to be bandleader. He told his father he wanted to learn to play the trumpet. The elder James agreed. Harry recalled:

> I borrowed a battered old horn and used to get out behind the bandstand and just blow and blow. A couple of years later my father presented me with a fine trumpet and began to give me lessons. He was a great psychologist. Even then I was crazy about baseball and always wanted to get in a game instead of practicing. So he would pencil off two or three pages in my practice book, and say when I'd mastered them I could play ball. Sometimes it would take two hours, but often I'd learn in fifteen minutes. In a year, I was good enough to play in the band, and I did feel important in a red uniform with gold braid. [34]

The James family spent several years with the circus, but in 1931, the business was suffering. They decided to give up and settle in Beaumont, Texas, where they had spent many winters. Harry played in the high school band which won a state-wide competition with Harry picking up an award as a soloist. By this time he was yearning to play something other than Sousa marches.

When Joe Gill's Band from St. Louis played Beaumont, Harry asked to sit in with them. Harry said later, "Joe treated it as a gag, but two weeks later I was still there earning $60 a week." James loved the experience and it fired his ambition to reach the top of the heap. From there Harry joined Ben Pollack and recorded "Deep Elm." When this recording came to the attention of the great Benny Goodman, he promptly added Harry to his band which also included talented musicians Gene Krupa, Lionel Hampton, and Teddy Wilson. In 1935, Harry met and married violinist Louise Tobin in Millerton, New York. They eventually had two sons, Harry Jefferey and Timothy Ray.

Her first pregnancy put an end to Louise's musical career and she retired to raise her first-born. Family matters didn't deter the ambitious Harry who wanted to form his own orchestra. He talked the idea over with Goodman. His boss not only gave his blessing, but invested $4,500 in the new band, taking as collateral a one-third interest. For a while James found the going tough. Harry James and His Music Makers took any jobs they could get — anything to stick together and be able to eat.

Harry was a musician — an ambitious one — but he was not a very good businessman. The money from various gigs came and went, and often Harry slept on the tour bus to save on hotel bills. On these trips, card games helped the boys in the band pass away the long nights, and the luckless Harry often found himself on the losing end. Like many musicians, he was also fond of a tipple. To add to his problems, he couldn't resist a pretty girl — and there were plenty of willing partners hanging around the bandstand, ready to sneak off to the bus when the band had finished their stint. These three major "vices"— gambling, women, and booze — plagued him all his life.

When the band became more organized and started to gain a reputation, they got work on a semi-permanent basis in Meadowbank, New Jersey. Harry stopped off in Hoboken one night, and a young singer so impressed him that he signed him up. He was Frank Sinatra, and Frankie's first successful record, "All or Nothing At All" was made with Harry James.

Some time later, after Sinatra had moved on and joined Tommy Dorsey, Harry was plagued by a tall young man who wanted him to hear some of the songs he had written. Harry finally agreed, and listened as the young man sang his compositions. Harry thought the songs only so-so, but he liked the voice. And so Dick Haymes was signed on as soloist. It was Dick's recording of "Old Man River" with the James band that started the outfit on the road to success.

In 1941, the band got its biggest break with a record in which Harry's trumpet, rather than the vocalist, won attention.

I picked a new tune called "A Sinner Kissed an Angel" for the A-side of the disc," said Harry. "For the B-side I chose the old standard, "You Made Me Love You." The A-side didn't click, but the flip side caught on like a prairie fire. That's when the juke-boxes started playing us. [35]

Fame followed quickly. The band played to capacity audiences across the country. Finally Hollywood beckoned with a season at the Palladium. It was a sell-out and firmly established James as one of the all-time greats in the world of popular music.

Harry was contracted to appear in eighteen cities throughout the States, so after the Hollywood engagement during which he and Betty became reacquainted, he was off again. Betty missed him, but wasn't sure yet of her feelings for the tall, rangy music man. So she resumed her dates with Raft when she wasn't busy at the Hollywood Canteen.

Her one consolation was her work. Despite repeated requests from Sperling and several others at Twentieth Century-Fox to use Grable's services in future dramas, Zanuck cast her in *Footlight Serenade,* again with Vic Mature (nurturing the public's notion that the couple were indeed a real-life romantic twosome). However, handsome John Payne was the romantic interest this time, and Jane Wyman (the first Mrs. Ronald Reagan) played Betty's girl-friend and roommate. Comedian Phil Silvers was also featured.

Jane and Betty had worked in the Goldwyn chorus lines years earlier and were good pals. Initially Betty had asked Zanuck to get Lucille Ball for the part. Miss Ball's career was going through a sticky patch and Betty thought it would be a nice way to repay her for all the help and encouragement (not to mention friendship) she had received from Lucy in the early years of their careers. However, Lucy refused the role and took a suspension at her own studio as a result. Betty couldn't understand why Lucy had turned the part down. It was a good role and would have done much to boost Lucy's stock, but the comedienne gave no reason for her refusal. Miss Wyman was happy to accept the strong supporting role.

It was another successful outing for Betty. She had the benefit of Gregory Ratoff's direction, a witty script, and Mature playing the "ham" for all it was worth. The storyline was slight, but it had a most authentic backstage atmosphere, faithfully recording the drama (and fun) of chorines auditioning for Broadway shows. Betty had some excellent numbers, particularly one called "I Heard the Birdies Sing," in which she had some fine footwork — including boxing with her own shadow! She claimed that Raft had helped her with the boxing moves required in the number. Once again, Hermes Pan was in charge of the choreography and accompanied Betty on-screen in a snappy routine.

On a topical note, Jane Wyman played a character who was forever consulting the cards for herself and Betty. When asked by Grable if she would ever get a starring part, Wyman replied, "You have about as much chance of that as I have of being First Lady!" Had Miss Wyman stayed married to Ronald Reagan, that's exactly what she would have become!

Zanuck took in the rushes every evening and had to admit that Betty was a natural when it came to musical comedy. His only regret over *Footlight Serenade* was that he didn't shoot it in Technicolor. Apart from adding nearly a third to production costs, color stock was in short supply due to the war effort, and his studio's quota for the year had already been allocated to other productions.

However, Zanuck was so pleased with Betty's work on this film that he called her into his office one morning toward the end of shooting and told her that in the future all her films would be photographed in Technicolor, inserting a clause into her contract to that effect. He also announced that her salary would be hiked to $2,000 a week. Betty left his office like a dog with two tails. She knew now that she had really arrived. She was the first star ever to have a color clause written into her contract — though a later rival, June Haver, had all thirteen films she made at Twentieth Century-Fox photographed in Technicolor.

Betty's fan mail had soared to about 5,000 letters a week. She was the studio's biggest box-office attraction in years. Not even Alice Faye had reached such dizzying heights. And still the publicity spewed forth. A group of Hollywood artists and sculptors voted her as having the most perfect figure on the screen. And, of course, her legs were always mentioned in the fan magazines. Because of the publicity over her gams, as she called them, she took to wearing slacks while out shopping. She was tired of hearing women say in a loud voice (to be sure that Betty would hear), "I don't know what's so special about her legs. . . I can fill a stocking as well as she can!" Betty dismissed such comments, realizing there were some unsavory aspects to being well known.

Meanwhile, Betty and her mother had purchased a Spanish-style house on Stone Canyon in Beverly Hills, finally establishing themselves as residents of the popular star colony.

Despite her mother's warning that there was no future in it, she continued dating Raft. At one low point in her unhappy love affair, she even mentioned to a girlfriend the possibility of moving in with him. Openly living together in those days was strictly taboo. Friends warned her that her career would take a nosedive if she took this step. Plus, the morality clause in her contract with the studio was a major consideration. Those close to her knew that Betty would never have seriously considered cohabitation and neither would Raft, but it demonstrates the depth of her feeling for him — and her desperation.

Alice Faye, who had married Phil Harris, was about to start a family. She kept refusing film offers, despite pleas from Zanuck and her countless fans. This led to a backlog of musical scripts for Betty to get to work on. In fact, Betty's workload was so heavy that Zanuck had to borrow Rita Hayworth from Columbia for *My Gal Sal*.

Another film Zanuck had earmarked for Betty was *Roxy Hart*, the story of a brassy chorus girl on trial for the murder of her boyfriend. It was an interesting black comedy, but Betty didn't appear too keen on it, so the boss hired Ginger Rogers. Grable wasn't unhappy at the decision; she felt on much safer ground in the musical scene.

With the runaway success of *Footlight Serenade*, Zanuck decided to exploit Betty's showgirl image fully in *Springtime in the Rockies*, a new film to be directed by Irving Cummings, co-starring John Payne, Carmen Miranda and Cesar Romero. For good measure Charlotte Greenwood and Betty's "good luck mascot" Edward Everett Horton were added to the starry line-up.

To Betty's clear delight, Harry James and his Music Makers were brought in to supply the music. She greeted him cheerily on his first day on the set of his first film. The bandleader appeared equally delighted to renew the friendship. Their mutual love of music gave them a common ground for developing their relationship, and Harry often dined at Betty's table in the commissary. They went out on a number of dates together; it was a change for Harry to be able to sit and enjoy the music of an orchestra rather than lead it.

The Queen of the Hollywood Musical and the King of the Bobbysoxers (as the fan magazines often labeled him during this period, though that title was really Frank Sinatra's) were soon featured in the gossip columns. The resulting speculation didn't do any harm at the box office.

One of their dates took them to the Hollywood Palladium where Benny Goodman was playing. After the show, they went backstage to meet Harry's former boss, and bought back Goodman's one-third interest in the band — for $20,000. If Harry had waited any longer, it would have cost him much more. Goodman wasn't complaining. A $20,000 return on a $4,500 outlay certainly wasn't chicken feed!

George Raft, who had been dropped by Betty when James arrived in town, confronted the couple as they were dancing one evening. After a heated exchange, the two men became involved in a minor scuffle, with Betty in the middle trying to separate them. Photographers were quick to seize the opportunity to snap Hollywood's top blonde in the midst of a romantic duel, and the flashbulbs popped. The next day, George, Harry, and Betty were splashed all over the gossip columns with the heading "Actor and Bandleader in Brawl Over Betty Grable."

The news could scarcely have been expected to escape Zanuck's attention, and it didn't. The next day he interrupted filming to call Betty to his office and reprimand her over the incident, reminding her that her wholesome image must be kept intact. Betty was angry at this invasion of her private life and was on the point of telling the boss where to get off when she remembered it would also involve Harry. He had barely started work on the film and could easily be replaced. She took the reprimand in silence and left the office. The event was quickly forgotten and Grable and Raft were never seen together again in public. The incident brought home to Betty the sad fact that film stars aren't allowed the privilege of a private life.

Raft sent roses and apologetic notes every day for weeks, plus a few expensive gifts like jewelry and a fur coat, but Betty was determined to end the association and didn't contact him. Except for their shared evenings at the Hollywood Canteen, Harry and Betty settled down to a couple of dates a week during the film's duration.

All in all, the making of *Springtime in the Rockies* seems to have been a pleasant experience for Betty. Her role was tailor made for her; she danced superbly with Cesar Romero, and each of her outfits seemed more glamorous than the last. She had a scene with Harry, but his dialogue was kept to a minimum; he looked much more at ease fronting his band. Carmen Miranda was her usual knockout self and had some good scenes, including a fractured rendition of "Chattanooga Choo Choo." Her natural vivaciousness made her an involuntary scene-stealer! Fans of both actresses often queried why they never made another film together — their powder-room sequence in the film was a hilarious piece of comedy. Unfortunately their busy schedules kept them apart.

Betty sang "Run Little Raindrop, Run" with Payne, and led the big finale, "Pan American Jubilee." The film also featured the song "I Had the Craziest Dream" which became Betty and Harry's theme song. Grable was disappointed that she wasn't given this lovely ballad to sing in the film, but that honor went to Harry's contracted band singer, Helen Forrest, who wouldn't have given it over graciously — she was rather jealous of Betty's fame, and besides, she carried a torch for Harry herself. (In a radio broadcast a year or so later, narrated by Cecil B. De Mille, Betty finally got to sing the song with co-star Dick Powell.)

When *Springtime In The Rockies* opened in New York, it broke all box office records and also won her another raise. By now she was Twentieth Century-Fox's highest-paid star — and nobody had worked harder than Betty to earn this honor. But her biggest surprise was yet to come.

With the film completed, Harry told Betty he was travelling to Texas to talk with his wife and sons; he wanted to tell them of his intention to marry her. Betty was speechless. Although she was fairly sure she was in love with him, he had never given any inkling that he was serious as well. He and his wife had split up long before he got involved with Betty and there had been many other women in between, but he had been in no hurry to divorce until he met the beautiful blonde actress. Louise James must have sensed the inevitability of the situation, for she agreed to seek a Mexican divorce as soon as her lawyer had drawn up papers to provide for herself and the boys.

With Harry away, Betty continued her stint at the Canteen, though some of the enthusiasm had left her. Not that she was wriggling out of her commitment to the servicemen, but she realized she was just as lonely as they were, and it depressed her. Friends like Dottie Lamour and Martha Raye tried to help, but with very little success. Although Betty had the capacity to make others laugh, she found that, in times of stress, there was little friends could do to cheer her up. After a couple of days on a downward spiral, she would suddenly snap out of it, acting as though she hadn't a care in the world.

Her pet director, Walter Lang, was preparing his next project — a musical set in turn-of-the-century New York — and he wanted Betty to take the lead. She was interested, but had misgivings about appearing in period costume. She read the script of *Coney Island*, however, and agreed it would be her best role to date. She was given lots of comedy pieces and a plethora of musical numbers, from low-down chorus girl bits to sophisticated song and dance routines, which pleased her immensely. To allay her fears of appearing in a period piece, Lang had the wardrobe department dress Betty for the part and he shot a few test scenes. He invited Betty to view the rushes; and was delighted with the result.

Before she reported for work, she asked Zanuck if she could take a few days off to visit some friends in New York. There wasn't much going on around the studio that he didn't know about, and he asked Betty point blank if she intended to see Harry, who had opened at the Paramount Theatre. Betty admitted her growing love for James. The boss listened sympathetically and agreed to her taking some time off. He asked only that she try to keep the romance quiet until the James's divorce was out of the way. Then they would be free to marry — with the studio's blessing!

Columnist Louella Parsons was after Betty for an exclusive story on her latest romance, but Betty played it cool. She told Louella: "I'm very fond of Harry, and our mutual interest in music brought us together. But there's no romance — we are both too busy with our careers." [36]

Before Betty set out for her trip to New York, her mother asked if she thought she wouldn't be better off single for a while yet. Betty blew her stack. "I'm 26 and single — and that's practically middle-aged. If Harry still wants me, we're going to get married."

Mrs. Grable didn't particularly like her daughter's intended (she didn't like anyone who could wrest control of Betty Grable from her), but she realized that, as the cream of America's popular musicians, Harry James was quite a catch. Betty could do a lot worse than marry James, but Lillian would much rather have Betty at home where she could still help to run her career. With Harry James around, she felt her power over Betty diminishing.

After checking into the Hotel Astor, Betty hailed a cab to take her to the Paramount Theatre. The driver didn't recognize her and told her he could only take her to the block before the theatre. "Why's that?" she asked. "Because, lady, police are out on patrol around the theatre trying to control thousands of bobbysoxers waiting to see Harry James," explained the cabbie. "I guess you're a fan too, huh?"

"Well, I have heard of him," replied Betty, trying to conceal a smile.

The cab driver was right. Betty had to trudge through freezing slush to reach the stage door where the doorman refused to open up and let her in. A mounted policeman came to the rescue. He recognized her, but demanded her autograph before he would give her the okay to go inside.

After a very affectionate reunion, Harry asked Betty if she would be able to cope with this type of fan worship after they were married. Betty laughed. "That will be the least of our problems. I'll just get Wells Fargo to escort you home from the theatre each night."

Despite her delight at seeing Harry, Betty was glad to leave the chilling cold of New York and head back to the perpetual sunshine of California. Now that her personal happiness seemed assured, she was ready and willing to go back to work.

Betty arrived back at the studio to find that she still had a week or so before reporting for work on *Coney Island*, as co-stars George Montgomery and Cesar Romero were still on other assignments. Many of the big stars were giving up their free time to entertain the troops at home and abroad. Betty liked the idea and volunteered her services. Immediately she was on the road with her personal hairdresser, Marie Brasselle, visiting war-wounded soldiers in hospitals in the Pacific area.

Marie Brasselle, who had quickly become Betty's best friend and confidante since being assigned to her in 1941, recalled the period.

> For all her shyness and terror of meeting new people, she can conquer it when the occasion arises. I've never seen Betty work so hard during those first shows she did.
>
> I particularly remember one night at Fort Bragg where she was scheduled for an outdoor show. It was pouring rain and not the kind of weather for the fancy white satin and sequined gown

she was wearing. The officer in charge suggested they cancel the show, but Betty gritted her already chattering teeth and walked on to the stage amid cheers of more than 5,000 soldiers waiting in the rain. 'If they can stand, so can I,' said Betty. And there she stood for almost two hours singing her heart out. Her hair-do was drooping and her dress was getting longer by the minute! But she seemed to be having the time of her life. [37]

Later that week Betty and Marie were asked to visit a hospital ward to talk to soldiers and airmen who had been badly burned in airplane accidents. Betty had never been around people who had been seriously hurt or maimed, and she was a little apprehensive. Marie said,

> I watched Betty as we walked into the ward. She was trembling, and at one point I thought she would turn back. She didn't. Instead she stayed some hours, chatting to every one of the forty soldiers there. When we came out, Betty said quietly, 'Y'know, Marie, I never thought I'd be able to do that.'
>
> Next morning she couldn't wait to get started all over again, and when we had covered the entire hospital, the largest in the country at the time, the soldiers who were able to leave their beds gathered in the auditorium to thank her and present her with some gifts of handicraft work they had made during their convalescence. I had never seen Betty so touched, and I was so moved by her reaction, I couldn't help crying. When Betty caught me, she tried to laugh it off, but the tears were streaming down her face as she chided me, 'Look at you, why are you crying? You are a real gooney!' A simple, undemonstrative person herself, she hates gushers. [38]

Betty promised the soldiers she would return, and she did — several times.

(After they were married, Betty and Harry, [who had been exempt from military service because of his childhood mastoid problem], volunteered their services with the U.S.O. to entertain the troops abroad. When Zanuck heard this he vetoed the plan, persuading Betty that she would be a much more valuable asset to the morale of the troops by continuing with her film work.)

She went back to work the following week, a much-changed person. For too long she had been protected by the studio, only half-realizing that there was another world out there. Zanuck liked this change in his top star and did all he could to help her keep her feet on the ground.

"When you have 5,000 people writing to you every week, it must be very difficult to lead an ordinary life. But Betty was pretty level-headed about her success," he said later. [39]

Zanuck respected that and rewarded her for it. During the filming of *Coney Island*, Betty had trouble negotiating the stairs from her second-floor dressing room in her heavy period costumes. Zanuck immediately ordered studio carpenters to build her a luxurious, ground-level bungalow which was to remain her dressing room for the rest of her career at the studio. The boss considered Betty's welfare at the studio to be of prime importance; not only did he like her personally, but he considered her a very valuable commodity.

Further proof of her worth to Zanuck and the studio were her frequent invitations to Zanuck's oceanside home in Santa Monica for fun weekends, as well as his luxury home in Palm Spring. Few of his stars were accorded this preferential treatment. Though she was never one of Zanuck's personal pets, she was always a popular guest. Zanuck's wife, Virginia, enjoyed her company — particularly as she knew that Betty was one of the few stars at the studio who wasn't having an affair with her philandering husband.

Whenever Harry was in town, he accompanied her to the Zanuck home. They both enjoyed the informality of the place and found Virginia to be a generous hostess. She was also very discreet, seeing to it that Betty and Harry had adjoining bedrooms during their stay. Zanuck approved of the romance with Harry who was almost as popular as Betty. Still he had a few misgivings about the union; it occurred to him that her popularity, particularly with the troops, might fade if and when she married. The studio had invested a lot of money in Grable, and the boss felt it would be disastrous if she started to slip after her marriage.

Beyond a doubt, Betty Grable's superstar days had arrived. In 1942 she was voted among the top ten in the Money Making Picture Herald-Fame Poll, and was to remain in the top ten for the next decade (a record unequalled by any other woman star before or since). During the shooting of *Coney Island*, Betty received further proof of her fame. The Nazis, in a series of radio broadcasts, denounced her as a "creation designed to take the enemy's mind off what they were fighting for . . . there was more to life than Pepsi-Cola and Betty Grable." [40]

The infamous Tokyo Rose spouted similar propaganda in numerous broadcasts in the Pacific war zone. Such "poison" didn't stop American and Allied troops from adopting Grable as their official pin-up girl.

Happily, that was no studio publicity stunt. Her popularity easily outstripped that of other glamour-girl notables like Rita Hayworth, Lana Turner, and Dorothy Lamour. In one week, requests for her pictures reached an all-time record of 25,000. [41]

Darryl F. Zanuck left Twentieth Century-Fox to enlist in the war effort. He became a lieutenant colonel and took charge of production of U. S. Army war-training films. Life carried on as usual at the studio under the new leadership of William Goetz, although George Jessel was acknowledged as the real head of production in Zanuck's absence. Betty's film was almost finished and it had all the makings of another winner.

Harry and Betty kept in constant touch by telephone, and he visited her in Hollywood for the New Year festivities in 1943. He was in town for *Two Girls and a Sailor*, an M-G-M musical starring June Allyson, so they were able to get together to plan their wedding. Betty didn't want the big affair the studio had in mind. She and Harry agreed that when his divorce came through, they would slip off quietly to Las Vegas and tie the knot. She was head over heels in love with the handsome bandleader and couldn't wait to be Mrs. Harry James.

Once Betty had completed her part in *Coney Island*, she went to the studio's "portrait gallery" for a session with top photographer

Frank Powolney. Apparently the studio needed a bathing suit shot for costume designers about to start work on her wardrobe for *Sweet Rosie O'Grady*, Betty's next film.

Powolney took several rapid shots of her in a white bathing suit, high heels, and a "good-luck garter." Recalled Betty: "The session wasn't going too well; Frank was trying to achieve something different. After about a dozen shots, he told me to turn my back to the camera and he would catch my face in profile. I obliged, turned my face toward the camera, and asked, 'How about this?'"

It turned out to be exactly what Powolney wanted. Many stories have circulated about the famous pin-up shot, including one that Betty was pregnant at the time. The truth is that there are several frontal shots of Betty taken on the same day (one is reproduced in the photo section of this book). She certainly doesn't look pregnant.

Powolney was so pleased with his picture that he dispatched it to Publicity; they airbrushed out the garter and released the picture to the press.

The shot caught on like wildfire and became the most-requested picture in movie history. No one knows exactly how many requests were made for the photograph, but close to three million copies were sent to the armed forces. (To advertise an exhibition entitled "Forces Sweethearts" at the Imperial War Museum in London, 1993, Betty's famous pin-up shot was used extensively on billboards and posters all over the country. Within the museum, it was stated that more than 10 million copies of the pin-up photograph had been distributed.) [42]

Certain sections of her anatomy were sectioned off into battle zones to enable bomber pilots to find their targets more accurately. Enthusiastic military artists painted the pin-up shot on the sides of aircraft. In the late 1980s, one aircraft was restored to its former glory — complete with Grable portrait — and is now on view at the Lockheed Aircraft Museum in Burbank, California. [43] The restoration work gathered much publicity and renewed interest in Betty Grable and her importance during World War Two.

In the spring of 1943, Betty started work on *Sweet Rosie O'Grady* with Robert Young, Adolphe Menjou, Virginia Gray, and Reggie Gardiner. The title had been purchased from Columbia Pictures which had used it for a 1926 movie starring Shirley Mason and Cullen Landis. It was a very amusing tale of a burlesque queen who had ambitions to marry into British peerage. *Police Gazette* reporter Sam McGee (Young) exposes her as a phony, and the fun is fast and furious.

Betty had some good songs — "Going to the County Fair," "Waiting at the Church," and a lovely new ballad, "My Heart Tells Me," which became a big hit. This number was filmed as Betty took her first screen bath. So anxious were the men around the studio to see "more" of Grable that director Irving Cummings ordered the set closed for the duration of the sequence. Nevertheless, many workers not directly associated with the production managed to smuggle themselves onto the sound stage anyway.

Midway through filming, Betty received a call from Harry, with the good news that his wife Louise had divorced him in Chihuahua, Mexico. He was free to marry! Betty sought out George Jessel, who was in charge of the production, and asked for time off to get married. He agreed and wanted Betty to let the studio arrange everything; it would make headlines all over the world. But Grable had had enough of studio publicity. She said no. She and Harry would marry quietly out of town — and she was adamant about it. She had already had her "big, splashy wedding" some six years earlier and, despite the ballyhoo during that ceremony, the marriage came to grief. It was an exercise she was not keen to repeat.

Jessel conferred with director Cummings, and it was agreed that Betty could be spared for a couple of days during the Fourth of July holiday. She immediately called Harry with the good news. They arranged to marry in a wedding chapel in Las Vegas. She would travel there on Sunday, July 4 (Independence Day), marry later in the day, and have a couple of days' honeymoon — Betty didn't have to be back at work until the following Wednesday.

Betty set off by train, accompanied by her friends, actress Betty

Furness (who was to be her witness) and Mrs. Edith Wasserman. Word got out that the couple were marrying in Vegas. By the time Betty got to the church, a loudspeaker relay system had been installed so that the crowds who couldn't get into the tiny church would be able to hear the complete ceremony!

Grable felt angry when she spotted some Hollywood press photographers at the scene. She was sure somebody at the studio had tipped off the press about her impending wedding. She hadn't told anyone in the cast that she was off to get married, but they must have guessed; it was common knowledge that she and Harry were planning a wedding. She trusted her work pals and felt sure they would respect her request for privacy. Only her mother, Jessel, and Cummings were in on the secret. Unfortunately, it was too late now; she would just have to brave it out. Betty thought Jessel was behind the leak and made a mental note to have a word with him when she returned to the studio.

As luck would have it, Harry's train was late, so the two Bettys sat as inconspicuously as possible in their hired car, parked near the chapel. Betty was in a state of near panic. "This isn't a wedding," she exclaimed. "It's a three-ring circus!"

Eventually she spotted Harry circling the church in his car. He hastily transferred to hers and they drove to their hotel where they called a Baptist minister, the Rev. C. S. Sloan, and asked him to come to their suite and perform the ceremony. By now it was into the early hours of July 5.

The groom wore a dark blue pinstripe suit, and the bride an ice-blue dress. In her excitement Betty forgot to wear her corsage of flowers.

After the ceremony, Betty telephoned her mother. All she could say into the phone was, "This is Mrs. Harry James speaking . . . this is Mrs. Harry James."

The only question Lillian Grable asked her ecstatic daughter was, "Were there many photographers there?"

The couple never left their hotel suite during their three-day honeymoon.

CHAPTER SEVEN

Betty returned to Hollywood a radiant bride. The press gave the marriage full coverage and the gossip columnists gave it six months at the most! Betty was quick to retort, "I aim to stay Mrs. Harry James for the rest of my life."

The couple settled down to wedded bliss at their new home at 2301 Beaumont Drive, Beverly Hills. Added to the happy home were Betty's two dogs; she maintained that home just wouldn't be home without them!

Her mother called to offer her congratulations, as did her father. Conn and Lillian were once again on friendly terms, and Betty still hoped they would get together again. She found it sad that her parents were really two lonely people now leading separate lives, although Lillian kept herself as busy as possible with Betty's career.

There was much gaiety on the set when Betty returned to finish work on *Sweet Rosie O'Grady*. The blushing bride had to take some flak from her co-stars and crew. But it was all good-natured high spirits. Co-star Robert Young threw a party for the newlyweds.

After filming was over, Betty settled down to a domestic routine appropriate to a forties wife, dutifully swapping her spangles and feather boas for an apron and a vacuum cleaner. She had to admit she was no great cook. "My mother never taught me to cook, simply because she herself never learned," cracked Betty. She agreed that some of her dishes had turned out disastrously. Consequently, she and Harry ate out often in the first few weeks of their married life, until they found a resident cook.

Later that summer, Zanuck returned to take charge of the studio. He had resigned his commission to resume his career in

Hollywood, feeling that he could contribute more to the war effort by turning out top-quality commercial films. He had seen first-hand how eagerly Betty's morale-boosting musical comedies were received by the troops overseas.

One of his first duties was to interview new contract artists hired in his absence. Two of the more spectacular newcomers were Jeanne Crain and June Haver. He had them assigned to Alice Faye's new film, *The Gang's All Here.*

Another bright newcomer to arrive at the studio was strawberry-blonde Vivian Blaine. She showed much promise as a future musical star, and Zanuck kept her in mind for the day when Betty would be too busy — or pregnant. The latter option materialized sooner than he thought.

Anxious to cash in on the Grable pin-up tag, the studio rushed together a flimsy script, titled it (naturally) *Pin Up Girl,* and immediately brought Betty, the blissful bride, back to work. She didn't mind. Harry had to go east to fulfill bookings arranged before their marriage.

James had promised as soon as his commitments were out of the way, he would be returning to Hollywood, using it as his new base. He also told Betty he was cutting down on traveling and would concentrate on a career in films, which he did with some success.

With Ty Power, Vic Mature, and John Payne all in active war service, there was a dearth of leading men in the studio. Most major studios were in the same predicament; even Clark Gable of M-G-M was overseas with the Air Force. Good-looking newcomer John Harvey, who was neither a singer nor a dancer (some unkind critics suggested he wasn't an actor either), was cast as Betty's leading man. He was a likeable if ineffective foil for Betty's charms.

Betty gamely accepted John and helped him all she could, realizing that his role was so bland there was little he could do with it. Martha Raye, Joe E. Brown, Dorothea Kent, the Condos Brothers, and the Skating Vanities filled out the line-up, with Bruce

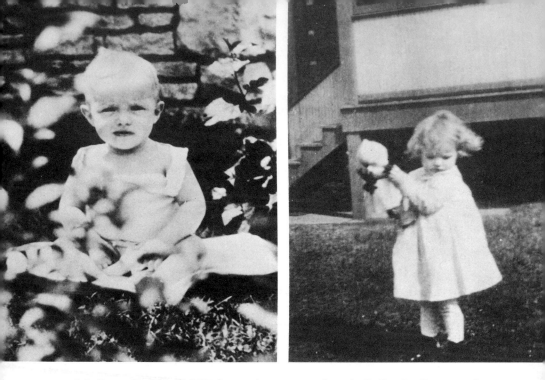

1-1 Betty Grable, age 13, dances in amateur show in St. Louis. *Courtesy of the Academy of Motion Picture Arts and Sciences.*
1-2 Betty Grable, age 14 months, in her hometown of St. Louis, MO
1-3 Young Betty Grable enjoys the outdoors with her doll
1-4 Five-year old Betty Grable on vacation in the Ozark Mountains
1-5 "Dolly with Dolly." Christmas, 1922 in St. Louis. Betty, age 6, and sister Marjorie pose with their Christmas tree and presents.

1-6 Betty Grable, age 13, fronts the chorus line in the Eddie Cantor musical *Whoopee*, 1930. *Courtesy of the Academy of Motion Picture Arts and Sciences.*

1-7   Betty Grable in a scene from Astor's compilation movie *Hollywood Bound* (1940). She was billed as Frances Dean and was about 14 years old here. She is at the left center, holding the dog.
1-8   Another scene from *Hollywood Bound* (1940).

1-9 A dramatic moment for Nancy Carroll and Betty Grable in *Child of Manhattan* (Columbia, 1932).

1-10 Dorothy Wilson, Mary Mason, Betty Grable, and Marion Weldon pose in an open car in this scene from *Fraternity House* (RKO, 1933).

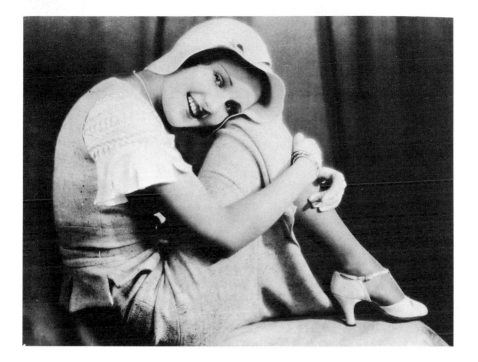

1-11 Early portrait of Betty Grable taken around 1932-1933.
1-12 Betty Grable, appearing as Frances Dean, in an early publicity shot
1-13 Wheeler and Woolsey with Betty Grable in the film *Hold 'Em Jail* (RKO, 1932). *Courtesy of the Academy of Motion Picture Arts and Sciences.*

1-14 A major breakthrough for Betty Grable as she "K-knocks K-knees" with Edward Everett Horton in *The Gay Divorcee* (RKO, 1934).

1-15 Lucille Ball, Harriett Hilliard, and Betty Grable in *Follow the Fleet* (RKO, 1936).

1-16 Judy Garland, Patsy Kelly, Johnny Downs, and Betty Grable
appear in a scene from *Pigskin Parade* (20th Century-Fox, 1936).

1-17 Betty Grable and basketball hero "Hank" Luisetti in a scene from
      the film *Campus Confessions* (Paramount, 1938). *Courtesy of the
      Academy of Motion Picture Arts and Sciences.*
1-18 Poster for *Campus Confessions* starring Betty Grable, "Hank "
      Luisetti and Eleanore Whitney

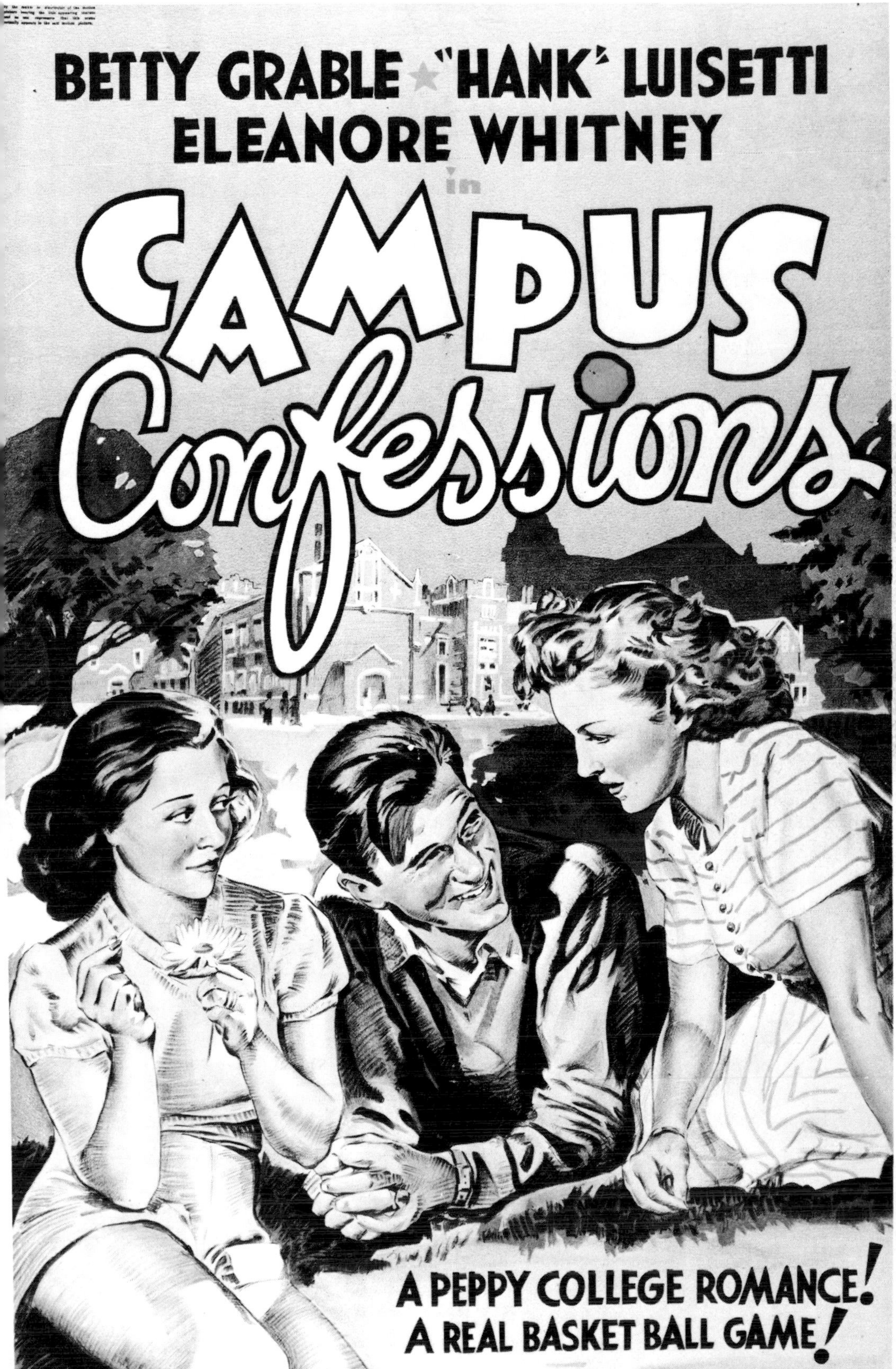
BETTY GRABLE ★ "HANK" LUISETTI
ELEANORE WHITNEY
in
CAMPUS
Confessions
A PEPPY COLLEGE ROMANCE!
A REAL BASKET BALL GAME!

1-19 Betty Grable and co-star Larry "Buster" Crabbe in a romatic close-up from *Thrill of a Lifetime* (Paramount, 1937).

1-20 Lewis Stone, Bruce Cabot, and Betty Grable in a scene from *Don't Turn 'Em Loose* (RKO, 1936).

1-21 Betty Grable and Johnny Downs in *Pigskin Parade* (20th Century-Fox, 1936) publicity shot.

1-22 Family group at preview of Paramount's *Thrill of a Lifetime* in Los Angeles. It shows Betty with fiancé Jackie Coogan. Her father is to her left and her mother to her right.

1-23 John Payne, Gracie Allen, George Burns, Martha Raye, Bob Hope, Florence George, Skinnay Ellis, Betty Grable, and Jackie Coogan in *College Swing* (Paramount, 1938).

1-24 Betty Grable - "the Quicksilver Blonde" - photographed at RKO, 1933.

Humberstone directing and Hermes Pan once more in charge of Betty's dance routines.

A month into the shooting of *Pin Up Girl,* stories were put out by wardrobe assistants that Grable was putting on weight, which she initially denied. Once the production was well under way, however, she announced she was, in fact, pregnant. Martha Raye thought this was a hilarious turn of events, and promptly rechristened the film "Pregnant Girl."

Zanuck was far from amused. If he postponed the production until Betty's confinement was over, he would have to pay full salaries to the other principals. Alternatively, he could abandon the project altogether, which would still be expensive even if it did cut down on production costs. Another alternative would be to replace Grable in the title role, but who else at the studio had pin-up girl status? No one. The whole point of the film would be lost.

At one point he toyed with the idea of substituting Carole Landis. She had sung a number entitled "Pin Up Girl" (nothing resembling the song to be used in the Grable film) in a war effort short made some time previously. But on viewing this curio, he decided against using Carole. There just wasn't anyone to replace Grable!

While all this was going on, *Coney Island* had gone on general release and was creating new box-office records wherever it played. It was her biggest hit to date. Audiences fell for Grable's "new look" in this winning costume musical. Its great score by Leo Robin and Ralph Rainger included two big hits, "Take It From There" and "Cuddle Up a Little Closer." Other numbers included "Winter" in which Betty danced with a pantomime horse, and "Danger in a Dance," actually three dance routines in one, partnered once again by the excellent Pan.

To further complicate matters, Betty had just been voted the number one box-office star, overtaking Bob Hope, Bing Crosby, and Abbott and Costello. The powerful executives in Twentieth's New York office informed Zanuck that the exhibitors were screaming for more Grable musicals. He had no choice but to continue with Grable in the lead and finish the film as quickly as possible. Betty had pre-recorded her songs for the film, so if they could get the star's dance sequences over before she began to show, they could shoot the rest of the film showing Betty from the waist up. Betty's routines were kept to a minimum and Martha Raye was given another number to fill out the film.

During the early weeks of shooting everything went smoothly. The star's pregnancy was progressing normally and she was proving a healthy mother-to-be, never losing a day's work. Early on she executed a spectacular adagio-type number, "Once Too Often," partnered by Pan and her dance stand-in Angie Blue, doing some of her best footwork to date. Then, with her dance routines out of the way, she romped through the rest of the film.

The story centers around Betty as a secretary in Washington. She is also a compulsive liar, which gets her into all sorts of jams. Through her fibbing she gets herself involved with a returning war hero (Harvey) and further complicates matters by appearing as a night club attraction. By day she is a prim, trim typist, but come evening she becomes the glamourous top attraction at Joe E. Brown's nightspot. Through her night club job she becomes the Official Pin Up of the Forces.

It sounds like a highly unlikely plot, but Betty made it work, and the only prop she used to change her image was a pair of glasses. She showed a fine sense of comedy, and in fact she was the only thing worth watching in an otherwise dull movie — with the possible exception of Dorothea Kent who played her long-suffering girlfriend. It was curious that Dorothea was prominent in the early scenes, but once Betty gained fame as a pin-up girl, Miss Kent vanished from the film. There was no explanation offered in the plot, so perhaps Dorothea's later scenes — if there were any — were deleted from the final cut of the film.

One big headache was that no one could dream up a suitable finale for this obviously morale-boosting tale. In their haste to get Betty's dances in the can, Humberstone and Pan had failed to shoot a routine that could have been used as a suitable ending.

They had thought of closing with the "Merry Widow" sequence, but Grable's pregnancy was all too obvious in the slit skirt costume she was wearing and her famous legs looked rather heavy.

Ever conscious of the war, producer William LeBaron suggested the idea of having Betty drill a platoon of chorus girls in some fancy military steps. The director agreed, and precision dance expert Alice Sullivan was called in to choreograph Betty in what might be the worst finale ever devised for any musical film.

Betty was filmed marching up and down the sound stage "like a drill sergeant" in a very unbecoming uniform and flat heels. Betty recalled, "To hide my by-now obvious pregnancy, they wrapped me in a Sam Browne belt — I looked so tough. I was very unhappy with that routine."

When Zanuck saw the rushes, he was also unhappy but was persuaded — much against his better judgement — to let the ending stand. Technically it was a perfect piece of precision marching, but totally wrong for Grable and completely out of place as the finale to this lightweight confection. Fans felt cheated watching Betty drill a platoon of chorus girls instead of leading them into a glittering dance finale. There wasn't even a final clinch with her leading man — merely a shot of Betty smiling behind a ceremonial sword!

By the end of filming, Betty was seven months pregnant, and she retired from the screen to await the birth of her first child. The studio kept her on full salary during the long lay-off, unprecedented in studio history. Zanuck's big worry was that Betty might abandon her career in favor of motherhood.

The studio boss wasn't too unhappy, though. *Coney Island* continued to do excellent business, and *Sweet Rosie O'Grady* was scheduled to be released toward the end of 1943. By the time *Pin Up Girl* would be ready for viewing, Betty should be back at work on her next film. This clever scheduling allowed a steady stream of customers into the theatres with no untimely gaps.

Early notices from *Sweet Rosie* were phenomenal. Said *Motion Picture Daily*, "Entertaining, tuneful, stunningly Technicolored musical starring Betty Grable, who delivers a first-rate performance. Emerges as a contender for top grosses." The *New York Daily Mirror* wrote, "Will gross millions. It's a bell ringer for escape pictures in wartime. It builds Grable to a new high in ability as well as appeal." The rival *New York Post* described Grable as "a blonde enchanting delight."

In his book, *The Heart of Hollywood,* James Cairn wrote,

> *Sweet Rosie O'Grady* . . . is the best musical ever to come out of Hollywood. If it were twice as long, I'd have enjoyed it twice as much. This musical is pure harmony linked to beauty, novelty and enchantment, all pleasing to the senses, making filmgoers see and hear beauty. I hope to see this picture again and again. [44]

Meanwhile the publicity department worked overtime to keep the Grable image very much alive in the minds of the cinema-going public. Betty helped out by making a guest appearance, along with Alice Faye and Carmen Miranda, in *Four Jills In A Jeep;* she sang "Cuddle Up a Little Closer" from *Coney Island.*

According to studio publicity, the Grable pin-up picture was now being mailed to servicemen, and requests were running at around 100,000 a month. The Hays Office (the all-powerful censorship group) was not thrilled; they thought the picture too sexy. While they did not object to its being used in the context of a film, they objected to its being distributed universally. However, the shot was so popular that the studio suspended requests for Grable photographs from civilians for the duration of the war, supplying only service personnel. This created a huge black market on the home front, and her faithful civilian fans had to pay hard cash on the black market for her latest portraits.

Betty took her pin-up image quite seriously. She said,

> Some of the boys write me and tell of their problems with their girls back home. I find it a grave responsibility being a pin-up girl. Our boys are in a war, fighting for the freedom of our country, and I think it is the duty of all of us to support them in

their awesome task. I answer as many letters as I possibly can; it is a duty that I cannot ignore, and I know that Rita, Lana, and Ann [Sheridan] don't shirk their duties either.

Her career and pin-up image had not suffered as a result of her marriage or her impending motherhood. The fact that she was now married only seemed to enhance the Grable legend. Many a weary soldier trudged into battle singing the parody, "I want a girl just like the girl that married Harry James."

Film roles scheduled for Betty were assigned to other stars. The studio was only too happy to welcome back Alice Faye, after her latest confinement, to star in the very successful *Hello Frisco, Hello* with John Payne, newly invalided out of service.

Newcomer Vivian Blaine was given her big chance opposite Carmen Miranda and young crooner Perry Como in a loose adaptation of the hit Broadway show, *Something for the Boys*.

Harry James was also working on a new musical over at M-G-M — an Esther Williams aqua-musical entitled, appropriately enough, *Bathing Beauty*, which shot its star into the pin-up league.

So while Betty languished in her beautiful home awaiting the birth of her first child, life was going on as usual in Hollywood. But she didn't quite escape the potshots of the gossip columnists. One wrote, "Wouldn't it be awful if the child of a certain blonde musical star and her bandleader husband were born with HIS legs and HER brains?" [45]

Betty was quickly quoted in reply, "Harry has good legs!" Such comments riled her, but she generally managed to see the humor in them — although if she thought for a minute that the writer of such quotes was being deliberately malicious, she could get fighting mad. "I've heard all the jokes made about my legs," she added, "and I have laughed at all of them. But what has Harry or my unborn baby ever done to merit such treatment?"

She didn't even mind the columnists knocking her movies, because she knew the public had the final say — and they said a resounding YES to Betty's films.

On March 4, 1944, Betty gave birth by Caesarean section to a daughter weighing seven pounds, twelve ounces. The baby was named Victoria, after the character Betty had played in *Springtime in the Rockies*. Harry was present when Betty gave birth. She said:

> I was feeling pretty uncomfortable, but I honestly think it was much tougher on Harry. The doctor kept asking him if he was all right, while I was lying there awaiting the birth! Once it was all over and the nurses took Victoria away to clean her up, Harry excused himself from the room.
>
> I was puzzled. I had seen him going several shades of grey, but I thought he was stronger than to run away from it all! I was feeling happy, but drowsy. I was anxious to hold my baby in my arms and have Harry by my bedside. But both of them had deserted me for the moment! Fortunately my mother and father arrived to keep me company — though, they too, were anxious to see the baby! A short while later, the nurse brought Victoria to me — and she was beautiful. I don't think I have ever felt so complete in my life. Everything else I had done seemed to pale into insignificance.

Harry reappeared about 10 minutes later — with a book of crossword puzzles. Betty said:

> I didn't know whether to laugh or cry. If he had brought me just one puzzle, that would have been understandable — but a whole book full! I remember wondering, 'Just how long does he think I'll be here?' But I didn't say a word, because I could see how his mind worked. Being desperate to get me something to cheer me up, and knowing that I loved crossword puzzles, he felt that they would please me more than flowers or perfume. I thought it was so sweet of him that, feeble though I felt, I tried to do one or two puzzles to show him that I really appreciated the thought.

That day, Betty said, was the happiest day of her life.

With Harry busy at M-G-M, Betty was quite happy to stay home with baby Victoria. Friend Alice Faye had given her a high chair and Lana Turner a bassinet set. Betty refused to employ a nurse, insisting on bathing, dressing, feeding, and changing diapers on her own. "I want to experience the joys of motherhood," she said simply. "This means much more to me than my career."

Her mother thought differently. Before her marriage, Betty had her legs impressed in cement in the forecourt at Grauman's Chinese Theatre, and Mrs. Grable was determined that Betty should continue "cementing" her impressions on the screen. She was anxious for Betty to return to work. "The public will quickly forget you if you don't resume your career," she warned her famous daughter.

Replied Betty: "If the public doesn't like it, then to hell with it. This is what living is all about."

Lana Turner and Rita Hayworth had also given birth to daughters recently. It seemed the fashionable thing to do!

Not only did motherhood suit Grable, it also helped to enhance her career. The month after Vicki was born, Betty's fan mail from the civilian public rose to an astronomical 90,000 letters a month — and a great number of the letters were from women. Betty's pin-up status had been mainly directed at men, but that didn't stop her female fans from writing her. This pleased Betty. "If you were a sex symbol, you only heard from the boys. Me? I had mail from just about everybody — children, mothers, grandmas and, of course — the boys! I guess I had something other than a pin-up image going for me. I don't know what it was. Perhaps some day someone will analyze it in depth. It would be interesting to find out just what I did have!"

Grable quickly got used to being a wife and mother, and enjoyed being a stay-at-home. One evening she mentioned to Harry that she was considering giving up her career. She had been in show business for fifteen years and had reached the top of the heap. Now all she wanted was to become just an ordinary wife and mother. Fame, now that she had tasted it, didn't mean that much to her. She maintained that her best production had been giving birth to Vicki.

The normally placid James blew his stack. Sweeping his arm across the beautiful living room he told her, "If you quit the movies, you can say goodbye to all this. I don't make nearly enough money to keep us in this style."

Betty was shocked at his outburst. Never being a person for grand living and acquiring possessions, she just couldn't understand his attitude. But she let the matter drop — for the moment.

Her otherwise blissful existence didn't last long, however. She was coaxed out of retirement to star opposite Dick Powell in a Lux Radio version of *Springtime in the Rockies,* directed and narrated by Cecil B. De Mille. She recalled that she felt a little rusty after the birth. Radio was a good way to ease back into show business — but she realized that in order to fully resume her career, a little more preparation was necessary.

> It isn't good for a dancer to get out of the habit of dancing. It's okay for an actress — but a dancer has to keep constantly in trim. So I started limbering up at home. It was hard going, but it soon came back to me once I had got rid of the stiffness. And the exercises didn't do any harm to my figure. I was so pleased to see my waistline return!

Zanuck called her constantly, hoping for a back-to-work date from his wayward star. Betty kept putting him off. Finally, he called her to the studio. He was very complimentary of her appearance, and presently told her he had the perfect vehicle lined up for her return to the screen.

It had been ten months since she had finished *Pin Up Girl* which had had its release delayed to coincide with the announcement of Vicki's birth. As Betty had expected, critics blasted both the film and its star, but the studio could not ignore the colossal box-office returns as the fans lined up at theatres throughout the world. It was one of the biggest money makers of 1944 and the studio's top grossing film. With this in mind, Zanuck was determined to get Betty into another hit as soon as possible.

The "perfect" comeback vehicle Zanuck was referring to was Billy Rose's *Diamond Horseshoe*. William Perlberg and George Seaton, the famed producer-director team, were given the responsibility of bringing the story to the screen. They were pleased to have Betty heading the show with a strong supporting cast including Dick Haymes, Phil Silvers, William Gaxton, and Beatrice Kay. Sensational new pianist/bandleader Carmen Cavallero was to make his screen debut. Grable and Haymes made a likeable screen team and there were several good tunes in the film, including "I Wish I Knew" and "The More I See You."

Haymes was a little unhappy with his role as a hospital intern. He especially disliked the ending where he appeared crooning at the side of the stage in his hospital outfit while Betty and the rest of the principals were in the spotlight. He thought the plot too contrived for the scene to work and complained to director Seaton.

Betty took Dick aside. "Listen, honey," she told him, "If Zanuck could have you center stage performing an amputation while Bill Gaxton and I go through our routine, he would. Believe me."

Haymes laughed at her zany suggestion. "She was a wonderful person and a great actress. Never upstaged anyone, never temperamental. I loved working with her," he said. [46]

Years later, whenever he appeared on stage, radio, or television shows, he always fondly mentioned his great times with Betty and how much he owed her in getting his film career off the ground. Although Dick wasn't very popular around Hollywood, particularly after his disastrous marriage to Rita Hayworth, Betty would never allow a bad word to be said about him.

In *Diamond Horseshoe* Betty was slimmer than in her previous films. To celebrate her new figure, she wore a succession of revealing costumes (particularly in the opening sequence) just to reassure the public that she had lost none of her glamour. Her best dance number in the film was "In Acapulco," backed by a chorus of six male dancers, and once again choreographed by Hermes

Pan. However, the highlight was her beautiful rendition of "I Wish I Knew" to Cavallero's accompaniment.

Apart from revealing her perfect legs and figure, Betty showed some nicely defined dramatic touches as the gold-digging showgirl who really had a heart of gold. Her scenes with Haymes, when she was trying to get him back into medical school, brought a touch of realism to this otherwise glossy piece of confection.

It was in this film that William Gaxton, who was always at loggerheads with Betty in the story, uttered the now-famous line, "You only have two reasons for being in show business — and you're standing on both of them! Put you in a long dress and you'd starve to death!" Betty used this line for many years while she was giving interviews; she thought it summed up her screen image perfectly!

Zanuck was very pleased with the final cut of the film and expected massive profits from it; profit was what his studio needed right now. Zanuck had bombed at the box office the previous year with his personally supervised production of *Wilson*, the story of the former U. S. president. Critics commented that it was fortunate the studio could always fall back on Betty Grable to make money for them, just in case Zanuck should want to make another *Wilson*.

With *Diamond Horseshoe* safely in the can, Betty went back to full-time motherhood. Harry had just finished another film at M-G-M and was in the middle of negotiations for a contract for his band with Twentieth. He also signed a deal with Columbia Records which would keep him busy in Hollywood for several months ahead.

The couple's happiness was short-lived. A letter arrived at the studio in March, 1945, stating, "You will not be alive on March 20 unless you meet me at Gower Street and Santa Monica Boulevard on March 19. Bring $5,000 in used notes with you."

The police were informed and they took the threat seriously. Out of the millions of letters Betty had received throughout her career, none had threatened her or her family, and very few were of an indecent nature. The police department called the F. B. I., just to make sure the star would come to no harm. They asked Betty to keep the appointment, but the studio flatly refused her permission to embark on such a dangerous "date."

The matter was resolved when Betty's stand-in, Betty Furness, volunteered her services. Betty didn't want anyone going out on a limb for her, and it was only when the F. B. I. agents assured her that they would have men posted all over the area, that she finally relented. The trap was set and Betty's double arrived at the appointed time with a brown paper package under her arm. A few minutes later a tall young man approached her. The F. B. I. moved in and he was taken into custody without any fuss or incident.

He turned out to be an 18-year-old high school dropout who admitted sending the letter. However, the young man denied he had any intention of harming Betty; he claimed he only wanted to meet her in person.

After this incident, Betty felt decidedly uneasy living in Beverly Hills, even though the suburb was well policed. She and Harry had bought a ranch in Calabasas which her father was managing for her, and Betty pleaded with Harry to move there permanently. He was quite willing, but reminded Betty that such threats could be just as easily carried out no matter where they were living — a prophecy which came frighteningly true some three years later when a woman demanded a huge ransom against Betty's second child's being kidnapped. Again the would-be kidnapper was apprehended without incident.

Her anxiety gradually faded as she studied her forthcoming movie project. It was *The Dolly Sisters*, a fictional account of the famous dancing sisters of the twenties and thirties. It was announced that Betty was to be reunited with her old friend Alice Faye for this film, and publicists said the stars looked forward to working with each other again.

But Alice, who was still technically under contract to the studio, was never seriously considered for the role. It was practically a remake of their earlier *Tin Pan Alley,* but now both stars were too top-line to play the secondary role of the younger sister. It had been okay for Betty to play second fiddle in 1940 when she was just getting established. Now she was Hollywood's top box-office attraction, and no one would believe for a moment that she would bow to Alice, no matter how strong their friendship.

Alice too had her own staunch legion of fans who would have been outraged if their favorite had to play second banana to anyone — particularly Grable (for some odd reason, dyed-in-the-wool Faye fans never really took to Betty). In any case, Alice was busy bringing up her two daughters and was not really interested in any more films, although she owed the studio two to fulfill her contract.

Zanuck had his problems; if it wasn't one blonde, it was another! Producer George Jessel decided on newcomer June Haver — practically a Grable lookalike. But this presented Zanuck with a real dilemma. Would Betty accept a virtual newcomer co-starring with her in a $2 million production?

With the war in Europe now over and Japan's threat dwindling in the Pacific, Zanuck feared that the returning servicemen would forget all about their number-one pin-up girl. Miss Haver, who was proving herself as a popular entertainer, was being groomed to step into Grable's shoes, should the top blonde fall from favor.

During Betty's long lay-off, Miss Haver had appeared in *Home In Indiana* and *Irish Eyes Are Smiling* which co-starred her with Dick Haymes. June received favorable notices for both these Technicolor outings and solidified her position as a top-flight entertainer. This pleased Zanuck whose policy was always to keep a threat on the sidelines, should the headliner become difficult. It usually worked. Most other big studios used the same tactic when they found one of their top attractions getting too big for her dancing shoes.

Grable obviously knew this, and in a press interview she was frank.

> I am first a wife and a mother — my career now comes a poor second to my home life. With the war over, I suppose I will go

into a decline. But no one will have to stay up nights worrying over my career. I'll quit while I'm ahead. The public can be fickle — and if the studio wants to promote some new star, then that's all right by me. I've had my good times, and it wouldn't worry me if I never saw the inside of a sound stage again. [47]

On reading the statement, a furious Zanuck sent for Betty. "You are Number One at this studio, and as long as you are willing to work, we can find the movies for you to do. There is no question of your being replaced. Your contract comes up for renewal next year, and I fully expect to meet your terms." [48]

That was what Betty wanted to hear. With very little effort she had forced her boss's hand. She hated the thought of returning to the studio with some starlet in the shadows waiting for her to break a leg — or worse! Betty wanted stardom on her own terms. It looked as if she had won the first round.

She never thought it would have been so easy!

BERNIE
FREEDMAN '93

CHAPTER EIGHT

Betty Grable had changed in her three years of marriage to Harry James. Apart from becoming a mother, she became a stay-at-home, shunning most publicity junkets, parties, and premières.

She said she'd had enough of them during her early years in Hollywood and maintained she much preferred an evening with Harry and Vicki to the bright lights. Betty had also fallen in with Harry's habit of relaxing before dinner with a martini and then a couple of vodkas after the meal. Smoking was another habit she picked up. Although she had for some time admitted to smoking on social occasions, she never believed she was addicted to cigarettes. However, since marriage she had gone from borrowing one or two from Harry's cigarette case now and again to smoking three packs a day. Whenever she stepped off the set from filming, there was always a "gofer" waiting to supply Betty with a cigarette.

Studio personnel noted many other changes in Grable when she returned to work on *The Dolly Sisters*. She behaved badly at times, often seeming snappy and querulous for no apparent reason. Instead of being her usual malleable self, she often disagreed — volubly —with director Irving Cummings over the interpretation of how a scene should be played. Their working relationship became strained, and Cummings vowed he would never work with her again. Marie Brasselle often took the full force of Grable's tantrums, but she knew Betty well enough to roll with the punches.

Onlookers put Betty's mood swings down to the fact that, despite her well-known belief that there was plenty of room at the top, Betty was most displeased with June Haver's being accorded the full star treatment alongside her in this big-budget musical.

The truth was that she was running scared. Haver was the most dangerous piece of competition she had come up against so far, and Betty knew that producer Jessel was doing all he could to promote her. And, at nineteen, Haver was ten years Grable's junior.

In addition, Betty simply didn't like June. They didn't socialize with each other off the set and kept to their separate dressing rooms between takes. Betty usually holed up with the chorus girls and others, enjoying a social drink in her dressing room. That in itself wasn't unusual; Betty was always happy in the gypsies' company, but usually her co-stars also were invited. In all her previous films, Betty never had a cross word with any of her co-stars, and most of them found her to be a very helpful person.

She was also unhappy that Hermes Pan wasn't available to choreograph the new film, although Seymour Felix did a splendid job with the dance scenes. Betty felt that she did her best screen dancing with Pan and complained to Zanuck about Pan's not being available. [49]

Despite Betty's churlishness during production, the film turned out to be a smash hit and one of the most fondly remembered of all Grable's films, even though the critics thought it too contrived and the girls too mechanical. Betty despaired of ever getting a good review, but the public flocked to Grable's first musical of the postwar era; apparently they were not as fickle as she imagined. The hit song, "I Can't Begin to Tell You," was nominated for an Academy Award, and Betty and June performed some lively song-and-dance numbers, notably "Darktown Strutters Ball," "On the Sidewalks of New York," and "Lipstick, Powder, and Rouge." Another hit song from the film was "I'm Always Chasing Rainbows." Betty duetted on "Give Me The Moonlight" with leading man John Payne, who remained a staunch ally throughout the film, though he too was puzzled by her erratic behavior on the set.

With completion of *The Dolly Sisters*, Betty's contract with Twentieth Century-Fox came up for renewal. She toyed with the idea of working for another studio. M-G-M had always shown an interest in her, and Warner would have been only too glad to have her services. At that time they lacked a big musical star of their own. However, Betty decided to have a good, long rest and enjoy life. She felt in need of it. It had taken seven months to get *Dolly Sisters* in the can, and it hadn't been a happy experience for Betty — often her own fault. She was by now twenty-nine years old and wondered just how long she could hold on as filmdom's top glamour girl.

Hayworth and Turner had spread their talents between musicals and dramas with great success, but Betty felt happier staying with musicals. She always believed she wasn't a "real" star and was simply there by default — much to her mother's despair. It would have been a good time for Betty to take the plunge, to alternate between musical comedy and straight acting parts. Her name was big enough to take a chance with other ventures. But she was too scared to take that chance. What Betty really wanted was to quit while she was at the top. But her mother wouldn't let her — and neither would Harry.

Harry had signed a contract with Twentieth Century-Fox and was scheduled to make his acting debut opposite Betty and Dick Haymes in *Kitten on the Keys*. It would be Betty's first film under the new contract which Zanuck hoped she would sign. The teaming of the glamorous married couple would enhance the film's box-office potential dramatically. As one studio wag put it, "They could have Grable playing opposite a nobody and it would still be a box office winner!" [50]

The Jameses had a few weeks together before they were to begin the new film. Christmas was approaching — the first since the end of the war — and Betty wanted to make it one to remember. She invited her mother and father, Harry's two sons by his first marriage, and Harry's parents. The reunion-cum-Christmas party went well and Betty was the perfect hostess. Betty was especially happy that her sister Marjorie, her husband David Arnold, and their son were able to come up from Texas (where

David ran a small business) to spend the festive season in Beverly Hills. Also present was her hairdresser, Marie, and her son Keefe Brasselle, a handsome teenager who would soon make his motion picture debut.

As a Christmas gift for her mother, Betty bought and furnished a house for her at 257 South Rodeo Drive, Beverly Hills. [51] She had spent a lot of money furnishing and decorating the house, and when it came to interior design, Betty had exquisite taste. She also hoped the the gift would win over her mother's love. Lillian Grable was delighted with her gift and was quite moved at her daughter's generosity. It was a very happy Christmas for the Grable family.

For New Year's, 1946, Betty and Harry joined producers Sam Wood, Edmund Goulding, and Irene Selznick for dinner. Afterwards the party moved on to a gambling den on Sunset Boulevard. Gambling was another habit Betty had picked up from Harry, and she became as enthusiastic about it as smoking and drinking — if not more so.

No sooner were they seated at their table than gunmen rushed in and told everyone to stand with their hands above their heads. While one of the masked bandits covered them with his shotgun, the others robbed the safe of more than $75,000. They raced away in conventional style in a black sedan, after wishing everybody a "Happy New Year."

The story of the hold-up circulated around Hollywood for days, but the management, evidently preferring the loss of the money to a charge of running an illegal gambling den, did not report the incident to the police.

Eventually, Betty admitted to a reporter that she had been present during the hold-up. "One of the men pointed a gun straight at me. It was very scary. I don't think he recognized me." The reporter was skeptical about Hollywood's top blonde not being recognized by the gangsters and said so. Betty came right back, "Well, I was wearing an evening gown, so he obviously couldn't see my legs!" Irene Selznick later confirmed the story but since the police had not been officially informed about the robbery, no action was taken. [52]

Twentieth Century-Fox signed Betty to a new contract early in 1946. It required Betty to make only two pictures a year (although Zanuck tried to hold out for three) with a say in the choice of directors. Her annual salary was an impressive $300,000. Under the terms of the new deal, she became the highest-paid female entertainer in the world. The only other female who came close to her was Olivia de Havilland. In fact, Betty's new salary was $40,000 a year more than Zanuck's.

The studio was glad to have her back on the payroll and enthusiastic in its plans for her future. No other star on its books brought home her colossal box office returns. With the huge success of *The Dolly Sisters*, Zanuck attempted to get the screen rights to a biography on the Duncan Sisters, two blonde all-American vaudeville artists who had also appeared in early movie musicals. The boss thought it would be ideal for Betty, and he planned to co-star her with Rita Hayworth who, he was sure, could be borrowed from Columbia. Both actresses appeared to be enthusiastic about the project, but the ambitious plan was abandoned when Zanuck ran into legal difficulties.

Blaine, Haver, Anne Baxter, and Linda Darnell, although successful in their careers, could never match Grable's earning power. After a disastrous drama entitled *Fallen Angel*, Alice Faye abruptly departed the studio in a rage, accusing director Otto Preminger and Zanuck of editing the film in favor of co-star Linda Darnell.

So the horizon was clear for Betty at Twentieth. She had no competition, a say in her choice of films, and an annual salary bigger than her boss's — at least on paper. Zanuck, a shrewd businessman, was also a major shareholder in the company (which paid good dividends), and as head of the studio he also came in for invisible earnings by way of bonuses, expenses, and other perks.

The first thing she did on signing her new contract was to turn down *Kitten on the Keys* which would have starred her opposite Harry. He was disappointed that Betty wouldn't play opposite him (as was Haymes, who was anxious to follow up his previous hit with Betty in *Diamond Horseshoe*), but she didn't like the script and said so. The picture turned out to be a dud.

With Harry busy on the film, Betty was called into a meeting with Zanuck to discuss her career. He had recently bought the screen rights to Somerset Maugham's best seller, *The Razor's Edge*, as a starring vehicle for Tyrone Power, newly returned from active service with the Marine Corps. Gene Tierney and Clifton Webb were cast in principal roles. The only role not yet filled was that of Sophie, a pathetic young alcoholic who eventually commits suicide. (Zanuck had asked Louis B. Mayer if he could borrow Judy Garland for the part, but the M-G-M boss refused. Judy's film schedule was heavily booked for the whole of 1946.) After a few cordial remarks, Zanuck offered the role to Betty, who was horrified. She'd read the book and knew of the Sophie character. She begged Zanuck to be let off the film. "The character is too much for me," she protested. "I can't act. You know it, I know it, and the public knows it. Leave me where I am. I couldn't handle this."

Undeterred, Zanuck told her that her friend Edmund Goulding was directing and would be able to get a performance out of her. In fact, said the boss, Goulding was enthusiastic about Betty in the role. Grable burst into tears. "No, no. This is wrong for me." She reached into her handbag for a tissue. Zanuck said. "That's exactly what we want, Betty." Drying her eyes, the tearful blonde cried, "You don't understand — this is for real!"

At least, that was the way the story was reported over the years, but Betty denied it. "It was ridiculous to ask me to play Sophie. My fans just wouldn't go for it. Grable committing suicide? No way. They would have expected me to come back to life for the final scene, singing and dancing as usual. There was no tearful scene in Zanuck's office. I simply refused, explained why, and he accepted it, though he was pretty mad at me at the time."

Realizing that Betty wouldn't change her mind, the boss handed the role to young actress Anne Baxter, who won a best supporting actress Academy Award for her performance.

Zanuck would have been well within his rights to have suspended Betty for her refusal. Any actor under contract who refuses a role is usually suspended, the suspension lasting until the disputed film is completed. But he didn't.

Betty returned to the domestic bliss of her Calabasas ranch where the couple had heavily invested in stud horses. It was, according to their accountants, a "tax haven" and the two stars were quite content in having to pay only minimal taxes for years. Towards the end of Harry's film, now retitled *Do You Love Me?* (which helped boost the title song to become a moderate hit), Betty was asked to do a cameo spot. In the storyline, Harry loses Maureen O' Hara to crooner Haymes, and the director wasn't too happy about Harry's exit from the film. They hit on the idea of having Betty waiting to greet Harry after he is discarded by O'Hara in favor of Haymes.

Betty fell in with the idea and was filmed sitting in a taxi in the final shot of the film. James opens the door, Betty smiles "Hello" and everyone is happy. This clever gimmick was re-used a few years later at M-G-M when Tony Martin loses the girl. They had his real-life wife, Cyd Charisse, waiting for him at the final fade-out.

Harry went on to make *If I'm Lucky* with Perry Como, Vivian Blaine, and Carmen Miranda, which was a step downward as far as his film career went. It was one of the studio's low-budget musicals — and didn't do much for Misses Miranda and Blaine either.

Zanuck then persuaded Grable to do *The Shocking Miss Pilgrim* with Dick Haymes, produced and directed by the Perlberg-Seaton team. The story revolved around a New York girl who has a tough time finding a job in staid Boston after graduating from a "type-writing" school. She eventually persuades Haymes, the boss of a shipping office, to take her on. It was a very early Women's Lib affair, and Betty enjoyed her role.

The film had a delightful Gershwin score — including "For You, For Me, For Evermore" and "Aren't You Kind of Glad We Did." The music had been lying around for some years, and when the film was suggested, surviving brother Ira added suitable lyrics which fit the plot. Betty looked radiant (once again in late 1880s costumes) and her hair was back to its natural dark blonde color.

Grable and Haymes were always a tuneful screen team and Zanuck searched around for a third vehicle for them. The publicity department issued statements that Dick enjoyed working with Betty, and said that of all his Hollywood films, his fondest times were his appearances with Grable. The feeling was mutual, Betty agreed.

But the film nearly died at the box office, though most of the critics enjoyed it. It was her fans who nearly killed it off. They wrote in the thousands, (the studio estimated close to 100,000 letters) complaining about the absence of the Grable legs. Despite the publicity blurb: "Shocking? She's Sensational!" the film was the only one in her career to barely cover its costs when first released.

The failure of the film jolted Betty. She had long realized that as long as her legs were prominent, and there was plenty of singing and dancing, her fans were happy. But she'd thought that her singing and acting performance in this one would have carried her through. She had enjoyed the change of pace in this film. This was working-girl Grable, stripped of her showgirl image, but shedding none of her glamour.

Just before she finished *Miss Pilgrim*, George Raft re-entered the fringe of Betty's social circle. He had been signed to star opposite Vivian Blaine in *Nob Hill* (a remake of Alice Faye's *Hello Frisco Hello*) at Twentieth. Betty and George met in the studio commissary and exchanged a few pleasantries, and that was it. Two civilized people passing the time of day, it appeared. But George Raft had never gotten over his feelings for Betty.

There had been other women in his life since they split up in 1943, including Grable's stand-in Betty Furness, but none came anywhere near the original as far as Raft was concerned. But he remained a perfect gentleman. Once the ice was broken between Raft and the Jameses, George was often asked to share their box at various race tracks in the state, and frequently accepted. Along with Harry and Betty, George took part that year in a documentary short, *Hollywood Park*, featuring many of filmdom's celebrities who frequented the famous race track. Also included in the cast was Jackie Coogan who had remained on good terms with Betty.

With Harry free for a few weeks, the Jameses went to the San Mateo horse sales and spent $75,000 for seven race horses. They also purchased a cottage at Del Mar where they could stay during the racing season.

More and more, Betty was turning her back on the film world and kept refusing social invitations. In the past she had attended premières for her own films, travelling to Miami for the premières of *Moon Over Miami* and *Song of the Islands* and to New York for *Tin Pan Alley* and *The Dolly Sisters*.

However, she ignored the première for *The Shocking Miss Pilgrim* and didn't even see the film until months later at a neighborhood theatre.

Said Betty, "Most of our friends are in the horse business. We seldom go out on the town any more. I had my fill of nightclubs in my starlet days, and Harry has to work in them. So it isn't any fun for us now."

Her best pals around this time were Betty and Harry Ritz. She had known Harry since the thirties when he was part of the famous Ritz Brothers comedy partnership. The two Bettys fast became firm friends. They had similar tastes and shared the same wacky sense of humor. The foursome were regulars at Del Mar, and when Harry was away on tour, Betty was often seen in the company of the Ritzes.

Even after the Ritzes divorced and Betty Ritz got involved with a Mexican bullfighter, their friendship endured. They had some crazy times together, and, as Betty Ritz said, there was never a shortage of laughs when Grable was around. [53] After her fun-filled vacation, Betty was happy to report back for work in her latest film, *Mother Wore Tights*, the true story of a vaudeville couple which had become a national best-seller. Betty loved the script, calling it "my best role to date." It was indeed a great part for her, and in many ways the story ran a close parallel to her own life. There were several big production numbers in the film which afforded Betty the opportunity to turn in some of the best dancing in her career. Betty was further delighted when she learned that Zanuck was negotiating to sign either Fred Astaire or James Cagney as her leading man. For the first time ever she would have a dancing leading man as opposed to straight leading men like Ameche, Payne, Mature, and Haymes.

Zanuck got thumbs down from Warner. They wouldn't hire out Cagney, though the star was anxious for a change of pace and believed he would have found it with Grable. Astaire, who was freelancing, was interested, and preliminary negotiations were entered into. Unfortunately, Grable and Zanuck couldn't agree on certain script changes Astaire wanted. Betty (it was believed) wouldn't accept second billing to Fred and Astaire withdrew from the project.

Years later, Betty flatly denied that she refused to accept second billing to Astaire. "I would have worked unbilled to have had the chance of dancing with Fred," she said. "Also it would have finally ended the rumor that Astaire's best screen partner was Ginger Rogers! Rita and Ann (Miller) were far superior dancers, but I am sure I could have matched any of Fred's former partners step for step." According to Betty the script change Fred wanted was to make the male the stronger role, but Zanuck wouldn't agree to altering the plot which was, after all, the story of a working show business woman-cum-mother.

At the time it was believed that Zanuck was too scared to take a chance. Dance-king Astaire had taken a knock in his career and his box-office drawing power had slipped a little. His dancing prowess and personal charisma had not diminished, but his dancing style suffered from comparison to Gene Kelly's — Kelly had already taken over Astaire's top slot at Metro.

However, much closer to the truth was the fact that Fred held a grudge against Zanuck for not putting him under contract in the early thirties when he was a struggling young dancer trying to break away from the brother/sister stage act and into movies. Zanuck had the chance to sign him then, but declined. It wasn't until after the success of *Flying Down to Rio* that Zanuck realized what a grave error he had made. An unforgiving Astaire never worked at Twentieth Century-Fox until the mid-fifties when he accepted top role in *Daddy Long Legs* opposite Leslie Caron — by which time Zanuck was no longer in charge of the studio.

It was a great pity that Fred and Betty never appeared together as dancing partners, and especially in a film as superior as *Mother Wore Tights.*

For the male lead in the film, Zanuck auditioned Dan Dailey, newly returned from the service. Dailey had played the "heavy" in several films — particularly successfully in M-G-M's *Ziegfeld Girl,* completed just before he was drafted. Dan had begun his career in the dying days of vaudeville and was a regular entertainer at various New York burlesque theatres. He then graduated to Broadway with a role in *Babes in Arms,* and was signed by an M-G-M talent scout in 1939. His first film for them was as a brutal Nazi troop leader in *The Mortal Storm.* After several insignificant roles, he was signed for the lead in *For Me and My Gal* with Judy Garland. But he was called for Army duty before the film got under way and was replaced by Gene Kelly.

With his vaudeville background, Dailey easily passed the dance auditions for *Mother Wore Tights.* All that remained was for the studio boss to convince Betty that Dan would make an ideal screen partner. Grable wasn't so sure. She had seen Dailey in several of his earlier films and thought he was more suited to heavy roles than leading man in a musical. She told Zanuck that she'd rather have John Payne, leaving her to carry the bulk of the dancing. Zanuck insisted the storyline called for a partner of equal dancing as well as acting ability.

The boss assured her that Dan was a highly talented song-and-dance man, and eventually Grable was persuaded to go into rehearsal with him. Betty insisted that she be allowed to exercise her option and veto Dailey if she didn't find him suitable. Zanuck conceded. The new partners went straight into rehearsals with dance director Seymour Felix. Betty found her leading man very talented, good-humored, and easy to get along with. Later that day she called on Zanuck before leaving the studio, saying how pleased she was with her new leading man. Zanuck heaved a sigh of relief.

On the first day of shooting, the press was invited to meet the new screen team. Betty was generous in her praise of Dailey. "Dan is a swell guy and a fine dancer."

Zanuck viewed the rushes each night and boasted that he had discovered the best screen dance team since Astaire and Rogers. Grable and Dailey worked well together and their easy styles and professionalism shone through in the finished film. Their warm, outgoing personalities blended beautifully and gave the film an extra touch of class.

The strong supporting cast included Mona Freeman, Connie Marshall, Sarah Allgood, and Robert Arthur. Anne Baxter narrated the story. Walter Lang directed this epic, the life and times of two young hoofers from vaudeville who make the big time and manage to raise a family without sacrificing their careers.

Betty loved the role, stating it was "one of the best I have ever had." She often recalled it as one of her favorite films. It certainly gave her the most demanding role she had ever tackled, but Grable rose to the occasion under the skillful eye of Walter Lang and turned in a fine performance.

Many critics thought that this was now the turning point in her career and that she would progress to more dramatic roles. Studio insiders were also claiming that Betty would be nominated for an Academy Award, but Betty knew better than to build up any hopes in that direction. In those days musical stars were never seriously considered for top awards.

Co-star Dan, who received much praise in his first major musical role, spoke highly of Betty.

She has never really believed in herself. She always had this thing that put it down to 'good luck' to survive on the little talent she claimed she had. I often had to remind her that although there were admittedly prettier girls around — and some of them were better actresses — it was Betty the customers paid to see. She was also one of the most natural dancers I had ever worked with. She was what I called an intuitive dancer — and always ready to adapt to any new style. [54]

So happy were Betty and Dan in their new-found partnership that she approached Zanuck asking him to buy the rights to a famous stage show *Sons O'Guns* in which the great dancer Jack Donohue made his last stage appearance. She thought it would be an ideal script, with Dan playing Donohue's role. The boss said he would consider it, but the matter was never pursued.

Many top Hollywood actresses envied the way Grable made musical comedy seem so easy. Years later when Ava Gardner switched to comedy in the film *The Little Hut*, she admitted she found the going tough. The raven-haired beauty said, "Comedy is the most difficult of acting tasks. Goodness knows how a star like Betty Grable can make people laugh, cry, and set their feet tapping — all in one film. That takes talent." [55]

Reporters often asked Betty if it wouldn't be easier for her to concentrate on straight roles instead of the demanding work required in musicals. Betty admitted, "Yes, it probably would. But you see, for me, all the hard work was done years ago . . . when I was four and went to dancing school and really worked. I was learning then to condition myself. Now it's fun. I love it. Lazy and lucky, that's me!" [56]

At long last critics were enthusiastic about a Grable film. They generally praised her performance in *Mother Wore Tights* (which Betty jokingly referred to as "Mother Was Tight"). The plot required her to age from a teenage high school girl to a grandmother — via great production numbers such as "Kokomo, Indiana," "Rolling Down Bowling Green" (which was cut from the finished film, and was only used as a reprise towards the end),

"This Is My Favorite City," and the hit of the film, "You Do," which Betty sang with great feeling. The song received an Academy Award nomination. Music directors Alfred Newman and Charles Henderson both won Oscars for their work in the film.

Considering the number of hit songs she introduced to the screen, it was amazing that Zanuck forbade Betty to make commercial recordings. She had to content herself with the fact that while she did indeed introduce them, stars such as Bing Crosby, Danny Kaye, Dick Haymes, and Peggy Lee — to name a few — were able to cash in on Betty's hits. Alice Faye and Carmen Miranda both managed to make commercial recordings, but Betty was never allowed to. It was one great anomaly in her career, and no one at the studio could give a reasonable explanation for this, particularly since Betty had a fine, if light, singing voice.

However, a couple of years later, she managed to sneak in a number with Harry. He was at the recording studio when his contract singer, Helen Forrest, took ill and failed to turn up for the session. He called Betty, who was home at the time, and she drove straight to the studio where the record was taped in a couple of hours. The song was "I Can't Begin to Tell You," one of the hits from *The Dolly Sisters*. To keep it a secret from the studio, she was billed on the label as Ruth Haag (the couple's middle names!). It fooled no one, and the record quickly became a collector's item.

Towards the end of filming *Mother Wore Tights*, Betty found she was again pregnant, quashing Zanuck's plan to follow up with another Grable-Dailey musical. The boss had big plans for his newest dance screen team and couldn't wait to get them together again. But it wasn't to be — at least not for another eighteen months. Film roles which had been lined up for her went to June Haver and Vivian Blaine, including a remake of *Moon Over Miami* — this time titled *Three Little Girls in Blue*. Unfortunately, the new version failed to live up to the earlier one and was only moderately successful.

Betty's mother stayed with her at the Calabasas ranch, as Harry was once more on the road, playing cities on the East Coast. Baby

Number Two decided to make her entry into the world a month earlier than expected. As Betty was preparing for bed one night, she felt that something "was about to happen." She called her mother who accompanied her to Cedars of Lebanon Hospital in Los Angeles where a few hours later her second daughter was born on May 20, 1947. Once again it was a Caesarean birth. The James newcomer weighed in at six pounds, four ounces, and it was announced that mother and daughter were both "doing fine." The star/mother's only disappointment was that Harry hadn't been present for the birth.

Betty telephoned the good news to Harry in Atlantic City, where he was appearing. He was a very surprised father. In Betty's haste to get to the hospital, she had forgotten to inform Harry of the impending developments.

He returned from the East when the baby was two weeks old — and as yet unnamed. "We had a few names planned for a boy, but we just didn't count on another girl," Betty explained to the press after the christening. "Harry said, 'We'll call her Jessica.' I shrieked, 'Jessica??? Oh, no Harry. They'll call her Jesse James, just as sure as the original who shot that Mr. Howard!'"

But Harry won out. Jessica James it was. Three-year-old Vicki was thrilled with her new sister.

Harry, Betty, and the children spent the summer at Del Mar, having fun at the racetrack. Betty's mother usually accompanied them, but stayed at a nearby hotel. She enjoyed the Del Mar season as a social outing, but was not much of a gambler. Lillian was, however, fond of a tipple, and would often be seen in one of the many bars where she wasted no time in telling those around her that Betty Grable was her "little girl." Occasionally Betty and Harry would join her for a few drinks. Harry and Betty Ritz were also regulars at the track.

Betty enjoyed the thrill of the race track. But her horses were only moderately successful, though one or two of them showed promise. It was an expensive hobby for the couple, but as long as it kept the tax man off their backs, they didn't worry too much.

Betty's $300,000 a year took care of their bills. Harry's annual salary was reputed to be around $100,000 which he used as "fun" money, squandering it on booze and gambling.

Their Calabasas ranch, named the Baby J, was important to them, too. At first it was just a pleasure thing — a place to ride and ramble through the hills. Then Harry suggested getting some brood mares, and by 1947 the Baby J had developed into a breeding farm, expertly managed by Betty's father.

They sold their home in Beverly Hills. Betty explained:

It would have been too small for us after Jessica came along," Betty explained.

We expected to build on the ranch right away, but now we find we need more property — flat ground where the mares and their babies can run, and where we can set up a half-mile training track.

Once the deal is finalized, we'll build a rambling stone and frame house in ranch style. Harry wants one huge room with a stone fireplace — the kind of room that will hold a pool table, bar, television and a shuffleboard. Anything Harry wants is all right by me. If it wasn't, I'd say so. Perhaps some women wouldn't like the idea of a pool table in the main living room. I don't mind. What does it matter how a room looks compared to its comfort? In another couple of months, the place ought to be in great shape, so we will move the whole shebang over there. That will be the James household for good. That's where we hope to spend our golden wedding anniversary. [57]

When Betty made that statement to the press, she was the most contented movie star in Hollywood and was coming up to her fifth wedding anniversary. She and Harry had disproved the cynics who had given their marriage only six months at the most. Betty's only regret was that she didn't have a larger family, but her doctors advised her to keep it to two. As both of her previous births had been Caesarean, they felt she would be taking great chances with her health if she tried for any more children.

Being Mrs. James was the most important thing in her life. Betty loved Harry so much that if he had asked her to quit the movie business, she would not have hesitated; her husband and children meant much more to her than her career. But Betty was working as much to maintain the James lifestyle as she was for her own enjoyment, although that wouldn't have been a "wifely" thing to admit in the forties. As she told the press:

> Harry has never said don't work. But I know he'd be much happier if I didn't. He's not in the least impressed with being married to a movie star. I can understand that.
>
> Harry's ideas about women are very old-fashioned. He doesn't care about seeing his wife constantly in the limelight. But he's very understanding too. He knows I enjoy making pictures, so he won't ask me not to. He knows I'll quit when the time comes.
>
> What really griped him at first was the Betty Grable thing. It shouldn't have, because his name is as big as mine — if not more so. But the fact remains that it has made him uncomfortable. As a matter of fact, it made us both unhappy at first. I used to squirm when people would introduce me as Miss Grable in his presence. When they'd call up the house and ask for Miss Grable, I'd always tell my secretary to ask, 'Do you mean Mrs. James?' Even at the studio, where I naturally expect to be called Grable, my chair is marked as 'Betty James.' And there is one director who always introduces me as Mrs. James. I never asked him to do this — he just sensed I liked it better that way. Somebody will come up to us and he'll say, 'This is Mrs. James.' It gives me a nice feeling. It's as it should be, and I know it makes Harry happier too.[58]

Betty James or Betty Grable — it didn't matter too much to Zanuck, who was waiting patiently to get his star back into harness. The early receipts from *Mother Wore Tights* had just come in and they were colossal — even better than her previous films.

And the exhibitors, as always, were anxious to know when she would be back at work.

Betty was lured back to the studio in early October. Zanuck was unable to come up with another Grable-Dailey starrer. Dan had been busy on other films during her pregnancy and lay-off, and was becoming one of the studio's most popular leading men. Zanuck hired the legendary Ernst Lubitsch, renowned for his frothy, romantic fantasy musicals throughout the thirties. He wanted Lubitsch to direct Betty in a screenplay he had bought, *That Lady in Ermine*.

Grable wasn't so sure about Zanuck's decision. She read the script, and in an interview with the boss, asked him, "It's very witty, but is it ME? And, more to the point, will my fans buy it?"

Zanuck assured her that with Lubitsch in charge, she would have no problems. "It's a complete change for you, Betty," he said. "Not a footlight in sight."

She found Mr. Lubitsch a charming man, but he was not in the best of health (having suffered several heart attacks in recent years). Any misgivings she had about the film were soon dispelled by the Lubitsch charm.

The story, based on the operetta *This Is The Moment*, was a romantic spoof on East European royalty, with Betty in a dual role as a ruling duchess whose "great-grandmother" (the Lady in Ermine, also played by Grable) surfaced around midnight with other ancestors to plot against the Hungarian invaders. It co-starred Douglas Fairbanks, Jr., and Cesar Romero.

Many critics thought that the casting of all-American girl Betty as a European countess was in itself a touch of satire on Lubitsch's part. The director had high hopes for Betty in this film. He believed she had promise as a talented comedienne. Hermes Pan was called in to choreograph the musical numbers; in the initial shooting script, eight musical sequences were called for, but in the final cut of the film, only four remained.

In charge of Betty's costumes was René Hubert. He conferred with Lubitsch on how best to dress Betty for the role. Lubitsch was in favor of frills and crinolines for part of the film, and black-and-white smartly tailored outfits for other sequences. As to the showing of the famed legs, Lubitsch asked Mr. Hubert to be discreet — "subtle revelation is what we are after," he said. [59]

Lightweight transparent nylon was used for the crinoline skirts, causing a problem for cameraman Leon Shamroy. After filming wardrobe tests, he reported that Betty's legs were clearly showing through the nylon against the strong lights. Technicians and lighting experts worked feverishly on the equipment to get the best of the costumes without revealing her fabled legs.

Betty was highly amused: "This is the first time anyone has gone to great lengths to conceal my legs. Normally, when a cameraman sets up a shot, he measures the distance between my knees and the camera — with most actors the nose is usually taken as the focal point!" [60]

Work on the film commenced on schedule and Betty found Lubitsch easy to work with. Lubitsch was equally impressed: "Betty's a complete professional." [61]

Two weeks into shooting, however, Lubitsch suffered a massive heart seizure, and died a few days later on November 30, 1947. Production closed down for a week, mainly out of respect for the celebrated Lubitsch, but also because the studio was in trouble. Who was going to finish the film? More than a million dollars had already been spent on the production and they couldn't afford to write it off. About thirty minutes of usable footage had been shot by Lubitsch.

Actor-director Otto Preminger came to the rescue. He had been a close personal friend of Ernst Lubitsch and volunteered to complete the film in tribute to his friend. He insisted that all credit for the film should go to Lubitsch, and his own name should not appear on the screen.

Zanuck really had no choice. The week-long shutdown unnerved Grable, and word was out that she was getting nervous over the delay. When Zanuck heard through the grapevine that she was thinking of abandoning the project, he gave Preminger the go-ahead. Work was eventually resumed on the jinxed film on December 5, and it was completed on January 5, 1948, after twenty-six days of shooting.

While there were no arguments or blow-ups on the set, Betty was decidedly unhappy with Preminger in the director's chair. She felt he was too heavy-handed in his approach to the story. She also knew Preminger was responsible for Alice Faye's fleeing the studio after the disastrous *Fallen Angel*. And for the second time in her career, she took a dislike to her co-star. She felt Douglas Fairbanks, regarded by many as the Prince of Hollywood, spent more time socializing on the set than working on his role.

He went to great lengths to befriend Grable, inviting his children to the set to meet her. Naturally, Betty chatted amiably with the children, but she was always wary of the Prince of Hollywood. She felt that his approach to the musical genre did not come up to her own high standards, and that he treated the whole film as a joke. If he gave that impression, it would have been most uncharacteristic; Fairbanks, a totally dedicated professional actor, was deadly serious in his approach to any new project.

Grable wasn't in the mood to be persuaded, and there was a decidedly cool atmosphere on the set. She objected whenever Fairbanks conferred with Preminger on certain scenes without her being consulted or even asked to join in on the discussions.

Off the set, she seldom mixed with Fairbanks; she thought he acted more regally than the King of England. They hardly ever lunched together, and Betty stuck mainly to pals Reggie Gardiner and Romero in their off-duty moments, leading to a certain amount of awkwardness on the set.

According to other actors in the film, most of Douglas Fairbanks "failings" were a figment of Betty Grable's imagination. Most co-workers found him a likeable person who was a little nervous about starring in a musical — particularly when he was cast opposite the undisputed queen of the lot. Betty's unreasonable dislike of Fairbanks was part of her hang-up of demanding star status around the studio whenever it suited her, while at other times being happy to revert to Betty the Chorus Girl, everybody's friend. It was a kink in her personality that surfaced from time to time, particularly when she thought she was under threat.

Betty was glad to see the film finished. She vowed she would never work with Preminger or Fairbanks again. The dance sequence had been a nightmare from beginning to end, even though the routine had been kept simple because of Fairbanks' lack of dancing talent. He was much more at home in swash-buckling roles, and for his only song in the film, his voice had to be dubbed. Betty also felt that Fairbanks denigrated her fame, regarding her as a chorus girl who got lucky. Yet years later she spoke warmly of Douglas Fairbanks.

Betty photographed beautifully and was particularly good in her dual role, especially playing her ancestor, a rather formidable lady. But the film wasn't allowed to develop as a whimsical Ruritanian fantasy. Not even the fine Shamroy photography or the stunning sets could save it. The finished film was described by some critics as "awful."

Zanuck was in a state of shock. *That Lady in Ermine* was the most expensive Grable film to date. It was rapidly turning into a dud, even though it received much more favorable notices in Britain and Europe. Despite the heavy publicity turned out by the studio, the film was not the blockbuster Zanuck had hoped it would be.

Betty had no trouble placing the blame. In addition to her problems with director and co-star on the set, she was angry that some of the musical sequences were cut, in particular the enchanting "There's Something About Midnight" number which Betty felt would have been the hit song of the film. The other big number, "This is the Moment" — the movie's original title — remained intact, and was a splendid piece of work on Grable's part.

Despite the huge following Lubitsch had among filmgoers, *That Lady in Ermine* did only moderately well at the box office. Only the magnetism of the Grable name (and her runaway success with *Mother Wore Tights*) kept it from becoming a financial disaster.

Wrote Howard Barnes, of the *New York Herald Tribune*, "Since

Miss Grable treats the whole proceedings as though she were appearing in a straight musical, the fanciful yarn of warriors and fair ladies gets short shrift."

Bosley Crowther of *The New York Times* was a little kinder:

> Credit Betty Grable with bringing to the title role a certain attractiveness of person which makes the Hussar's dreams entirely plausible. Even wrapped in ermine, Miss Grable looks sharper than most girls in bathing suits and the flashes she gives of territory for which she's noted are few but rewarding . . .

British critics were much more receptive to *That Lady*. Campbell Dixon, of the *Daily Telegraph*, wrote:

> It has many things we expect of Lubitsch — elegance, charm, buoyant gaiety and style. He has embroidered it with lavish sets, colour, song and dance, pleasant humour, charming touches . . . and some good acting.

Said Fred Majdalany, of the *Daily Mail:*

> Forever Grable! There is a blonde in every man's life. Even if she exists only in the suspicious imagination of his wife or the wishful imagination of himself. And what she looks like is unquestionably Betty Grable.
>
> Miss Grable is the apotheosis of blondeness. She is what schoolboys sneak into local theatres to see when they are supposed to be watching their school play cricket. She is the girl the middle-aged export driver hopes to meet on the Queen Mary.
>
> There are musical comedy queens with more pronounced gifts: singing ones like Kathryn Grayson, clowning ones like Betty Hutton, and dancing ones like Judy Garland . . . but Miss Grable's, I fancy, are the slippers from which the most champagne would be drunk in open competition.

Stephen Watts of the *Sunday Express* was less eloquent but just as enthusiastic: "What a first-class comedy actress Betty Grable is, and Douglas Fairbanks is best when his heroic swagger is not meant to be taken seriously."

And Ewart Hodgson of the *News of the World* summed up: The whole thing is gay, carefree and utterly irresponsible. A wholly delightful soufflé."

While not a musical in the typical Grable mould, it did have lots of charm. It would have been interesting to see how the finished product would have turned out had Lubitsch seen the film through. Today (particularly in Europe) it is regarded as a fine example of imaginative film-making.

Even Grable confided to friends years later that she was secretly pleased with her performance, but she always maintained that it would have been an even better film if Lubitsch been able to complete it. [62]

Zanuck hastily conferred with George Jessel and Betty's favorite director Walter Lang, hoping to come up with something good for Betty. The New York office was screaming for blood over Betty's latest picture, and Zanuck's head was firmly placed on the chopping block. To make doubly sure of success, he told Jessel to get a story which would reteam Grable and Dailey. Jessel bought the rights to a show-business story from Columbia which had plans to turn it into a Hayworth-Kelly vehicle.

The new film turned out to be *Burlesque,* based on the novel by George Maker Watters. Betty and Dan went straight into dance rehearsals. Grable was just as anxious as Zanuck to maintain her hold on the box office. She was terrified of failure. Jack Oakie, June Havoc (sister of Gypsy Rose Lee) and old-timers Richard Arlen and James Gleason were added to the cast.

Always the clown, Jack Oakie walked up to Betty on the first day of the set and, with a serious look, asked her: "Pardon me, but haven't we met before?"

Indeed they had. This was their fourth film together. Jack had brought along a scrapbook of memories from their first film together, *Collegiate*, over at Paramount. He and Joe Penner had been the stars, with Betty playing a pretty co-ed. Oakie recalled:

> We had Betty, Virginia Gray and Eleanor Powell in that film. They were just kids then, but with the talent that put them where they are today. I would have remembered Betty, even if she hadn't been the cutest blonde in town. She worked very hard in that film. And she hasn't changed a bit. [63]

Glamorous newcomer Jean Wallace, the lovely young blonde wife of Franchot Tone, was also added to the cast. She played Sylvia, who tries to woo Dailey away from Grable.

The film concerned the romantic problems of a burlesque queen (Betty) and her man (Dan), when he gets his big break on Broadway as a solo act and then turns to booze. By the final reel, Betty has sorted him out, with much tear-spilling and some excellent dancing. Dan drew on his early experiences in vaudeville — particularly the several seasons he did in New York — to add substance to his role.

There were several good numbers in the film, some specially written by Mack Gordon and Josef Myrow, including "When My Baby Smiles at Me," and "By the Way." Betty had three big numbers — "What Did I Do" (a solo spot), "Oui, Oui Marie," and "In Spain They Say Si-Si" — all expensively mounted production numbers in which she was backed by a girlie chorus. Dan Dailey shone in his rendition of "Birth of the Blues."

The film was released as *When My Baby Smiles at Me*, and the public, happy to see Betty back in more familiar territory, flocked to the cinemas. Zanuck was off the hook with the New York office.

Hollywood Reporter placed it in the "hit class" and the *Los Angeles Times* regarded it as "one of the best ever films made about show business." Another critic said it was "a honey of a musical . . . packed with entertainment."

Dan Dailey was nominated for an Oscar for his performance. Betty was delighted for her hardworking co-star, but unfortunately he lost out. However, it did show that the Academy occasionally took in a performer's work in a Grable film now and then. She often felt her films — apart from music, costume and art awards — were largely ignored by the Academy.

Many people thought that Grable, who had been topping the box office polls for the past six or seven years, should be recognized by the industry. She had made millions for her studio, and the profits enabled many less successful, but highly prestigious films to be financed. Betty never let her feelings be known on the issue. She maintained that she was well paid for her work, and as long as it kept the fans coming into theatres, that was reward enough. As George Jessel said, "Every Oscar statuette should be inscribed — 'Betty Grable helped pay for this.'" [64]

It was during the making of *When My Baby Smiles at Me* that Betty and Dan became really close friends. When they worked together on *Mother Wore Tights,* she had suspected that Dailey was bisexual, but had never brought the subject out in the open. She regarded it as his own business.

Dailey married beautiful Los Angeles socialite Elizabeth Hofert in 1942 and they had a young son, also named Dan. At the studio, as would happen in most workplaces, rumors abounded about Dailey's sexual preferences. Eventually, during the shooting of *When My Baby Smiles at Me,* Dailey confessed he was having problems in his marriage. Betty sincerely liked the tall, blond actor, and Dan knew this. They were like brother and sister. He eventually opened his heart to her and poured out his sorry tale.

Dailey was living a double life, and he was afraid of how it might damage his career if the press or some malicious gossipmonger latched on to his problem. Though not a great believer in analysis, Betty advised him to seek professional help — for the sake of his young son, and to try to save his marriage. She had nothing against homosexuals (many of whom, she knew, were some of her most loyal fans) and told Dan this. Dan was close to having a complete nervous breakdown, and she urged him to get help before things went too far. He promised that he would, and their shared secret cemented their private and professional relationship.

Many gossips were sure Dan and Betty were enjoying an affair behind their spouses' backs, but nothing was further from the truth. Even had Dan been interested, Betty Grable never believed in adultery; she had seen first-hand what misery it could wreak, and she always put her marriage first. Occasionally "friends" informed her that Harry played around while on tour, but Betty point-blank refused to believe it. She never even discussed the subject with him; there was no need to. Their marriage was based on trust, and since she knew that Harry trusted her, she implicitly trusted him.

However, Betty did help Dan find friends (and lovers) among the young dancers around the lot. She kept a discreet silence about it all — except on one occasion when she visited the studio unexpectedly and found Dan on a sound stage, done up in "Grable gear" doing a take-off on her for the benefit of his gay friends on the lot. She was infuriated and felt betrayed. It took Betty a long time to get over this.

Betty was glad when work on her latest film was over. It had taken six months to film *When My Baby Smiles at Me,* and all she wanted to do was go back to Harry and the children and enjoy a long vacation.

The studio had nothing lined up for her in the immediate future, but Zanuck was scouring the bookshelves for another Grable-Dailey epic. *When My Baby Smiles at Me* had been a remake, previously filmed as an early talkie, *Dance of Life*, in 1929, and again in 1937 as *Swing High, Swing Low*. For her next film, Zanuck wanted something more original, but nothing he had looked at had fit the bill so far.

Over at M-G-M, Louis B. Mayer was having problems of his own. His top star, Judy Garland, was working on *Annie Get Your Gun* and having difficulty with her role. Judy had pre-recorded her songs for the soundtrack and Mayer was decidedly unhappy when he heard the playback; her voice was lackluster and missing the usual Garland magic. She was also suffering weight problems and was under great emotional stress — two factors which haunted her for the rest of her colorful career.

Judy's film, based on the Broadway hit which had starred Ethel Merman, was eight days into production when she failed to turn up for work. Mayer viewed what had already been filmed and decided to drop Miss Garland.

On May 20, 1949, Mayer notified Judy that she was fired. Hollywood went into a frenzy. The role of "Annie" was a real plum, and almost every musical comedy actress in town wanted it. It was reported that even Ginger Rogers called Mayer, informing him she was free to take on the role; Mayer declined her offer. To make matters worse, director Busby Berkeley also left the film through differences of opinion with the front office. Berkeley was replaced by Charles Walters — Betty's co-star in *Du Barry Was a Lady* — who suggested to Mayer that Grable would be an ideal Annie. Knowing that she was between films, Mayer contacted Zanuck and asked to borrow her on loan-out.

Betty was approached privately by Walters who wanted to gauge her reaction. Not unpredictably, she was ecstatic. A ready-made hit was within her grasp, if only Zanuck would agree. Surely he wouldn't stand in her way. Hadn't she been the good little girl all these years, making millions of dollars for the studio? Zanuck sat on it for a few days, then announced his decision: Grable was not for loan-out. The studio had big plans for her, and working in *Annie Get Your Gun* would only upset her busy schedule.

To put it mildly, Betty was upset. She had been so sure the boss would have consented just this once. Walters was equally disappointed; he felt sure Betty would have been great in the role. Her name would add millions in receipts.

Instead, the plum of the year went to another blonde — Betty Hutton, whom Paramount had no hesitation in lending out. It was to prove the highlight of her not inconsiderable career, and added a lot of clout to Hutton's box-office drawing power, which had slipped somewhat after one or two film flops.

It was later said that Hutton bullied and cajoled Paramount's top brass to free her for the role. Perhaps if Grable had put up a fight against Zanuck, she might have been successful. But that was not her style. Making films was strictly business to her. She never involved herself in the politics of gaining power over her bosses; she left that to her agents. In rare interviews during her movie-queen reign, she often trotted out the "I just got lucky" routine, which many of her fans believed, but luck — apart from a few streaks of it during her early days — had little to do with it. It was her talent, her spunk, and her ability to give the public what they wanted that put Betty among the elite of Hollywood's top-draw stars. She was unique, not a carbon copy of Alice Faye; a genuine all-round entertainer — a blonde with loads of sex appeal, but always an aura of niceness about her.

Now, however, rot had set in. Things would never be the same again between Twentieth Century-Fox and Grable. As long as Betty's films made money — and they usually did — Zanuck was quite happy to use her as his bread-and-butter star while keeping an eye out for newer talent who would be groomed to replace Grable when the time was right.

Grable knew the workings of Hollywood and was well aware of her precarious relationship with Zanuck. But in all her years at the studio, Betty never once had a major Broadway show bought especially for her, and very few parts she could really sink her teeth into. The studio felt safe relying on hackneyed backstage musical plots as long as customers kept coming to see them. This had probably bothered Betty for a long time, but she never made her feeling public. She simply got on with the job.

While Zanuck was aware of the weak plots of many of Betty's films, he did nothing to remedy the problem. As long as she was making money for the studio (and she made mega-bucks), he didn't appear too keen to lift Betty's career out of the rut in which it was embedded. He was quite happy to use her profits to finance more prestigious films like *Gentleman's Agreement*, a story he had bought about anti-Semitism. Although he wasn't Jewish, this was a subject close to Zanuck's heart.

Many observers maintained that Zanuck used Grable for her box-office clout, and the moment any of her films went into the red, she would be dropped. He wasn't particularly fond of her at this point, but he did respect her undoubted talent and drawing power. At times she could be difficult — usually over minor details like costuming. But on larger issues he found her malleable, and played on this to get his way over scripts and co-stars. The fact that one of two of her films showed signs of her losing her grip on the box office seemed to make her work even harder on her next project. He liked that. It kept a star in check, too scared to make a move unless the boss okayed it.

Despite her earlier protestations at being pushed into dramatic roles, Betty felt she would, at this point in her career, have bene-fited from a change of pace, like a romantic comedy or a witty sophisticated comedy-thriller, with perhaps one or two musical interludes woven into the script. But nothing was forthcoming — and Zanuck had an ironclad contract with Grable. There was no way he would release her to work for another studio.

The press didn't blame Zanuck for wanting to hold on to Grable, who was known as the "Solid Gold Blonde" in film circles. Said one columnist over Zanuck's loan-out refusal, "Who wants to let go of a gold mine?!" [65]

BERNIE
FREEDMAN '04

CHAPTER NINE

Zanuck hired director Preston Sturges on a two-picture deal. The famed Sturges was now freelancing after a number of years at Paramount where he had turned out such box office winners as *Hail the Conquering Hero, Miracle of Morgan's Creek,* and *Sullivan's Travels.*

He arrived at Twentieth as a firmly established and highly successful producer-director, and Zanuck was anxious to put him to work. One script which Sturges had written himself and planned to direct was *The Beautiful Blonde from Bashful Bend,* and he wanted Betty Grable for the lead. It was a western comedy with musical sequences to be added for the star.

Having received no other offers, Betty had little choice but to accept the new assignment. Cesar Romero, Rudy Vallee, and Olga San Juan were top-billed in a talented cast which also included several comedy notables from the past — Hugh Herbert, Porter Hall, El Brendel, and the marvellous Margaret Hamilton.

From the beginning, Betty didn't like the script. Although she approached her role with her usual professionalism, she thought she deserved better than this farcical offering and told Zanuck so. Zanuck was unmoved and said, "This is a visual comedy — the lines don't matter so much as the action." However, he told Sturges not to alter the Grable image too radically and insisted that her legs be clearly visible. Zanuck was pleased when he saw that that the red costume Grable would be wearing in the opening scene had a thigh-high split skirt. So much for visual comedy!

Prior to meeting Grable, Sturges spent hours at the studio's private cinema, viewing many of her films. Aware for the first time of her untapped abilities, he restructured the script to suit her.

Sturges enthused in a major fan magazine:

> She's a director's dream. Sure, she has the most beautiful legs in Hollywood, but that isn't all she's got. Her legs only detract from her talent. . . . Betty is a talented actress with a long and successful career as a comedienne ahead of her. She quickly kids herself, an example of her genuine modesty. But, believe me, she hasn't anything to be modest about. She is one of the few genuine talents in Hollywood today. Take her singing, for example. A girl who can sing for the screen with the fine tempo and shading she puts into it, is surely in the same league as the straight dramatic actress who knows the nuances of inflection. [66]

Such flattery from an important director would have gone to many actresses' heads, but it actually made Grable more nervous than she was before. She had grave misgivings about journeying into unknown territory — farce. Her mother was not keen on it either, but was in no position to say so. When Betty tried to discuss the script with Harry, he seemed quite unconcerned with her plight. In fact, he couldn't have cared less about his wife's career, but he did like the money she was bringing home. He agreed with others around the studio — namely, that the public would pay to see Grable in anything. She should have held out against the studio this time and refused the role, even if it would have meant taking a suspension. Unfortunately, she didn't obey her gut feeling and went back to work.

Betty had only two numbers in the film — and no dancing. She played a saloon girl who accidentally shot the town judge while aiming for philandering Romero. She breaks jail, skips town with girlfriend Olga San Juan, and finds refuge in a small town posing as a school teacher, Miss Hilda Swandumper. Although it was claimed to be an original Sturges story, the character Betty played bore more than a passing resemblance to the character Mae West played in the 1940 hit, *My Little Chickadee*, particularly the episode where Mae poses as a schoolmarm. Coincidentally, Sturges often likened Grable to Mae West.

Grable had a bad chest cold during most of the shooting. In one scene she was required to lift 182-pound Romero and injured her back. She was out of filming for a week until the pain eased, but it caused no disruption to the production schedule. Sturges shot around her until she was fit again. [67]

The picture was shot in eight weeks — one of the quickest-ever Grable epics. After filming was over, Sturges continued to beat the drum for Grable. He told a columnist,

> Betty takes direction superbly. She plays a scene over and over identically. This is what a director needs, while adding or subtracting other elements. A player who delivers differently each time lacks technique and defeats you.
>
> She proved a perfect sport about the falls she had to take in some scenes and refused to use a double. I also liked the way she never tried to manoeuvre her leading men into the background — and there are very few actresses one can say that of!
>
> She is anything but lazy, and works as hard as every other man and woman on the set. We never once had to wait for an entrance — she was always on time and always prepared for what she had to do. She does her job as an actress with a minimum of flurry and without any pretense. She has a logical, earnest mind. Knowing Betty Grable is an experience I wouldn't have missed for anything. You can count me in as a fan. [68]

If Grable was a director's dream, Sturges wasn't Grable's idea of a dream director. When Sturges went into print, stating that Grable's legs got in the way of her career, she was astounded. "He must be off his rocker," she remarked to friends. "My legs made me!"

(A couple of years earlier one of her directors told her in all sincerity, "Betty you are a wonderful film actress." Betty replied sweetly, "I know, honey — but I'd hate to do it without my legs.")

According to Cesar Romero, at the start of filming Grable and Sturges got on well and things ran smoothly. Midway through shooting, Grable got a call to the front office. She was there for over an hour. When she returned, there was a marked change in her demeanor, and for the rest of the filming she seemed very somber. She never discussed with anyone what was said to her at the meeting with Zanuck, and the details of the meeting remain a mystery. [69] But from the moment she stepped back onto the set, she never spoke another word to Preston Sturges.

A studio insider claimed that Sturges had gone to Zanuck, and complained that Betty wasn't giving her all to the character she was playing, and the boss called her in and put her in her place. However, this cannot be confirmed. What is known is that Zanuck was most displeased at what had been shot so far. He hauled Sturges into his office, threatening to take him off the picture if things did not improve. In a panic, Sturges is said to have put most of the blame on Betty's shoulders for being uncooperative.

Grable ignored the end-of-filming party and walked off the set without a goodbye to Sturges. A studio publicist recalled attending a sneak preview of the film with Zanuck and Sturges:

> Harry and Betty also attended, which was very unusual, but Harry was a Western fan and was eager to see the finished film. When the screening was over, there was an awful silence in the theatre. The studio chief left quickly. Betty and Harry rushed to their car. Zanuck walked round the block several times. He couldn't believe what he had just seen. Sturges had crucified Grable, that's all he kept saying to himself — he crucified her. [70]

The critics were not wild about it either. They planted most of the blame in Betty's lap for not entering wholeheartedly into the spirit of the Sturges farce. Betty retired to lick her wounds. She was bitterly disappointed with the film. "They've made a laughing stock of me, Harry," she complained to her husband. "I'll never live this one down. Especially when the critics compare it with *Annie Get Your Gun*."

In later years, *The Beautiful Blonde* has gained a cult status among film buffs. It has been shown in specialty movie houses in London and New York, playing to packed audiences. Avant garde fans see the film as it is played — a mixture of slapstick and farce. When Key Video released it to the home market in 1989, it was eagerly snapped up by Grable — and Sturges — fans. There were some fine comic performances, particularly from Hugh Herbert, Sterling Holloway, Margaret Hamilton, Richard Hale, Danny Jackson and Chris-Pin Martin. Many critics see it as Grable at her zany best, and never fail to point out the take-off characteristics of the film. It is a Western where the baddies are worse than bad — bullets fly but no one is ever hurt (except the hapless judge) and everyone ends up happily ever after — well, almost!

Betty couldn't understand the studio's attitude; she was at a crucial stage in her professional life. At thirty-two, she knew she was pushing the glamour-girl image to the limit, and she wanted a shot at a good comedy that would point her in the right direction for the remainder of her career. But Zanuck seemed to be content with a one-hit, one-miss pattern of movies for her.

She and Harry attended the Hollywood Park race track season, then vacationed once more at Del Mar. Betty shunned the press when she was on vacation, and later found she was being labeled uncooperative. This news surprised her; she had always had a good relationship with the press.

The studio then announced that she would star in *The I Don't Care Girl*, based on the life of Eva Tanguay, and that they had several other properties lined up for her, including *With a Song in My Heart*, the story of crippled singer Jane Froman. Betty showed almost no interest in these projects and kept away from the studio for several weeks. (One of the reasons she wasn't interested in the Froman project was because she would have to lip-sync [mime] to a playback recorded by Miss Froman. The role went to Susan Hayward.)

Many other stars had been dropped in massive economy cuts at other major studios. Her pal Dorothy Lamour was unceremoniously dismissed by Paramount when sarong movies seemed to be going out of fashion. Despite Dottie's success with both comedy and drama, the studio just wasn't interested in her any more. After a couple of years working for Columbia and United Artists, it was the influential Cecil B. De Mille who brought her back to the fold when he cast her in *The Greatest Show on Earth*. Betty Hutton was also dropped by the same studio when it appeared she had out-lived her madcap usefulness.

However, Fox held on tightly to Grable. Her films, despite one or two duds, were still earning a lot more money than other stars of her era, and she had once again been named the highest-paid woman in the United States. She was listed every year since 1942 among the Top Ten money makers — the only woman in show-business history to achieve such a record.

Why, then, Grable asked herself, was Zanuck continuing to shove her into one dud after another? He was surrounded by some of the best writers in Hollywood, yet he didn't use them to get to work on a suitable Grable vehicle. Betty began to wonder whether Zanuck was trying to give her the push. It certainly looked that way to her. The publicity department, though, was working flat out to sell her latest film to the public, and Grable knew that publicists could make or break you. For the moment she still seemed to be in favor — but only barely!

Fortunately *The Beautiful Blonde From Bashful Bend* was much better received by the public than it had been by the critics. It soon recovered its costs and went on to make a profit, though it was by a much narrower margin than *When My Baby Smiles at Me*.

Betty appeared to be much happier staying at home with her husband and family. She enjoyed taking Vicki to school each day and spent quite a lot of time with Jessica, taking care of her daughters without the aid of nannies. Grable had enormous problems holding on to domestic staff; she didn't know how to handle them. She was either too soft with her staff and they took advantage of her, or she was unreasonably hard on them, only to find herself accused of being a tyrant.

Her mother was disappointed at Betty's lack of ambition. She told Betty, "You owe it to yourself to get back into movies — and you owe it to your fans!"

But Betty was just not interested. She felt jaded and seriously considered abandoning what had been, up until now, a glorious career. She had told her mother she wouldn't mind going out while at the top. But after the disaster of *Beautiful Blonde*, it would have been on a low note. Betty knew it, and so did Lillian — and that may have been the only thing that kept her in show business.

Betty announced to the press,

> I am enjoying my life now. Harry is at home and we are a complete family unit. It makes such a difference — movies no longer seem important to me. Harry's the breadwinner of the family — and that's the way it should be. When he's away, I don't care about being with a lot of people. Once in a while, some friends will take me to dinner, or have dinner at home with me. But they don't do this thinking that I am lonely and need cheering up. They know me better than that.
>
> Of course, I get lonely. But I don't get frantic over it, wondering what I should do to pass away the evening hours. Maybe I'm just lazy, but I'd rather eat dinner with the children, watch some television, and climb into bed around nine with a good book. When I am working I have to be in bed by then, but working or not, I prefer to be lonesome by myself instead of having people trying to entertain me and get my mind off Harry's being away. I miss him terribly. But he has to go on the road for so many weeks in the year — I have to accept that. Gosh I'm lucky. Look at the girls whose husbands and boyfriends were gone for years during the war. What have I got to complain about? [71]

The magazine article quoted above portrayed Betty as a happy and contented person. In real life she was having problems — and not just with her career. Ranch neighbors Perry and Virginia Snow sued the James family, complaining that a fence between their adjacent properties interfered with the Snows' use of communal water rights. Betty was also summoned to appear in court, alleged to be in breach of contract when she changed her agency representation from MCA Artistes to Nat Goldstone. However, the studio's legal department sorted out the latter problem.

Eventually, Zanuck met with several top screenwriters in an effort to salvage the dangerously sagging Grable career. There were a few stories on the shelves. Actress Billie Burke, widow of Broadway producer Florenz Ziegfeld, had completed her memoirs, entitled *With A Feather on My Nose*. It had been submitted to Twentieth Century-Fox as an ideal screen vehicle for Betty Grable. Zanuck declined the offer, though several other studios showed interest in the property.

The studio's stockholders were anxious to get Betty back to work in a sure-fire hit. In the right sort of role, there was no one to equal her box-office drawing power. To add to their frustration, she had recently been crowned "Queen of the Dance" by Frank and Yolanda Veloz, on behalf of the U. S. Ballroom Operators Association, and a newspaper opinion poll of Latin American countries had named her "South America's Most Popular Blonde." With all this good publicity, it seemed a waste to have their top money-making star sitting around on the sidelines.

The studio had loaned out its other top blonde, June Haver, to Warner Bros. on a two-picture deal. (Warner had originally asked for Grable to portray Broadway star Marilyn Miller in their top-budgeted biopic *Look For the Silver Lining*, but as usual, Zanuck refused.) The only other musical talent Twentieth had on the payroll was a pretty nineteen-year-old dancer of Hungarian descent named Francesca Mitzie Marlene de Charney von Gerber, who later gained much fame under the more familiar name of Mitzi Gaynor.

Zanuck kept Mitzi waiting on the sidelines. He didn't want to entrust a virtually untried newcomer with a big-budget production. Mitzi was a talented dancer, but Zanuck put her under the tutelage of a studio drama coach while he searched around for a suitable role for her.

The studio had recently purchased a property based on the lives of Chicago songwriters Gus and Grace Kahn. Zanuck had taken an option on it, thinking it might be suitable for June Haver. Filming would start on the picture, entitled *Wabash Avenue*, as soon as she returned from Warner Bros. He reasoned there would be no point in having two blonde musical stars lazing around until something was found for them to do. But Grable was his biggest problem.

Director Henry Koster, a long-time admirer of Grable's work, said he would be prepared to direct her next picture if a suitable vehicle could be found. Years later Koster said, "Betty was the funniest, certainly the most natural movie actress I ever saw . . . certainly not the greatest. She was not a great dancer, not a great singer, not a great actress, but altogether such a likeable personality. She couldn't say a phony word." [72]

Zanuck assigned scriptwriters Harry Tugend and Charles Lederer to dream up something suitable for Grable. The two men retired to their office, but after several days they had to admit stalemate. In desperation, they decided to view some of her earlier films in the hope that it would spark off something between them.

One of the films viewed was *Coney Island*, a major success for Grable in 1942. The writers liked the smart script but thought it could be improved on, and took the idea to Zanuck. He wasn't very impressed. He couldn't imagine that people would pay to see Grable in a blatant remake of her own film. Furthermore, *Coney Island* had been reissued over the years and was still fresh in the memories of her legions of fans. Meanwhile, Zanuck had come up with a story, *Storks Don't Bring Babies*, by S. K. Lauren. He thought it had possibilities as a musical.

Betty's fans kept writing to the studio, asking what was in the pipeline for their favorite star. Her fan mail was still astronomical, reaching around 12,000 letters a week. This fact was enough to keep the studio bosses busy in their frantic search for suitable projects for their evergreen star.

Over lunch in his office, Zanuck mentioned the scriptwriters' idea of a remake of *Coney Island* to director Koster. The director asked to see the original film and he and Zanuck viewed it that afternoon. After the showing, Koster was cautiously optimistic. "It has possibilities," he admitted.

Zanuck also told him of the Kahn story, *Wabash Avenue*. He wanted the director's opinion regarding its suitability for Grable. After reading a synopsis of the script, Koster turned it down. He stated that it would be most unsuitable for Grable. "It is the story of a partnership, with the man (Gus) the stronger of the team. Betty would only be a secondary character to the plot. She needs a vehicle to showcase her talents, with others supporting her." Zanuck agreed, and the two men decided that a remake of *Coney Island* was their best bet. The studio head's only worry now was, "How will Grable match up to her image of eight years ago?" Koster assured him that he envisaged no problem in that department.

Zanuck had a meeting with Grable at the Baby J ranch, and outlined the idea of remaking her earlier film. He expected fire-works — Betty had recently been demanding more originality in her future films, and she was tired of those backstage storylines. Although she was deeply disappointed in the results of *Beautiful Blonde*, she still wanted to come up with a top comedy. She knew she could handle it. Much to his surprise, Zanuck found her quite receptive to the idea of remaking her earlier hit. Perhaps it appealed to her ego, showing that she could appear just as youthful as she was eight years ago. "Fine", she told him. "Get some new songs and plenty of humour, and I'll do it."

The boss got his scriptwriters together to work out details altering the original film. "But not too much — that film was a big grosser. No point in killing the goose, if you know what I mean," he told them. He also assigned top song-writers Mack Gordon and Josef Myrow to come up with some new songs.

To ensure the success of the new project, Grable asked for Dan Dailey as her leading man, but he was busy on another sound stage with yet another musical western, *A Ticket to Tomahawk*. The studio settled on Victor Mature, reunited with Betty for the first time since 1942. He was one of the studio's most popular leading men of the time and Betty was pleased to be working with him again. It was a happy reunion.

The Girl With the Million Dollar Legs

Alice Faye's husband, bandleader/comedian Phil Harris, was her other romantic interest. The turn-of-the-century period of the original was retained, but the locale was switched from the New York pleasure beach to the Chicago World's Fair. With Phil in the film, it brought Alice and Betty back into each other's lives. They hadn't met for a couple of years. Now they were happy to catch up with each other.

The studio decided to title the new film *Wabash Avenue* and discard the contents of the original story. (Warner bought the property a couple of years later as a vehicle for Doris Day and Danny Thomas, filmed it under the title *I'll See You In My Dreams*, and proved Henry Koster's earlier statement that the man was the central character. Doris came off second best.)

If the studio chiefs worried how their top star would compare with the original film version, they worried needlessly. At costume tests, she was slimmer than she had been during her *Coney Island* days, the legendary legs remained supreme, and her face was still unlined. Head of make-up, Ben Nye, went on record as saying that Betty used much less make-up on camera than many of her contemporaries. Her only make-up problem, he said, was a slight bone protrusion on her nose, which he covered with highlight grease.

The cameraman assigned to *Wabash Avenue* was Arthur Arling, and Betty was pleased with his work on the film. She was particularly happy with the way he photographed the dance sequences. Mr. Arling was equally complimentary. He said that Betty was a dream to photograph. "A natural," he said.

During the course of filming, Betty invited Dan Dailey and Anne Baxter to lunch. They talked at length about their families and what was new around the studio. Dailey remarked that a new girl on the lot was announcing to anyone who would listen that one day she would oust Grable from the throne at the Fox lot. The girl was Marilyn Monroe. Dailey went on to say that Miss Monroe was a very ambitious young lady who openly declared that she was a good friend of the studio president Joe Schenck.

Marilyn had been given a contract at Fox in 1946, but had been dropped at the end of her first year. After some modeling work and freelancing at other studios, she was again taken on by Fox, but to date she had very little film footage. She spent a lot of her time on the Fox lot viewing early Grable films, modeling herself on the studio's top star. "There's an awful lot of Grable in Monroe's early films," said one studio technician. [73]

Naturally, Grable had heard of Marilyn, but the two had never met. By this time, of course, Marilyn had created quite a reputation for herself around the film colony and had many influential people working to promote her. Columnist Sidney Skolsky was one of the first to champion the new starlet. He wrote, "Two words keep Marilyn Monroe from becoming a major star — Betty Grable." [74]

But if Betty was worried by this latest usurper to the "throne" she didn't let it show. "There's always plenty of room at the top," she still maintained.

The gamble with *Wabash Avenue* paid off. Betty looked as youthful as she had in the earlier version. But the more mature Grable delivered her lines with a fine sense of comedy timing and her overall performance was much more polished than in *Coney Island*. Apparently Preston Sturges was right about Grable's having the talent for comedy, but not in the farcical vein of *Beautiful Blonde*.

Betty played a gaudy saloon singer who makes the big time on the musical comedy stage, and director Koster brought her through the slight though highly amusing plot. She was helped along with a smart script, Mature's deadpan playing, and Phil Harris's wry humor. The trio worked well together. The fans loved Betty's first film of the new decade. It showed their favorite star just the way they loved her — flashy costumes, plenty of leg show, and a musical score that suited the Grable personality perfectly. Betty had several numbers in the film, including "Big, Red, Rosy Apple," "Baby Won't You Say You Love Me," and the popular "Wilhelmina" which was destined to become a big recording success for Danny Kaye (and was nominated for an Academy Award). As usual, Betty lost out when it came to recording her own hit songs.

A newcomer to the studio was Billy Daniel, a talented dancer/choreographer who had worked at Paramount and Columbia as a dance director. He was being groomed to replace Hermes Pan who had recently left Twentieth Century-Fox. Betty and Billy got on famously, and the two of them did some fancy footwork in the film's big production numbers, "Billy" and a flashy jazz-type number entitled "My Honey Man." Not only was Daniel a clever choreographer, but he adored working with Grable. [75]

Many fans thought this was the best number in the film; it certainly showcased Betty's singing and dancing abilities to perfection. It was in this sequence that Betty's complete professionalism shone through. Towards the end of the vocal, Betty was caught off-guard as Billy was about to swing her into the main dance routine. She realized her left foot was positioned wrong for the next series of steps, and quite casually she shuffled the offending foot into the correct position. Her action saved her having to stop the filming, saving thousands of dollars in production costs. The casual viewer would be hard-pressed to spot the shuffle which stayed in the final cut of the film.

One other number — a beautifully executed version of "Shimmy Like My Sister Kate" — caused a few headaches. The scene had to be refilmed several times because Betty's gold lamé, fringed leotard caused problems with the censors who felt too much of her anatomy was on display.

In her dance sequences Betty needed three identical costumes because during strenuous routines she perspired profusely; this constantly embarrassed her. She also used up to eight pairs of opera hose each day, specially made for her at a cost of twenty-five dollars a pair.

During the making of *Wabash Avenue*, a team of motion study experts were called in to time Betty at work. No one is quite sure whether the studio was becoming more cost-conscious about musicals, or if they anticipated good publicity when they announced their findings. According to the experts, it took Betty thirty-two hours of rehearsal to get one minute of useable footage in the final film. They also determined that she worked as hard as a Pennsylvania coal miner, burning up as many calories per hour during rehearsals and final takes — no wonder, they declared, she kept her figure in such fine trim.

Betty's allies in the publicity department made sure the findings were released post-haste to all major trade papers and fan magazines; they were always grateful for copy on Grable. Her picture on the cover, with a good meaty story inside, always ensured a high volume of sales.

Regarding her figure, Betty was much more down to earth. "When I had a weight problem in the early forties, Zanuck used to call me into his office and bawl me out. I became so afraid of those Monday-morning arguments that I tend not to put on any weight these days. I'm sure it's psychological."

Grable was one of the very few stars who ever recreated an earlier film role successfully. The critics loved *Wabash Avenue*. *Variety* noted that Betty was at her sparkling best, while *Film Daily* announced that the film should cause much healthy activity at the box office. Fans also went overboard for the new film — with one notable exception. A man wrote to Betty saying that he had seen *Coney Island* seventeen times and loved it. But he expressed "great disappointment" when he paid to see *Wabash Avenue* and ended up watching a rehash of the original. Betty wrote a personal reply to the fan, apologizing for causing him so much disappointment. She promised that her next film would be more original and hoped he would liked it. He was the only fan known to sound a sour note on *Wabash Avenue*.

Betty never forgot her fans. She said:

I never allow myself to forget that it is the public who made me . . . not the studio . . . and those fans could just as easily break me. Since the end of the war, I found that many of the fan letters were coming from Australia and New Zealand, as well as my faithful band of followers in Britain and Europe. I suppose that because of the war, the Australians didn't get a chance to see my movies. And I have recently started getting letters from Germany, where some of my old films are having their first run.

Of her fan mail, she added,

Most of the letters simply ask for an autograph or portrait. Others can be a bit personal. For instance, I received a letter from one woman who stated that she wanted the name and address of the plastic surgeon who molded my legs! 'Nobody was born with your legs," she wrote, 'and I would like to know how much the operation costs . . .' I just ignored that one. [76]

Delighted with the runaway success of *Wabash Avenue*, Zanuck brought Betty and Dan Dailey together for *My Blue Heaven* (the new title for his *Storks Don't Bring Babies* project). Also in the cast was the young Mitzi Gaynor. Grable strongly suspected that Mitzi was being groomed to replace her, but she didn't begrudge the youngster her chance. And she found Mitzi a charming girl, never acting pushy or trying to upstage anyone.

Prior to shooting the film, Betty insisted on several rewrites to script. She also insisted that director Claude Binyon be replaced by a director more familiar with her style. Onlookers felt Grable was going out of her way to be difficult. Betty denied this, saying she only wanted what was best for the final film. "I don't want the success of *Wabash Avenue* to be frittered away in this new film. I want to consolidate its success with better quality musical scripts. It's important that the public gets what it wants from a film."

Louella Parsons, normally kindly disposed to Betty, thought that she was going "high hat" and hinted as much in her column, adding that she could be heading for trouble over the fuss she was making over the new film. The columnist also revealed that there was talk of her being replaced by Ginger Rogers, whose mother,

Lela, denied the story, but added that her daughter would love to dance in a picture with Dan Dailey at some future date. [77]

The truth was that Ginger had slipped in popularity the past couple of years, and columnist Parsons was doing all she could to keep her friend Ginger in the spotlight. Rogers had never been considered as a replacement for Grable in this or any other film.

As it happened, Ginger got lucky when the ailing Judy Garland had to bow out of *The Barkleys of Broadway* with Fred Astaire. Ginger replaced her and there was much publicity over the re-teaming of the old dancing partnership. The film gave Ginger's career a much-needed boost. (It was also rumored that M-G-M had tried to borrow Grable for this film.)

Nevertheless, Zanuck let it be known through his aides that he wasn't too happy about the way Grable was behaving. She went into her new assignment fully realizing that all was not well between her and the studio. In answer to Louella Parsons' allegations, Betty gave her an exclusive interview in which she said, "There are far more talented singers and dancers out of work right now who would give anything to be where I am. I guess I owe it to my fans, my mother, and myself to keep on working." [78]

With that, Betty reported on schedule for *My Blue Heaven*, with Dailey, Gaynor, David Wayne and Jane Wyatt. Cameraman Arthur Arling was once again in charge of photography, and the new director was the more-trusted Henry Koster.

Mitzi Gaynor and Grable became good friends right from the start. Betty helped the newcomer with her scenes, and as there were several dance sequences, she insisted that Mitzi be given the big "Live Hard, Work Hard" routine. It contained too many ballet steps — and ballet just wasn't Grable's forte. She was glad to be out of the routine, feeling that she had more than enough to do and that the loss of the ballet sequence wouldn't do her any harm.

Said Mitzi, who underwent a name change from Gerber to Gaynor on completion of this film:

Betty was the bread-and-butter star of the studio. Without

her, we'd all have been out of work. She particularly impressed me with her no-nonsense approach to her work — and she took trouble to point out many technical details and helped me in every way possible. Considering I was a raw newcomer to movies, she was very generous to me. [79]

If Mitzi was enthusiastic about Grable, it didn't quite work the same way for the star. While Grable worked on her musical numbers, Mitzi was always around watching her. This unnerved Grable so much that she spoke to Dailey about it. "She watches every move I make — it's as though I am being understudied," she complained. Otherwise, work progressed normally.

The story concerned Betty and Dan, a successful radio team, who move on to television. Betty gets pregnant, loses the baby in a car accident, and has all sorts of problems trying to adopt. There were some good numbers in the the film, including "Don't Rock the Boat Dear," "Deductible," "I Love a New Yorker," "Friendly Islands," and, of course, the title song. A number Betty enjoyed doing was "Halloween," aimed at her younger fans. Betty was partnered by Dailey and Wayne. In their third film together, Betty and Dan again proved to be a winning combination.

Betty wore Dior's "new look" outfits for the film — longer skirts. In a veiled reference, she had been chided by the famous Parisian dress designer. He said that a woman's knee was the ugliest part of her anatomy and should be kept hidden. Betty replied, "I haven't had any complaints from my fans — or my bank manager." Earlier in her career she had been criticized for showing too much leg and encouraging male admiration. Defensively Betty said: "Any girl who says she doesn't like wolf whistles is a liar!" Either way, Betty couldn't win.

Before the wrap of *My Blue Heaven*, Zanuck announced that the couple would be re-teamed in *Call Me Mister*, a new film due on the floor in four weeks. Betty was exhausted after her six months on *My Blue Heaven*, and told her boss she needed a rest before committing herself to another gruelling term on the sound stages.

Filming a musical was vastly more time consuming than a straight comedy or a drama. Weeks of dance rehearsal preceded the actual shooting, and then the filming of a three-minute dance sequence could take as much as a month; the routine would be photographed from every angle and stopped for close-up shots, medium shots, and, of course, leg shots! In addition, the stars had to spend several days in the recording studios putting their voices on the master tape to be looped into the final soundtrack.

Betty felt she needed some time off, but her mother (who had gradually worked her way back into her daughter's career) disagreed. She kept insisting that Betty prepare herself for the new film, but Grable was in no mood to be coaxed — or even threatened — into work. It led to several serious arguments between them. Finally Betty phoned Harry, who was appearing in New York, and complained that the studio was working her too hard. "I need a break," she told him, "but I have to be at the studio a week from Monday to start this new film."

Harry seemed sympathetic. He suggested that Betty fly to New York with the children for a few days and forget her studio problems. A few days later, when she should have been at the studio to discuss costumes for her forthcoming film, Betty and her daughters departed from Los Angeles International bound for New York. Once in the city, they checked into the St. Moritz where Harry was staying. Word quickly spread around town that Grable was in New York. Crowds gathered on the pavement outside the hotel, hoping to catch a glimpse of the blonde actress. Because of her stint on Broadway, New Yorkers laid first claim to Betty as their very own star! After a quick nap, a shower, and a change of clothing, Betty and the children emerged from the hotel doorway to hail a cab to the Astor Roof where Harry was playing. It was a rare treat for Vicki and Jessica to be able to watch their father perform.

The doormen outside the hotel quickly attempted to clear a path for the threesome. Betty clasped her children's hands tightly as she made her way to the waiting taxi, but several people with autograph books got in the way. In the ensuing stampede, little

Jessica, who hadn't been noticed by the crowd, was nearly trampled underfoot. After what seemed like a century, they eventually reached the comparative safety of the car. Some onlookers grumbled that the star was rather "uncooperative" in refusing autographs.

Betty was incredulous. "How could I risk the lives of my children just to sign an autograph? I know they are my fans, but the safety of my family must always come first."

After the incident, Betty was very careful about venturing out onto the city streets with her children. The next day Harry rented a car and took them sightseeing — the Empire State Building, the big stores on Fifth Avenue, and a buggy ride in Central Park. They were mobbed wherever they went, particularly the day they visited the city zoo. Betty returned to Los Angeles after only five days. However, she had enjoyed the break and was now ready to face the music at the studio.

She arrived the next day for the belated costume conference. Zanuck took her aside and emphasized to her that he was sympathetic to her problems of overwork. But he added, "You are at your peak now and it is to your advantage to gain as much screen exposure as possible. You know, Mitzi [Gaynor] is already at work on her first starring musical, [*Golden Girl*] and she is shaping up pretty good." [80]

Grable got the message. If she didn't work, she would find herself out in the cold. She would be in breach of contract if she didn't report on schedule.

With that, Betty turned up for work on her new film, *Call Me Mister*, a freely adapted version of the famous Broadway revue which had starred Betty Garrett. Being a revue, it had no plot to sustain it as a film project. Zanuck simply rehashed the plot he had written for an earlier Grable film, *A Yank in the RAF*, and instead of dwelling on the beginning of World War II as in the original film, updated the plot to the immediate post-war period in Tokyo. Betty played a civilian actress on tour in the Far East who meets up with her estranged husband Dailey (in the Tyrone

Power role), and dallies between Dan and handsome newcomer to films Dale Robertson in the part originated by John Sutton.

Just after production began on Betty's film, Harry and his band were contracted by the studio for work on yet another musical just starting production. It was *I'll Get By* (a remake of Betty's *Tin Pan Alley*) with June Haver and Gloria De Haven.

The Jameses enjoyed being at work at the same studio at the same time. Their housekeeper took care of the children, and they were able to travel to and from work together — and had the added luxury of sharing the same lunch table. Those lucky enough to join them in the commissary were usually musicians, dancers, and production workers. Haver and Grable appeared to have let bygones be bygones and were often seen lunching together. It was an unspoken rule that shop talk was forbidden at these daily gatherings. It also gave Betty a brief respite from her long day — and though she ate very lightly during filming, she could never resist the dessert course. Not that she worried about it — "I can usually burn off the calories with my dancing."

Harry's work on *I'll Get By* was completed in four weeks. The couple was disappointed that his part had been whittled down to a few lines of dialogue and two or three appearances fronting his band. The film was only moderately successful and didn't stand up well against the original Faye-Grable version of 1940.

Betty, too, was having problems with her film. She was disappointed in the rushes she viewed and suggested to Zanuck that certain scenes should be re-shot. Zanuck maintained that director Lloyd Bacon knew what he was doing and vetoed her suggestion. He didn't want to add to the costs of an already-expensive production. Grable was also disappointed with dance director Busby Berkeley. Since her early days at the Goldwyn Studio, she had been waiting for her chance to work with him again, but the maestro was past his prime by the time they got together and the end product was less than satisfactory. She did, however, have some good routines; dressed in sailor's whites with the identically costumed Dunhill Trio, she did some excellent tap work, and executed lively steps in "I Just Can't Do Enough for You, Baby," with Dailey.

For a Grable-Dailey film, it was not quite successful enough at the box office, and the critics were merely lukewarm. Even though it was a tuneful show, the songs were not up to the high standard of her previous films. One hit of the original revue, "South America Take It Away" was a big recording hit for the Andrews Sisters. It would have been an excellent comedy number for Grable, but it was not used in the film.

Betty came over well on the screen, and she was ably supported by Dailey, Danny Thomas, Benay Venuta, and Dale Robertson. However, it seemed that public taste was shifting away from the glossy musical confections that had done such fantastic business during and immediately after the war years.

Other studios noted the winds of change, too. M-G-M and Warner Bros. were having only moderate success with their formula musicals. Two notable exceptions in this period were *On the Town* and *Singin' In the Rain*, both starring Gene Kelly. These two films were among Betty's favorite musicals because they took the musical to new heights of originality and gave a new look to the genre with their verve and energy.

Bright newcomer Doris Day, at work on her second musical for Warner, was the only threat on the horizon as far as Grable was concerned. In fact, Miss Day's first role, *It's Magic*, was such a steal from earlier Twentieth Century-Fox confections — ocean-going liner, blonde sassy showgirl/singer, S. Z. Sakall, and exotic locations — that one expected Carmen Miranda and the Bando de Lua to pop up at any moment. It was a huge success and catapulted Doris into the big time.

Grable watched Miss Day's progress with professional interest. Betty's fans, however, remained loyal to their favorite musical star and continued to bombard the studio with requests for pictures and information. *Life* ran an article on her entitled "The World's Most Popular Blonde."

At the end-of-filming party for *Call Me Mister*, Dale Robertson told Betty that he appreciated all the help she had given him during the film, and that he hoped to work with her again some day. Betty was flattered. She liked Dale. He had a freshness about him which she found appealing; besides, he shared her love for dogs and horses.

Betty left the studio telling everyone she was going to sleep for a week before embarking on her long-awaited holiday. She had worked for thirteen months straight (apart from her week in New York) and was looking forward to a break. However, the studio had other ideas!

Writer-director Richard Sale and his wife, Mary Loos, had come up with a script called *Don't Fence Me In* as a suitable story for Betty. They had aroused the interest of producer George Jessel and he agreed it was tailor-made for Grable. It was a modern-day backstage comedy about a Broadway star who discovers her producer-husband cheating on her, feigns amnesia and leaves his show stranded. She eventually turns up in Miami, a honky-tonk singer in a fifth-rate night club.

Jessel dispatched a messenger with the script to the Baby J ranch, with a terse note urging Betty to consider it. She read the script and admitted she was interested in the role. It afforded her the chance of playing in a light sophisticated comedy, but not at the expense of dance routines.

Zanuck, who was full of enthusiasm for the new project, got all the interested parties together into the front office for urgent discussion on the script and casting. He insisted the film would have to go into production immediately, as he was anxious that studio space should be fully utilized during these economic times.

Grable wasn't sure. She had been promised a long vacation after *Call Me Mister*, but she was also smart enough to realize that a script as fresh as this could be a long time coming her way again. She knew the studio was working her flat out, but she agreed to do the picture because she had a feeling the film would be a great big personal triumph for her. Zanuck promised he would try to get a big-name leading man for her. He had already approached Cary

Grant who showed a keen interest in appearing in a musical with Grable. Betty also asked the boss to cast Dale Robertson in the new film, not as the leading man (as yet he had not much experience in movies) but in a supporting role.

Pleased that his top star was keen on the project, Zanuck wasted no time in setting up the production. He gave director Sale carte blanche. Jessel didn't like the title and Zanuck agreed: "Too much like a western." One of Zanuck's henchmen (as Grable referred to her boss's aides) came up with *Meet Me After the Show* from one of the songs in the film. It seemed to please everyone and it was accepted. Like Betty, Zanuck seemed to feel it would be a smash hit — and there weren't too many musicals making top money at that time.

Betty reported for work only three weeks after finishing her last film. At costume fittings she tried on more than 150 pairs of shoes before finding the right pair to match an outfit she would be seen wearing on screen for about thirty seconds. Zanuck blew his top and confronted Betty about wasting time in wardrobe. The actress retorted, "My fans are entitled to see me at my best. After all, my pictures still make money, so what's all the fuss over a pair of shoes?"

She also insisted that the sound stage where she was to perform a barefoot routine be swept with a magnet before she set foot on it. She further insisted that Arthur Arling photograph the film. Zanuck complied with her every wish — "anything for a quiet life," he muttered. He warned his aides to be on the lookout for any tantrums on the set and to report them to him immediately. He could be tough. No star, not even Grable, was bigger than the studio. If this was her idea of revenge for the studio making her work too hard, there were remedies for that, too.

When Zanuck announced that Cary Grant would not be free from other commitments in time to start the picture, Betty suggested that they close down production until Cary was available. No way, said Zanuck, and promptly cast Macdonald Carey, new at the studio, in the leading male role. He also refused her request for Dale Robertson — that part went to another husky newcomer, Rory Calhoun.

Principal photography was started without delay. The big problem for Betty was the tough schedule for dance rehearsals. In her last film, the dance sequences were filmed at the end of shooting, Busby Berkeley style. In the new film, dancing was filmed first, allowing Betty no breathing space. New choreographer Jack Cole and his pretty assistant Gwen Verdon were assigned to the film, and put Betty through a gruelling rehearsal period.

In an interview with film historian John Kobal, Cole said Grable was a very talented lady, ". . . but having been a child performer, she was just the old tired gypsy as a young girl. And the problem was that she could do all those pictures forward and backward. She never looked at the script, she'd just come in, put on her make up, look at the three pages they were going to do that day and then go, ready. She could do it all in a haze, you know, while thinking about what horse was going to win that day."[81]

Up-and-coming comedy actor Eddie Albert was added to the cast along with Calhoun, Fred Clark, Lois Maxwell, and Irene Ryan in support. The stars worked well together and had a professional rapport that came over well on screen.

One day on the set Mac Carey picketed Betty's dressing-room, carrying a placard which read, "Unfair to Actors." Betty watched him for a few moments, but couldn't contain her curiosity any longer. She opened the door and called, "What's up, Mac?" Carey continued his pacing. "You are." She asked, "What have I done?" Carey kept a straight face ."Just look at you — that's what's wrong. Who's going to look at an actor on the screen when Betty Grable is around!" Betty dissolved with laughter.

Carey said,

We knew Betty was having a tough time with the studio — and with Zanuck in particular. Keeping her amused and entertained was just the tonic she needed. Eddie Albert, a very funny man, was also a big help in relieving potential tense moments. We were all rooting for Betty. After all, she was the biggest name in films and we felt we owed her at least that for keeping us in employment. The industry was going through a very bad time during 1951.

Betty was a fun-loving woman and often kept us laughing. She had a keen wit and a very dry sense of humour. She was friendly, but never fawning or gushing.

She could also take a joke. For a gag the electricians wired up a stuffed polar bear she had to dance around in one scene so that it would "growl" every time she touched it. At rehearsal we all stood at the side of the set as Betty went into her number. As planned, the bear growled the moment she leaned on it. We were doubled up with laughter. Betty immediately realized she had been set up but continued with the rehearsal, growling back at the bear each time she touched the animal. [82]

Carey was also impressed with her dramatic ability,

... considering she had no dramatic training for either the stage or screen. She jolted me as a performer as well as a person. Working with her convinced me she has a genuine talent for acting and a fine, self-developed technique for playing comedy. This is my first comedy role in years and comedy is harder than straight emoting because the timing has to be trigger-accurate for effect. Grable has it down pat. I was awed by the speed with which she understands a script, by her intelligent conserving of her energy during rehearsals, and by her reliable habit of never fluffing her lines. [83]

Betty grew very fond of Carey and Albert. She felt they contributed a lot to the success of the film. And a success it was. The critics reacted very favorably. Don Smith of the *Los Angeles Daily News*, said, "She's back again and she's got everything she ever had — and more!" *Variety* wrote, "The film should be a good tonic for the flagging box office." John L. Scott of the *Los Angeles Times* stated, "Betty really turns on the charm in this one, and works hard in her production numbers." *Box Office* said Betty "was at her singing and dancing best." And the Los Angeles *Citizen News* critic noted, "Miss Grable works hard in this one. That the picture is at its best when she is performing is a compliment to her talent and personal charm."

It was all true. She did work very hard on the film. She had some highly original dance routines, thanks to the imaginative Cole choreography. She looked slim and sexy in the barefoot number, "No Talent Joe," which had her backed up by a chorus of leopard-skin-clad muscle men. Other numbers included "It's a Hot Night in Alaska" in which the fur-clad star hoofed amiably around a Polar Bear; the bluesy "Bettin' on a Man," wrapped in gold lamé; and the title number in which she fronted a chorus of "elderly" gentlemen. This number included a fast tap routine with Gerry Brandow and her old pal Steve Condos — like Betty, still going strong since he had first worked with her in *Moon Over Miami*.

Superb Broadway dancer, Gwen Verdon, partnered Betty in two sequences, including the "I Feel Like Dancing Tonight" finale, which many critics thought ahead of its time. Betty came over as nimble-footed as Gwen who was several years her junior.

The finished product gave Zanuck no cause for concern. It was obvious the studio had another hit on its hands — and that was all that mattered. The film was completed on time, despite Betty's being out of action for a few days when she suffered from lumbar trouble, a recurring problem which often caused her great pain.

The only sour note came from Britain. Twentieth Century-Fox's London office decided, in its wisdom, NOT to showcase Betty's latest hit in the West End, refused to hold a press preview, and sent it out on release almost immediately. London critics were incensed at this, but caught the film on release and reviewed it, much to the Twentieth Century-Fox London office's embarrassment. They were all in favor of Grable's latest hit.

Director Richard Sale was delighted with Betty's performance and wanted her for his next assignment at the studio, *Father Does a Strip*, due to start production in a month. Betty was at home preparing for her much-postponed vacation when Zanuck called her to the studio, telling her to report for a script conference on the new Sale film. She was to be co-starred with Dan Dailey and Dennis Day. She was angry and thought the boss was deliberately trying to upset her. She told him, "You have been promising me this vacation for the past eighteen months. I have hardly had a day off in that time. I won't do it."

Zanuck was adamant. "It's a good script and Dan is anxious to work with you again. " Betty was equally adamant and left his office — furious! The studio sent a legal letter to the reluctant actress, reminding her of her contractual obligation and telling her to report for work on *The Girl Next Door* (the film's new title) on May 1, 1951. Betty ignored the letter and set off with Harry and the girls for her vacation cottage at Del Mar.

Director Sale, so anxious to have Betty in the film, persuaded Zanuck to delay the start of the film by a week, in the hope that she might change her mind. When Grable didn't show up on the rescheduled date, the studio announced, "Twentieth Century-Fox has placed their top star Betty Grable on suspension for refusing to report for work on *The Girl Next Door*. The actress will remain on suspension until the completion of the film." The obligatory letter had been sent out by the studio's legal department informing Betty she was in breach of contract and was therefore on suspension.

It was the first time in her twelve years at the studio that she had received such a letter. It jolted her, but she maintained that she had made her own bed and she couldn't expect anything but suspension. Nevertheless, such a move left her feeling not a little uneasy. She couldn't understand why Zanuck refused her the long-awaited vacation. She claimed she was tired and therefore felt she couldn't give her all to the new production.

A journalist on a Hollywood newspaper recalls the day the press release reached the newspaper's offices. "The editor opened his office door, beckoned to me, and said: 'The world is coming to an end — Fox just suspended Grable!'" [84]

CHAPTER TEN

Back among her racing cronies in Del Mar, Betty Grable began to relax. Her mother had also arrived for the series of race meetings, but kept out of Betty's way. She knew better than to tackle her rebel daughter on the suspension. At first, Grable was angry about the studio's attitude, but she understood fully the consequences of refusing the film role. "No use crying over spilled milk," she claimed, whenever any of her horse-set friends came to sympathize.

Gossip columnists hounded her day and night at her holiday home, trying to get the "inside story" on what had gone wrong between the studio and its solid-gold blonde. It was her first-ever suspension in her twelve years at Twentieth, and it was also the first public mention of friction between her and the studio.

Hedda Hopper was on a story-gathering stint at a film location in Colorado at the time, but one of her staff writers managed to get access to Betty and quiz her on the suspension. The star talked willingly. It was a ploy often used by Betty to get the press on her side whenever anything went wrong.

The unrepentant star explained that she had just finished *Meet Me After the Show* and was told to report for work the following week on *The Girl Next Door*. She added:

> I didn't refuse to do the picture. In fact, I hadn't even seen the script. I had been working on three films for the past eighteen months without a break. I needed a rest and a vacation before starting back to work.
>
> I was told I could have the vacation but I'd be suspended if I took it. After being at Twentieth all these years I was hurt by the

studio's attitude. Then Zanuck asked me to do another picture in two months time — after my vacation. My reply was,'So long as I'm being taken off salary, I'm promising you nothing!' [85]

When Zanuck read the column, he was furious. He insisted on speaking with Hedda personally. Sensing that there was an almighty feud heating up between Grable and Zanuck, the writer hot-footed it back to Hollywood. It had the makings of a good lead story for her widely syndicated column.

In a lengthy (for a studio chief) interview, Zanuck said he was irked by Grable's attitude. The studio had been good to her over the years. He took great pains to explain that Betty had been kept on full salary while she had both her children. Usually when a studio learns that a star is pregnant, she automatically goes on unpaid lay-off until after the baby is born. He said:

> Betty had made so much money for the studio that we made an exception in her case. The studio is on the verge of dramatic cuts. Television is making big inroads in movie audiences, and theatres all over the country are beginning to take in less money. The star is not so important as the story, and that is the line the studio is going to take in order to win back audiences. [86]

Despite a last-minute plea by Dan Dailey, Betty remained adamant that she was going to have her holiday with Harry and the girls.

It was the beginning of the end for the Grable-Twentieth partnership, but neither of the two parties would give in gracefully. The scene was set for a long and bitter fight. All Hollywood knew what the outcome would be — stars never won battles against the all-powerful studios.

June Haver, newly returned from her stint at Warner Bros., was cast in the role, but fell from a table during a dance sequence early on in the shooting and injured herself. Production was held up for almost eight months while she recovered. Dailey and Dennis Day both went on to work in other films during June's indisposition.

Haver's accident was doubly costly for Betty; it meant that her suspension continued for a year, instead of the four or five months it normally would have taken to complete the disputed film.

Ironically, Grable had just been announced as one of the top-ten box-office champions for the tenth year in succession, whereas her replacement in the film had never achieved such distinction. Betty didn't appear terribly worried by the long lay-off. She was enjoying her lazy summer vacation, dividing her time between the race track and the beach, where she had fun with her daughters.

Her horses were on a winning streak; her favorite, Big Noise, romped home a $100,000 winner at one track, so lack of earnings wasn't a great problem to her. Harry had been contracted by Warner Bros. to act as technical advisor for the Kirk Douglas-Doris Day starrer, *Young Man With a Horn* (also known as *Young Man of Music*) in which he dubbed his trumpet-playing on the soundtrack as well as coaching Douglas on how to handle the instrument. [87]

Betty was pleased Harry was working again in Hollywood. She still maintained that Vicki and Jessica were brought up to realize that Harry was head of the family. To them, she claimed, Betty Grable was just a studio product seen in cinemas from time to time. "I took Vicki to see a reissue of *Mother Wore Tights* recently," she said, "and I don't think she was very impressed!"

When Harry finished his work at Warner Bros., the family left Del Mar and accompanied him on a tour with his orchestra. They spent some time in South Dakota — "to see where the REAL corn grows," said Betty. "It was nice to be among the folk in a rural community. We visited the Corn Palace in Mitchell and were given a really heartwarming reception. They didn't appear in the least concerned who we were — and it was good to be accepted as just ordinary people ... which is what we are. It gave me peace of mind — and [reminded me] that there was more to life than making movies."

The family returned to the Baby J ranch where Betty settled down to being a full-time mother. Various newspapers had printed stories claiming Betty to be the world's most glamorous mother. Worldwide polls voted her among the top ten of Hollywood moms. Betty didn't regard herself as such; she said she was much too strict with her children. Asked if they would embark on film careers when they were older, Betty said:

> I wouldn't push them into it. Vicki is taking piano lessons and shows a lot of talent. If they decide when they are older that they want to try for a career in show business, I would not stand in their way. And if they showed any talent for it, naturally I would encourage them. But there's no way I would force it on them. So long as they are healthy and happy, that's all that matters.

The girls were never allowed to go around basking in their parents' fame. Betty was determined that they wouldn't become typical Hollywood spoiled brats, and tried to set firm guidelines for them. Vicky's best friend during this period was Candice Bergen, the lovely unspoiled daughter of Edgar Bergen.

While Betty was absent from the studio, the ambitious Marilyn Monroe was working hard, trying to consolidate her success in her latest picture, *All About Eve*. She had received favorable notices despite being up against such female competition as Bette Davis, Anne Baxter, and Celeste Holm.

Marilyn played a girlfriend of George Sanders, who took a great delight in introducing her as a "graduate of the Copacabana School of Acting." It was a first-class movie and Marilyn's role, small though it was, proved instrumental in bringing her to the attention of the studio boss. However, Marilyn didn't endear herself to the other female stars. Miss Davis had only one scene involving Monroe, and the superstar was not amused that the scene was held up while a wardrobe woman made last-minute adjustments to Monroe's gown. [88]

She was quickly utilized in a number of films — *As Young As You Feel*, *Love Nest*, and *Let's Make it Legal*. Her fan mail was growing steadily and the publicity department was quite happy to promote the publicity-conscious newcomer. Monroe had been signed by Twentieth after a showy performance in M-G-M's *Asphalt Jungle*.

Zanuck still didn't have much faith in the studio's latest blonde. She had been screen tested in 1946 (ironically, on a Betty Grable set), renamed by then-head of talent Ben Lyon, and practically signed up without the boss's knowledge. Her option was dropped after six months. In that early period Marilyn had come to the attention of Joseph Schenck, the studio's president, who had taken a personal interest in the blonde newcomer. As Dan Dailey had told Betty so long ago, it was Schenck who did all he could to promote her, but since Monroe was without much talent or acting experience, Zanuck had no hesitation in dropping her. It was her new agent/lover Johnny Hyde who had inveigled the studio to sign Marilyn once more. Zanuck's argument was that he had Grable, and could sign Betty Hutton if he wanted to, so what did he want with untried and unproven Monroe? However, the persuasive Hyde eventually convinced Zanuck that Monroe would be an investment. Zanuck capitulated.

The knowledge that Zanuck had little faith in her made Marilyn all the more determined to make the big time. She was twenty-four years old and realized that at that age, Grable already had a well-established career covering film, band-singing, vaudeville, and Broadway, as well as a couple of top-notch movies to her credit. Monroe adored Grable's screen persona and viewed her movies at every opportunity.

(When Grable was filming a musical sequence, actors and technicians from other sound stages would stop work to come and watch Grable "strut her stuff." She was so popular among other stars that director Walter Lang once remarked: "I don't know why I bother looking for extras for audience shots. There's a ready-made audience right behind the camera!") [89]

Time was against Monroe, and she knew she had to work that much harder to achieve her goal. She also had to prove herself against other newcomers to the studio — Jean Peters, Anne Bancroft, and Debra Paget in particular.

The furor over her suspension having died down, Betty Grable agreed to be interviewed for *Movie Life*. In the article she went to great pains to explain that a film star's working life was not all champagne and caviar. She told the interviewer:

> If you could get a little closer to my job, you'd see what I mean. During filming I have to be up at five o'clock each morning. At this unearthly hour I have to set about trying to make myself look glamorous. My films all call for that sort of thing.
>
> I do my own make-up while Marie fusses over my hair. Around eight o'clock I go in for body make-up and get dressed for my scenes. It's after nine before the camera starts rolling — but that doesn't get away from the fact that I started rolling at 5 a.m. Musicals are the most difficult movies to work in. Apart from spending weeks rehearsing dance numbers, the filming of the number is a long, slow process. After the initial run-through, the cameraman then has to get close-ups of footwork, body movements, etc. It seems to go on forever.
>
> My work day lasts until six o'clock. Although it isn't in my contract, I've been lucky with directors who have in theirs that they can knock off at six. I arrive home around 6:30 p.m. Till now it's been a thirteen-hour day, but that isn't the end.
>
> Like any worker who has to take a shower to remove the grime, I set about getting cleaned up for dinner. It takes about forty-five minutes to complete my ablutions before I settle down to a meal and a quick evening of leisure. A very short playtime with the girls, a hurried look at the script for tomorrow's work, and it's off to bed in preparation for the same old routine next day. That goes on for five or six months, which is the average shooting time of my pictures."

Grable continued:

> I hope this is beginning to make some sense as to why I needed that rest. I am not looking for sympathy. I tried that once when I told a group of people how little of my salary I was

allowed to keep. One of them remarked: 'Well, now isn't that a shame. Do you mind if we all break down and cry?' Instead of urging them to do this, I just laughed. And I've been laughing ever since at how absurd I must have sounded. The truth is that a movie star just doesn't command any sympathy. That's the main reason why I have come to accept this long suspension — to indulge in a little practical sympathy for myself, on my own time. [90]

Apart from the headway Monroe was making at the studio, Zanuck was quite happy to promote the talented Mitzi Gaynor who was proving to be a very popular youngster. She was enjoying considerable success in a series of musicals, notably *Golden Girl* and *Bloodhounds of Broadway*. But the combined grosses of both Mitzi's films didn't bring in as much money as Grable's *Meet Me After the Show* which was doing great business on its general release. Still, Zanuck considered that at thirty-four, Grable was pushing the glamour-girl image and it was time she had a change of pace. Her contract with the studio still had five years to run and at $320,000 a year (around $3,330,000 in 1994 terms), he had to get her back to work if he were to appease the stockholders.

The Girl Next Door was eventually completed and Grable was put back on the payroll. The film, though pleasant, wasn't a runaway hit. Perhaps if it had been the fifth Grable-Dailey starrer, it may have turned out differently — though the mediocrity of the film certainly wasn't Haver's fault. The songs and dances she was given to perform were simply uninspired.

Grable and Zanuck buried the hatchet and it was announced that several scripts were being prepared for her to star in, including *Mother Was a Marine*.

The studio had recently purchased the screen rights to the hit Broadway show, *Gentlemen Prefer Blondes* as a showcase vehicle for Betty. She was excited about this. "The studio must still have faith in my drawing power to put me in this one. I am really looking forward to playing in it. It will make a pleasant change from all those backstage stories," she enthused.

Gentlemen Prefer Blondes, written by Anita Loos, was a lightweight musical comedy set in the Roaring Twenties. It had been bought by Jesse Lasky in 1927 for Clara Bow who refused it, then it was offered to Laura La Plante and Esther Ralston, but the project never came to fruition. Zanuck's plan was to bring it up to date, and mould the central character, Lorelei Lee, to suit the Grable personality. Despite his own personal feelings about Grable, he had been particularly impressed with her "new look" performance in *Meet Me After the Show,* and thought she would be perfect as Lorelei.

First of all, Betty had to get her latest assignment out of the way. It was *The Farmer Takes a Wife,* a remake of the 1935 Janet Gaynor-Henry Fonda hit, now set to music. To please her, Zanuck lined up Dale Robertson as her leading man, with Thelma Ritter, John Carroll and Eddie Foy, Jr. heading the supporting cast. They spared no expense, and built a replica of a canal — complete with working locks — on the backlot. It was Grable's first outdoor musical and she was pleased with the change of pace.

Betty believed *Farmer* was the studio's top-budget musical for its 1952 release schedule, and she approached it with her usual enthusiasm.

The Harold Arlen songs, although not show stoppers, were pleasant, and one of them "Today I Love Everybody" is still sung by various artists. Gwen Verdon once again partnered Betty in a couple of routines which, despite being choreographed by Jack Cole, were spirited but not very inspired. Betty thought that Jack, who excelled in fast-moving modern routines, couldn't do his best work on this film because he was hampered with the costumes and sets required for the 1850s storyline. He was much more at home in a contemporary environment.

To overcome the old-fashioned set, Betty and the principals spent four weeks rehearsing a "modern" dream sequence dance with Cole, and a further two shooting it. It ran for seven minutes when slotted into the final cut. Betty was bitterly disappointed when the sequence was taken out completely. She was never officially told why and had no say in the matter. Director Henry Levin said he thought it slowed up the action, although it wasn't his idea to scrap the sequence. Without it, the film's running time was reduced to seventy-five minutes compared to the usual of ninety minute running time expected of a Grable musical.

Betty was anxious to get the film (for which she had now lost her initial enthusiasm and referred to as *The Farmer Takes a Dump*) out of the way, so she could be fresh to start work on *Gentlemen Prefer Blondes*.

The second male lead in *Farmer*, John Carroll, got on well enough with Betty, but he kept quiet about the fact that he and his wife, talent scout Lucille Ryman, had been "involved" with Marilyn Monroe. Miss Ryman had signed her to a personal management contract, and for a few months Monroe had moved in with the couple. During this period, Monroe developed a crush on Carroll, a fact that eventually persuaded Miss Ryman to cease promoting Monroe. Although any personal involvement between Carroll, Ryman, and Monroe had long ceased, Carroll still felt uneasy, knowing that Monroe had always nursed an ambition to replace Grable at the first opportunity.

There were no major hold-ups on *Farmer*, but filming a musical is a long, slow process and the production ran slightly over schedule. In the interim, the studio's New York executives had been doing some quick arithmetic, totaling up the returns from the releases of Marilyn Monroe's latest films, *As Young As You Feel*, *Monkey Business*, *Don't Bother To Knock*, plus her first starrer, *Niagara*, in which she played a scheming wife desperate to have her husband killed off. Although these films did not get rave reviews, Monroe emerged from them unscathed. She was making a lot of money at the box office and it was obvious she was also developing into Hollywood's newest sex symbol. The public was clamoring for more.

The East Coast bosses began to put pressure on Zanuck to star

Monroe in *Gentlemen Prefer Blondes*. Although Zanuck had purchased the Broadway hit for Betty Grable (beating off competitive bids from M-G-M, as well as Paramount, who wanted it for Betty Hutton, and Columbia, who thought it would be ideal for Judy Holliday). Apparently, the New York brass no longer regarded Grable as top box office security.

To complicate matters, Joe Schenck had fallen for Monroe in 1946 and had begun a "platonic" affair with the young blonde, but that ended after she was dropped by Zanuck in early 1947. Now, however, Schenck was putting pressure on Zanuck to use Marilyn in more prestigious films and to give her the big studio "build-up." Marilyn's relationship with Schenck was well chronicled by the gossips around the studio. It didn't escape Betty's attention either. She neither liked nor trusted Joe Schenck and often referred to him as Joe Skunk.

It was obvious that Monroe's star was on the ascent but, on the surface, Betty appeared to be quite unconcerned. Her work output was good, her health excellent, and she had lost none of her glamour. Plus she had years of experience behind her . . . "too many," cracked Grable dryly!

The critical panning of Marilyn's first top-budget starrer, *Niagara*, lulled Grable into a false sense of security. In Toronto, Liberal Party representative William Houck called for the banning of Monroe's film, stating it was the worst movie of the year and that Marilyn was the "worst actress." Grable should have known better than to allow herself to believe this would harm Marilyn. She knew there was no such thing as bad publicity. Cinemagoers flocked to see the latest Hollywood glamour girl in her first major film in Technicolor. Apparently, they liked what they saw.

Zanuck didn't want to entrust Monroe with the studio's biggest film of the year, and said so. But he could not ignore the excellent business *Niagara* was doing or the fact that Monroe's fan mail was rising steadily. Grable's fans weren't deserting her, but clearly Monroe was on the brink of stardom. Her name was in practically every show-business column in the United States and photo agencies wired her pictures to every newspaper office. She was good business for them.

Before he made a final decision, Zanuck wanted to view a film Marilyn had made at Columbia in 1948. It was a dreadful B-musical called *Ladies of the Chorus*, co-starring Adele Jergens, then queen of the B-movies. Marilyn, however, came off best in an otherwise trite film. In this film, Marilyn had a couple of songs which she managed to put over very well under the musical direction of Freddy Karger, head of music at Columbia Studios. (Karger was also romantically involved with Monroe.)

Zanuck watched the film in the company of Sol Siegel and Howard Hawks, producer and director of the new film. The trio agreed that Monroe could hold a tune and if the sound engineers could boost her voice, there shouldn't be any problems.

Schenck was delighted. He "suggested" that Grable had let the studio down with her recent suspension. It was rumored her name would be missing from the top-ten box-office attractions when their listings would be released in a few weeks. Schenck thought it was time she was put out to pasture.

Since she had an iron-clad contract with several years to run, that could have proved difficult, but Schenck came up with a plan. If Grable were sidelined into a run-of-the mill programmer, she would slip even further from the top rung of success and hopefully quit, instead of hanging on to a career that was on a dangerous downhill slide. Zanuck eventually agreed. Monroe was tentatively penciled in for the lead in *Gentlemen Prefer Blondes*.

With Monroe now practically accepted as the lead for the film, the studio wanted a "name" to bolster her in the other female lead role. Someone suggested that Betty Grable be teamed with Monroe, and the script altered to suit their individual talents. This idea was quickly quashed. Zanuck felt it would look like a remake of *The Dolly Sisters* or *Tin Pan Alley*, which had already been remade several times over the years. It was a ludicrous suggestion.

The boss decided to look beyond the studio for a name to co-star in their top budget production. He approached Howard Hughes who still had Jane Russell under personal contract, to find out if she was available. She was. But Hughes, reminding Zanuck that Miss Russell was already a major star, insisted that Miss Russell be given top billing over Monroe, with some songs specially written for her and her part fattened. Zanuck agreed; it would help keep Monroe in check if Russell were billed over her.

Meanwhile, Betty was a couple of weeks into her work on *Farmer*, but she was so enthusiastic about *Gentlemen Prefer Blondes* that she was already planning a two-week vacation, plus a couple of weeks at home to relax before the all-important call from the studio to report for costume fittings for the big one. She was blissfully unaware that her career was perilously close to a skid — a skid from which she might never recover.

Zanuck took a perverse delight in the knowledge that Grable was out of *Blondes*. Not that he particularly favored Monroe, but his immediate problems with his Number One box office champ were solved for the time being. The studio — and its head — could always determine the future of any wayward star.

It seems incredible that Grable never met up with Monroe or Russell (who was a long-time pal) in the commissary or elsewhere in the studio, but apparently such was the case. The very unlikelihood of the situation led one columnist to believe that Grable knew all along that Monroe was in for the lead in *Blondes*, and, aware of her now-precarious position at the studio, went along with the "secret." Such secrets are almost impossible to keep in the film world. But Betty always claimed she never knew of the plot. The supposedly unsuspecting Grable continued her work on *Farmer* while practically everybody at the studio knew Marilyn was set to play the role of Lorelei Lee.

Eventually Grable was called from the *Farmer* set to Zanuck's office. Betty claimed she fully believed she was to be told that the studio was ready to announce her start date for *Gentlemen Prefer Blondes*. Nevertheless she was suspicious. Their meeting was "cautiously cordial." They were playing a cat-and-mouse game with each other. Betty knew she could no longer trust the studio.

Zanuck complimented her on how well she was coming across in *Farmer*. Always to the point, Grable cut him short: "You didn't bring me all the way from the set to tell me that. What's on your mind?" The boss told her *Gentlemen Prefer Blondes* was going into production without her. Grable's heart dropped into her lap when he added that Monroe had been cast as Lorelei, the role she had so badly wanted — and needed.

That week, Jane Russell and Marilyn Monroe reported for work on the film that Betty Grable had pinned all her hopes on. It was just the role she needed to revitalize her career. Unfortunately, that career had been all but abandoned by the studio in its enthusiasm over Monroe, and there was nothing she could do about it. She returned to the *Farmer* set, told director Henry Levin she was feeling "unwell," and went home.

She returned next morning as though nothing had happened and resumed her role as Molly Larkin. Filming continued without incident with a totally professional Grable completing her assignment. All that was missing was her sense of humor and her enthusiasm for the role. Even the filming of Betty's second bathtub sequence in a film passed without any great publicity.

The two-week vacation now seemed pointless. It had been planned that Betty would have a complete rest, build up her tan (she was an avid sun-worshipper) and be fighting fit to start work on *Gentlemen Prefer Blondes.* Now that the world knew she had lost the top musical role of the year, what was the point? Grable was terribly depressed during this period — and small wonder.

The press was most interested in how she felt about losing the plum musical role of the year, and Betty had to drum up a response. "It's true that *Gentlemen Prefer Blondes* was bought for me," she told reporters. "But if Messrs. Schenck and Zanuck decide that Miss Monroe is more suitable, then that's all right by me. Making movies is their business, and I won't argue with them."[91]

Grable's vacation ran into three weeks before the studio called her. Zanuck, who had his finger on the pulse of everything that was happening around the studio, knew how she felt. But she was under contract and costing them $6,000 a week. He had to get her back to work.

He had a script by Samuel Fuller, based on a story by Dwight Taylor, which he found interesting in the light of the ever-vigilant American government's fears of Communist infiltration. Fuller was also contracted to direct the movie, entitled *Blaze of Glory*.

Top contract player Richard Widmark had already been penciled in for the lead. The female lead required an actress who could display a flashy cheapness, yet a vulnerability that audiences would believe in. First choice was Shelley Winters who was keen on the part — but she was also pregnant. Zanuck thought that Grable, with a little persuasion, could play the role.

Grable was invited to meet with the studio boss over lunch. A wary Grable, knowing full well she would have to get back to work soon, arrived at the studio commissary and was escorted to the Cafe de Paris, where the cream of the studio's top stars and executives dined. Writer/director Fuller was also present. He was keen to have Grable in his film and felt that his presence at the pre-production meeting might help coax her into it.

Zanuck came to the point. "You are at the crossroads in your career, Betty. Leave the glamour and tinsel to Monroe and her like. I want to build you up into a dramatic actress. It will open up a whole new career for you." Betty stopped him dead. "Forget it," she said. "We've been all through this before and you know my answer. You'll have to come up with something better than this. I know my time is coming to an end in the glamour roles. I'd like to venture into comedy — not farce. How about those films that made Carole Lombard such a famous comedienne? Why don't you get a scriptwriter working on something like that for me?"

Zanuck said he would, but meanwhile he was assigning her to an espionage thriller, called *Blaze of Glory*. "It's a skid movie, isn't it?" asked Betty. "No. It is a big-budget production and has Richard Widmark and Thelma Ritter with a strong supporting cast," replied the boss. Betty interrupted, "If you insist on shoving me in this dud, my fans will stay away in droves."

Zanuck took a deep breath. Whatever his feelings for Betty Grable, their professional relationship went back a long way, and what he had to say wasn't made any easier by her outburst. He told her that the New York office was frantic for more pictures starring Monroe. Officially, Betty was now no longer regarded as the studio's top attraction. Betty felt she had been hit with a hammer, but didn't let it show. Although she was deeply affronted, she kept her cool and listened quietly. But Zanuck's cruel words kept running round in her head.

He said the role in *Glory* wasn't too demanding, and insisted she at least read the script. Betty relented and left the studio with the script under her arm. That night she read it, and was "horrified" to find that she was expected to play a call girl involved with a pickpocket. The plot concerned Red spies operating in New York and showed the seedier side of the world of espionage.

The film was to be made in black-and-white and had a six-week shooting schedule. (The fact that the film was to have been shot in black-and-white was contrary to Grable's contract, which stated that all her films be filmed in Technicolor. Perhaps if she had referred this matter to her lawyer, she could have gotten out of the film on this technicality. But Betty didn't pursue the matter.)

More than ever, Betty was convinced it was indeed a "skid" movie — a film that a studio often shoved a fading star into to get rid of him or her once and for all. The star would begin a fruitless revolt, end up in breach of contract, and be dismissed, usually never to work in films again.

Not even the enthusiasm of director Fuller, who wanted her in the film, convinced Grable. She telephoned Zanuck and told him she was not interested in the film. He wasn't surprised; he expected her to refuse. Betty was hurt and angry at Zanuck's seemingly insensitive handling of her career at this crucial stage. He knew, she told herself, that she would accept a light comedy. But no heavy stuff.

She also telephoned Harry, who was in San Francisco. After listening to her tale, the only advice he could give her was to follow her own instincts, but he felt a mild panic set in when she told him what Zanuck had said about the New York office wanting more of Monroe, and that Betty was no longer top banana at the studio.

The only person who was enthusiastic about the role was Lillian, but she had no say in the matter. Once Betty had made up her mind, nothing would change it. She had never faced such a career dilemma before and had no one to turn to for professional advice. In all her years at the studio she had trusted Zanuck implicitly in his choice of vehicles for her.

As expected, she received the official letter from the studio's legal department, informing her if she did not report for work on the said date, she would be once again in breach of contract and would be suspended. Grable scanned the letter and threw it in the trash can.

A week or so later, she decided to return to the studio and face the music. She telephoned her agent who arranged to meet her at the gates. As she was preparing to leave home, she switched on the television set for the children.

During a local newscast, the announcer's voice jumped out at her. On the screen was a still of herself. "For the second time in her career, Betty Grable has been suspended by her studio," read the announcer. "The blonde pin-up star refused to report for work on *Blaze of Glory* which would have been her first dramatic role in eleven years."

Grable had been angry earlier, but now she was beside herself with rage. Immediately after the news bulletin, her telephone began ringing. Friends were calling to commiserate with her; others were anxious to find out what had happened between her and her boss. Of course, the press was always eager for a statement.

After answering a few calls, Betty redialed her agent and prepared a press release. Then she disconnected the telephone and checked her mailbox. As she feared, the letter from the studio's legal department was there.

It was official; she was indeed under suspension. Numbly she poured herself a large vodka. Normally she didn't drink so early in the day, but she was in shock. She mulled over this latest development. She couldn't have expected anything other than suspension, but the speed at which it was implemented left Betty feeling that Zanuck was desperate to get rid of her.

To the press, Betty appeared to be more calm about her latest censure. She had decided to be as benevolent as possible. Said Betty in the statement:

> The studio suspended me for refusing to play the part of a call girl. I felt such a part was not in keeping with my image, on or off the screen. My name sells family entertainment, and the character I was asked to play, however disguised, was not fit for family audiences. It is not the kind of film I would take my kids to see.
>
> The role was originally scheduled for Shelley Winters — and she is a heavy actress. God knows I am not in her league. And I will never be a Davis or a Crawford, so I don't understand Mr. Zanuck's reasoning when he insists on handing me these roles. I'm a song and dance gal. It's what I do best and what my fans pay to see. I'm sticking to the formula. The strongest line I usually have to say in my movies is 'Hi-ya, Joe'. I'll never understand why Mr. Zanuck picked on me. There are plenty of actresses in Hollywood who would have been happy to accept *Blaze of Glory*. [92]

Grable garnered favorable press for her gracious account of why she hadn't accepted the role, although she didn't do herself justice in "playing down" the caliber of the career she had worked so long and hard to mould.

The fact that Fox had once again suspended its top star left other big names around the various studios feeling decidedly uneasy. The only musicals of any importance shooting at the time were Warner Bros.' *Calamity Jane* with Doris Day, and Paramount's *Red Garters*, being completed by bright new singing sensation Rosemary Clooney and top ten recording star Guy Mitchell.

Hedda Hopper arrived on the James doorstep seeking an exclusive interview with Grable. She sympathized with Betty over her latest wrangle with the studio and asked her if it were true that she was scared to tackle a dramatic role.

"No," replied Betty, "not really, although most of my most dismal failures were in dramas. Of course, my biggest successes have been in musicals. Let's face it, Hedda. Very little acting is required of me in most of the films I do. However I'd welcome the opportunity to do comedy, the kind of parts that Carole Lombard did so well. But I suppose nobody believes I can do comedy."

"No plans for retiring then?" pursued Hedda.

The question appeared to startle Betty. "Oh, no," she answered. "I love working on pictures. In fact with Harry away on tour, and the children in school, I'd love to be making one right now."

Hedda sought out Dan Dailey in order to complete her feature, which would be published under the heading "Is Grable Quitting?" Dan was generous in praising his troubled co-star. "In real life Betty's shy and does not reveal her true personality," he said.

> I've always felt that what we see on the screen is not the actress, but Betty Grable herself. She has the greatest natural gift for dancing that I have ever found in a woman. She makes it looks so easy, but she has never developed it. The same applies to her acting. Making motion pictures is strictly a business with her. She likes the money and does enough on the sound stages to get by in a big way. But her chief interests lie in buying the family groceries and bathing her children! [93]

The disputed part went to Jean Peters and the film was retitled *Pickup on South Street*. It wasn't a bad movie and the role of the call girl could quite easily have been played by Betty, but no one would have believed her in it. It was too far removed from her usual screen image. As it was, Thelma Ritter stole the film by giving the best performance of her career. She was nominated for an Oscar as best supporting actress. The film was completed in two months and Betty was once again back on the studio's payroll.

Insiders knew what a blow Betty had suffered by losing out to Monroe in *Gentlemen*. It was the first time the studio had bought a major show for her, and she had lost it. Grable kept out of the limelight for a few weeks, shunning all publicity and social gatherings. She couldn't face people. "My career has taken a nosedive. And, in this town, once your slip is showing, you are out in the cold," she said.

To make matters worse, the 1952 box office poll results had been released. As earlier rumors had predicted, Grable had slipped to 20th place — out of the top ten for the first time in a decade. This was a devastating blow to the already beleaguered star. There was more bad news for Betty when she found that *Farmer Takes a Wife* was going out on general release as the lower half of a double bill, underneath a feature entitled *Dangerous Crossing* which starred Zanuck's current pet Jeanne Crain.

Yet many critics thought *Farmer* Grable's most charming picture in years; one even likened it to a scaled-down *Oklahoma*. Others felt that it was too "cozy" and "a glossy piece of Americana."

She looked good in the film and sang with great gusto. Grable apparently adapted easily to her first movie with an outdoor setting, and it looked as though she had at last shed her showgirl image. It is still regarded by her fans as one of the better films of her career. In fact, Betty's performance couldn't be faulted. She acted as though she had been around canal boats all her life. Despite several critics comparing it unfavorably with the "wonderful" original of 1935, Grable made a more spirited and lively Molly Larkin compared to Janet Gaynor's interpretation of the role. The only bad spot in the film was the overblown theatrical finale in which the cast appeared in a surreal stage setting, thus detracting from the original outdoor concept. It was the only scene in the film that failed to work.

Since the film had gone out on a double-bill basis, it was

difficult to judge just which film audiences were paying to see, so there were no financial returns available for *Farmer*. (After its initial release in Great Britain, Twentieth Century-Fox's U. K. executives re-released it a couple of years later to bolster Marilyn Monroe's *Bus Stop,* which was not doing very well at the box office.) Betty felt the double-bill release was a dirty trick on the part of the studio and that the bosses were determined to oust her with their tactics.

Meanwhile, the publicity machine worked overtime on Monroe. After all, the studio had cast her in a three-million-dollar musical and was quite happy to spend a few thousand dollars more to make sure the public knew all about her. Every quotable quote was wired around the world. When asked how she felt about playing second fiddle to Jane Russell, Monroe replied, "Whatever the billing, remember I am the blonde of the title."

Lost in their enthusiasm over the sexy newcomer, the publicists spared little time feeding the press stories or features on Grable. *The Farmer Takes a Wife* was lost in the deluge of pre-launch publicity being turned out for *Gentlemen Prefer Blondes*. The publicity department was exercising its all-powerful authority in promoting — and demoting — whomever they felt deserved such treatment. They could make or break stars with the tap of a type-writer key. Or so they thought.

With *Blondes* now in the editing stages, the studio was even more enthusiastic about Monroe. Even Zanuck admitted he was "pleasantly surprised" at the results. News advances stated that when the public saw Marilyn in her new image as a musical comedy actress, she would oust Grable from the throne — just as Marilyn had predicted in 1950!

The studio half-heartedly announced that Betty would be reteamed with Macdonald Carey in a marital comedy called *My Wife's Best Friend*, but the part went to Anne Baxter. Shooting began on this film before Grable even got a chance to see the script. Apparently, Richard Sale changed his mind about working with Grable again, and insisted the part be given to

Miss Baxter. There was nothing in the pipeline for Betty.

Her fans remained totally loyal to her, but the studio ceased to announce the amount of fan mail Grable received in its monthly press releases— though it wasted no time in letting the media know that Marilyn's mail was rocketing.

Asked about how she felt about toppling from the Top Ten, Grable appeared philosophical. "I hadn't had a picture released during 1952. There is nothing wrong with my career that one good film won't put right. And that's up to Schenck and Zanuck!" Unfortunately, the "one good film" was obviously *Gentlemen Prefer Blondes*. And that was a once-in-a-lifetime opportunity.

Grable stayed away from the studio for a couple of weeks. Officially, she was on vacation. Zanuck knew how upset she was at losing *Gentlemen Prefer Blondes* and that she was in a huff. Eventually, she was called to his office.

This time, there was no "welcome back to the fold, Betty" pep talk by Zanuck. There was no assignment for her, and she hung around cooling her heels. She felt she was still being "punished". Zanuck was in no hurry to cast her, and with good reason.

Monroe had finished her work on *Gentlemen Prefer Blondes* and word had it that she had emerged the new box office champion at the studio. Zanuck had no alternative but to search for new scripts to keep her busy. In his eyes Grable was now an also-ran. He hoped she would quit, but she refused to throw in the towel.

The studio boss had other problems. Hollywood was once again going through changes — this time, in its battle against television. Studios were experimenting with three-dimensional films and wide screens. Twentieth had perfected its own wide-screen process, CinemaScope ("You see it without the use of special glasses!" ran the publicity blurb) and Zanuck was anxious to try it out on a full-length feature film. There were several Westerns and dramas on the shelves, but Zanuck wanted something really spectacular to show off his CinemaScope process.

He had bought Lloyd Douglas's *The Robe*, and it was ready to go into production with Richard Burton, Jean Simmons, and Victor

Mature. The new screen process would bring out all the spectacle of the biblical epic. Zanuck was confident *The Robe* would be a winner, but would the new process adapt itself to contemporary sets and storylines? What he needed now was an intimate comedy to further test the new system.

A year or so earlier he had bought a story entitled *How to Marry a Millionaire,* but found it unsuitable for filming. However he liked the catchy title and handed the assignment to writer/producer Nunnally Johnson, who came up with the idea of remaking *Moon Over Miami* with three girls seeking millionaires in Manhattan.

Jean Negulesco was hired to direct the film, and the studio announced that they were starring Monroe in her first CinemaScope comedy, with two other actresses yet to be named.

Joe Schenck conferred with Zanuck. He told him he wanted Grable alongside Monroe in the new film. It was a business move, he said. "Grable is ten years older than Monroe, and it will show up on the big screen. She'll never be able to match up to her new rival in a straight comedy. Let Monroe carry the film, and we can say goodbye to Grable." That is what Grable truly believed when she was told of her new assignment.

> After pleading for two years to do a light comedy, suddenly it was handed to me on a plate. After all the rows and suspensions . . . I was immediately suspicious, but I read the script and liked the job Nunnally Johnson had done. The only problem was Marilyn. It wasn't her fault that she took off in a big way, that's the way the cookie crumbles. It happened to me all those years ago and, let's face it, we worked hard to get to the top.
>
> No. I was mad at the dictators and the politicians around the studio. Did Zanuck and Schenck really think I would sit back and let all the years of work I had put in for the studio, just slide away from me? I knew this would be my last chance to prove myself without any singing or dancing — and I wasn't going to let go that easily. It had gone beyond a studio wrangle. My professional reputation as an actress and entertainer was now at stake.

The third girl in the trio turned out to be the sultry Lauren Bacall, who had to be tested before the studio finally decided on her. She had never played comedy before.

Scriptwriter Nunnally Johnson worked a deal with director Jean Negulesco which allowed him to rehearse the actors with their lines before each scene. The plan worked well. Johnson said the actors were pleased with this arrangement.

> Betty Grable was well capable of delivering a line very well. She was a very good comedienne. I didn't know what Bacall could do because I'd never seen her play comedy, but she played it first rate. And Marilyn, I didn't know what to look for there. It was a good story. But everyone at the studio went around with their fingers in their ears guessing at what tantrums there would be on the set, and the gossip columnists did everything they could to make trouble for us.
>
> I don't think Grable and Bacall had ever met before. But Betty Bacall fell in love with Grable and thought she was the funniest clown she ever had the pleasure of knowing. Which was not far from the truth. Miss Grable was a real hooligan, and a fine, salty, bawdy girl without an ounce of pretense about her. She referred to Lauren on the set as Miss Bagel! In addition, Grable was turning in a better performance than anything she had ever done before.

Of Monroe, the writer recalled:

> The two Bettys had gone out of their way to help and make friends with Marilyn, but Miss Monroe was generally something of a zombie. Talking to her was like talking to somebody underwater. She was very honest and ambitious and was either studying her lines or her face during working hours. There was nothing to be said against her but she wasn't material for warm friendship. [94]

Now that the rival blondes were set to battle it out on the same film, the press conjured up all kinds of feud angles between them. But they were disappointed. There was no feud. As usual, Betty surprised the columnists by befriending Monroe. Grable was now thirty-six years old and fully realized she was no longer the youthful, leggy blonde of her pin-up days. She also knew she had had a good long run for her money during her illustrious cinema career. She and Marilyn got on famously.

The first day on set, the press men were out in force. Bacall and Monroe were in Grable's dressing room — since it was the nearest to the set — preparing to meet the press.

As Bacall coolly brushed her hair and checked her make-up, Betty painted her nails. She glanced across at Marilyn who was staring into the mirror in panic. "Get a hold of yourself, Marilyn," urged Betty." It's you they've come to see." Lauren Bacall stood up. "Ready, girls? Let's get it over with." Betty rose, adjusted her skirt and followed Bacall to the door. She turned, gave Monroe an appraising look, noticed that her feet looked rather shoddy and stopped in her tracks. "You can't go out there like that!" she exclaimed. Betty reached to her dressing table and opened a bottle of nail polish. Casually, as if she were dressing her children for school, she got down on her expensive knees and started lacquering Monroe's neglected toenails which were peeping out through her sandals.

If the gentlemen of the press could have witnessed that single incident — one glamour queen helping her rival — it would have quashed feud stories once and for all.

The trio of beauties eventually emerged from the dressing room and moved to the sound stage. Bacall and Grable were treated to the usual fanfare and were immediately surrounded by photographers and scribes. Monroe, who was last to leave the dressing room, almost turned back in fright as the cameramen mobbed her. It was Bacall who held on to her and brought her down the few steps to the studio floor.

The studio's newest sensation was suddenly mobbed by journalists, falling over each other to record some new quotes

BETTY GRABLE
Paramount Pictures

2-1 Early Paramount Publicity Photo, 1937.
2-2 Happy couple Betty Grable and Jackie Coogan in 1937, just months before their wedding.
2-3 Out on the town with George Raft in 1932.
2-4 Proud parents Betty Grable and Harry James pose with infant Vicki (March, 1944).

2-5   Early Paramount publicity shot of Grable in 1936. *Courtesy of the Academy of Motion Picture Arts and Sciences.*

2-6   Betty Grable eavesdrops in this scene from *The Day The Bookies Wept* (RKO, 1939).

2-7   Charlotte Greenwood and Betty Grable look glum in this scene from *Down Argentine Way* (20th Century-Fox, 1940).

2-8 Alice Faye and Betty Grable display their charms in this scene from
      Tin Pan Alley (20th Century-Fox, 1940).

2-9 Betty Grable stands by Victor Mature as he is arrested by detective
      Laird Cregar in this scene from *I Wake Up Screaming* (20th C, 1941).

2-10 Betty Grable dances up a storm here with the Condos Brothers in
      Moon Over Miami (20th Century-Fox, 1941).

1786-3

2-11 Betty Grable and Jack Benny in *Man About Town* (Paramount, 1939)

2-12 Lucille Ball and Betty Grable try their hand at hot-rod racing (1934).

2-13 George Montgomery, Betty Grable, and Cesar Romero in the film *Coney Island* (Twentieth Century-Fox, 1943).

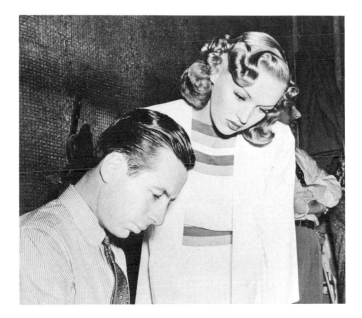

2-14 Betty Grable in a publicity shot for *Down Argentine Way* (20th
     Century-Fox, 1940).
2-15 Betty Grable goes over her lines with assistant director Joe Leffert
     for the film *Give Me A Sailor* (Paramount, 1938).
2-16 Broadway star Grable enjoys a romantic evening with wealthy
     Scots-American playboy, Alex Thompson (1940).

2-17 Boosting World War II morale, Betty Grable in a scene from *Pin Up Girl* (20th Century-Fox, 1944)

2-18 Betty Grable and Tyrone Power in a tender scene from *A Yank In the RAF* (20th Century-Fox, 1941).

2-19 Songsheet from the film *Footlight Serenade* (20th Century-Fox,1941). Unfortunately, this number was cut from the final film!

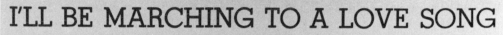

I'LL BE MARCHING TO A LOVE SONG

2-20 Starry line-up on the Fox Lot. From left: Cesar Romero, Carmen
Miranda, John Payne, Betty Grable, Edward E. Horton, Charlotte
Greenwood, Jackie Gleason, Helen Forrest, and Harry James on
the first day's work on *Springtime in the Rockies* (20th Century,
1942). *Courtesy of the Academy of Motion Picture Arts and Sciences.*

2-21 "The Other Side of Betty Grable" taken by Frank Powolney during the same shoot as THE famous pin-up shot which appears on the spine of this book. While it was said that the rear view was used because Betty was pregnant at the time, this front shot shows that if Betty was pregnant, nothing was showing !

that would spill from those highly glossed lips. By now, Marilyn realized that literally anything she said would be syndicated all over the world. So she played along with Bacall and Grable and kept the small talk very small.

The girls received fair coverage in the world's press over the next few weeks. And while Grable and Bacall were somewhat overshadowed by Monroe, several columnists believed that Marilyn should be wary of the "cute little blonde Grable," that Marilyn would have to use all her resources to upstage her, and that the studio had lost its marbles in favoring Marilyn over their Number One box-office queen. Of course, in those days, Marilyn was regarded as a joke by the press. Good for copy, but not much else, and Monroe knew it. She was determined not to be slotted into the dumb-blonde image that so many people thought she was in real life.

Grable took aside one newsman who was a particular friend and advised him, "Go easy on Marilyn. She's a good kid. She's the biggest thing that's happened in this town in years. She'll make it to the top." (Was this a wily ploy by Grable to keep in the press men's good graces, since Monroe was already the hottest new name in town?)

Some writers likened the casting of Monroe and Grable in the same film to a title fight. "Grable vs. Monroe," "Which Blonde Do Gentlemen Prefer?" and "The Battle of the Blondes" ran some of the headlines. Much of the fodder for these articles was provided by the studio's own publicity machine.

In reality, it was history repeating itself. Zanuck himself had co-starred Betty with Alice Faye in *Tin Pan Alley* to gauge public reaction (and preference). Alice had foiled the mean-spirited rivalry rumors by befriending Betty, as Betty did now with Marilyn.

Several incidents occurred during filming that proved beyond all doubt that Grable and Monroe were on the best of terms. In one sequence the girls were leading a fashion parade. After their "walk," they had to take up positions leaning against tall stools.

Betty had taken up her position and was posing prettily against one of the stools when Marilyn accidentally nudged her and Grable promptly toppled over. Co-star Cameron Mitchell, who was at the side of the set, rushed to Betty's aid, but Betty brushed everyone aside, saying, "It was my own fault — I was standing off balance." Marilyn was profusely apologetic, but Grable dismissed the incident, and continued filming.

Betty's genuine concern for Marilyn was completely mutual. Midway through the film, Betty received a call that her daughter, Jessica, had taken a bad fall at school. Director Negulesco advised her to leave immediately and, if everything was all right, to report for work next day. Fortunately the fall was not as bad as was first suspected and after a check-up, the child was given some aspirin and put to bed. Betty and Harry decided to turn in around 9 p.m. He was leaving next day on tour, and she would have to be at the studio at 6 a.m.

Shortly before they retired the telephone rang. Harry answered. He put his hand over the mouthpiece. "It's for you, Betty," he said, adding, "It's Marilyn." (Betty always had a joke at Monroe's expense whenever she telephoned. "Marilyn? Marilyn who?" Betty would always ask. Exasperated, Marilyn would say, "You know — MONROE!" "Oh, that Marilyn," Betty would laugh. Marilyn never caught on. It wasn't a malicious joke on Grable's part, just an example of her quirky sense of humor.)

Fearful that something had happened on the set in her absence, Betty took the call. Monroe and Negulesco were not getting on too well and many times Bacall and Grable had to intervene on Monroe's behalf when things became difficult. Over the phone Monroe said, "I just called to find out how your daughter was. Is she . . . is she all right?" Breathing a sigh of relief, Betty assured Marilyn that Jessica was fine. "Oh," said Marilyn, "That's good. I was sick with worry. Good night, Betty. I'm sorry if I disturbed you."

Grable replaced the receiver thoughtfully. Of all the people on the set that day — some eighty or ninety actors and technicians —

Marilyn Monroe, the world's newest sex symbol, was the only person who took the time to call and inquire about her daughter.

She defended Marilyn many times on the set, and her zany humor often dispelled awkward moments. Negulesco often found his patience stretched to the limit, particularly when Marilyn consulted her drama coach Natasha Lytess on how to play a scene.

It is true that Betty did say to Marilyn on their first day on the film, "Go get yours. It's your turn now. I've had mine." But, like Monroe, Grable was no dumb blonde. She genuinely liked Marilyn and felt a little sorry for her. Said Betty:

> The poor girl was listening to everybody and anybody, taking advice here and there. But very few folks really liked her. Some used her like a meal ticket, and I thought if I gave her a few words of encouragement it would help her to assert herself and rely on her own judgment.
>
> In one scene we had together, Marilyn was in a panic. She had no lines to speak — just react. It was a simple scene in our apartment just as Betty (Bacall) was about to be married. She said she didn't know how to handle it, despite several suggestions from her drama coach Natasha Lytess, which I am glad Marilyn ignored. I took her out of earshot of Lytess and told her: 'Just exaggerate — do what I have been doing all along. But exaggerate it about a hundred times.' She did, and the scene worked. I liked Marilyn. She had a lot going for her, it's just a pity that she fell into the clutches of others who were simply out to exploit her.

As Pola, Monroe had by far the showiest role in the film. With her nearsightedness, she had plenty of comedy business like walking into walls, following waiters instead of her escort, and ending up on the wrong plane. According to one source, Monroe initially objected to the role, as she did not want to wear glasses in the film. She preferred Grable's role of Loco. Marilyn felt that the studio was favoring Grable by giving her the better part. Director Negulesco convinced her that the role of Pola was the better one for her. [95]

Bacall played Schatzie, the brains behind the gold-digger plot, and she played the cool, quick-witted model to perfection. She was a joy in her first major comedy and opened up a whole new career for herself.

Betty's character, Loco Dempsey, was a slightly over-aged model, with nothing but sawdust in her head. She didn't have many funny lines to speak, but she used what she had to great effect in combination with some brilliant facial expressions, and made it all come together in a performance which she intended to make the movie moguls sit up and take notice. Grable was far from washed-up, and she showed it.

As Loco, she is the manhunter who brings the men back to the Sutton Place penthouse. First off, she meets Cameron Mitchell at the cold cuts counter and is instrumental in pairing him off with Bacall who treats him with disdain ("a gas pump jockey," she calls him). So gorgeous Grable is out on the town persuading handsome men back to the apartment while Monroe and Bacall languish around the living room appearing moody and pondering their predicament. Just as things look bleak for the man-hunting trio, Betty finds Texas millionaire William Powell in the fur department at Bergdorf's and he sees her home.

On being introduced to the other two girls he too falls for the Bacall charm! Powell promptly invites the three beauties to a function he is attending in town with several other millionaires. The girls eagerly accept, and just after Powell exits the scene, Grable, Bacall and Monroe turn to face the camera, each locked in her own thoughts at what delights the evening will bring. It is in this shot that Betty's star quality shines through. She has a lovely expression on her beautiful face that puts her co-stars in the shade.

In fact, viewing the rushes, Zanuck must have queried the wisdom of listening to Schenck. Grable was stealing the film from under Monroe, scene by scene. She had some fine comedy with that great supporting actor Fred Clark. He inveigles her to his lodge in Maine. Dizzy Grable, believing it to be an Elks convention, exclaims in blue-eyed amazement as she views the empty log cabin, "But where are all the other people?" And one of the biggest laughs comes when she contracts measles, then passes them on to Clark. Their weekend stretches into a two-week vacation. She also had several romantic interludes with handsome hunk Rory Calhoun, whom she subsequently marries.

It was too late to alter Grable's role at this stage, although he could have manipulated director Negulesco's work, as he had often done with other directors in the past, he didn't. Zanuck could only hope that the film editor's scissors would come down in favor of Marilyn Monroe. They didn't.

In the modeling sequence, Betty and Marilyn both had to display their legs, and the older star won hands down. She strutted across the sound stage in a show of confidence, and Monroe suffered by comparison. Her legs look heavy and flabby. However, it was for other parts of her anatomy that Marilyn gained the most publicity. As far as Hollywood was concerned, legs were out!

With *How to Marry a Millionaire* finished, Betty waited for her next picture. The publicity department announced that she would star in a comedy, *Mother Was A Marine*, which had been announced for her a year or so earlier. Nothing came of it, though it was made a couple years later with Sheree North and Tom Ewell as *The Lieutenant Wore Skirts*. There was also talk that she and Dan Dailey would reteam for a musical entitled *Show Business*, to be directed by Walter Lang. (It was made in 1954 with Dan, Ethel Merman, Mitzi Gaynor, and Marilyn Monroe under the new title *There's No Business Like Show Business* — and turned out very similar to Betty's earlier hit *Mother Wore Tights*.)

Harry Cohn, boss of Columbia, commissioned a script entitled *The Pleasure Is All Mine*, a musical remake of Jean Arthur's comedy *Too Many Husbands*. But he didn't have a star. Rita Hayworth was unavailable, and the Columbia chief didn't want to entrust it to newish stars Kim Novak or Constance Towers. He wanted a big name to carry his studio's first 3-D musical. He asked Zanuck if he could borrow Betty Grable. Amazingly, the Twentieth boss finally said yes. He was gearing his film schedule around Monroe, and there was nothing lined up for Grable, who was sitting around collecting her $6,000 a week paycheck. Therefore he was quite willing to off-load his former box-office champ to another studio. It was the first time in her long reign at Twentieth Century-Fox that Zanuck agreed to loan out his top star.

Grable, while flattered that she was Cohn's choice, refused. She was angry at Zanuck over *Gentlemen Prefer Blondes*, the shabby treatment given to *Farmer Takes a Wife*, and had still never really forgiven him for refusing to loan her to M-G-M for *Annie Get Your Gun*.

Besides, she was angry that the studio would get a full year's salary for her loan-out. Zanuck, enraged at Grable's attitude, suspended her for the third time in eighteen months. Betty realized she was now in deep trouble with the studio. Three suspensions in eighteen months was very bad news indeed — no matter how big the star.

The lay-off lasted several weeks which was a much shorter period than her previous suspensions, mainly because Columbia was not quite ready to go into production with the disputed film — and Harry Cohn was still anxious to have Grable in the role.

Critics around town began saying Betty was finished; she had grown too big for her dancing shoes. She defended herself. "I am interested in doing *The Pleasure Is All Mine*, but I haven't even seen the script yet, and I don't know who will be co-starring. I have to be very careful in my choice of acting assignments."

No sooner was Betty put back on salary, than she stormed into Zanuck's office and tore up her contract in front of the bewildered studio chief. After almost 14 glorious years — and they had been glorious — with Twentieth Century-Fox, Betty Grable had decided to call it a day.

Betty could quite easily have sat it out at the studio collecting her $320,000 a year salary until her contract ran out in three years time. But she wouldn't do that. Other big stars had been dropped recently at the studio, including Tyrone Power. Betty was the last remaining big name from the forties remaining at the studio. She knew it would be professional suicide to sit around collecting the money with nothing to show for it in on theatre screens. In fact she didn't even consult Harry James — or her mother — on her momentous decision to quit. She just couldn't stand being ignored by the studio and treated with so little consideration. She knew Twentieth had no plans for her and all she could see on the horizon was a series of skid movies which she would reject, resulting in the usual suspensions.

A short press statement was released by the studio on June 3, 1953: "Twentieth Century-Fox announced today that the studio and Miss Betty Grable have amicably agreed to end their contract."

Amicably! The word made Betty smile ruefully. She admitted she cried as she cleared out her dressing-room, which was being taken over by Monroe. "All the little mementos, personally auto-graphed photographs of famous co-stars, personal notes, gifts and souvenirs, record albums I had collected over the years came tumbling out of drawers and closets. I felt very sad."

Several press men were waiting for her as she made her way to the parking lot for the last time. They were expecting a rather sad figure to emerge. Not Grable. Dressed in figure-hugging white top and slacks and high heels, with her blonde hair shimmering in the afternoon sunshine, she looked great as she walked to the parking lot. She claimed that she was "very happy" with the way things had turned out. "I don't think it is a good thing to stay with the same studio for too long. They lose interest in you and concentrate on newcomers. I've no complaints though, I've had a good long run for my money."

With that, she put her familiar red Cadillac into gear and drove off through the studio gates onto West Pico Boulevard. She didn't stop to say goodbye to the security guards, most of whom she had known during her long stay at Fox. Although it was only a seven-minute drive to her home, she made a detour heading towards

Santa Monica and pulled into a diner parking lot where she burst into tears. Nobody paid much attention to the beautiful blonde in the red convertible drying her eyes. It had been a very traumatic day.

Nonetheless, the future didn't look too bad for Betty Grable. She had a good track record at the box office. Harry Cohn wanted her for a starring role, which she announced she would consider — as a freelancer. Perhaps a change of studio would be good for her at this point. She had burned her bridges at Twentieth Century- Fox, ignoring her mother's pleas to make her peace with Zanuck. She knew the studio wasn't big enough to carry her along with Monroe, and there was no way she was going to play second fiddle to anybody!

However, she did know that she had *How To Marry a Millionaire* in the bag, and she was confident it would open up a whole new chapter for her. Nunnally Johnson had told her he was very pleased with her performance. He felt that it was time to concentrate on expanding her career as a comedy actress and had promised to use her again at the first opportunity. Good advice, reasoned Betty, but who would give her the opportunity? Certainly not Zanuck.

She had to look elsewhere for such an opportunity. M-G-M and Paramount had been after her for years. She would instruct her agent to let it be known to these major studios that she was now available for work. Plus, she had many friends in the business. Gene Kelly had always told her when they met on social occasions that he would love to work with her. New-wave choreographer Michael Kidd, now at M-G-M, had been a long-time pal and often expressed a wish to choreograph her. For years she had been asked to headline a Broadway show, a move she had never seriously considered, having been away from live theatre for so long. Now it was a distinct possibility.

As the beautiful blonde dried her eyes and re-applied some mascara and lipstick in the diner parking lot, she began to feel more optimistic. She gunned the car out onto Arizona Boulevard and headed home — to Harry and the children.

The Girl With the Million Dollar Legs

The sun, as usual, was shining. It was a beautiful California day. She was still a very attractive woman at the peak of perfection, her figure was still the envy of millions of women, she was wealthy, and, more important, she enjoyed good health. She should be happy and count her blessings.

Yet she had a nagging feeling at the back of her mind that her long run of good fortune was coming to an end.

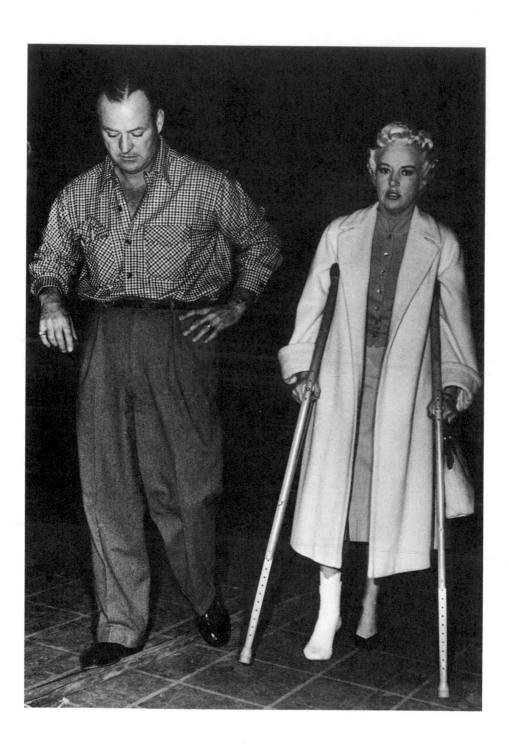

CHAPTER ELEVEN

The accession to the throne of the new queen of Hollywood, Marilyn Monroe, was accomplished in a bloodless coup. There was no battle, despite the best efforts of studio publicists to create one. The loser merely threw in the towel. It was a simple abdication without any hysterical drama being played out for all the world to see.

On the screen credits for *Millionaire*, Betty was top-billed — one of the conditions of her now-discarded contract. Zanuck fulfilled his part of the deal by at least obeying the studio's final contractual obligation to her. But for the first time since 1941, a co-star's name appeared over Grable's on the billboards.

The crown of the Queen of Hollywood sat easily on Marilyn's tousled locks, though Zanuck nervously hoped he would get as much mileage — and profit — as he had from her predecessor. He was right to be worried. Marilyn had her own ideas — aided by Natasha Lytess and others — on how her career should be handled.

Ex-queen Grable left final proof of her immensely successful reign over Twentieth Century Fox in the form of her performance in *How to Marry a Millionaire*. Instead of stealing the crown jewels, she'd simply stolen the show! And Zanuck knew it. No amount of cutting or re-editing could erase her stamp of royal authority on the finished film. Betty knew it, the critics knew it, and her fans knew it. *Millionaire* was the highlight of her career so far — a career that she hoped was far from over.

Millionaire was the world's first film to be completed in the CinemaScope process, but the studio held up its première, leaving *The Robe* to take all the plaudits. Once the biblical epic was premièred and out on its roadshow, however, Zanuck decided to go all out on *How To Marry a Millionaire*. He declared it would be premièred at the Fox Wilshire, and studio publicists were given the go-ahead to make it an evening to remember. Monroe would most certainly be there. Co-star Bacall was bringing husband Humphrey Bogart and — "oh, you might as well invite Grable," added the boss, almost as an afterthought.

The studio's publicity department called to invite her to attend. Betty hesitated. She said she'd like to go, "but Harry is out of town and I wouldn't have an escort." It was true that Harry was on tour, but Betty could quite easily have made the première. Monroe was attending without an escort (her boyfriend Joe DiMaggio was in New York promoting a baseball fund), so it was a lame excuse. The truth was that Betty just didn't want to be there. She always claimed she was "terrified" of premières.

It was a grave tactical error on Grable's part not to attend this glitzy première at this crucial crossroads in her career. The Los Angeles papers were full of double-page spreads on the event and the stars garnered quite a bit of coverage. Betty's name wasn't mentioned once! Apparently, she was not conspicuous by her absence. It was a successful night out for the stars who did attend, and Grable's no-show did her career irreparable harm. She needed all the good publicity she could get. Many fans attending the première expressed their disappointment at Grable's absence — as far as they were concerned, she was still Hollywood's top glamour-girl and Marilyn would never overtake her.

Betty's mother was furious with her. She knew Betty needed all the help she could muster. She accused Betty of handing over the reins to Monroe without putting up a fight. Betty disagreed; she felt she had no quarrel with Marilyn.

There was no animosity between Monroe and Grable. With Joe and Harry out of town so much, Marilyn called on Betty several times. "We used to cook up a couple of steaks, drink some champagne, and have a load of laughs. Marilyn was easy to get along with. She was a much wittier person than she was ever given credit for, and it used to make me so angry when I read some of the stories put out about her. She was a hard-working actress determined to consolidate her success, and she was determined to succeed in drama. Already she had proved what a fine comedienne she was."

Betty had some advice for her new pal when she learned that Marilyn was going on location with her next picture, *River of No Return* which was to be directed by Otto Preminger She told Marilyn that Preminger was a bully and that she should stand up to him. "He's all mouth and he doesn't like actresses," she stated.

Millionaire was critically acclaimed and even though Marilyn was officially named Queen of the Fox Lot, Betty got excellent notices for her performance. Many critics thought that she was the funniest of the trio. Dorothy Manners, writing in the *LA Examiner*, praised the film. "WHAT girls," she said, "Monroe, Grable, and Bacall . . . Grable is a doll as Loco, a fur-bearing blonde of the type most certainly preferred by gentlemen." Journalist Louis Berg also came out strongly in favor of Grable. He wrote that ". . . the public cannot have too much of Betty Grable. She is all over the place in *How to Marry a Millionaire* despite competition from co-stars Monroe and Bacall. Betty, conceding not a line and not a wrinkle to the years, plays one of the models, matching the younger girls in glamour and cheesecake. For our money, Betty overshadows all."[96]

Not long after the première of *Millionaire*, Marilyn and Betty were among dozens of stars invited to celebrate famed columnist Walter Winchell's birthday at a lavish party. Monroe called to ask if Grable were attending. Betty said she hadn't given it a thought, with Harry off on tour. Marilyn suggested that since Joe was also unavailable (he was in San Francisco this time) they should attend together. "OK," said Betty. "I'll pick you up around eight, so be ready!" (Marilyn's reputation for tardiness was legendary.) Then, as an afterthought, Betty added: "Since I am going to be your escort, do you think I should rent a tuxedo for the night?" Marilyn laughed heartily at the typical zany Grable suggestion.

Betty arrived at Marilyn's house at the appointed hour, and sounded the horn to signal her presence. Marilyn came to the window and waved. Five or six minutes passed without another sign of Marilyn.

Betty gave another toot on the horn, and Marilyn again came to the window and waved. This scene was enacted several times more over the next 10 minutes. Growing impatient, Betty got out of her car and rang the doorbell. Marilyn opened it at once. Betty saw she was dressed and made up. "What's the hold-up?" she queried.

"Come on in, Betty," said a flustered Monroe. "It's these damned gloves." Apparently Marilyn had spent the last hour trying to button up her evening gloves. "But they are out of fashion, Marilyn, they're impractical!" said Betty.

An exasperated Monroe said they were the only gloves she had and they would have to do. Betty patiently buttoned up the offending gloves so they could be on their way to the party.

Driving to the function, Betty asked her pal how she was going to manage to eat with those gloves on. Marilyn pondered the situation and said she would cross that bridge when she came to it.

Betty recalled the Winchell party as one of her happiest outings in years. Friend Lucy Ball was there, along with Dan Dailey, Liz Taylor, and many more of her showbiz friends. So too was Robert Mitchum who, according to Betty, was one of the sexiest men she had ever met. (Late in the evening Mitchum declared his undying love for her!) Zanuck also attended, engaging Betty in a long — and apparently friendly — conversation.

According to Betty:

The funniest incident of all was when it came to the buffet. Marilyn and I both had chicken drumsticks with a side salad. And the only way to enjoy drumsticks is to eat them with your fingers. Marilyn and I were seated at the same table with a couple of crusty old matrons. When Marilyn had finished eating, she casually dipped her gloved fingers into the fingerbowl of water, swished them around a couple of times and then proceeded to dry them on her napkin. She had kept her gloves on while eating as she knew she would have problems trying to get them off.

One of the old dears raised an eyebrow at Marilyn's table manners. Marilyn and I exchanged glances. I was dying to laugh. Like a scene out of one of her films, Marilyn shrugged innocently at the old ladies, then she turned to me and winked. We both dissolved with laughter. It was very rude of us, and I am sure the ladies thought we were bombed. But it was a great night, and I hadn't had so many laughs in ages.

As someone who made her own friends laugh, Betty found that Marilyn could and often did have the same effect on her. "She was very funny in a natural sort of way — she didn't deliberately set out to make you laugh, but, like me, she saw the funny side of everything — and made the most of the situation," recalled Grable. As Betty always maintained, "That's the only way to go through life!"

Harry's singing tour came to an end in August, and the family was reunited for the racing season at Del Mar. Although it had been some months since she had seen her friend, Betty Ritz, the two made up for lost time at the race track. It was one long round of fun for the foursome.

Said Betty Ritz:

> My husband was a very funny man, but nobody could make me laugh like Betty Grable did. She was a knockout once she got going. But she could also be a very angry lady. Once we both went to the powder room. I asked if she would lend me her comb. She hesitated. I said 'Come on Betty, I don't have lice.' Eventually she pulled out this big comb with half the teeth missing. She said: 'Take good care of it — it's my lucky comb.' Well, as luck would have it, I dropped the thing and it broke in two. She hollered and raged at me and left in a huff.
>
> I didn't know what to do. I went back to her box and she refused to speak to me, moaning to Harry James that I had

broken her good luck comb. Later, I went to the local store and bought up all the combs I could find and had them gift-wrapped in a beautiful box, then had them sent to her. I think the whole race track heard her screaming with delight as she unwrapped the box. She had forgiven me. She was quite a lady. [97]

Back in her home surroundings, Betty took life easy. She and Harry celebrated their tenth wedding anniversary in the company of old friends, including the Ritzes, Lucy and Desi Arnaz, Betty's mother and father, sister Marjorie and her husband, and a bunch of their racing friends. Betty was immensely proud of her ten-year marriage. It was the focus of her life, and she loved Harry deeply. She always maintained that her husband and daughters came before anything else.

When Harry was on tour, he called her every night. And Betty made sure to always be there for that call. It didn't matter if she was out with friends; she always made sure to leave in time for that call, much to the annoyance of her table partners who felt that the evening ended when Betty left. She felt it was her duty to be there for his call, but friends believed that Harry was, in a way, checking up on her. Although he himself played around, he was extremely jealous of her. He should have known better. Betty would never have put her marriage at risk for a one-night stand. Not that she didn't have her share of unwanted suitors. She had many!

One such suitor was a contract player at Fox. He had appeared one afternoon on the *Wabash Avenue* set and quickly sought out Betty. She recalled, "The usual smooth talk followed and he asked me out to dinner. He knew Harry was on tour so to get rid of him I said brightly; 'Why don't you come over to my place and I'll fix us something'." The actor couldn't believe his luck!

Betty, always the practical joker, hatched a plot with her hairdresser Marie that would fix the young man's unwanted advances once and for all. After rehearsal she went home, showered, removed her make-up, tied her hair up in a scarf and dressed in a loose wool sweater. The children had been in bed since 7:30, which gave Betty half an hour to prepare the "romantic" dinner for two.

Just before her "date" arrived she slapped on some cold cream — "just enough to show it was there" — and took some hamburgers and french fries from the refrigerator and put them in a pan to cook. When her suitor appeared on the front porch, he was greeted by Betty — and the smell of burnt food. She acted as if everything were fine, seated her guest, and offered him a drink. After the usual small talk, she got up to go to the kitchen to "prepare" dinner. The telephone rang. Marie Brasselle carried out her part of the plan by talking nonsense to Betty. They gabbed for about ten minutes; then Betty apologized, saying she would have to go, or dinner would be "simply ruined."

Blithely she tripped into the kitchen, telling the young man dinner would be ready in a few minutes. Presently, she returned with a plate of cremated hamburgers and soggy french fries, and set them on the table as though it were a Cordon Bleu meal. Her date seated himself at the table, as Betty encouraged, "Help yourself, there's plenty more in the kitchen if you are hungry!"

Dumbfounded, he helped himself to a hamburger which fell on to his plate with a decided clunk. Betty paid no attention, as she garnished the inedible meal with an assortment of relishes.

"Betty," he said at length, "I know you've had a busy day at the studio. Why don't we call a babysitter and we'll eat out?"

Betty hadn't anticipated this, and started to make all sort of excuses. As if on cue, the dining room door opened and in walked young Vicki, complaining of tummy ache. Although this wasn't part of the plan, Betty welcomed the diversion. She soothed Vicki, asked her guest to warm up some milk, and took Vicki upstairs to bed. When she returned, the actor was in the kitchen heating the milk. Betty thanked him, but he had had enough. Making some lame excuse, he left in a hurry. Betty sighed with relief, but her humor deserted her as a twinge of guilt took its place; she felt she had been leading the poor man on. She attended to Vicki, threw the "meal" into the garbage disposal, and retired for the night.

The amorous actor never returned to the set and steered clear of Betty in the commissary. However, the following Christmas she received a cookbook, beautifully wrapped with a jolly greeting card — unsigned.

Years later, Betty was at a social gathering when she ran into the "wolf." He was by now happily married, raising a family and in the production side of the business. She confessed that he had been set up that night. He took it well, admitting that the events of the evening had puzzled him considerably. He told Betty he had confided the incident to some friends, who laughed and told him that Betty Grable was just the kind of girl who would play such a trick on an unwanted suitor. However, he steadfastly denied that he had sent the cookbook. Betty never did find out who had played that trick on her!

Most would-be suitors weren't so easily put off, and many times Betty resorted to being downright rude to get rid of them. Betty was no fool when it came to spotting phonies.

I can spot them a mile off. It makes me uncomfortable to be around such people. Actors seem to draw them like magnets and I have had many good friends go under financially through their association with such people.

It's a shameful thing to say, but it does make one wary of making new friends. Often I find myself thinking, 'Why is he/she interested in me?' It can take me some time to decide to cut a person dead in his tracks with a look or some unsubtle remark. More often, I remain polite but distant, and if the person saw he wasn't getting through to me, he would concentrate his 'talents' on some other personality.

With Harry away so much, I guess some of the wolves around town thought I was fair game. Even if I had been interested in playing around, there just didn't seem to be enough time in the day for such activities. For me it was all work and sleep. Once I am in bed, I can nod off in seconds — not very romantic, is it?

Columnists were interested in Betty's future. She had accompanied Bob Hope on a visit to a U.S. Air Force base in Alaska and was also spending a lot of time touring veterans' hospitals, chatting with wounded soldiers who had just returned from the Korean War. At this point in time, she had nothing more definite planned. "Maybe Harry will give me a job with his band — have pierced ears, will travel!" she joked.

As it turned out, Harry was interested in employing her. He had been contracted to a week's engagement at the Chicago Theatre in November, 1953, and suggested that Betty appear on stage with him. He felt it would help her get reacquainted with the feel of a live audience. At first Betty wasn't sure, but Harry warned her: "If you don't do it now, you never will."

Harry James and His Music Makers on stage were a good enough draw, but Harry backing Betty Grable in her first live stage appearance in years was a stroke of genius. It would ensure sell-out performances wherever they played. Betty fell in with the idea, but instead of fronting his band, she suggested they make it a variety bill, with other acts opening the show, and Betty and Harry's band taking over for the second half.

Harry agreed. Betty immediately set to work. She contacted choreographer pal Billy Daniel, and they began rehearsing. Eventually the show grew to include Betty, Harry and his band (including famed drummer Buddy Rich), accordionist Tommy Gumina, and tap dancers Lewis and Van.

Betty's idea was quite revolutionary and ahead of its time. Many stars later took big shows on the road, mostly under heavy financial backing, so that no matter if they flopped, they still came out of it with no loss to themselves. Betty and Harry were not very business-minded and didn't stop to think of the risk of staging such a show — especially when it was financed with their own money!

There were other risks as well. Betty felt she was taking a tremendous gamble with her career. If the show flopped, word would quickly get back to Hollywood and any hopes of continuing a screen career would vanish. In films it was much easier to cope with a flop. The studio would protect their investment by putting her into a sure-fire hit as had happened to Betty a couple of times in the past. Stage work was a different proposition. She would get only one chance before the critics to do her best singing and dancing — and she felt a little rusty. It would be a hard grind to perfect an act for the show. But she was keen to work with Harry and went along with it.

"Just after we were married," said Betty, "I used to accompany Harry wherever he was playing when I was between films. I used to sit backstage until word would get out to the audience that I was around. They began calling for me, and eventually I had to do a couple of numbers — dressed in an old pair of slacks and no make-up!"

However, Betty was very well made-up and outfitted for her Chicago appearance. Her costumes were created by her favorite dress designer from her film days, Billy Travilla, and cost a cool $20,000.

Queried about the wisdom of staging such a lavish show for only one week, Betty said, "We want to see how the show goes in Chicago. Then if it works out as we hope, we can plan further dates. We have an idea that this is the type of show we can do every year in theatres all over the country."

The revue was a roaring success, but financially it didn't recoup the money spent on staging it. If the couple had played Chicago for a month, they would have seen a handsome return on their investment. As it was, the week-long show had been sold out weeks before it opened and could easily have supported a longer run. Chicago critic Sam Lesner wrote that it was the "smoothest and best balanced revue seen in the city for some years. Betty sings and dances effectively and looks [like] a million dollars." [98] *Variety* also covered the show and agreed it was a success, describing Betty as an "elegant" dancer.

One night Betty arrived at the theatre and noticed a tall slim youth who had been hanging around the stage door each evening. She suddenly remembered who he was, and approached him. "It's Mikey, isn't it?" The surprised youth stammered affirmatively.

Betty invited him backstage to watch the show, and introduced him to Harry.

The young man was a fan named Mike Levitt, and he recalled how he had first met Betty.

> As a kid, I used to go down with some pals to the La Salle Street station, autograph hunting. Many of the stars had to stop over there changing stations en route to New York. One day we asked the car attendant if there was anybody famous on board. He told us Betty Grable was aboard with her children. I immediately gave him my autograph book and asked him to get Betty to sign it . . . 'to Mikey' She had always been my favorite. The attendant returned a few minutes later and asked: 'Which one of youse is Mikey?' I was taken aboard and got to meet my idol.
>
> She was charming, dressed in a man's shirt and slacks with her blonde hair tied back in a bandanna. She asked me all about school, my favorite films, and my home life. Before I left, she introduced me to Vicki and Jessica, and asked for my home address and my birth date. I left that train walking on air. Imagine — getting to meet your favorite movie star! I was the envy of all my school friends. [99]

Betty had written Mikey often in the interim — sending him birthday cards, Christmas greetings, an expensive camera, and a cashmere sweater. Mikey faithfully continued to write to his favorite film actress.

Now the friendship was being renewed four years later. That friendship lasted until Betty's death. There is no doubt she was very fond of the young man and often paid for his trips to visit her at home.

Harry and Betty returned to Los Angeles just after Thanksgiving, in time to prepare for their annual Christmas family reunion. This year, however, the get-together was not so happy. Betty's father had been ill for some time, with heart and bladder problems. The festive period passed quietly, and her father was hospitalized early in the New Year.

Before the holiday Columbia again approached Betty with its film offer. It had now been re-titled *Three for the Show*, and Harry Cohn wanted Betty to co-star with William Holden and Henry Fonda in the new CinemaScope musical. Betty decided to keep Cohn waiting.

So, Betty took her first tentative step into television. The Chrysler Corporation, anxious to secure glamour names for their prime-time slots, approached Betty, offering her top billing with Mario Lanza in their first-ever color spectacular. This offer she accepted. As was usual for films, Grable and Lanza pre-recorded their songs prior to live transmission. Unfortunately the standards of sound technology in those early days were not up to the present highly skilled technical levels, and mime flaws were obvious throughout the telecast.

Betty got more publicity for the stunning low-cut, revealing gold lamé gown she wore for the show than she did for her performance. Her legs were well in evidence in the "Digga Digga Doo" number, though her stand-out number was "One For My Baby," which she sang with great feeling.

Louella Parsons quizzed Betty in an interview about her reluctance to report for work on the film at Columbia. Replied Betty:

> I know I have been often criticized for the delay. I liked the story and I thought it was right for me. Besides, I had been on suspension for months and I know it's not good for me to be off the screen for so long. [But] when I couldn't find out who was going to be playing opposite me (since the studio last approached her, Holden and Fonda were now busy on other pictures) I said to myself, 'This is not for me'. I was very annoyed when people said I took this step because of the money. Columbia and I had settled all that. (Her fee was $200,000.) [100]

Betty's father died of uremic poisoning in February, 1954. He was 70 years old. It was a very sad time for the Grable family. Betty loved her father dearly. Her hopes that her mother and father would get together again had never materialized although they had been considerate and tolerant of one another.

Conn's death ushered in a time of reflection. Betty realized she had shown an amazing lack of foresight in the early fifties at Twentieth Century-Fox. She should have quit the studio then, instead of going through all those suspensions and incurring all the resulting bad publicity. Very few stars were under long-term contracts now — most of them set up their own deals and traveled to wherever the work was. Practically the only musical star left working under a long-term contract was Doris Day, and even she was about to part from her parent studio, Warner Bros..

In February, 1954, Grable at last reported to Columbia to begin work on *Three for the Show*. She was to be paid the agreed-upon $200,000 fee, and was happy to be able to bring in her own cameraman, Arthur Arling, as well as choreographer Jack Cole, and her friend and stand-in Angie Blue.

After Betty signed the contract, she found the script had undergone several changes. Instead of a light, sophisticated comedy, the studio had come down heavily in favor of the double-entendre. The story concerned the exploits of a Broadway star who believed her first husband had been killed in action in the Korean War. She remarried, only to find husband Number One turning up just as she was about to set off on her honeymoon with husband Number Two.

Up-and-coming Broadway actor Jack Lemmon was installed as her new leading man, and the other top roles went to dancers Marge and Gower Champion. Betty had known the Champions for several years and got on well with them. The thought of working with Jack Lemmon, however, terrified her. Betty, ever self-conscious of her "acting limitations," later admitted she had seen Jack in his first film, the Judy Holliday comedy *It Should Happen to You*, and had been so impressed with his performance that she worried that she wouldn't be able to match up to him. But on their first meeting, she and Lemmon got on famously. His wacky sense of humor and likable personality put her at ease right away. She later learned that he had been just as nervous about meeting her!

Recalled Lemmon:

> Betty was one of the most helpful co-stars I ever worked with. Had she been like some of the other leading ladies I had later in my career, I think I would have quit the film business. There was no big-star pretense about her.
>
> She was a very co-operative worker and never kept anybody waiting. A true professional. And what a looker! Betty, Judy (Holliday) and Rita (Hayworth) were my favorites. [101]

By the time filming was over, she was far from happy with Columbia in general. She felt it an impersonal place and was appalled when she was summoned to the set via the public address system. No way to treat a star! And if she had thought Zanuck was a monster, there were no words to describe her feelings for Harry Cohn.

One telling incident involved an important close-up with Jack Lemmon, set in the back of a car. On her way to the studio that morning, Betty had been bitten on the cheek by a mosquito and the resulting welt was quite obvious. Her make-up man did what he could, but cameraman Arling told her the mosquito bite was showing up on his view finder. Betty asked director H.C. (Hank) Potter to shoot around her until the offending bite mark disappeared. Potter said he would have to consult Cohn, and went off to confer with the boss. He returned some minutes later. "We carry on filming — there must be no delays." Lemmon and Grable went into their scene, and the offending blemish showed up on the final print of the film.

Betty said Zanuck would never have permitted any of his stars, male or female, to go before the cameras with any kind of facial disfigurement showing.

According to Betty, she was later offered a role in Columbia's *Pal Joey* opposite Frank Sinatra, but she vowed she would never work there again. The part went to Rita Hayworth after Marlene Dietrich also refused.

Generally the critics were kind to Betty in her first film in two years, but not to the film itself. The direction was poor, and the finished product proved disappointing, especially to Betty, who was hoping this one would revitalize her film career.

It wasn't a total flop; the musical numbers were lively, particularly the opening number played over the credits — a Harlequin/Columbine sequence in which a stunning Betty fairly strutted across the CinemaScope screen displaying her still-perfect legs. Marge and Gower Champion also appeared in this lavish scene. In another big production number, "Down Boy," Betty appeared as the queen of a male harem. And the finale, "How Come You Do Me Like You Do," was pure Jack Cole magic. Grable danced as she had never done before — sexily, sensually and very erotically in this arresting Latin American number.

(In this sequence, Grable was unfairly accused of "doing a Monroe" as the number was reminiscent of Marilyn's "Heatwave" routine in *There's No Business Like Show Business* — which should come as no surprise, since that, too, was choreographed by Cole. Betty's number was both more vivacious and more professionally executed; her terpsichorean training shone through.)

It was the script that let the stars down. There were long pauses between lines — possibly in hopes for laughs, but the script did not have many — and the story moved along at a snail's pace. More numbers and more inventive comedy situations would have helped enormously. (To be fair to Columbia, the studio had had to alter their script in order to please the Hays Office and the Catholic League of Decency, which insisted on certain restrictions and even had the film temporarily banned. Apparently they were not pleased with the polygamy theme. The film's principals had to be recalled to re-shoot several key scenes, making it one of the longest projects Grable had ever worked on.)

In the end, what should have been a successful comeback vehicle for Betty turned out to be a routine backstage musical with all the usual cliches. It had little going for it except its distinction as Betty's first musical in CinemaScope and the first-ever release of a Grable movie soundtrack. (It is now a rare collectors' item).

Considering the reviews, the film did quite good business and seemed to please Grable fans, who were delighted just to see her on the screen again. Some critics felt that Grable looked much older than she should have (she was thirty-eight on the film's release), but an English reviewer summed up most fans' sentiments with one of the shortest notices on record: "Never mind the plot, gorgeous Grable more than makes up for it." [102]

For Christmas, 1954, Betty took her mother and the children to Lake Tahoe for the holiday. Harry was appearing there, and she wanted her mother away from the usual festive surroundings of Beverly Hills, since this would be their first Christmas since her father had passed away.

While the family was on vacation, the Internal Revenue Service impounded the Baby J ranch and all its stock for non-payment of taxes due a few years previously. To their horror, Harry and Betty found that their "tax shelter" had sprung a leak, and their accountant had disappeared! They needed money — and fast.

Betty's unlikely rescuer came in the shape of Twentieth Century-Fox. They, too, were having their problems.

Marilyn Monroe was firmly ensconced as the studio's top attraction due to the departure of most of her competition — Mitzi Gaynor was now freelancing, and June Haver, who had married Fred MacMurray after a spell in a convent, had left the scene. Unfortunately for Zanuck, Marilyn was also refusing roles right, left, and center.

Unlike Grable, Marilyn was determined to be accepted as a dramatic actress and quite rightly refused to be moulded into a model of her predecessor. After only a couple of years of top stardom, she was suspended for refusing to report for work in *How To Be Very, Very Popular*. It was her second suspension since Grable had departed the lot, and the studio threatened to sue her for breach of contract. Zanuck was reported to have admitted that he had been a fool to ever have let go of Grable.

Another newcomer, Sheree North, fresh from her brief but

triumphant showing in Paramount's *Living It Up* (a one-spot dance number which had caught the eye of the critics, rather similar to Betty's show-stopping routine in *The Gay Divorcee*), had been signed up by Twentieth as a replacement lest Monroe become temperamental. Old habits died hard at Twentieth Century-Fox.

But they couldn't tether the free-spirited Monroe to a post. She simply walked out. Marilyn had first been suspended by the studio for refusing to star in *Pink Tights*, stating that it was a "rehash of an old Grable movie." A promotion preview of the film, which was to have co-starred Frank Sinatra, Dan Dailey, and Mitzi Gaynor, was set up starring Sheree North, executing a dance number originally planned for Marilyn. But Sinatra also walked out on the project and it had to be abandoned.

Now, the studio didn't want to risk the untried North carrying *Popular*, and was looking for a "name" to help sell the big-budget comedy at the box-office. Had Marilyn accepted the role, there would have been no problem with a co-star not being a top name; the public would have flocked to see the film on the strength of Marilyn's billing alone. But with Sheree still an unknown quantity, the studio knew it had to have a big name to help sell the film. And Nunnally Johnson was instrumental in naming that name —what better "name" than Box-Office Betty?

But would she return to the studio that had given her such a hard time over the past few years? Her agent was contacted, and Betty signed on the dotted line a few days later — for a fee of $200,000 plus expenses. And, of course, top billing. Trusting Nunnally Johnson implicitly, she hadn't even read the script.

The film was purported to be a bright, witty comedy in the *Millionaire* vein, and there would be dance routines added for both Grable and North. They were to play a couple of chorus girls/strippers who were on the lam after witnessing the on-stage murder of one of their stripper friends. (A much funnier variation of this plot, entitled *Sister Act*, was made in 1992 as a vehicle for Whoopi Goldberg.) Unfortunately, Nunnally Johnson's latest script was not nearly as witty as its predecessor —and, unbeknownst to

Grable, Marilyn Monroe had been warned off it just in time.

A sample of the dialogue went something like this:

Cummings: What happened?

Grable: Well, he shot the stripper — that's what happened. Shot her — right in the middle of her act!

As a firm believer in omens, Betty should have had ample warning that things were not going to go well. Shortly before the film's anticipated start date, she stepped out of bed, not realizing her foot was still "asleep", and sprained her ankle. The first day of shooting had to be delayed a week until her ankle healed, and she missed a television appearance on NBC's "Shower of Stars," having to be replaced on the program by the youthful Shirley MacLaine. Even so, Betty reported to Twentieth Century-Fox for costume fittings on crutches, probably the only star ever to do so. She met Miss North and, predictably, they became good friends.

On her first day back at work, the studio pulled out all the stops to make her welcome. As she entered the elegant 1930s-style commissary for lunch, Betty gaped open-mouthed at the sight before her. A huge banner stretched the length of the entrance area, proclaiming "Welcome Back, Betty!"

Other diners and staff applauded as she walked to her table. Betty was visibly moved at the gesture; she had kept the studio going almost single-handed through some very rough periods, but it was nice to have that fact recognized.

Sheree was delighted for her, and later said: "I remembered to be as nice to the lowest worker on the set [as Betty always was]. That was one of the reasons Betty lasted so long — she never made an enemy on the crew." [103]

Comedy actor Robert Cummings (they had starred together in *Moon Over Miami*) was delighted to be reunited with Betty. However, on studying the script they realized they were expected to behave like a couple of teenagers. The character Betty was to play was called Stormy Tornado! Sheree was the more sedately named Curly Flagg. Nearing forty, Betty expected a role with a little more sophistication, instead of being saddled with the part of a dumb-blonde stripper. She felt the part wasn't as witty or classy as it should have been, and quickly became disenchanted with her "triumphant" return to her home studio. But she needed the money, so she stuck with it and gave the role her usual professionalism.

Grable looked good in the early scenes, particularly in the chorus routine, but as filming progressed it was obvious that she was handing the film to Sheree North. Some of Betty's lines were very funny and she made the most of them. According to the critics, she raised most of the laughs in an otherwise lackluster film.

Understandably, Sheree received the bulk of the publicity during the filming with the studio enthusing about her potential as the "new" Monroe. At this time, the studio didn't know that Sheree had no intention of being the "new" anybody, and was biding her time till the day she could emerge as a dramatic actress — which she did later, very successfully.

Once Betty did make the columns, but purely by accident. During a rain sequence, she had to wear a pink head scarf. After removing the wet scarf, she was about to speak her line when the director yelled "Cut!" She looked beyond the camera to Johnson, wondering what had gone wrong with the scene. The "rain" had washed the dye from the scarf onto Betty's blonde locks, which were now a bright pink! There was nothing to do but rebleach her hair on the spot. The cast and crew waited around all morning while the hairdresser got to work on the Grable tresses. A dollar scarf had cost the studio a $30,000 production delay.

On the film's release, the critics blasted Grable and North. One pointed out that the darling pin-up of the forties was now hardly able to bend at the knee. The comment was rather unfair considering Nunnally Johnson had cut Betty's dancing to one chorus number with Sheree and two other girls, and throughout filming she had suffered a lot of pain in her recently sprained ankle.

However, there were several positive reviews. Wrote A. H. Weiler, of the *New York Times*: "Sheree North, as the somnambulistic blonde, and Betty Grable, her equally blonde wisecracking partner, are a treat to the male eyes. They handle their dialogue with ease and zest." *Variety* noted that "the wild and wacky doings dreamed up by Nunnally Johnson are dressed up considerably in eye appeal by having the Misses Grable and North running through most of the footage in costumes appropriate to their striptease profession. The CinemaScope lensing does justice to the ladies."

But Betty's personal assessment of the film summed up the feelings of the majority of the critics. She described what should have been a bright, wacky, freewheeling comedy romp in the *Millionaire* vein as "incredibly bad . . . a turkey!"

The only real winner on the film was Sheree North; her rock 'n' roll routine at least proved what a great dancer she was. Sheree also received top billing over Betty on the posters, even though Twentieth Century-Fox lived up to the letter of their agreement by giving Grable top billing on the credits. By the time the movie came out, however, Betty claimed that she would have been much happier if her name had been removed from the film altogether!

The truly sad thing about the film was its wasted potential. It should have been a hit, given its talented cast — Betty's old pal Fred Clark, new funny man Orson Bean making his big screen debut, Tommy Noonan (so good in Judy Garland's comeback film, *A Star is Born*), and of course the polished playing of Bob Cummings, whose scenes with Betty came over very well considering the material they had to work with. Another highlight of the film was wonderful comedy actress Alice Pearce, who gained great notices for her cameo role in *On The Town*, and later became an internationally known personality when she played the neighbor in the hit TV series, "Bewitched." There was no shortage of hit-making talent in *How To Be Very, Very Popular*, but it just didn't come together.

Betty retired to lick her wounds She knew that two poor films in a row — no matter how loyal her fans were — was bad news indeed. Only months after Betty completed her latest assignment at Twentieth Century-Fox, it was announced that Darryl Zanuck had resigned as head of the studio. It gave Betty no great pleasure to read of his resignation. She realized that she owed her big break to Zanuck and, that for the most part, he had guided her through her career with great professionalism. "He was a star maker," she admitted, "and if he hadn't given me my big chance in 1940, goodness knows where I would have ended up."

For the next couple of months Betty refused all offers of work, although television companies had become very interested in her. It appears that she was keeping to the statement she had made years earlier: "I'll quit while I'm ahead . . ." She maintained that she had been sincere when she'd said that, but she hadn't reckoned on the power of television, which by now had superseded movies as the top entertainment outlet. She hadn't reckoned on her mother still pushing her. And she hadn't reckoned on her fans.

Thousands of them wrote to her, suggesting ideas for movies; many wrote to network chiefs asking why her old films weren't shown on television. Many fans wrote from Britain asking her to make an appearance at the London Palladium, which had become a mecca for American stars in the post-war years. Danny Kaye, Dorothy Lamour, Betty Hutton, Judy Garland, and Carmen Miranda all had outstanding success at the famous theatre.

Coincidentally, Moss Empires, the largest theatre chain in Britain (and owners of the Palladium) approached the Jameses' agents inquiring if Betty and Harry would be interested in a two-month tour of Britain. The tour would take in Birmingham, Manchester, Liverpool, Glasgow, Edinburgh, and Newcastle, ending with a two-week top-of-the-bill stint at the Palladium. The couple agreed and everything looked set for the trip. Betty was enthusiastic that the children would also be able to visit Europe with them. Another plus for Grable was that the Rank Organization had made tentative approaches to her agent asking if she would be interested in a film deal.

Then the British Musicians' Union stepped in. They claimed they were tired of British musicians going without work because of the influx of big bands from the United States.

Apparently Betty and Harry were most welcome, provided Harry conduct an orchestra made up of top British musicians for the tour. Harry refused to travel without a guarantee that his band would be allowed to play; Betty refused to travel without Harry; and Moss Empires refused to book Harry without Betty. It was Grable they were really after to top the bill!

The result was that the tour was called off, and Betty's British fans would have to wait another fifteen years or so for their idol to set foot on their island. Instead, Harry negotiated a tour of the Eastern States, while Betty remained home to fulfill her obligation to NBC's "Shower of Stars" spectacular.

In an interview, the young director of the show described his working relationship with Betty — with tongue planted firmly in cheek:

> This girl is a problem to any director. She has no confidence in herself. She has never realized just how great she is. She thinks it's done with publicity!
>
> But nobody set her box-office records without a touch of the real thing. I can name you a dozen blondes who had bigger build-ups than Betty — but where are they now? Last year Betty was hurt and missed one of our shows. Shirley MacLaine stepped in and overnight became a television star. Now we were asking Betty to do a number called "Swinging the Muses." It had a catchy tune and bright lyrics, with Betty dressed in the costume of a Greek goddess. Rita Hayworth first did it in a movie — (*Down To Earth,* in 1947).
>
> It was bad enough asking her to use another star's material, but we had Shirley (MacLaine) on the same show. I don't see how we could have made it tougher on Betty. But all she asked was: 'Please give me a real showy set and lots of pretty girls. That's how the public expects to see me — surrounded by beautiful fluff. I've got to have the setting. I can't sing or dance well enough to carry it alone.'
>
> Well, we gave her the meringue — the prettiest chorus girls in Hollywood and a $7000 set that would be used for just four

minutes. We made her enter in a cloud of smoke made by deto-
nated flash powder. I died a thousand deaths worrying that
something would go wrong and we'd singe those million-dollar
legs. The worst we did during rehearsal was half-strangle her on
smoke. But she never complained once.

The evening we went on the air (the show was telecast live)
one of my cameras swinging round to another shot gave me a
glimpse of Betty waiting behind some scenery. She looked tense
and frightened. My assistant also caught the shot and said: 'I
don't think she's going to make it!' I was scared silly. Then came
her cue — and here was Betty fancy-stepping through that puff
of smoke. The control booth was bedlam and out the stage they
were whacking each other's backs and cheering silently.

Betty, with Gene Nelson, went through her routine without a
flaw and richly deserved the applause. Maybe they are more
blase nowadays, but in live television, we were always a little
surprised when it worked out right! [104]

Betty's successful television outing kept her in the public eye
and she quickly followed it up with appearances with Bing Crosby
and Dinah Shore. She was paid $40,000 for each "Shower of Stars"
appearance.

Paramount announced they had secured screen rights to the
current Broadway smash *Guys and Dolls*, a musical based on
stories by Damon Runyon. Bob Hope was cast as Nathan Detroit,
and Jane Russell signed on for the role of the mission girl, Sister
Sarah Brown. Betty was asked if she was interested in playing the
top role of Miss Adelaide, a part created on the stage by Vivian
Blaine. She was offered a salary of $200,000, with an option for a
further film at the studio if she agreed. She was definitely
interested.

Paramount also wanted Clark Gable for the Sky Masterson role.
It was a studio publicists' dream casting: "Gable and Grable —
King and Queen of Hollywood — together for the first time
ever!" Everything looked set for Paramount's musical of the
year. However, independent producer Sam Goldwyn beat the

Paramount bid and gained the screen rights. When the studio realized it had lost the property it had no option but to drop its plans.

Betty was so disappointed. She had been looking forward to working with Gable. But the battle was not yet lost; Goldwyn cast Marlon Brando and Frank Sinatra in the top male leads and British actress Jean Simmons (in her first musical) as Sister Sarah.

The role of Miss Adelaide was still up for grabs, and Goldwyn made it known that he was interested in Grable. He had never forgiven himself for failing to spot her star potential in the thirties and releasing her from her contract. Through Betty's agent, an interview was set up between the star and the producer to discuss the terms of the deal. Normally all the business would be left to an agent, but Goldwyn, one of the last of the genuine moguls, liked to "interview" his stars personally.

On the day of the meeting, Betty was preparing to leave home when one of her dogs yelped sharply on the lawn. Betty was at the animal's side immediately. The dog had injured its paw, and was in some pain. All thoughts of the interview went out of her head as she carried her pet to the car and drove to the veterinarian's office. Once her dog had been sedated and attended to, she asked if she could use the office phone. She made a call to Goldwyn who, when he heard he had been stood up for a dog, hung up on her.

She then dialed her agent and explained the situation to him. He told her not to worry. He would go round and speak to Goldwyn personally and "soften up the old man." However, the "old man" was still in a huff and refused to see the agent, who then called Betty suggesting they wait until the next day when they would both go to the studio and explain the circumstances to Goldwyn.

The meeting never took place. Goldwyn felt slighted, and his ego was badly dented when the story got out that he had been stood up for a poodle! It was regarded as one of the funniest situations to hit the film colony in years, and gave the Hollywood insiders a good laugh. At the time, Betty also appreciated the "joke," although she realized the serious implications it had on her career. A few days later it was announced in *Film Daily* that Vivian Blaine would be joining the cast of the film — as Miss Adelaide.

What would have been an excellent comeback vehicle for Betty was now out of her reach. She was a three-time loser as far as films based on Broadway hits were concerned — first *Annie Get Your Gun*, then *Gentlemen Prefer Blondes,* and now *Guys and Dolls*. Her only consolation was that her dog was now out of pain and was managing to limp around the lawn. Animal-lover Betty always maintained she made the right decision.

As it turned out, *Guys and Dolls*, while financially successful, was not all it should have been — partly due to mis-casting. Vivian Blaine, though, was excellent in her screen re-creation of Adelaide, even though one of the stage version's best songs, "Bushel and a Peck" was cut, with a nondescript substitute, "Pet Me, Poppa" served up as a replacement.

A disheartened Betty joined Harry in Las Vegas where he and the band were playing. Film offers were still coming in but she turned her back on the film city. As far as she was concerned, she truly believed she was all washed up in movies. In a situation like that, Hollywood was not the place to be. Hollywood was (and still is) afraid of failures. And so was Betty.

It was quite true that she was still receiving film scripts. But she was a freelance artist now, and not having the backing of a studio made a big difference. However, Twentieth Century-Fox did approach her once again, this time to play the mother of Tuesday Weld in a generation-gap drama, *Teenage Rebel*, in late 1955. Betty showed no interest in the project.

The role went to Ginger Rogers, with Betty Lou Keim as her teenage daughter and British actor Michael Rennie playing her husband. It seemed strange that Betty should refuse this kind of role, considering she already played such a role *(Mother Wore Tights)* when she was only thirty-two years old. When asked about this, Betty laughed: "It was fun acting older than I really was playing Mona Freeman's mother. That was make-believe. Now that I am older, it doesn't seem such a good idea!"

She was accustomed to being handed assignments from her boss and in most cases she accepted his judgment. Now, without a major studio behind her, she was forced to rely on her own (or her agent's) judgment in accepting new projects. Even when a script with great potential came along it was not a sure thing for she had seen first-hand the way script changes and/or bad direction could turn a potential hit into a dud.

Grable, who had spent far too long under the protection of Twentieth Century-Fox, was afraid she wouldn't be able to survive another dud movie. Was this the end? Would her glorious reign at the top of the heap continue its downward spiral?

Her mother wanted her to sit it out in Hollywood. "Something will turn up, Betty," she advised her worried daughter. "It always does."

Grable disagreed. She had witnessed too many big-time stars, from the early thirties to the present day, waiting for that all-important call from the studio. Sometimes the call came — but sometimes all they wanted was your name to add some clout to an already shaky project. Betty wasn't going to wait for that to happen to her. Against her mother's advice, she decided to head for Las Vegas where Harry was working steadily for six or seven months of the year.

Apart from benefit appearances and a couple of "roasts" at the Friars Club, Betty had little experience working in nightclubs. But Las Vegas was screaming out for big names to keep the customers coming in, and Betty felt she needed a complete change of scene. Before making a final decision on this crucial career move, however, she tentatively sought the advice of her choreographer pal, Billy Daniel. He was so full of enthusiasm for Betty to make her nightclub debut that he offered to choreograph it for her. His enthusiasm rubbed off on Grable. Las Vegas it was!

But first, she said, she was going to take a good long vacation to recharge her batteries. She now had no financial worries (or so she thought) and she felt in need of a rest.

CHAPTER TWELVE

Betty couldn't afford to take a very long break from show business. The Internal Revenue Service was demanding almost half a million dollars in unpaid taxes — money the Jameses simply didn't have. Within the next few years they would be forced to sell both Betty's beautiful, Hawaiian-style home (it was purchased by Carol Burnett), and the Baby J ranch, along with Betty's beloved horses. Grable had little business acumen and Harry even less; it had been estimated that during her years with Twentieth Century-Fox she had earned around $10 million, and she had no idea where most of it had gone.

Typically, Betty's career luck held out; she and Harry were offered a season at the El Rancho in Las Vegas at a salary of $12,000 a week — double her weekly pay check at Twentieth Century-Fox.

At rehearsals for her Vegas opening, however, she wasn't too happy with the presentation. The "spectacular" floorshow was very much in vogue, leaving little for Betty to do except flash her legs and look gorgeous. She worried that the customers might think she was just cashing in on her name. "I never believe in living on my laurels — I'm not quite over the hill yet, so give me something to do," she asked the producers.

Betty got to work on building up her act with the help of her old friend Jack Cole (Billy Daniel was otherwise engaged). Her revue consisted mainly of favorite songs from her films and a blues medley, with plenty of dancing and leg show. First-night critics acclaimed her debut, noting that she appeared to be a much better dancer on stage than in her movies. Betty became the biggest draw of the season, her nearest rival being Orson Welles who was doing a one-man show at the Sands. To advertise its star attraction, the Frontier management erected a huge neon-lit version of the famous pin-up pose, leaving the gambling fun-seekers in no doubt that the show to see was Grable's.

The James family liked life in Vegas and decided to look around for a home in the area, with a view to settling down permanently. Harry could still tour with his band if he wanted to, but if he didn't, there was always plenty of work in the desert town. With her daughters at school, Betty was free to pick any number of the engagements offered her.

Television offers were also coming in, and Betty commuted regularly between the gambling capital and Hollywood to make appearances in "Shower of Stars" and "Hollywood Palace." Betty liked television, but was still nervous about it. She told a *TV Times* journalist, "Every time I appear before a TV camera I'm terrified. But it's good for me — it keeps me on my toes. Fluff one line and you have millions of viewers asking why."

Betty met Orson Welles socially during their season in Vegas. He was contracted to direct and star in a television version of *Twentieth Century*, the Ben Hecht play which had been filmed in the mid-thirties. He asked Betty to play opposite him. She eagerly accepted. It was just the type of role she had been waiting for, recreating a part made famous in the 1930s by her comedy idol, Carole Lombard.

The two returned to Hollywood to rehearse the play which would be transmitted live. They worked well together, and one critic stated that she "was particularly good in light comedy and should do well in similar roles in the future."

Though Betty received a number of good notices, most of the reviewers said that she and Welles were mismatched, one stating that he could not for a moment imagine Grable falling for some-one with Welles's looks! All in all, however, Betty was pleased with her performance and said she was considering making a new career for herself in television.

In addition, the appearance with Welles led to a new offer; an independent television company cast her in the title role of

"Cleopatra Collins." She played a scatter-brained housewife-cum-model. It was a pilot for a series, and Casey Adams (later known as Max Showalter) was her leading man. She had known Casey from his days as a contract player at Fox; his most important role had been as Jean Peters' husband in Monroe's *Niagara*.

Unfortunately, although the pilot had some funny moments and the role suited Betty perfectly, the backers decided against going ahead with additional episodes. Betty was disappointed when she learned the series had been cancelled. Most Hollywood producers knew Grable was a very funny woman with untapped comedy talents, but none of them seemed able to come up with a television format to suit her outgoing personality.

Her friend, Lucille Ball — by now the biggest name on television with the "I Love Lucy" series — also couldn't understand why Betty had never been given her own TV series. Lucy had often asked Betty to appear in guest spots on her shows, but she had always refused. But now, Grable's recent flings with the television medium had given her new confidence in herself, and when Lucy repeated her invitation early in 1958, both Betty and Harry took her up on it.

The resulting hour-long episode was entitled "Lucy Wins a Racehorse," and centered around Betty's favorite spectator sport. Partnered by Desi Arnaz, Betty got to dance "The Bayamo" — a Latin routine reminiscent of her film production numbers. It was another successful outing for Betty, although one critic complained that Grable and James ". . . had little to do but play along with the hossy capers." At the end of the taping, Betty stated she was happy the "Cleopatra Collins" project hadn't materialized. "Television is a much harder grind than the movies ever were. You have to work that much faster."

However, she continued her television appearances — mainly guesting in variety shows headlined by friends like Bob Hope and Dinah Shore, as well as the occasional spectacular. A reviewer wrote of the "Bob Hope-Chevy Show," which also starred Harry, Eddie Fisher, and Rowan and Martin (before their "Laugh-In " fame): "The shapely Grable stems and torso activated in rhythmic motion. Grable fronted a big production number in spangles that gave the viewer fleeting glimpses of her curvy chassis and let Hope play off her for some high humor." [105]

She and Harry also had a memorable show with Perry Como, who was then at the top of the ratings. Betty and Perry had a delightful musical sequence in which they sang many of their old hits. Betty also did a live TV show — transmitted direct from Las Vegas — with comedian Jerry Lewis. Though she performed well, she found she couldn't cope with the hyperactive Lewis. He was involved in every scene and hogged the limelight during Betty's musical routine. She felt more at home on the lower-keyed "Andy Williams Show," where she fronted a bevy of young chorines for a lively "Night Life" number.

The Jameses had often been asked why they didn't set up their own spectacular series on TV — Harry and his band with Betty and an assortment of guests. Betty said Harry much preferred working before a live audience, and there wouldn't be much time to tape a show with Harry being on tour so much.

But the band tours were dwindling, thanks to a young man named Elvis Presley who changed the whole face of the music business. The big band era was coming to an end, and James was finding difficulty in getting bookings. Rock 'n' roll had taken over, and it was — at the time — cheaper for management to book a group of four or five youngsters than to hire the Harry James Orchestra which consisted of around forty musicians plus additonal personnel. So Harry James found himself more or less home-based in the late fifties — and he wasn't too happy about it.

However, Betty was pleased with the arrangement. The couple had settled into their $100,000 home on Country Club Lane, close to the Desert Inn Golf course. Despite her glamour image, Betty had always been fond of sports. She was an expert horsewoman and an excellent skater and tennis player. If she hadn't become a movie star, she might easily have found fame in the sporting world. Now, with her new proximity to the golf course, Betty took up the sport, gaining points more for enthusiasm than for her prowess on the greens. She enjoyed her golf outings and settled down to a couple of games a week with some new-found golfing girlfriends.

Harry seldom joined her, preferring to sleep late after a show. Rumors that Harry was "playing around" abounded, although when Betty confronted him about the stories, he flatly denied them. Betty was still deeply in love with her husband and tried to give him the benefit of the doubt, believing that most of his dalliances were the result of his drinking problem. Betty Grable once stated, "The basis of a happy marriage is a double bed." But now she found herself relegated to not only a separate bed, but a separate bedroom.

To Betty, the only cure seemed to be her work. She renewed her efforts to salvage what was left of her career. Impresario Frank Sennes encouraged Betty to create her own nightclub act, promising to book her into the Moulin Rouge in Hollywood whenever she was ready. Now she was. In this act, entitled "Memories," she was backed by strong supporting talent, and her own routines were unashamedly based on nostalgia, closing with a rousing "Katie Went to Haiti." The show was a sell-out and brought excellent notices. The critics, though, concentrated more on her figure than on her performance, noting that the chorus girls couldn't hold a candle to forty-two-year-old Grable. In early 1959, she took the show to Miami, again to rave notices.

Later in the year she was booked into the plush Latin Quarter, New York, with the same act. The management admitted they booked her purely on nostalgia, but Grable — clad in practically nothing but sequins — packed them in.

Word of her success in New York quickly filtered back to Las Vegas where booking agents were anxious to get her signature on a contract. Any star who could pull in the customers — and Betty had proved she could do that — was most welcome in the gambling town. But she turned down an offer to stage the show at the Tropicana because of "personal problems."

Betty had resigned herself to the fact that Harry would be absent from their "happy home" two or three nights a week. There was nothing she could do about it, but on one occasion, she did ask him to be discreet. His response was to turn on her and hit her hard across the face, giving her a black eye. Betty felt then that her marriage was coming to an end.

Her new career was taking a great toll on the famous Hollywood marriage, and after seventeen years of near-bliss, Harry took an apartment at a nearby hotel. As if to disavow any significance to the move, he claimed that after a show, he and the boys liked to eat a late dinner, play the tables, and have a few beers before retiring. He felt that it was only fair to Betty who liked to be up and about during the day, attending to her various household chores, which she claimed she enjoyed.

"How considerate of you," Betty hissed sarcastically at him during a row over his decision. [106]

She was lonely — lonelier than she had ever been in her life. She felt she had no one to turn to for advice. During her frequent visits to Lillian's home in Beverly Hills, the subject of her marriage was never brought up. After seventeen years together, Harry was like a stranger to her now, and her "foundation" seemed to be crumbling around her. Her children were her only consolation, and although she tried to be a real mother to them, it was too late for that. Vicki, now 16, and Jessica, 13, had become accustomed to being cared for by nannies and housekeepers, and they felt that their mother was like a stranger. This upset Betty enormously and she blamed herself for the situation.

It wasn't totally her fault. Considering her own upbringing, she didn't know how to react lovingly to her own children. Betty's childhood had consisted of theatres and dressing rooms, and a mother who had little or no time for displaying love or affection. Although Betty had shielded Vicki and Jessica from the rigors of show-business, she found she could not respond spontaneously to any show of love or affection from her own children. She tried, but it was an uphill struggle to forge a relationship with them. It led to many disagreements between mother and daughters, particularly with Jessica, who had a rebellious streak in her.

An added difficulty was the onset of menopause. Deep down, like most women, she resented this time of her life — the passing of her long-lasting youth. Whereas most women have to cope with physiological changes and anxieties at that time of life, film actresses, particularly sex symbols, have a double dose. And there was no quick cure for either problem.

Betty took refuge in an occasional vodka. It didn't make her immediate problems go away, but it helped dull them for a little while. She would be the first to admit she enjoyed her "social drinking," particularly her pre-dinner martinis, but she never became a problem drinker and never missed an engagement because of alcohol. The same thing could not be said for Harry, however. He seemed to be going steadily downhill, thanks to the bottle.

Suddenly it all became clear to Betty. Those rumors she had ignored about Harry having a girl in every town seemed to have more than a grain of truth in them. His gambling losses were getting heavier and heavier, and Betty had to settle the bills. During her Hollywood heyday, she had never bothered herself with money matters. She knew her studio check was banked every month, and both she and Harry could draw on it at will. Apparently Harry had been using it for years to cover his gambling fever and pay his booze bills. Betty never gave a thought to her bank balances. The fact that the couple's tax haven had disappeared now left them in a precarious financial situation.

She was also fond of a flutter herself and thought nothing of placing thousand-dollar bets on "sure things," but they were usually also-rans. The Jameses became known as the "bookie's friends." They seldom came up with a winner — although Betty could quote form guides better than any bookmaker.

There was nothing to do but to lose herself in work. Her finances were still rocky, but as long as she was able to earn a living, Betty Grable decided it was much better to go it alone than to suffer a bad marriage. At this period she often told younger friends in various shows who asked her for career advice: "Be as independent as you can. Your best friend is your wallet — always remember that."

When Betty learned that United Artists was to film *The George Raft Story* in 1960, she had her lawyer make discreet inquiries to see if she were to be portrayed in it. Much to her relief she wasn't. Young actor Ray Danton played Raft, with Jayne Mansfield his blonde starlet girlfriend.

She took a booking headlining the show at the El Rancho Hotel. Once again she became the hottest ticket in town. Betty was glad to be back at work; it helped her keep her sanity. And it helped to pay the bills.

But "hottest ticket" proved to be an unfortunate phrase!

One night, just after she had finished her final performance of the evening, a fire started backstage, and Betty and the cast had to flee for their lives. The hotel was destroyed in the blaze and arson was suspected, but no one was ever arrested. There were no serious casualties, but Betty and several of the other girls in the show had to be treated for smoke inhalation. When Betty fled her dressing-room she was clad only in a blanket; municipal firemen volunteered extra blankets for the choking star! This frightening episode worried Betty. She had never had such a close call, and for weeks afterwards her nerves were raw.

In the summer of 1960, Betty and Harry seemed to be getting along much better and arranged to vacation in Del Mar. Betty stopped off to visit her mother and Marjorie. Harry said he would follow after his show closed and be there in time for the start of the racing season. He had cut down on his drinking, and there were far fewer arguments when they were together. Betty lived in hope.

Back in circulation in Hollywood, Betty received a call from Charles Walters, who was about to direct a new comedy for M-G-M. "It's a great story, Betty, and it would be ideal for you. I'll send you the book. Read it and tell me what you think."

The book was *Please Don't Eat the Daisies* and Walters was

anxious to have Betty play the female lead opposite David Niven. His bosses at M-G-M were interested, and felt that five years away from film making was far too long in Betty Grable's case. It was time she came back. Betty read the book, telephoned Walters, and told him: "I love it." Presently she arrived at the studio and was about to sign on the dotted line, when she suddenly asked: "When does filming begin?"

On being told, Betty replaced the pen in its holder and informed Walters that it was right in the middle of the Del Mar season and would upset her vacation plans with her family. She walked out on what would have been an excellent comeback vehicle for her. At least, that's how one account of the story goes.

Another version is that she was asked to play second lead to Doris Day in the film. That is possible. Grable refused to play second-lead to anybody. But whichever version is correct, Betty confirmed that Charles Walters wanted her in the picture and she turned him down. She said years later that "I get scripts submitted frequently. Trouble is that I'm typecast. They only want me for the same part I've played for years. They wanted me to play the vamp (second lead) in *Please Don't Eat the Daisies*, but I didn't like the part. However, if I get something interesting I'll do it."

Perhaps she was too scared to take the chance having been so long away from the cameras. Or perhaps she was determined to patch up her shaky marriage, which still meant more to her than her career.

Harry eventually caught up with Betty and they set off for Del Mar. But the magic was missing. Her old friend, Betty Ritz wasn't there. She had divorced her husband, and was now living with her new spouse, a Mexican bullfighter, in Acapulco.

Over the next couple of years, Betty alternated between television and cabaret with equal success. Her old friend, Dan Dailey, arrived in Vegas for a holiday. He called on Betty, who was delighted to meet up with her famous co-star. She was between shows so they had plenty of time to catch up on their lives. Dan seemed to have come to terms with his own personal problems, and Betty was pleased to see that he was looking so well.

Dan, like many song-and-dance men, found earning a living solely in films becoming more and more difficult. After his professional association with Grable had ended, he continued working with Twentieth Century-Fox, then moved to M-G-M where he was featured in a few more films. Some of them were less than successful. M-G-M had tried to team up Grable and Dailey in the late fifties, but Betty always refused to talk terms.

Dan toured in summer stock and appeared in several TV spectaculars (often with Betty), where his dancing feet and a new comedy routine received a favorable reaction. From time to time, their old studio would issue publicity releases saying it was thinking of re-teaming Grable and Dailey in a new musical film. Whether this was to test public reaction for a further series of musicals or just a publicist's fanciful imagination will never be known. The public had swung away from from musicals and showed no sign of ever returning to the golden days of the innocent backstage romantic confections of the past. Hollywood, too, had changed, with a crop of new stars taking over.

Grable and Dailey took in several shows together and generally had fun. They enjoyed a nice warm relationship, and Betty felt completely at ease with the amiable Dailey. She felt she was able to confide in him, and she poured out all her marital problems to Dan. He listened sympathetically, and Betty felt better getting it all off her chest. Dan felt sorry for her and said she deserved a lot better than she was getting and should divorce James. Betty said no. She could never go through another divorce.

Betty confessed that up until she had come to live in Las Vegas, she had been living in "Cloud Cuckoo Land," believing that her life was just like one of her film scripts . . . happy ever after! She said she would be made to look like a fool divorcing James after twenty years of marriage. Dan let the subject drop, as Betty appeared to be distressed.

On an evening out, Betty and Dan came to the attention of director Ed Greenberg who had the idea of bringing famous

Broadway musicals to the Las Vegas nightclub circuit and various dinner-theatres which were taking off all over America. It was the latest form of entertainment, combining good food with first-class Broadway shows at an all-inclusive price.

He introduced himself to the couple and put forward a plan he had to co-star them in *Guys and Dolls*, for which he was negotiating. They were immediately enthusiastic and agreed they were keen to work together again. After lengthy negotiations with the management of the Dunes Hotel, it was announced that Grable and Dailey had been signed for the Christmas season in the new production.

The cast went into rehearsal six weeks before the scheduled opening. Betty and Dan were happy to be working together again. It was a shrewd move on Greenberg's part. With their names on the marquee, he was virtually assured of a successful season. He ran ads in the the local papers announcing: "Grable and Dailey — together for the first time on stage."

Betty worked as never before preparing for this show. She was determined to prove to herself and producers that she had what it takes to go "legit." She told the director she had never played in a "real" play before, ". . . so you'll have to teach me everything — word by word!" She proved a quick learner.

Guys and Dolls opened in December, 1962, for a four-week engagement. It was more than Greenberg had hoped for; the couple was so successful that the show was held over time after time. When the curtain came down for the last time, it had played a record-breaking eight months! Betty loved the role of Adelaide, and proved to audiences and critics how sensational she would have been had Mr. Goldwyn forgiven her over the dog affair. She was particularly good in the "Take Back Your Mink" number, and also "Adelaide's Lament," which was encored at every performance. The production numbers were expertly staged by choreographer Roy Wilson.

A few weeks after the close of *Guys and Dolls*, Dailey returned to Los Angeles for a nightclub booking. The show was briefly reprised in Anaheim, California, a month or so after the close of the Vegas run, with the handsome Hugh O'Brian, TV's Wyatt Earp, as the male lead.

A year later, in September, 1964, Dailey was reunited with Betty. A new production of *High Button Shoes* was being prepared, and the producer wanted them for the leading roles.

Grable accepted. She left Las Vegas — and Harry — to travel to Los Angeles. *High Button Shoes* played a limited engagement back at the Melodyland Theatre, Anaheim. While it was a critical and financial success, nobody backed the producer with a financial package which would enable him to take the show into a theatre in the heart of Los Angeles. It closed after a solid three-week run.

Betty stayed on in the movie capital for a couple of television spectaculars. Producers were pleased to book Betty on their shows. The nostalgia boom was gaining momentum throughout America, and she was regarded as one of a "dying breed of genuine sex symbols," as one network man put it. "Her name on the bill helped to boost the ratings."

While in the city, she learned that her former studio was casting *High Heels*, a teenage romantic drama about the problems of a mother and her young daughter growing up in the rock 'n' roll era. They approached Betty asking her to consider playing the part of the mother. She read the script and this time she agreed. Apparently, she now felt mature enough to try such a role. It would have been her first film role in eight years, and once it was confirmed that she would accept the part, the studio's publicity office got to work on stories of the forty-five-year-old pin-up queen's comeback. She was quoted as saying: "I have two teenage daughters, so I think I have some experience in the character I am going to play."

The project did not come to fruition, however, mainly because of money problems at the studio. Twentieth Century-Fox had not yet recovered from the financially disastrous Elizabeth Taylor epic, *Cleopatra*. Zanuck was no longer in charge and the board of directors was going through a bad time.

Grable was disappointed. After all the publicity she had received for the forthcoming film, she thought she had been made to look foolish. In truth, Grable would have loved a splashy comeback film, but everything seemed to be going against her. On hindsight, she regretted not having taken the M-G-M offer, and now Twentieth had cancelled this latest chance of her making it big in the movies once again. Fans had written to her applauding her comeback and wishing her well for future film roles.

She stayed on in Beverly Hills with her mother, who was not in the best of health. Nevertheless, Lillian still tried to counsel Betty on her career — and had a few things to say about her marriage, too. Mrs. Grable knew that all was not well between her daughter and Harry. She also realized that Betty was still very much in love with him and was reluctant to end the marriage. She told her daughter that she should do what was best for herself — and not to consider anyone else. "The children are grown up now, Betty, and have lives of their own to lead. You could stay married to Harry and make the best of it — or you could end it and try to seek happiness with someone else. You are still young enough to make a new life for yourself."

Not wishing to worry her mother unduly, Betty said she was "perfectly happy" with the way things were at the moment, and she was not in the slightest worried about her life. She also said she had no intention of divorcing Harry.

Betty took a season at the Mapes Hotel, Reno, in the summer of 1962. While rehearsing her show the news of Marilyn Monroe's death was announced. Canceling her rehearsal, Betty said she was "most upset. Marilyn and I were good friends. We were never really rivals. That was just studio talk. I shall miss her. She did an awful lot to boost movies when Hollywood was at a low ebb. There will never be anyone like her again — for looks or for attitude. She had it all."

Betty returned to Las Vegas with Harry. For the past year or so, regardless of what she had told her mother, Betty had been seriously considering divorcing him, even discussing it openly with him whenever he was sober enough. Harry's drinking and womanizing problems had escalated dramatically, and he had been seen around town with Las Vegas snowgirl Joan Boyd, throwing discretion to the wind. Betty was hurt and humiliated by his attitude. Despite several pleas — which usually ended up in blazing rows — he continued to see the girl quite openly. Betty made up her mind. When she felt the moment was right, she would proceed with her plans for the divorce.

First of all, she had to get through the forthcoming marriage of Vicki to fellow University of Arizona student William Wiley Bivens. Betty was a radiant mother of the bride, and to the outside world the James marriage seemed as solid as it ever was.

Harry seldom stayed at the James home, but they kept in touch regularly. Betty always appeared in the audience wherever Harry was playing. Whether she liked it or not, the fact was she loved him.

With time on her hands, Betty took to having nights on the town with the girls. She had plenty of girlfriends and plenty of willing escorts, usually dancers from the various shows. One big pal at the time was British actress and one-time sex symbol Diana Dors, who recalled her outings with Betty:

> I was appearing in cabaret in Las Vegas, in 1960, when I first met Betty. She was doing a show too, but also lived there permanently with her adored husband. We hit it off right away, and every time I went back to Vegas, we would always get together and have good times.
>
> La Grable was a star in the true sense of the word, but like all true stars she was the last person to think that way about herself and never pulled the star routine on anyone.
>
> One of the things we had in common, was that she felt as I did about the tiring aspect of two shows a night in Las Vegas. She would arrive at the club, with her hair in rollers hidden under a head scarf, and begin the tedious business of getting made up when really all she felt like was staying at home and watching television.
>
> She used to say, 'Diana, I never feel I can get through the

evening, but as soon as the damn shows are over I come alive, and I'm ready to go to the first party anyone suggests.' I knew exactly what she meant, as it is a recognized fact that once the adrenaline begins flowing on stage, any performer brightens up no matter how bad they feel at the start.

A nasty incident occurred when the two glamour-girls had a night on the town with a couple of male dancers from Betty's show. They were having fun at the Thunderbird Hotel. Diana, a non-drinker, and Betty, sipping on a vodka martini, were enjoying each other's company when a drunk came up to Betty and asked her to dance. Grable declined politely and he went away for a while. He returned later even more intoxicated. On being refused a second time, he started harassing Betty and calling her names. Continued Diana:

> Steve, one of our escorts, stood up and asked him to leave us alone. Without any word of warning, the drunk punched him on the nose and ran off leaving poor Steve on the floor with blood pouring from his face.
>
> Betty screamed and pandemonium broke out, sheriffs appeared from all sides and, of course, we were the center of attention. We had to take Steve to the hospital, and Betty was genuinely very upset, as I do not think she had been involved in such a thing before and was worried that it would hit the papers.
>
> One can imagine the headlines — Diana Dors and Betty Grable in bar-room brawl with three men. Thankfully it did not make the headlines, and sadly it was the last time I ever saw her.
>
> Somehow I will never be able to believe she is gone, those beautiful legs, and the pin-up blonde looks, still dancing and dazzling whenever they show her old wartime movies on the television screen.
>
> Betty Grable was a star, and there will never be another one like her. When she went, they destroyed the mould! [107]

Betty returned to Hollywood with Harry to tape a "Hollywood

The Girl With the Million Dollar Legs

Palace" special. She was the M.C. and topped the bill among such stars as Diahann Carroll, the Smothers Brothers, and Henny Youngman. The television reviewer in the *San Francisco Chronicle* welcomed her return to television in his column: "Betty Grable returned to television last weekend showing no visible scars for a decade of backstage musicals. The brevity of her costume in the opening number closed any arguments that the lady's structure might be sagging. It was clear in an instant that her figure is still equal to the best on display today."

To outsiders the Jameses still seemed the ideal couple. It was a successful television appearance for Betty, and well-timed from a domestic point of view. The show took her mind off her personal problems and led to appearances in several other programs.

Betty still maintained that she was very happily married, and few outside her close circle of friends suspected otherwise. One network boss had the information that she was about to divorce James and tried to date her several times. She was flattered, but since he was already married, he was turned down flat. She didn't want to become the subject of gossip columnists at this crucial stage in her life.

Just after the Thanksgiving holiday, Betty received a call from Marjorie that Lillian had suffered a major heart attack and was hospitalized. Betty flew immediately to Los Angeles.

Lillian Grable was being treated at St. John's Hospital in Santa Monica. A few weeks later she was declared fit enough to be discharged. Betty and Marjorie (who was not in the best of health herself) took turns nursing their mother. It was a bleak Christmas for the family.

Lillian Grable died on January 1, 1965, at the age of seventy-four. Harry, Vicki, and Jessica returned to Beverly Hills for the funeral. After putting the house up for sale, the Jameses headed back to Las Vegas. Superstitious Betty felt it was a bad omen for the rest of 1965. She was sure it wasn't going to be her year.

Grable was a much saddened woman. Of her Number One Fan, she said: "She wasn't really the typical show business mother. She just cared about me and my career, and helped smooth all my domestic arrangements. I shall miss her terribly." It took a long time for Betty to get over her loss. Years earlier Betty had said, "Some day I'll meet something head on, something I won't be able to brush aside. I will have to face up to it without any help from anyone." Many friends thought this reference was about her career problems. However, it appeared to have nothing to do with her professional life. It went much deeper than that. For quite some time now she had been delaying the decision to divorce James. But he was now living quite openly with Joan Boyd and it was common knowledge around town.

She told a close friend, "I don't believe in washing my dirty linen in public. I suffered agonies when I divorced Jackie Coogan and I vowed I would never go through that again. Contrary to what outsiders think, divorce is still a traumatic experience — even for us movie people. It is one of life's most unpleasant aspects."[108]

No matter what she had vowed earlier, Betty Grable had to do something. Harry James telephoned her quite casually that summer, informing her that Joan (Boyd) was pregnant. Grable was shattered. She felt this announcement left her no alternative but to go ahead with the divorce. No matter what she thought of Harry, she couldn't bear the thought of an innocent child coming into the world to an unmarried couple.

Betty became reclusive, staying home most nights, seldom venturing from her pleasant garden. Some of her friends thought that the announcement of her retirement was imminent. However, she wouldn't do this; she would have preferred to slip quietly out of the show business scene. She didn't like the jokes made about other stars who were forever on their farewell performance tours.

A telephone call from Broadway producer David Merrick's agent altered her monastic lifestyle. He had arranged to stage an abridged version of his hit musical *Hello, Dolly!* at the Riviera Hotel, and was anxious that Betty should play the leading role. Betty referred him to her agent and all but ignored the deal.

Several weeks went by, and she still showed no interest in the role.

Her private life was still in a mess and she felt she needed time to sort it out before committing herself to any more work. She did go so far as to play the Carol Channing soundtrack of the show, and, with her typical lack of self-confidence, thought she wouldn't be able to match up to Miss Channing vocally.

When her decision was relayed to Merrick he immediately telephoned her and pleaded with her to at least go into rehearsal and get the feel of the show. He was particularly anxious to secure Betty for the Vegas production (he had also considered her when he was casting the original show for Broadway). He felt her name would ensure box office security, and his backers for the Vegas venture insisted on Grable. No Grable — no show. [109]

Betty still refused to discuss it.

A week or so after Merrick's latest offer, she ventured out with Vicki and her husband to attend Eddie Fisher's opening at the Riviera. During his performance, he welcomed Betty and told the audience what a great Dolly she would make. The audience showed their approval with a round of applause duly noted by the hotel management.

Tony Zoppi, the hotel's public relations man, was in favor of Betty, and suggested a call to Tom Hughes, pioneer producer of Dallas's booming summer musicals, to ask his advice about the starring role for the forthcoming show. A list of names was run off to Hughes, including Edie Adams, Nanette Fabray, Janis Paige, Ann Miller, and Gwen Verdon. Betty's name was slotted in somewhere in the middle of the starry line-up. Mr. Hughes's first choice: "Get Grable!"

The Riviera's booking agent, Harry Silbert contacted Betty's friend and next-door neighbor, Cecil Simmons, a major executive at the Desert Inn, to enlist his help in coaxing Betty into accepting the role. After much persuasion, he was successful. Betty finally signed and flew to New York to see Carol Channing in the part. Afterward she went backstage to meet the star, and tried on several of the hats that were used in the show. She gasped at her reflection in the mirror: "I look like I just stepped off the *Coney Island* set!" [110]

The Las Vegas production of *Hello Dolly* was the most expensively mounted show to be seen outside a Broadway theatre. The staging and seating arrangements at the Riviera were altered and redecorated at a cost of $400,000.

Before Betty committed herself to the grueling rehearsal period, she asked for time off to attend to some private business. She had finally decided to end her marriage. Betty telephoned her daughters, and informed them that she and Harry had a date for the court hearing. He was playing an engagement at Harrah's in nearby Lake Tahoe at the time.

On October 8, 1965, she appeared with attorney Carl J. Christensen before Judge John Mowbray at Clark County courthouse. Betty sought her divorce on the grounds of extreme mental cruelty. One of the most celebrated marriages in show business ended quickly in a six-minute hearing. The Jameses were regarded as one of Hollywood's wealthiest couples, and no alimony settlement was discussed. The truth was that Harry had no money. Grable had subsidized him for years, so alimony was a moot point.

Betty Grable was now forty-seven years old, and she looked every day of her age as she left the court with a wide-brimmed white hat pulled low over her forehead.

The hearing had been planned to coincide with a newspaper strike, but the press and photographers were waiting outside to put on record one of the saddest days of her life. She refused to answer any questions. Her lawyer drove her to her home where more journalists were waiting. She was driven straight through the gates and smuggled into the house by a side door. Once inside, she thanked lawyer Christensen, then immediately unplugged the phone and retired to her bedroom. Friends maintained that she was still very much in love with Harry and was deeply hurt at having to end their once-happy marriage; however, she had confided in them that it "had been coming on for a long time." [111]

How lonely Betty must have felt that day cannot be imagined — remembering all those happy years together wiped out in just a few minutes in a cold, impersonal courtroom. And all those statements to the press! "I aim to be Mrs. Harry James for the rest of my life. . . " "This is where we hope to spend our golden wedding anniversary. . . ." "Harry is the breadwinner in the family, and that's how it should be. . . ." How hollow those words, spoken all those years ago, must have sounded to her that afternoon. Twenty-two years of a (mostly) happy marriage gone in a flash.

The irony of the whole episode was that it was later claimed that Harry wasn't the father of Joan's child, that she had found herself pregnant by another man whom she had been seeing behind Harry's back, and that she used her condition to force Harry into seeking a divorce and marrying her.

A few days later Betty flew to New York to rehearse *Dolly* with the principal cast. She threw herself into rehearsals; it was, she said later, therapeutic.

Recalled Robert Hultman, a singer with the show, and Equity deputy: "Betty's first word to the company was 'HELP!' We loved her for it. When Ginger Rogers took over the Las Vegas production, it was a different story. When Miss Rogers came in, the company manager lined us up on each side of the stage and announced: 'Company, this is your STAR.' Ginger acknowledged it graciously!" [112]

The Las Vegas production of the show was to try out in several cities before being brought into the Riviera for Christmas Eve. The company played to capacity audiences in Tennessee, Texas, Kentucky, and Colorado. Betty found the role demanding and her voice gave out several times, but she soldiered on, captivating audiences with her warmth and vitality. William Leonard, of the *Chicago Tribune*, said: "Betty's a knockout as Dolly . . . perfection."

Old friend Dan Dailey caught the show in Chicago, and was overheard to remark to his companion: "That darned woman . . . how does she do it? She looks just the same as she did when we were making *Mother Wore Tights!*" [113]

The production opened right on schedule in Las Vegas on December 23, 1965, for a four-month run. The critics were kind to Betty. Said John L. Scott, of the *Los Angeles Times*: "As Dolly, Miss Grable comes on strong, although somewhat handicapped at the press opening by an ailing throat. She gave a spirited performance and for the most part avoided a carbon copy impression of the original Dolly."

At an after-the-show party, a hoarse but happy Betty received congratulations from Carol Burnett, Liza Minnelli, and several other show business luminaries. Noticing her lighting her umpteenth cigarette in a short space of time, Miss Burnett scolded Betty, "You really ought to give up smoking, Betty. No wonder your voice is so throaty." Betty laughed and promised she would. But she was addicted — and despite all the advice of doctors and friends, she would not even try to break the habit.

Hello, Dolly! was an immediate success with the paying customers and became the top draw of the season. Despite stiff competition from international stars like Frank Sinatra, Tom Jones, and Shirley Bassey, the show was a big draw.

In his "Vegas Daze and Nites" column, Ralph Pearl wrote:

> The first thing the county will have to do now that Betty Grable and company have opened for a long run, is to put up traffic lights and a police patrol in front of the Riviera in order to maintain law and order and keep life and limb intact as nightly mobs storm the doors.
>
> The hotel has a gold mine on its hands and it could run for as long as the show wishes to stay here . . . and let no one compare Betty to the incomparable Carol Channing. It has already been firmly established that Betty Grable won't have to take a back seat as the Las Vegas version of *Dolly* . . . the title number in the latter part of the show with Betty [starts] goose pimples on every human anatomy in the room. She not only looks like a Dolly, she even sounded like one. Betty struggled with a slight case of laryngitis. Having been in show business for most of her life, we didn't have to ask Betty after the show how she felt about

grabbing off the prize role in the best Broadway musical since *My Fair Lady.* She glows happily with the heavy applause still ringing in her ears.

One of the highlights of the show was when the legendary Louis — Satchmo — Armstrong sang to Betty during a special performance. The audience loved this "impromptu session" so much that it was retained in the film version.

The run of the show was extended indefinitely, mainly through Betty's still considerable drawing power. It was hard work — two shows a night. But Betty was back in the mainstream of show business and loving every minute of it. She was once again living life to the fullest. The show finally came to an end in September, 1966, after a record-breaking ten-month run in the gambling capital.

Back in New York, Merrick had noted the Las Vegas receipts, which were colossal, and kept Betty in mind for the national tour of the show he was planning — covering all the major cities in the South and mid-West, and running for approximately twelve months. After a short break, Betty accepted Merrick's offer, and was off on the road with leading man Max Showalter who had co-starred with her in the "Cleopatra Collins" TV show.

As expected, the show did standing-room-only business in each city it played. The critics and audiences loved it, and noted how well Betty looked and how little she had changed (on stage) from her cinema queen days. Of course, the press also managed to mention that her legs were as lovely as ever — a fact that continued to embarrass her. To one journalist, who asked how she managed to keep the legendary limbs in such great shape, she replied: "I'm sorry to disappoint you, but there's no secret formula — they just grew that way!" However, the leg show was purely for the stage. Whenever she was seen at after-the-show parties or afternoon galas, Betty either wore a trouser suit or a long dress, much to the disappointment of her fans.

Although she loved performing *Dolly* on the road, Betty was disappointed in Gower Champion, the director. Only once during her long run did he ever come backstage to talk to her — and then only for a few minutes. Betty felt she didn't merit this treatment, and she often wondered what had happened to the happy young man who had worked so well with her in *Three For The Show.*

It certainly couldn't have been due to lack of industry on Betty's part; even Merrick had to concede that Betty was the hardest-working Dolly of them all. Her replacements in Vegas were Dorothy Lamour and Ginger Rogers who shared the show between them, doing only one show a night each. Poor Betty had slogged away twice nightly for the same money as Lamour and Rogers were getting. The behavior of Gower Champion was a puzzle to Betty — one that she never solved. [114]

The cast she headed had just returned from Vietnam where they had performed *Dolly* for the forces. One cast member was a handsome young dancer named Bob Remick. At first, Grable, though flattered by his attention to her, thought him "fresh." She was stunned when he asked her out; most of the young cast treated her as one of the gang, but never got too personal with her.

Betty, who was still basically shy, felt so much older than the others. She kept mainly to herself at the start of the tour. While appearing in Fort Wayne, cafe owner John Spillson threw a party to mark her fiftieth birthday. She had arrived in town just the day before the show's opening, and was thrilled with the surprise gesture. The cast and many prominent townspeople turned out for the occasion. Since they would be playing Fort Wayne over the Christmas period they made the most of the occasion by turning it into a double celebration. A local journalist described Betty as a most charming person and a "gracious guest of honor."

During the party, Betty and Remick got talking together and when the formalities were over he presented her with a gift of Shalimar, her favorite perfume. Betty was very touched by this gesture. [115] They found they had a lot in common. She was fascinated by his experiences in Vietnam. He had a maturity she found appealing. He was obviously younger than she (he claimed to be thirty-five, but twenty-five would have been nearer the mark).

They were often seen out together after the show. Betty also grew dependent on him for various tasks she couldn't handle on her own; he was especially useful for keeping unwanted suitors at bay. She was thought to be a very wealthy woman and, at fifty, was still extremely attractive. Also she was still a "name" in show business circles and attracted the usual crowd of hangers-on — publicity seekers who would go to any lengths to get their pictures in the papers with a star of her magnitude in order to further their own ends, whether show business or otherwise.

Bob, however, was genuine in his feelings for Betty. A pleasant, easy-going young man who had drifted into show business after his tour of duty in Vietnam, he had trained as a classical dancer as a child, but his career never got under way due to his draft status. He was attentive to Betty's every need, but kept out of the limelight on big occasions. Bob was exactly what Betty needed.

When the tour ended [by which time Betty had chalked up her nine hundredth performance as Dolly] she invited the cast back to Las Vegas, where she hired the Riviera for a late-night party. The breaking up of a cast is always a sad affair. Betty had enjoyed working with everyone and bought each of them a parting gift. One young girl dancer who had been with the same cast for several years remarked that it was the first time any Dolly had ever bought gifts for them.[116]

Bob Remick was particularly sad; he wanted to stay near Betty. They discussed the situation at length. Betty was worried that Bob would be tagged as a gigolo and told him so. However, Bob was a determined young man and managed to stay on in Las Vegas, just to be near Betty. He helped Betty with her house hunting. After much searching they found the ideal house at 164 Tropicana Road, close by the Tropicana Hotel, and — once again — overlooking the golf course! He escorted her around town to various events, and the romance blossomed. Betty was very proud of her handsome young beau.

Obviously, Betty still had "what it takes!"

CHAPTER THIRTEEN

Grable was now without any show business commitments for the first time in almost two years, and she was enjoying the break. Her lengthy spell with *Dolly* had enhanced her legend and her old films were being shown regularly on late-night television. She was receiving fan mail and requests for photos from a whole new generation of fans. This upturn in her career life thrilled her. It took her mind off other problems — including Harry James.

He was still around Las Vegas and it was impossible for them to avoid each other. Betty maintained they were "still good friends. There's no animosity — how could there be after all those years together?" The truth was she was still very much in love with Harry, despite his faults, and she felt that if she could curb his drinking problem — and his womanizing — they could get together again. Bob Remick knew how she felt about Harry, but he, too, was in love with her, and hoped one day they would make their own arrangement permanent.

It was also rumored, around this time, that she was being wooed by multi-millionaire recluse Howard Hughes. Betty laughingly denied this. It did flatter her, though, that someone took time to dream up such a wild rumor — it was always good publicity!

Without any help from publicists, Bob Remick was welcomed into Betty's circle of close friends, once they realized he was sincere in his feelings for her.

Betty was now a grandmother, both Vicki and Jessica having started families of their own. Vicki and her husband had a little boy, and Jessica had married Ron Yahner and was expecting her first child. Neither daughter approved of Betty's openly living with a much younger man and told her so. Betty was firm. For years she

273

had always had to obey someone — her mother, the studio, or Harry. Now, for the first time in her life, she was her own person, and told her daughters that it was none of their business. She had fulfilled her obligation to them as a mother, and she was free to do as she pleased. The girls saw the sense in this; the matter was never brought up again. Betty was pleased that, at last, she was able to relate to her beloved daughters.

In New York, comedienne Martha Raye was due to finish her run of *Hello, Dolly!*. Box office receipts were sagging after the show's three-year run at the St. James Theatre, and the show needed a massive injection of excitement to revitalize it.

Producer Merrick was determined that *Dolly* would beat *My Fair Lady* as Broadway's longest running show. Every now and again he freshened up the show with a new leading lady — not always with the results he expected. He wondered whether Grable, so successful in Las Vegas and the national tour, would be interested in the Broadway spot.

He called her, but Betty was unsure. "It's a long time since I appeared before a Broadway audience," she told him. Replied Merrick: "They loved you then — they'll love you even more this time. If you are interested you start rehearsals in three weeks time." Betty talked it over with Bob. His youthful enthusiasm won her over. He was very proud of Betty and knew she would be a knockout on Broadway. Betty wasn't so sure. But she took his advice and called Merrick, telling him of her acceptance.

She and Bob traveled to New York. She was excited, yet nervous about once more facing Broadway audiences — to say nothing of the critics, who could be the cruelest in the world. It was no wonder that they were known as "The Butchers of Broadway."

Upon arrival at the Warwick Hotel on Sixth Avenue, they were greeted by waiting press men, always eager for a light-hearted story in the trouble-torn Big Apple. Betty posed willingly for the cameramen, but refused to comment on her private life. Bob Remick stayed quietly in the background. She was concerned that their relationship, so calmly accepted in Las Vegas, might not be looked upon so easily by the mighty New York press corps.

Grable had about a week's rehearsal before she took over the part from Martha Raye. As usual, Betty went out of her way to make friends with the cast members and invited them to her hotel suite on the Sunday afternoon prior to the opening for a "getting-to-know-you" party. The afternoon was a great success.

Her costumes were not ready until the dress rehearsal on opening day. The final rehearsal broke up around 3 p.m. — and it had been terrible. Co-workers reassured her with the old showbiz cliché: a bad dress rehearsal means a good opening night.

New York was at its hottest, with high humidity. Betty showered and changed and was driven to her hotel to rest up before the opening. She was tired and told Bob she was going to bed, asking him to call her around 5:30. However, she couldn't unwind and the all-important sleep eluded her. She kept worrying about the show. Supposing she was the first Broadway Dolly to flop? Despite Bob's reassurances, she couldn't shake her depression.

Betty got out of bed, showered and dressed in a pale blue linen trouser suit. When her chauffeur arrived, he found the couple waiting in the lobby. He said the star remained silent on the journey to the theatre, "just staring straight ahead," apparently oblivious to her surroundings. [117] When she arrived at the theatre, there were no fans waiting to greet her at the stage door, however, there were good luck telegrams from Vicki and Jessica and several bouquets of flowers from her Las Vegas friends.

Betty was quickly made up and dressed for her first appearance in the show. Opening night was a sell-out. Soon she would be facing her first Broadway audience in twenty-seven years. Many in the audience would be regular theatre goers, and would probably recall seeing her in *Du Barry Was A Lady*. They would be comparing her to how she had looked all those years ago.

When her call-boy knocked on her door, she called out a "thank you" to his good-luck greeting and made her way to the wings. Bob whispered encouragement to her all the way to the side of the stage, where she stood behind some scenery awaiting her cue line.

Backstage crew members noticed she looked nervous and uptight.

On cue, she stepped onto the chorus-filled stage to be greeted with rapturous applause. The ovation lasted for several minutes, and was reputed to be the "best since the show first opened with Miss Channing in the lead." Betty was a splendid sight at center stage dressed in her turn-of-the-century costume. It was indeed *Coney Island* all over again.

The audience, too, noted that she appeared nervous at the beginning of the show, but her confidence grew with each round of applause. Said one of the theatre's ushers: "I've never seen anything like this. I've seen all the other Dollies, but this is something else — such cheers!" [118]

Drama critic Guy Savino wrote:

> A new Dolly, hoarse but nimble, received an uproarious salute last night. . . . the men in the audience gave her a standing ovation when she first appeared. When she demurely gathered up her skirts and let the slim, shapely legs show there was another ovation. The show was stopped several times while cheers and whistles filled the theatre. One woman shouted 'We love you, Betty' — while the men said it with whistles. As the show ended, the men swooped towards the stage and gave her another tremendous ovation. Somebody handed her a bouquet of roses.
>
> . . . the strange thing about the audience was that it was filled not with men who seemed veterans of World War II, but young men who might have been their sons. They sat in house seats close to the stage and rooted home a favorite who must have been familiar to them only because of the late TV movies. [119]

The critics were very fair to the former film star who had returned to the city that had given her the first heady taste of success. One critic noted that "she lacked a certain freewheeling wackiness the role demanded," but added that the first-night audience loved her. *The New York Times* reviewer stated, "Betty Grable returned to Broadway as 'Dolly' — there was hardly a dry eye in the house as the audience, according to the lyrics, welcomed her back to where she belongs — it was fun!"

Earl Wilson commented, "Grable opened in *Dolly* to a standing ovation. The best-received Dolly of them all, say her adherents about blonde, bouncy Betty." *Variety* enthused, "Betty Grable lights up the St. James Theatre with charm, humor, high spirits and sex appeal, and that's the best possible news for *Hello, Dolly.*" Wrote Rebecca Moorehouse, of *Women's News Service*, "Those Betty Grable fans who made her a box office champion are now saying hello to her in *Hello, Dolly*, Broadway's musical champ. It took five mounted policemen to clear a path for her as she left the theatre after her first wildly-cheered performance."

The next day, publicity agents for the show put out the blurb: "'Hello, Betty!' screamed New York last night as Betty Grable took over in the smash musical *Hello, Dolly!*"

Famed nightclub owner, Cryin' Joe Kipness, of Kippy's, threw a party to celebrate Grable's latest success. Among the invited guests was her former Broadway co-star, Bert Lahr. Planting a kiss on the old man's cheek, she stated: "It isn't every day I get to meet one of my good luck charms."

Her celebrity status in New York prompted the producer of "What's My Line" to invite her to appear on the show as the mystery guest, reprising an appearance she had made a couple of years earlier. Unfortunately, she failed to fool the panel.

With Grable in *Dolly*, it quickly became a winner, and she was delighted with the success — but no more delighted than Merrick (who found that since Betty had taken over, the box office receipts had gone up by an average of $40,000 a week). The nightly audiences reached near capacity midweek, and the show was a sell-out on weekends.

One Saturday evening, two young Englishmen arrived at the St. James Theatre booking office only to be told that all tickets for that night's performance had been sold. Disappointed, the two men turned from the booking office window. The clerk asked them where they were from and they poured out their story. They had both written to her over the years, but had never met their idol.

While on holiday in Toronto, they had decided to fly to New York on the spur of the moment to watch their favorite film star in action.

The clerk was sympathetic. He took down their names, and said that if any tickets were returned, he would see that they got them if they reported back to the theatre a half-hour before the show. "But," he warned, "I can't promise you anything definite."

The visitors thanked him and said they would come back in the evening. They spent the rest of the day sightseeing, but always their thoughts and conversation returned to the show. Despite the many interesting things to do in that fascinating city, the afternoon seemed to drag by. Eventually, they returned to the theatre and waited in a small queue of other hopefuls at the ticket desk. Their chances looked slim. As they were discussing whether it was worthwhile to wait or to try to get seats for another show, one of them was tapped on the shoulder. It was the ticket clerk, who had spotted them in the crowded lobby. "For you," he smiled and handed them a plain white envelope. He disappeared before the astonished men could thank him.

Still not believing their good luck, when they turned the envelope to open it, they saw the bold red monogram "BG" on the flap. Inside were two tickets — row B on the center aisle — and a note which read: "Am delighted you could come to see me in New York. Please call backstage after the show." It was signed by Betty Grable.

Apparently the ticket clerk had told Betty of the English visitors and she had immediately instructed him to give them her own personal "hold" tickets for the show. Few people ever enjoyed a show as much as they did that night, sitting in the best seats in the house, watching their pin-up girl for the first time in person. Afterwards they went backstage and came face-to-face with the star in her dressing room. They spent some time chatting about her career. She seemed amazed that they should know so much as they seemed far too young to have remembered her in her heyday.

Betty took an immediate liking to the young men and invited

them to have supper with her and Bob — an invitation they readily accepted. The next day, the two men left New York with fond memories of their visit that would stay with them for the rest of their lives. [120]

For a major star, Betty Grable took a great delight in meeting her fans — especially those who had written to her over the years.

Millie De Palmer, of Portland, Maine, a one-time treasurer of Betty's official U. S. A. fan club, traveled extensively to see her idol in action. She was invited backstage every time. Millie's home was a shrine to the star, and Betty appreciated her devotion, always making her welcome whenever Millie and her family turned up at a venue she was playing.

Another fan who entered Betty's life at this time was Bob Isoz of Kew Gardens, New York. Working with Pan Am, Bob took every advantage of his concession fares to travel the States (and later even London) to catch up with his favorite star. He saw her in every one of her stage shows with the exception of *High Button Shoes*, an omission which remains the one big regret of his life.

Said Bob:

> She was a fantastic lady. No pretense about her. I'm sure it was this facet of her personality that kept her in favor for so long. I was able to see her play Dolly in most American cities, but she was definitely Broadway's greatest Dolly. Audiences loved her. Yet she never thought she was anything special.
>
> One night in some mid-West town Betty asked me out to dinner with her and other members of the cast. She was in great spirits when we reached the restaurant. One of the actors in our party of six went up to reception to ask for a table. The young female receptionist told him the restaurant was fully booked and it would be impossible to get a table that night. On being informed of this, Betty said she would have to eat soon or she would faint. We decided to look somewhere else. Quickly. Just then the maître d' appeared and apologized profusely. 'Of course we have a table for Miss Grable's party,' he said. 'Please, come this way.' As we turned to enter the dining-room, Betty went into

a mock theatrical gesture and laughingly said, 'See what it is to be a great big movie star?'

We had a great meal and a load of laughs. Betty was in great form and when the young receptionist came by the table to apologize for not recognizing her, Betty told her to forget it — and in a nice gesture signed the menu card and handed it to the delighted girl. Betty Grable was one of a kind. Although she played it down, she really was a great big movie star! [121]

Yet another fan, Ralph Dykstra, who hailed from Betty's home town of St. Louis, traveled with some friends to see her perform in *Born Yesterday* in Chicago. On telling the theatre's manager, Guy Little, in a casual conversation at the interval, of his two-hour drive just to see his favorite star, he was astounded to be asked to come backstage and meet Betty at the end of the show

Ralph later recalled:

We were all a little nervous. When we entered her dressing room she flashed her beautiful smile and greeted us warmly. She talked about her career, and spoke warmly of Tyrone Power. Then she autographed our programs and thanked us for coming. It was a great night and the glow of Betty Grable's personality has remained with me ever since. I am so happy that I have my own special memory of a beautiful, talented lady who brought happiness to millions. [122]

And Bernie Freedman, an executive with Canadian Tire in Toronto, was so desperate to meet his pin-up idol that he flew to New York to see her. He telephoned the theatre from his hotel, asking for an interview with Betty, but was put off by the theatre management. A chance meeting on a New York beach with one of the dancers from the show helped him realize his dream. The dancer invited him backstage after a matinee performance. He told Bernie that he could swing a meeting with Betty.

Bernie sat through the matinee performance enthralled.

She was just wonderful, and when she hitched up her skirts to reveal those legs saying: 'Look at the old girl now, fellas,' it was the Betty Grable of the old days. After the show I made my way backstage. [The dancer] had left my name at the stage door. I was ushered in and after a few minutes came face to face with my idol. A momentary hesitation. What was I going to say to her? Betty dispelled the moment. She took the initiative. 'Where did you get that tan?' she asked me. From then it was easy. She was a delightful person — and when I looked into those beautiful blue eyes, I was well and truly hooked! [123]

Once she had got over the heady excitement of her tumultuous reception in New York, Betty settled down in the city. She told friends, "I love New York! I've always wanted to live here but was never able to before. I love the restaurants, the shopping, the people. I'm grateful to *Dolly* for bringing me here. Now you couldn't pay me to live anywhere else!"

She was once again in the news when a columnist reported that, when asked her opinion of the other Dollies, Grable replied, "Ginger Rogers looks like Harpo Marx in drag!" Needless to say, Miss Rogers was far from amused. Betty wouldn't confirm or deny that she had uttered the statement. She just laughed!

Said Betty of her newly-regained Broadway fame: "Despite my years in Hollywood, I still find new challenges an ordeal. *Dolly* was an ordeal at first, but now I've settled down to the part, and the audiences have been wonderful."

Of her future plans:

I don't know what's in store for me. I haven't made any plans and frankly I'd rather let things fall into place as they may. I like surprises. However, I don't need a crystal ball to know that the trend is away from the type of movies I used to make. Now the trend is [toward] heavy, meaty dramas — and I'm not one to knock trends. I might make a movie if the right one came along. In fact I'd love to play the movie version of *Dolly*, but time will tell.

I don't regret leaving Hollywood when I did. I'd had a couple of bad pictures, so I quit to spend more time with my daughters and I enjoyed seeing them grow up. Now they are older, and I can leave them to fend for themselves, so I'm ready to go back to Hollywood.

But first there are some things I want to do. I want to finish up in *Dolly* by the end of the year. Then I am going to tour the world before I do anything else. It's something I've always yearned to do. Do you know, I've never been to Europe. In fact, I've never been as far as Mexico. During all those years in Hollywood, I was too busy making movies to travel. So I am going to make up for lost time. It'll be like starting all over!

Asked about the new crop of Hollywood stars, Betty said: "They're great. They are independent and have minds of their own. What if young actresses do appear nude these days? I don't see anything wrong in it. Nudity is a trend, that's all. Show business is all trends. And gimmicks — and let's face it — I've been standing on my gimmicks for years!" [124]

During her Broadway run, Harry James arrived in town to fulfill an engagement at the Riverboat Inn. At the same time, old pal Frank Sinatra turned up to see *Dolly* and afterwards went backstage to congratulate Betty on her performance. She was pleased to see him; they hadn't met in months. Sinatra suggested that that he take Betty to see Harry's show and have some drinks. Betty was a little apprehensive about the meeting. Harry had long since divorced Joan Boyd (the marriage had lasted only months) and they were both free. However, she gamely accepted Sinatra's invitation and arrived with him at the Riverboat. After his show, Harry sat at their table and the trio talked over old times.

"It was all very civilized," said Betty later. "I don't know if Frank had planned this get-together trying to reconcile Harry and me, but I knew it just wouldn't work out. We did end the evening on a friendly note, though. Harry said he would come and see my show as soon as he got the chance." [125]

It was never recorded if Harry actually got to see his ex-wife in

Dolly, but the couple were never seen again in public in New York.

Her enthusiasm for New York diminished somewhat with the city's first snowfall of winter. "I dislike snow," she said. "I haven't seen any for years, but I still remember the dreadful cold sleet and slush of St. Louis winters when I was little, and I never want to see any more!"

Betty was due to leave the show at the end of the year, but Merrick was hopeful she would extend her successful run. She had no future plans, but she was keen to follow up her success with *Dolly* (apparently the world tour had taken a back seat). She was back in the big-time and realized just how much she had missed the limelight — especially the attention she was receiving from her fans.

She approached Merrick, and asked him what her chances were of replacing Mary Martin in the London run of the show. Betty had received many letters from her British fans asking her to bring the show to London. A British newspaper even went as far as to say she would be the London *Dolly*. Betty was enthusiastic about meeting her loyal British fans. Merrick sounded optimistic. He advised her to wait until nearer the end of Martin's six-month run and he would review the position. Later, she realized she was foolish to ask a favor of Merrick.

Much to Grable's disappointment, Merrick's British agents signed Dora Bryan for the remainder of the West End run, and also for the show's national tour. Miss Bryan, a well-known comedy actress, played the role in a "North of England" accent, admitting that she could never sustain an American accent for the perform-ance. The tour was successful but not nearly as much as it probably would have been with a star like Grable enhancing it.

British producer Freddie Carpenter, famed for his spectacular revues, wrote in the *London Daily Express*:

> I have seen Channing, Rogers and Raye in *Dolly* and for my money Betty Grable is the best of them all. She has that extra dimension that the role needs — warmth.

I have asked her to appear in "Five Past Eight" (his annual spectacular showcase which was always built around an international star) at the Glasgow Alhambra next year, and she said she would consider it as she has never appeared on a British stage. I guarantee you the biggest audience of middle-aged men and women if and when she does appear. [126]

Strangely enough, the Glasgow Alhambra was to be the venue of Betty's European debut — but not in the role of Dolly Gallagher Levi!

Twentieth Century-Fox had acquired the film rights to *Hello, Dolly!*, and Grable's fans wrote to the studio by the thousands demanding that she be given the lead in the movie version. Betty's agents were also active on her behalf. Linda Schreiber, head of casting at the studio, said: "We didn't realize just how loyal Miss Grable's fans were. Their worship of the blonde pin-up of the forties appears to be just as strong in the late sixties. Quite a remarkable achievement considering she hasn't made a film since 1955." [127]

The studio discussed the casting, and at one time it was suggested to the board at Twentieth that Betty be teamed with Dan Dailey for the film version. The idea was a short-lived consideration. New members on the board didn't think the Grable name now big enough (as far as films were concerned) to carry the expensive production. (If Zanuck had been in charge, it is believed there would have been no hesitation in the re-teaming of the famous screen couple. Zanuck knew what it took to bring folks back to the cinemas.) After much debate, the role went to Barbra Streisand. For the fourth time in her career, the screen version of a top Broadway show eluded Grable.

Betty remained in the Broadway production until December. Merrick offered her another national tour, but she refused. She admitted she was disappointed at being "overlooked" for the London season. He again asked her to extend her contract and remain on Broadway. Again she said no. She was replaced by Ethel

Merman, who kept the show running for another six months, but with less spectacular box office returns — which was amazing, as Merman was always regarded as the Queen of Broadway.

But David Merrick had succeeded in doing what he had set out to do; he took the longest-running record from *My Fair Lady*. In that time the show had used five leading ladies on Broadway, and countless others on tour. After Merman, Merrick — desperate to keep his show at the top of the heap — even considered a drag Dolly for Broadway, and approached first Jack Benny, then British star Danny La Rue to play it, but both refused and the plan was abandoned. Undeterred, Merrick installed Pearl Bailey and an all-black cast to continue after Merman's stint with the show. The black *Dolly* was a huge success, giving a further lease on life to the already successful show.

After completing her run on Broadway, Betty and Bob left wintry New York and headed for the sunshine of Las Vegas. Throughout 1968, Betty — always accompanied by Bob — traveled regularly between Las Vegas and Hollywood for television shows. She was a popular panelist on shows like "Hollywood Squares" and was also often asked to appear on talk shows to chat about her career. She often expressed disappointment that after the success of *Hello, Dolly!*, nothing had materialized for her to be able to identify as "my own show," as she put it.

During that summer, she prepared herself for her first-ever trip "abroad." Her agent had secured her an offer of a three-week production of *Guys and Dolls* in Hawaii. She was a guest of Honolulu's Civic Light Opera Company. Betty enjoyed the vacation-cum-engagement and proved to be a big draw among the tourists and locals alike. She and Bob had fun on the island, attending many parties and functions to celebrate the success of the production. She met another superfan, Neil McAuliffe. She was delighted with his knowledge of her career and presented him with several personal mementos during her stay in the Pacific islands. She was the biggest draw among the many attractions in Hawaii.

On returning to mainland America, she agreed — after much persuasion — to go back into *Dolly*. It was a limited engagement, taking in four cities. One of the cities was Chicago, and Betty renewed her friendship with her ardent fan, Mike Levitt. He joined Betty and Bob for drinks and dinner several times, and Betty made him promise to visit her in Las Vegas.

Back in Vegas, she and Bob attended a revue to celebrate the frontier town's 100th birthday. The revue was called *The Piecefull Palace*, written by Warren Douglas. It was a fun-filled, fast-moving hour-long show concerning the antics of notorious outlaw Belle Starr, the James brothers, and Calamity Jane.

After the show, Betty offered her congratulations to author Douglas. He was impressed with Betty and remembered her fantastic drawing power in *Dolly*. He got together with revue lyricist Steve Allen and discussed the possibility of enlarging the revue and moulding the leading character of Belle to make it a starring vehicle for Betty. Steve agreed to work out some new songs, while Warren Douglas returned to Hollywood to rewrite the script. [128]

Betty and Bob had been living together for about three years now, and he had often asked her to marry him. She always refused — not outright, but she put him off with one excuse or another. Friends believed she was worried about how the public would react to the news that she had married a man some twenty-five years her junior. Undeterred, Bob continued to propose at regular intervals. He was sincere in his love for Betty, and said he would never stop asking until she accepted. There must have been a deeper reason for her refusing Bob. Her concern with public opinion was a lame excuse; she wasn't under a studio morals clause, and she didn't have to answer to anyone. All her family and friends knew they were living together as man and wife. All she had to do was make it legal, but she never did. The truth was she was still in love with Harry James.

But regardless of her marital status, it appeared Betty was completely footloose and fancy-free for the first time in her life. She regularly took in various shows in Las Vegas, and found herself at the other end of "fan worship" when she saw British singing sensation Tom Jones in action at one of his shows. She was in the audience several times over the next few weeks to watch the sexy Welshman with the powerful voice gyrate on stage. Eventually she plucked up the courage to visit him backstage.

Tom remembered the visit well.

> I couldn't believe it when someone came into my dressing room to say Betty Grable was outside waiting to meet me. Betty Grable, the biggest star of Hollywood musicals . . . waiting to see ME! I didn't believe him . . . but it was true!
>
> She was a lovely lady and I asked her a lot of questions about her career and the old days in Hollywood. I was amazed that she had never worked outside America. I found this incredible, her having been such a famous film star for so many years. I found her completely unaffected — unlike some other stars I had met. But I have found that the bigger the entertainer, the less affected they seem to be. Stars like Grable who had been in the business for many years are very basic people. They love what they are doing, and get a lot of enjoyment out of it — doing what they really want to do, and having fun doing it! Like I said, she was a lovely, friendly lady, so full of life. When I later met Lauren Bacall, I got the same impression. They were both very similar in their outlook. [129]

Meanwhile, Warren Douglas had been busy for the past couple of months rewriting *The Piecefull Palace* as a showcase for Betty Grable. He'd enlisted the aid of actor Rory Calhoun and television director Jerry Schaffer. Between them they found enough backers for the venture, provided they could get Grable as their star. Calhoun flew to Vegas to tell her of the plans. He reminded Betty how much she had enjoyed the original revue, and assured her the enlarged version was even better, with new songs written especially for her. He stressed that with her headlining the show, it would be a guaranteed success. Betty was intrigued to learn that the show would open in London's West End early in the New Year

— providing she signed. Douglas' chosen director, Jerry Schaffer, began telephoning her constantly, urging her to accept the deal. The final script wasn't quite finished, but with Warren Douglas working on it there should be no problems. (He was already an established writer, with TV shows such as "The High Chaparral" to his credit.) [130]

Betty was tempted; it would be the first show especially written for her. She discussed the proposal with Bob who advised her to read the script before making a final decision. She was due to fly to Los Angeles to discuss a deal for a series of TV commercials for the Playtex Corporation. Her friend Jane Russell was already successfully advertising the "bra for us bigger girls" on television, and Betty had been asked to model a new line of panty girdles. She told Schaffer she would meet him in Los Angeles in about a week or so, and discuss Douglas' proposal then.

An announcement in *Film Daily* helped Betty make up her mind. Ginger Rogers had been signed for a year's guaranteed run in London's West End in the new musical *Mame*. Betty was more than a little envious of Ginger, who would be assured of success in this tried-and-tested Broadway hit.

In Los Angeles, while staying at her sister Marjorie's, Betty conferred with her agent, Gene Yusem. Yusem arranged a meeting with Calhoun, Schaffer, and Douglas, and Betty temporarily put the show at the back of her mind while she discussed the Playtex deal with a TV advertising company. Within a few days, Betty's agent advised her that he had sorted out the details on the Douglas show, and that the contract which would take her into London's West End early in 1969 was waiting for her signature at his office.

Betty signed a day or two later. Calhoun and Schaffer were present and the group celebrated with a bottle of champagne . . . drunk out of plastic cups! Once she had signed, Betty was ecstatic about making her European debut and couldn't wait to get started. Calhoun told her he was flying to London in January to audition singers and dancers. Betty would travel to the English

288

capital in mid-February, and the show was scheduled to open in April or May, depending on the availability of a theatre. An announcement in the *London Times* that "Miss Betty Grable, the actress, would make her European stage debut in a Western musical entitled *The Piecefull Palace*..." brought the world's press to Betty's doorstep in Las Vegas.

In an interview she said:

> To be honest, I haven't even seen the script, and I'm not bothered about the money — it hasn't been mentioned. But the London stage sounds exciting and I've never been to England. The part sounds marvelous — Belle Starr was a very tough lady, and I'm looking forward to playing her. I'm not obsessed with working, and I'm not poverty stricken. I feel good when I'm on a stage, and show business has been so much a part of my life that I can't stop. When you've worked as long as I have, you can't suddenly sit down and turn on the television set, or settle down to playing two leisurely games of golf a week. Not me!

She added, with a touch of pride:

> "You know, my figure is exactly the same as it was when I was making two or three pictures a year in Hollywood." Betty admitted that news of Ginger Rogers' fabulous reception and incredible box office advance sales had impressed her. "Ginger will wow them, and I hope I will too." [131]

Betty went back to Los Angeles in January, 1969, to prepare for her forthcoming trip to Britain. But first she had a sad duty to perform. Her faithful basset hound, Hitchcock, was now 15 years old, had a heart condition, and was almost blind. A year or so earlier she had bought herself a a black Tibetan terrier, Kato, when Hitchcock appeared to be on his last legs. For a while, the arrival of the new puppy gave Hitch a new lease of life, and Betty was pleased her old pal seemed to be enjoying his new companion. However, her visits to the vet had increased during the last couple of months as the old dog's condition worsened. The vet advised her to have him put to sleep, but Betty maintained that so long as he wasn't suffering, she would look after him. "You don't put down people just because they go blind," she reasoned.

She realized that the strict British quarantine regulations would require Hitch to be kept six months in kennels while she did her London run, and Hitch would never survive being kept in a compound. Now she had to decide what was to become of him. She knew he would miss her terribly, and this could bring on a fatal attack. Betty knew the only answer. It was a sad day when she returned from the vet's office — alone. For the next few days she was inconsolable.

Vicki informed her mother that she was once again pregnant; the baby was due in late May or early June. Because of this new addition to her family — it would be her fourth grandchild — Betty consulted her lawyers and drew up a new will to include the new baby. The last time she had changed her will was when she'd divorced Harry James.

Betty shopped for a new wardrobe for her forthcoming trip. She had been advised she would suffer "agonies" in the English winter, and purchased several heavy sweaters. She also took time to write to several of her English fans, informing them of her plans. She was so excited about the whole venture. It was like a whole new beginning for her, a new adventure, and a chance to meet all the British fans who had been writing to her for years.

All during the preparations for her departure, she had never once asked writer Warren Douglas how the script was coming along.

CHAPTER FOURTEEN

On February 27, 1969, Betty, accompanied by Bob and her dog Kato, waved goodbye to her family as she boarded the Pan Am 747 flight to London. Always nervous about flying, Betty took a long time to settle down on her first transatlantic journey. She slept a little, played cards, and read travel magazines to while away the hours. She also chatted with several other first-class passengers who were clearly delighted to meet the amiable star and share reminiscenses with her. It was party time in the first-class lounge!

After a long night in the skies, the aircraft touched down at London's Heathrow Airport at 7 a.m. Tired, but happy the flight was over, Betty made her way down the walkway from the aircraft to be greeted by a battery of press and television cameramen. It was a welcome she didn't expect and wasn't prepared for. Every national newspaper in Fleet Street and all the television news-rooms had been notified of the date and time of her arrival — but even Frank Rainbow, head of the public relations company engaged to publicize the show, was surprised at the amount of coverage. [132]

Clearing through immigration, there was a mix-up over Kato, who was going to have to be impounded for six months because of the strict British regulations regarding the importing of dogs. Betty expected this, but the Customs official was so overzealous that he took the dog from Betty before she had time to give it a goodbye cuddle! The moment was captured by TV news crews, who jostled with each other for shots of the distressed star.

The official relented and Betty knelt down to bid farewell to her pet. Kato seemed not in the least bothered by the fuss or popping flashbulbs as photographers urged: "Just one more pose please,

Miss Grable." Eventually the dog was led away, leaving Betty more than a little upset.

Cleared of officialdom, there was another surprise waiting for her as she entered Terminal Three. Fans who couldn't wait a moment longer to meet their favorite star had traveled from all over England to welcome her. Betty was thrilled at this, as she shook hands with people she had written to over the years and knew only by name. She was later quoted in the press as saying: "I didn't think anyone would remember me."[133]

Some press men expressed disappointment about her appearance, particularly the fact that her legs were concealed by knee-high fleecelined boots. Replied Betty: "I was warned that it would be very cold over here, so I dressed for your weather — not for fashion!"

Betty chatted with her fans for more than a half hour and signed pictures and autographs for them (as well as several curious passers-by who had stopped to find out what the commotion was all about). Baggage handlers and taxi drivers called out, "Welcome to London, Betty!" as she made her way to the limousine that would take her to her rented luxury apartment at 42 Upper Grosvenor Street in Mayfair, close by the American Embassy and facing the famous square.

Betty was too excited to sleep when she and Bob reached the apartment where she drank her first cup of real English tea. She was entranced by London; the first thing she noticed on the drive to the apartment was the quietness of the traffic. "Much more civilized than in New York!"

After a couple of hours spent unpacking her luggage, she wanted to do the "whole tourist bit," as she put it: Buckingham Palace, St. Paul's Cathedral, the Houses of Parliament, the Tower of London . But jet lag quickly caught up with her. Instead of doing the "tourist bit" she decided, sleepily, to go to bed, making Bob promise to call her in time to go out on the town and have dinner and some fun. While she was preparing for bed the telephone rang. It was Eamonn Andrews of Thames Television. He hosted a weekly talk show and had prematurely announced in the previous week's program that Betty would be appearing on his show.

Betty took the phone and thanked Mr. Andrews for his call, but said she was "too tired" to appear that evening. "Perhaps we can make it next week, once I have settled in and returned to a more normal semblance of living," she added. That night Mr. Andrews went on the air apologizing to millions of viewers for the non-appearance of La Grable on his show. As a Grable fan, Mr. Andrews was said to be "most disappointed." (Despite many requests to appear on talk shows, Betty declined all offers of television work during her trip to Britain.)

The next day, Betty officially met the press in the luxurious Upper Grosvenor Street apartment. At noon the drawing room was packed with news reporters, fashion writers, magazine interviewers and, of course, photographers.

Director Schaffer talked at length ("Most boring," one journalist whispered audibly) about the show, *The Piecefull Palace*, describing it as a Western extravaganza with music. He said he hoped the show would eventually reach Broadway after a lengthy stay in the West End. The highlight of the evening would be the burning-down of the "Palace" — a spectacular event which proved very expensive and most difficult to mount, according to Schaffer.

Eventually he introduced Betty — not a moment too soon, for the press men were growing restless. Dressed in a modest black mini dress, she emerged from a side door. Her hair was swept off her forehead and tied with a black bow. Soon she was answering the same questions she had been asked many times over the years.

My legs? I never give them a thought, she told one reporter, then glanced down — horrified to find she had a 'run' in her stockings.

My films? Well, I guess I am not too proud of any of them — well, perhaps I do have one or two particular favorites. I never watch them on the late TV. I find it too embarrassing.

My figure? I don't diet, and the only exercise I get these days is driving to the golf course. My handicap? About twenty-four . . . terrible! (Betty had a true handicap of around twelve.)

Referring to her lack of film-making in the past decade, she said:

From time to time I am asked to accept roles, but some of them are really tasteless. I don't want to be a part of the movies that are being made today. Who wants to go to a movie to hear some actor utter four-letter words that you can hear free on any street corner? But I do admire some of the films that are being made, if only for their honest approach to life.

It's a sad fact they don't make escapist entertainment any more. The war made me a star. I came along at the right time — when people wanted to escape from their hum-drum lives. Today Hollywood is a factory. I had fun making films. I came in right between Alice Faye and Marilyn Monroe. There's no fun in film-making now. I'm glad I had my good times.

One magazine writer asked if she would change much in her past life if it were possible. Betty thought for a moment. "No. I had a great career, a happy marriage — for the most part — and a good life, thank God." About her divorce from Harry James, she was reticent. "I won't talk about it."

But pressed further, she said quietly: "With Harry always on tour somewhere or other, we just grew apart from each other . . . Yes, I still see Harry from time to time. We are still good friends."

Asked about her favorite co-stars, Betty mentioned she got on well with Alice Faye, Marilyn Monroe, and Lauren Bacall, but she wouldn't be drawn on her male co-stars, which was what the press wanted to hear. However she did admit a fondness for Tyrone Power and John Payne. Of course, Dan Dailey also came in for his fair share of praise. Of the stars she never got to work with, she admitted she was disappointed she had never appeared with Clark Gable.

She claimed the only time she "met" him was in the 1930s when she was at the dentist. She said her mouth was full of cotton and clamps when her dentist called a patient in from a side room. "'Come here,' he said, 'I want to show you a beautiful set of teeth.' Clark peered at my teeth. 'Very nice,' he said, and stepped back out of the office. That was my only encounter with my idol."

To further questions on her career, she said: "For a woman with no talent, I've been very, very lucky. I can sing and dance a little, but I'm nothing compared to a real actress. I've always considered myself a song and dance girl, and I've never taken myself seriously. How could I, when *Harvard Lampoon* voted me the worst actress of all time!" (She had cabled the magazine, agreeing with them.) "I was a star, but I could take it or leave it. I was never fooled, like some actresses, into believing what I read about myself in the fan magazines. Once you start doing that, you might as well give up. I treated the magazines as a joke, but they were usually very fair to me."

Of her fans, she said:

I have the loyalest fans in the world. We have been corre-sponding for years. I know some of the newer stars don't bother with their fans — that is all wrong. Some of them forget it is the fans who put us where we are — not the studio. The studio can only build you up — package you, if you like — and try to sell you to the public. The fans do the rest — they either buy the product or they don't. And if they don't, there is nothing the studio publicists can do about it. I'm always pleased to hear from my fans, and I spend about a month writing and sending out Christmas cards every year. It is well worth the effort!

During the interview, Bob Remick remained in the background, and he was introduced to inquisitive journalists as Betty's personal secretary — which no one believed for a moment! Betty wanted the details of her love life played down in the press, however, and did not discuss her relationship with Bob.

The Girl With the Million Dollar Legs

A journalist representing a Scottish national daily asked her how she felt about opening the show in Glasgow. "Glasgow?" she echoed, glancing over her shoulder at Schaffer, who gave her the merest of nods. "It's the first I've heard of it. But that's fine by me — it will be my first visit to Scotland."

A short while later, Betty posed for photographers in the wintry sunshine in Grosvenor Square Gardens. She laughingly but emphatically requested "not too many legs shots — save it for the show!"

One enterprising photographer later lined up several pretty secretaries, out on their lunch break from nearby offices. He posed them in the same way as he had posed Grable earlier. His paper ran a "just-for-fun competition" with about a dozen pairs of legs, asking the readers to spot the Grable gams. Betty was the outright winner — even though she was twice the age of the secretaries.

Betty received full coverage in the next day's papers. Most articles described her as charming, unaffected, and with an amazing lack of big-star pretense. As one writer summed up, "Miss Grable came over with considerable charm and good humour." A female scribe found her "quite sophisticated and exceptionally elegant."

The following Monday, with a cast of British singers and dancers already assembled, Betty reported for the first full rehearsal of the company at the London-Welsh Association halls in Holborn, close to the famed Covent Garden. Again the press was anxious to see Betty at work. They got an added bonus when they caught her in the middle of a dance routine wearing slacks under a taffeta skirt with a broken zipper, her blonde hair covered in a bandana. Betty wasn't in the least bothered. She said, "I'm saving the glamour thing for the show — that's when I'll sock it to them." [134]

Journalists were surprised to see her get in line with the cast for coffee and donuts. Said singer-dancer Valerie Walsh, who played Calamity Jane in the show: "Betty is a lovely person. Nobody has to wait on her. She asked us to treat her as one of the gang — that's the way she wants it." [135]

After lunch, she and Bob slipped out of the rehearsal to have a look around the Covent Garden market. "Gosh," she exclaimed, "It's just like it was in *My Fair Lady*!" But they had to beat a hasty retreat when the market porters recognized her and gathered around her for autographs. Before she left, she was presented with a beautiful bunch of roses. [136]

During her twice-weekly visits to her dog, Kato, who was living a life of luxury in a Surrey kennel, Betty and Bob would often stop at country pubs and inns for lunch. But word would quickly get around that she was in the dining room and she would be beseiged by polite but eager autograph-hunters. She almost always knew the line they would give when they approached her. "It's not for myself, Miss Grable, it's for my wife (or son, or daughter)." [137] Grable found this highly amusing, remarking that Englishmen were so bashful, as if they didn't want to intrude on her privacy. She didn't mind in the least. She enjoyed meeting people.

The show was scheduled to open at the Glasgow Alhambra on April 1. And, after five weeks of rehearsals, Grable and company flew to the Scottish city on Saturday, March 29. The aircraft landed at Glasgow Airport at 1 p.m. Only a dozen or so fans greeted her and she was quickly whisked away towards the city by car. Accompanied by Jerry Schaffer and publicist Frank Rainbow, she remarked on her lack of welcome to Glasgow. Rainbow smiled, "Just wait until you reach the center of the city."

At St. Enoch Square, in the heart of the city, a float and two huge Clydesdale horses stood gaily decorated, causing no end of puzzled looks from passers-by. The float had been loaned by the Black and White Scotch whisky company and, in conjunction with an electrical and television firm, was decorated in the style of a covered wagon of the Old West.

By the time the star's car arrived at the square, there was a crowd of around two thousand waiting to greet her. Those closest to the car noted the look of surprise on her face at the enormity of the crowd. She stepped out of the car into the warm spring sunshine — blonde hair sparkling, an expensive sable coat draped over her shoulders. The crowd was quick to let Hollywood's "greatest ever musical star" [as she was billed for the show] know she was welcome in Scotland. Betty waved happily to the crowd, shaking eager, outstretched hands as she was ushered by Calhoun and Schaffer. It took her several minutes to reach the comparative safety of the wagon.

However, Betty — well-known for her love of horses — spotted the magnificently groomed Clydesdales and insisted on petting them. The waiting photographers quickly pounced on the idea of getting some shots of Grable standing with the horses. She good-naturedly obliged and stood between the animals, fussing over them and whispering in their ears, while the press got their pictures. Her escorts hovered around, fearful that the cheering crowds would make the horses bolt with the million-dollar blonde standing between them. But Betty and the horses looked far from nervous. Grable knew her horses!

Eventually the press had enough pictures and the star was escorted to the wagon. She was helped aboard, and stood on the front platform acknowledging the crowd, which was now blocking traffic. Police were anxious to get it over with, and Mr. Calhoun and company were asked politely, but firmly, to "move along, please."

Just as the wagon was about to move off, a man in the crowd shouted: "Show us a leg, Betty!" She laughed, parted her fur coat and hitched up her skirt. "How about this?" she asked revealing a shapely knee and thigh. The crowd loved it. Betty added, "Come to the show next week and you'll see a lot more." She winked, sat down, and prepared for the half-mile ride to her hotel.

Her welcome at the hotel was as tumultuous as her earlier one. The main foyer of the staid Central was packed with people anxious for a glimpse of the blonde legend. Although they were mainly middle-aged, there were many young folk present who could only have known Betty through re-runs of her films on television. Judging by the applause as she entered the hotel, the fans were impressed with their first sight of the star. Grable again signed autographs, and had to be led away to the elevator to her second floor suite, far away from the noise and bustle of the main-line station below.

The hotel switchboard was instructed not to put through any calls to Miss Grable's suite. There was to be no press conference, and Betty would rest for the remainder of the day in preparation for the first full rehearsal of the company on Sunday afternoon.

She arrived at the theatre dressed in rehearsal clothes. The set was in place and the orchestra ready for its first run-through of the show. Journalists were still anxious to interview Grable and the stage door attendant had a tough time keeping them at bay.

Daily Express fashion writer Molly Kelly, accompanied by a photographer, got a lucky break. As she was pleading with the doorman, the show's choreographer, Jack Card, passed by. Molly had brought along her dog, Jet, a loveable black Labrador. Mr. Card stopped, turned to Molly and inquired: "Is this your dog?" Before she could reply, the young man asked: "What's his name? I'd like Betty to meet him." And that was it. Molly and her photographer were in! Jet disappeared with Mr. Card for some twenty minutes, and was fussed over by Miss Grable, who was still unhappy about having her own dog in quarantine. However, the lucky dog was the only one to "interview" her that day, although the photographer was allowed to take pictures of her during rehearsal.

During one sequence, Betty was dancing in front of an all-female chorus line when a trumpeter hit a wrong note. The star did a "double take", which seemed to please director Schaffer. "Great Betty, I like it. Keep it in!"

After rehearsal, Betty and Bob walked back to the hotel. Betty seemed disturbed, and at last confided, "I'm worried, Bob — I'm not being directed. You know I need good direction."

Back at the hotel, Betty placed a call to agent Gene Yusem in Los Angeles. He listened to her version of the way rehearsals were shaping up, and promised he would catch a flight over. He told her not to worry in the meantime; Glasgow was only a try-out, and the show should be in great shape by the time it reached London. Betty wasn't so sure.

She met the Scottish press in the theatre's lounge on the day of the show's opening — April 1. Betty remarked: "I hope everything goes well for the show. April 1 doesn't necessarily mean we will make fools of ourselves." She admittted to being superstitious, but when asked if she would be wearing a good luck garter, Betty laughed: "In all my films there was nearly always mention of a good luck garter." Fingering her pendant, she continued: "I shall be wearing this — it's a Chinese good fortune omen."

Although technically the Glasgow opening was a try-out for the West End, glamour-starved Glaswegians treated it as a world première.

Opening night was a glittering occasion at the magnificent Alhambra, one of the most decorative and best-equipped theatres in Britain. Civic dignitaries, local show business personalities, and a sprinkling of international stars who had traveled from London and the USA gave the theatre an air of expectancy, the like of which the city hadn't experienced in years. And, of course, Betty's fans were out in full force.

Backstage, Betty was nervous. Good luck telegrams had arrived from all over the world. Her dressing-room suite was swamped with flowers. A few last minute well-wishers called to wish her good luck. Betty thanked them quietly. She looked tense and anxious — worried about how the audience would take to her.

"Five minutes, Miss Grable," came the announcement over the loudspeaker system.

In the usual hurried flurry, her dresser made a few last-minute adjustments to her black-beaded costume. Betty added a final touch of rouge to her cheeks, picked up her red feather boa, and made her way up the stairs at the back of the set for her entrance.

The curtain had gone up on the show and the brief introductory lines had been spoken, when the orchestra struck up the show's theme tune, "Belle." The stage lights dimmed and a spot lit a doorway on an elaborate balcony high up on the set. Behind the double doors, Betty fidgeted. Two stage hands were poised ready to swing them open on cue. On impulse, one of the men whispered to her: "You're still my pin-up girl!"[138]

Betty smiled at him, the doors swung apart, and there she was — once more in the limelight, a fifty-two-year-old grandmother under the scrutiny of 2,500 pairs of eyes. The orchestra paused, and Betty's smile froze momentarily — had she failed to live up to the audience's expectations? She was soon to find out.

The waves of applause that came across the footlights were deafening. Orchestra leader R. V. Brand again struck up the title song, the chorus tried to go into its routine, and the lighting man brought up the full stage lights while retaining the spot on the lone figure on the balcony. The applause came thundering across, completely drowning out the musicians.

It was music to Betty's ears. She smiled and waved to the audience, looked down at the waiting chorus, and shrugged her shoulders in amazement. "What can I do?" she seemed to be saying to them.

The reception lasted fully five minutes. Many in the audience rose to their feet in homage to the legendary queen of Hollywood musicals. They were paying tribute to the girl who had brought them through a world war, the blitz on Clydeside, rationing, black-outs, and all the other factors the war had brought. This was a salute to Betty Grable, the brightest of all the stars, and here she was in the flesh. Glaswegians weren't going to let her forget how much she meant to them!

Eventually the cheering died down and the show at last got under way. Betty, husky-voiced, sang and danced her way through the show. She looked incredibly youthful on stage — the face and figure stood up to the rigors of time. And those legs! Every time they appeared from the slit of the beaded gown, the applause would start again. It was a fun night. However, the show was light-weight to say the least. The mainstay of the production was Grable, and the enthusiastic — if uninspired — dancing.

Betty was very nervous during this performance although it was not obvious to the audience. But the cast and crew knew when she didn't use any of the gun-totin' tricks she had rehearsed for weeks with stunt arranger Dick Shane, who had coached many stars in the art of handling guns for various Western films and TV shows. Shane said, "Right up until the opening night she handled the guns expertly but I guess she lost her nerve — which was a pity because she was perfect in every movement at rehearsal." [139]

At the finale, the audience rose in a body. When the curtain went up again, Betty was missing from the line-up. The cast took several bows before the curtain descended. When it rose again, there stood Grable — a lone figure on the massive stage. Once more, the applause reached a crescendo. Betty smiled, waved, blew kisses, and bowed. Theatre attendants approached the stage with bouquets of flowers, which she accepted. The curtain descended again. Betty walked off stage, only to be told by Schaffer: "Get back out there — they won't let you go!"

Betty handed the flowers to her dresser and again took up her position. Schaffer called to her: "Make a speech." The star turned to him: "I have nothing prepared. What can . . ." In mid-sentence, the curtain rose again and she was treated to another round of applause from an audience who just didn't want to let her leave the stage. Betty acknowledged them, and held out her hands in front of her in an attempt to quiet them. It was a minute or so before the storm abated. Many of the audience were in the aisles and around the orchestra pit, anxious to shout their greetings.

When the tumult finally subsided, Betty falteringly began, "Hello . . . this is such a surprise . . . I'm at a loss for words." Those close to the stage noticed the tears running down her cheeks, but she quickly regained her composure. "Ladies and gentlemen," she began. "I have played many theatres all over the United States, and I must honestly say that I have never, never had a welcome like this in all my life. This has been the highlight of my career. God bless you and thank you. You are wonderful. I love you."

The musicians, usually anxious to get home after a show, again struck up with "Belle." The cast, who had witnessed the moving scene from the wings, came onstage applauding the star of the show. That night Betty Grable belonged to Glasgow — and certainly Glasgow belonged to Betty Grable!

When the curtain finally fell, so ended one of the most nostalgic nights in Glasgow's theatre history. Backstage there was the usual crowd waiting to congratulate the star, an event that was to occur nightly. Betty thanked them as Bob ushered them from the dressing room, while she took a shower and changed. Outside the stage door, a hundred people waited to catch a glimpse of her as she left for her hotel. Again, Betty smilingly obliged the autograph hunters, then went on to an after-the-show party at the hotel.

The reports in the following day's papers were generally good, paying more attention to Miss Grable's youthful looks and legendary legs than to the show itself.

Wrote Mamie Crichton in the *Scottish Daily Express*:

> Flowers and curtain calls, storms of applause, and floods of nostalgia made Glasgow's salute to Betty Grable last night 'the highlight of her whole career'. As Belle Starr, the spirited madame of the *Piecefull Palace* saloon, Betty Grable kicked up still-shapely legs, sang in a husky voice and swaggered bravely in feathers and spangles.
>
> More stridency and vulgarity might have been even more convincing in the character of this very tough lady. But being a musical send-up of all the legends of the Old West, the show makes no pretense at either fact or fiction. Rory Calhoun's production of some intricate effect ran very smoothly on the first night, as did all the vigorous dancing staged by Jack Card. This should be a swift and enormously zestful show when it reaches London under the title of *Belle Starr*.

In the *Scottish Daily Record*, Ruth Wishart was equally enthusiastic in her praise:

> They stood and clapped and cheered at Glasgow's Alhambra last night. Not just for Betty Grable, the superstar who cried a

little as she thanked them. The show itself is the rootinest, tootinest package of mock Western madness.

Betty Grable is a revelation. I saw the lady rehearsing in London and, to be honest, the drab surroundings and daytime gear did nothing much for her. Fully made up and clad in revealing black velvet that they didn't buy in any sale, she looks sensational. Her low, husky voice is more than sexy enough. She is on stage virtually non-stop and doesn't put an elegantly-turned ankle wrong.

Glasgow Evening Citizen correspondent Archie McCulloch was also enthusiastic about the show, adding, "I bet the ladies in the audience, many of whom were only half Grable's age, wished they could look half as good as she does!"

The only sour note came from *Glasgow Evening Times* writer Jack House, who said: "Betty Grable can't act for toffee, and she can't sing either. But she has personality and beautiful legs. Maybe that's enough." Several letters were received (and published) by the *Evening Times*, all stating that Mr. House was out of tune with the show, and missed the whole point of the send-up aspects.

Changes were made nightly during the Glasgow run of the show, and by the last night it had been tightened up considerably. *The Piecefull Palace* did better than average business, considering the West of Scotland was enjoying an unseasonal heat wave, and cinema and theatre attendance was down.

One cinema, however, attracted crowds by showing Grable's *Three for the Show* during her first week in the city. Said cinema manager John Wright: "We are doing good business with people who come to compare Grable in the 1950s. Most of them have spoken to me on leaving the theatre saying that she looks better in real life than she does on film." [140]

Betty managed to fit in some sightseeing during her Scottish visit. One memorable Sunday, she and a few of the cast visited Inveraray Castle, the Duke of Argyll's ancestral home in the Western Highlands. On the drive north she stopped to chat with some shepherds and watch their dogs in action. She was most impressed with the intelligence of the animals. Betty also took some film of Highland cattle, but when one of the shaggy beasts decided to have a closer look at a Hollywood film star, she retreated to the car. Unfortunately, the Duke of Argyll was not in residence, but Betty and friends were shown through the castle's magnificent galleries and viewed its priceless paintings and treasures. They came away feeling that they had "stepped into the past," as Betty put it. "This is where the writers of *Brigadoon* must have got their inspiration."[141]

On April 5, Gene Yusem arrived from Los Angeles. He immediately conferred with Betty and Bob. She was to the point:

> Schaffer thinks he's got a hit on his hands. He is going to fall on his ass when we reach the West End unless something is done to save the show. I've talked with Warren Douglas, and he agrees with me that I should have some new material written in for me. There is nothing for me to do in this show except look pretty and flash my legs now and again. If this situation continues we won't last a week in London, let alone a year.

Her agent made sympathetic and understanding noises. "I'll wire Hollywood and see if we can get a good script doctor over. But first I'll have to get agreement with Calhoun and Schaffer."

"Screw them," retorted Betty. "Just you go and do what you have to do. I can smell a turkey. I've been too long in this business to be kidded along. There is nothing for me to do in this show."[142]

Betty's trepidations were not shared by director Schaffer, steering his first big musical onto a West End stage. It had cost around $750,000 to mount, and he allowed himself to believe that Grable's personal charisma was enough to pull in the crowds. He told scriptwriter Douglas that he was pleased with the way the show was going and saw no need to re-write or add any new bits of dialogue for Grable.

Another ongoing disagreement concerned Betty's costumes for the show. Her total wardrobe consisted of a beaded black velvet

Hello, Tommy
Greeting and
best wishes
from
Betty

3-1 Betty Grable smiles in this 1953 studio portrait (with autographed inscription to the author).

3-2 Betty and Harry James with their daughters, Vicki and Jessica in 1952.

3-3 Betty Grable with daughters Jessica, age eight, and Vicki, age eleven, on the set of *How to be Very, Very Popular* (20th Century-Fox, 1955).

3-4 Betty and daughters Vicki and Jessica shown at home at their Calabasas ranch in 1949.

3-5   Marilyn Monroe, Lauren Bacall, and Betty Grable pose for this
        publicity photo for *How To Marry A Millionaire* (20th Century-
        Fox, 1953).

3-6 Betty Grable and June Haver meet up with songwriter Harry Fox
     (played by John Payne) in this scene from *The Dolly Sisters* (20th
     Century-Fox, 1945).

3-7 Jane Wyman, Betty Grable, and Victor Mature from the film
     Footlight Serenade (20th Century-Fox, 1942).

3-8　Phil Harris and Betty Grable between takes of the film *Wabash Avenue* (20th Century-Fox, 1950).

3-9　Co-stars Betty Grable and Marge Champion greet visitor Loretta Young on the set of *Three For The Show* (Columbia, 1955).

3-10　Dan Dailey and Betty Grable in a cut scene from *Mother Wore Tights* (20th Century-Fox, 1947).

3-11 Marilyn Monroe and Betty Grable shown having fun at the
     Winchell birthday party, July 1953.
3-12 Betty Grable reads at poolside in a cut scene from *Three For The
     Show* (Columbia, 1955).
3-13 Betty Grable and Dick Haymes console each other in this scene
     from *Diamond Horseshoe* (20th Century-Fox, 1945).

Hello, Tommy—
Greetings and
best wishes
from
Betty

3-14 1953 autographed publicity shot for *How To Marry A Millionaire*.
3-15 The cut dream sequence from *The Farmer Takes A Wife*.
3-16 Betty Grable and Dale Robertson from *The Farmer Takes A Wife*.

3-17 Director Henry Koster with Betty Grable on the set of *Wabash Avenue* (20th Century-Fox, 1950).

3-18 Preston Sturges with Betty on the set of *The Beautiful Blonde From Bashful Bend* (20th Century-Fox 1949).

3-19 A stunning Betty Grable steps out with Robert Cummings and Tommy Noonan in *How To Be Very, Very Popular* (Fox, 1955).

917-A

3-20 Betty Grable in tremendous form in her final screen dance spectacular from *Three For The Show* (Columbia, 1955).

3-21 Betty Grable appears with Dick Haymes in her last television singing and dancing appearance – "The Fabulous Forties."

3-22 Betty Grable and Bob Remick at the 44th Annual Academy Award
Presentation (1972).

3-23 "The Last Hurrah!" Betty Grable signed and mailed this shot to
thousands of her faithful fans in December, 1972 – only six months
before she died of lung cancer .

For Tommy –
Best wishes
for the best of
everything.

Betty Grable

gown with a slit skirt; a silver and green outfit with a tear-away skirt; and a purple cowgirl outfit with matching boots. Many people wrote to her saying how unbecoming the purple outfit was, and she agreed with them. She insisted it be taken out. Schaffer was reluctant, but Grable was in no mood to be crossed. He obliged, somewhat ungraciously. [143] Her lack of spectacular costumes was amazing; the fans expected to see her dressed as she had been in her heyday. Schaffer promised her several new outfits to wear for the West End opening. Betty told him that it would take more than a few new costumes to save the show!

But his promises of new costuming came too late. The word had already filtered into London that *The Piecefull Palace* was a very shaky show.

There was no love lost between Grable and Schaffer. When two Scots fans, who met Schaffer in the theatre's bar at intermission, asked if it would be possible to go backstage and meet Betty after the show, Schaffer replied, "Sure, if she's not too bitchy."

The fans did go backstage to have their programs autographed, and when one of them blurted out Schaffer's comment about her, the smile froze on Grable's face. Later that night in the Central Hotel, she had a full-fledged battle with the director. She was furious and told him so, in no uncertain terms.

Closing night was again an evening of nostalgia. In fact, it was practically a re-run of the first night. Her fans cheered themselves hoarse. Many of them knew that Betty was unhappy with the show and did their best to encourage her to continue and face the West End in a few weeks time.

However, it was now a much slicker, livelier show than it had been on opening night. In one scene, Betty — in order to control a "fight" — had to fire her six-shooter at a chandelier. At each performance, the sound-effects man synchronized the "tinkling" of the chandelier to coincide with the shot. But on closing night, Betty fired the gun as usual — only to be left with an awful silence. Around fifteen seconds or so later, the chandelier "tinkled." Betty, her back to the audience, looked over her shoulder, blew into the barrel of her pistol, winked and said: "This must be the slowest gun in the West!" The audience loved it. It was the biggest laugh of the night, and it wasn't even in the script!

The songs for the show were, at best, ordinary. Some of the numbers Betty had to sing embarrassed her no end, such as "I've Got the Biggest Pair of 38's in Town," (referring to Betty's guns, of course!), "Ladylike Lady Like Me," and "It Takes One to Know One." Her voice was amplified with a tiny microphone sewn into her costumes which caused much technical trouble during rehearsals. During freak weather conditions one evening, it picked up local police radio messages.

Many of the audience at the final Glasgow performance went round to the stage door to say a personal farewell to the blonde star. She spent at least half an hour signing autographs and chatting to fans before Bob managed to lead her to the waiting car.

Once in the hotel, Betty and Bob made straight for their suite. There was no final night party. She had to be up early to catch the 10 a.m. London train — to face her first West End audience.

CHAPTER FIFTEEN

The title of *The Piecefull Palace* had been changed to *Belle Starr* for the London opening. The producers thought that the original title might cause confusion since they were opening at the Palace Theatre. That anyone would have been confused is debatable; but unfortunately, everything besides the title remained the same. For the West End production, director Schaffer decided to revert to the original version of the show — in other words, the same one they'd opened with in Glasgow. Betty was furious and told him so. He argued that the Scottish critics loved it and so would the Londoners.

Betty dreaded the West End opening. The advance publicity for the show was poor. Betty herself was partially to blame for this; she had shunned pre-show publicity which hadn't helped advance ticket sales. She also had a terrible premonition that the show was doomed.

On opening night, at least, Schaffer's optimism seemed vindicated, as the audience's reaction to Betty's first entrance was as genuine and heartwarming as it had been in Glasgow. Betty knew, however, that the response was based purely on nostalgia — "and my legs." The show was simply not up to the usual West End standards. It was badly lacking in substance and style; although supposed to be a send-up, the script stopped short of high camp, and that was a mistake. If, as Grable had often suggested, they had done the show as straight burlesque instead of stooping to vulgarity, it might have had a better chance of success. As it was, the only reason the show didn't fold after the first performance was Grable. The rest of the cast, mainly newcomers to the West End, knew it too.

The company had to wait an extra day to read the reviews because of a one-day strike on Fleet Street. It was an agonizing wait, particularly for Betty. As she expected, *Belle Starr* was given the thumbs down, though some critics were kind to the star herself.

Not so the *Daily Mail*, which claimed that "Miss Grable has nice legs, well-matched . . . and able to dance for several seconds at a time."

Milton Schulman, of the *Evening Standard*, condemned the show by personally focusing criticism on Grable. It was one of the most vicious attacks to be made on any star in years. He wrote: "Grable has about as much sex appeal as Miss Vanilla Ice Cream of 1936. She has a timid little wiggle purporting to pass for voluptuousness, and a voice that barely reaches across the footlights."

As had happened with the *Glasgow Evening Times*, the *Standard* received and published several letters defending the show. One man wrote saying that Schulman had missed the whole point of the exercise. It was a "fun" show, and not to be taken seriously. The writer of the letter went on to say that others in the audience appeared to have enjoyed themselves, according to comments he had heard on leaving the theatre.

But the rot had set in. Many British showbiz personalities believed that the overkill publicity Ginger Rogers had received when she arrived for *Mame* had turned the critics sour, and that Grable was on the receiving end of the backlash of a Fleet Street anti-American campaign.

Bette Davis, in London for a new film, visited Betty after one performance and told her not to worry about the critics. "I've had trouble with them all my life," she said. [144]

Plays and Players magazine did not like the show as a whole and said they would rather have seen Grable in something more suited to an undoubted star of her magnitude. "A star without a show," was how they tagged her.

Well-known singer Frankie Vaughan, a good friend of Betty's, had had great chart-topping success with songs like "Hello,

Dolly!" and "Mame." He offered to record "Belle" — which was quite a catchy number — and rush-release the disk in the hope that it would help save the show. However, the producers decided not to accept his generous offer. Personally, Betty felt that nothing could save *Belle Starr*, and her mood was decidedly gloomy. It was an anti-climax to her previously successful stage ventures.

Yet, despite the pulverizing notices, Betty and the cast went through their performance each night — often to a half-empty theatre. Business just wasn't picking up.

Bubbly blonde British actress Barbara Windsor went backstage to visit Betty after one performance. When she emerged from the dressing-room after their chat, Barbara seemed upset. When asked about it, she replied: "I *am* upset. There's Betty Grable, one of the greatest stars of all time, in a show she knows is going to fold. Yet she gives it one hundred percent at each performance. She's a real trouper." [145]

Betty again confronted Schaffer and demanded that she be allowed to bring in her own scriptwriter to help save the show. "I'll pay all my own expenses, so you don't have to worry on that score," she told him icily. She also demanded and was given two extra costumes to wear. The press was invited backstage to photograph her in the new outfits to boost flagging ticket sales. But it didn't help much.

Author Warren Douglas approached Betty about what he could do to help, and she put forward several ideas for him to work on. Outside her dressing room, Douglas walked into Schaffer, who "tore the author to shreds over the failure of the show," according to one eye-witness. Betty overheard the row and was on the point of opening her door to go out and defend Douglas, when Bob intervened. [146]

"Keep out of it," he advised her. "You have a show to do tonight, and you can't let yourself get upset." She knew Bob was right. She had had her say with both the director and the author and they knew how she felt about the whole disaster.

The next day, Warren Douglas and his wife Bonnie, flew back to the U.S. Said Betty later, "They crucified that man. It wasn't his fault. If only Schaffer and Calhoun had listened to some good advice, they might possibly have had a hit on their hands."

Superfan Bob Isoz flew in from the U.S.A. to see the show and visited Betty backstage. He said: "The show was disappointing. It wasn't Betty's fault, but there were lots of things wrong with it. She felt bad about letting down her British fans, although audiences seemed to love her." [147]

A couple of days later Schaffer himself flew back to the States, leaving Betty and the cast stranded with a mass of unpaid bills. Top photographer Anthony Crickmay, who had done all the stills for the show in Glasgow, hadn't been paid.

Said Betty, "I had to go to the front office myself to find out what was going on. Nobody seemed to know anything. What a fiasco it had turned into. The debts were escalating daily. Then someone in the cast came to my dressing room and told me the show was closing the following Saturday."

The theatre management confirmed the show would close on May 17, after twenty-one performances. Said a sad Grable:

> I don't think I disappointed my fans. The critics killed the show, but they have a right to their opinion. Mail has poured in praising it, and my fans are very honest. Sure, there were some things wrong with the show. We were trying to improve it right up to the last night. Some of the things I had to say were downright embarrassing. Jokes were in bad taste — these things upset me a bit. But we were not the only show in London without packed houses. If we could have held on for another two weeks, we would have been in for a long run. You know, this is my first-ever flop."

Betty admitted that she had done more fighting backstage during the brief history of *Belle Starr* than she had ever done in her long career.

She was due to attend the prestigious British Variety Club luncheon as guest of honor, but she cancelled the engagement due to the bad publicity the show had received. Variety Club officials were very disappointed, as they were eager to pay tribute to one of the biggest names in the history of show business. But the truth was that Betty was too embarrassed to attend in the face of all that had happened over the past couple of weeks. She felt that she, personally, had let everyone down.

The closure notices brought a flood of ticket sales, and the last two nights of the show were completely sold out. Betty faced the last packed house with mixed feelings. She knew her fans were out in full force, and despite feeling very sad about the whole affair, she sang and danced her way through the evening as though she hadn't a care in the world. At the final curtain, she was crying, but not with happiness this time. She was embarrassed, she felt she had let the cast down. There were also tears of anger that the producers had fled, leaving her holding the most expensive West End flop in years.

Hundreds of fans lined the perimeter of the orchestra pit, anxious for their last glimpse of Grable. They were shouting: "Come back in *Dolly*"; "Revive *Guys and Dolls*"; and there were shouts of: "We love you, Betty." She acknowledged them all with a sad little speech.

But still they kept shouting, urging her not to take any notice of the critics and the hurtful personal remarks in the press — particularly those of Mr. Schulman.

Through all the noise, the blaring siren of a passing fire engine was heard throughout the auditorium. Putting her hand to her ear, Betty summoned a smile and said, "Listen. We'll have to go — I think they're coming to take us away." She managed a final wave before the curtain fell for the last time on *Belle Starr*. In her dressing room, there was pandemonium. Most of the cast were calling to say their goodbyes and there were lots of tears and hugs for their favorite leading lady.

Outside, she found that hundreds of fans had mobbed the stage door and it was nearly an hour before Betty had signed her last autograph. She was visibly moved by their loyalty, and promised them she would return to London someday — "... but next time, with a hit!" [148]

Eventually Betty reached her waiting car, and sped off to her London apartment. When the couple arrived, a few friends were waiting to greet them. Betty invited them to stay for drinks and appeared to be quite cheerful, despite the sadness of the whole affair. Actually, she was glad it was finally over; she had been expecting closure notices, and the uncertainty was much more of a strain than the actual announcement.

The Starlight Club, a luxurious private cinema in the May Fair Hotel near Betty's apartment, had planned a "Tribute to Betty Grable Week." Unfortunately, it commenced two days after the closing of *Belle Starr*. The poor timing did not deter her fans; they turned up for the week-long Grablefest anyway. Theatre manager John Hickey telephoned the star inviting her to make an appearance after the screening of one of her films.

"What's playing?" she inquired. When told it was *The Beautiful Blonde From Bashful Bend*, she declined the invitation. She had had enough of musical westerns to last her a lifetime! [149] Mr. Hickey was disappointed, but the screening was very successful and played to capacity audiences. Normally, Betty would have been happy to oblige her fans, but in the wake of the *Belle Starr* disaster, she knew she couldn't watch herself on the screen in what had been another near-flop.

Following the closing of *Belle*, the papers carried stories of the expensive West End fiasco. A theatre spokesman had informed the press that they had made the decision to close after studying the advance booking lists. The show needed to take between £6,000 and £7,000 a week to pay its way, but the spokesman said, "Takings were slightly below that level."

Naturally the press was anxious to record Betty's feelings as well. She wasn't at all keen to see them, but Bob advised her to do so and clarify her position. That afternoon Betty once more met with journalists who, only three short months earlier, had welcomed her to London. She told them:

The worst thing that happened to us was receiving good notices in the Scottish press. The producers thought they had nothing to do but sail into the West End with a ready-made hit. Naturally, I'm distressed. But it's not the end of the world . . . I'll get over it. I am only sorry for the others in the show; those poor actors and dancers who have been thrown out of work. As far as I understand they haven't been paid either. It's shameful. I want to get across that I have never seen anyone work harder than the kids in the cast. Any of them can be a star in his or her own right.

It was typical of Betty Grable to worry more about the young people in the show than about her own predicament. Even at the height of her career in Hollywood she always made sure her co-workers got a fair deal. Often, she deliberately held up a scene in a movie as it neared shutdown time so the chorus boys and girls would qualify for some overtime. Blayne Barrington, who played Billy the Kid in *Belle*, maintained that Betty Grable was the most helpful and compassionate star he had ever worked with. "She took time to help the cast with little bits of business. It was a pleasure working with her." [150]

Betty declined to pose for pictures for the post-*Belle* press interview, but she did promise one cameraman a photo-session of her with dog Kato at the Surrey kennels. True to her word, they drove down to the Hackbridge boarding kennels the following day. Betty was welcomed by owner Alan Hackbridge, who gave her an up-to-date report on her dog. Soon she was reunited with her beloved Kato, who leapt at his mistress. Betty made a great fuss over the dog, and the photographer got his shots. "Who said it isn't a dog's life?" laughed Betty, happy to be with her faithful friend. Next day the newspaper had pictures of Betty playing with Kato, with the caption: "Betty Grable can still manage a smile . . .".

The out-of-work star spent the remainder of her stay in London enjoying herself. She visited several night spots, including Danny La Rue's Club in Hanover Square. She and Danny — Britain's most famous drag artist — had become good friends during Betty's stay in England. He was one of Betty's most ardent fans, and they had plenty of laughs together, with Danny's equally outrageous sense of humor matching Betty's.

Her co-star in the show, Valerie Walsh, had been instrumental in introducing Betty to La Rue. She had worked with him for several seasons, and had kept her late-night revue job during the run of *Belle Starr* in the West End. Grable was very fond of Valerie, and predicted she would be a big name in the musical theatre. Typical of Grable, she always beat the drum encouraging newer, younger talent. Miss Walsh later had a great success in the West End, playing one of the strippers in the musical *Gypsy*.

One journalist friend suggested Betty take her own show on the road. Before he could continue, she interrupted, "No. I can't carry a show on my own. I need to be surrounded by all the glamorous trappings." But the journalist went on to suggest a sort of "Celebrity Talk-In" — "like a lecture show," he told the astounded Grable — with the first half of the show consisting of clips from her best-known films, and the second part allowing Betty to field questions from the audience. Betty said she didn't own any of her films, and as far as she knew Twentieth Century-Fox had sold them to Seven Arts Productions. She thanked the journalist for his suggestion, but felt it would involve too much legal work to borrow the film clips.

The journalist was simply way ahead of his time. Since then, many stars, such as Bette Davis, have earned a lucrative living doing such shows. It helped to keep them in the limelight when no other work was forthcoming.

Betty was undecided about whether to travel through Europe or head back to the States. She said to Bob, "It's a pity to be so near the European capitals without getting a chance to see them." "After all," she joked, "in many of my films I was the toast of the Continent — but that was all recreated on the Fox backlot! It would be nice to be able to visit the cities I was supposed to have [seen] in my movies!"

Bob spent an afternoon browsing through a travel agent's office in Bond Street. It was Bob, with his experiences abroad in the U.S.

military, who had given Betty this desire to travel. He was pleased about this, and always maintained that Betty Grable had a very youthful approach to life. His enthusiasm for living had smitten her.

An early morning phone call from Las Vegas put an end to the couple's plans for a grand tour of Europe. Vicki's husband phoned to say that she had given birth to a healthy son. That decided it for Betty. She was eager to see her new grandchild, and told Bob to make reservations to return to the States.

Bob suggested that they travel back to the U.S. by ship, stating that the sea voyage would give Betty a much-needed break. The liner *France* was sailing from Southampton on Friday. She agreed with his suggestion, and told him to go ahead and make reservations. To her English secretary, she was less enthusiastic. "I've never been on an ocean-going liner before," she confided. "I just hope I'm not seasick!"

The day before she was due to leave London, she received a call from Hollywood. Producer Robert Aldrich, who had resurrected the careers of Bette Davis and Joan Crawford with the highly-acclaimed *Whatever Happened to Baby Jane,* was on the line. He had a starring role for Betty in a new film he was preparing to shoot on location in Israel. It was a female version of *The Dirty Dozen*. He wanted Betty for the role of a tough lady Israeli sergeant, and it would be "only lightly dramatic, with lots of comedy touches."

Betty thanked him for the offer, and said she would give him her answer as soon as she returned home. She talked over the new offer with Bob. It had come as a complete surprise to her as it would be her first film role in fourteen years. Bob advised her to read the script first. She assured him she would never again make the mistake of not doing so. "A lady sergeant," she pondered. "No false eyelashes and no lipstick. I'll look terrible."[151] (On her return to the the States, she rejected the role, and the part ultimately went to Elke Sommer.)

The couple left Waterloo Station next day on the boat train to Southampton. There were only a few fans to see her off, as Betty hadn't revealed her plans to the press. On that day, the *Stage* newspaper carried a front page ad which read, "Goodbye and good luck, Betty Grable. Thank you for being such a super lady as well as a Superstar — from the cast of *Belle Starr*." The previous week's edition of the show business newspaper had carried a similar message from Betty to the cast.

The *Evening Standard* also carried a small paragraph on the inside pages of its first edition that day, "Betty Grable sails to New York on the liner *France* this afternoon. Someone should ask her back to London soon." It appeared as though they were trying to make amends for Schulman's blasting of the show. Of course, it was all too late.

The five-day Atlantic crossing was a delightful trip for Betty. She loved life on the high seas and mingled freely with the other passengers. No one mentioned the *Belle Starr* disaster. Betty appeared to have forgotten the drama of the past few weeks. She and Bob visited the ship's discothèque, and Betty proved herself adept at all the latest rock 'n' roll dances. They also often danced ballroom style and, much to Betty's embarrassment, there was always a round of applause when she and Bob took the floor. The sea was calm, the weather fine and sunny. And Betty Grable wasn't seasick once — much to her relief!

On docking in New York, the press was waiting for them. A rumor had circulated that Betty and Bob had married in London. The couple denied it, and the press men went on to ask what had happened with *Belle Starr*. Betty replied, "I'm used to this. None of my films ever received rave notices — that's a fact I've had to live with for years. But I want to go on record as saying this is my first-ever financial flop — and please underline the first!"[152]

The couple remained in New York for three days, visiting Bob's mother in Brooklyn. Mrs. Remick, although only a dozen or so years older than Betty, liked her and hoped one day that her son would make her his bride.

Bob again proposed over dinner one night in the city. Betty asked, "Why marriage, Bob? I'm a three-time loser, first with

Jackie, then George Raft, then Harry. Let's just go along as we are — then nobody gets hurt." She genuinely loved him, and she could tell he loved her by the way he had stood by her and protected her during the disastrous trip to Britain. But she still held back. Bob didn't believe she meant what she said about being a loser. And he didn't care what people would think. He loved her and that was all that mattered to him.

Their relationship had altered since their stay in London. Previously Betty had definitely been the shy, retiring type, depending on Bob for everything. Now she was much more assertive, she was drinking a lot less, and her general disposition was much more amenable. Perhaps the fact that she had come through menopause also helped.

The couple flew on to Las Vegas and settled back into a domestic routine — Betty smilingly noted that Kato had "fallen in love with the garden trees all over again." When her Las Vegas chums asked her about London, all she would say was: "Life must go on. There is no point in feeling sorry for myself. Everybody is entitled to one big mistake in their career — and now I've had mine. In fact, I've had plenty, but I'd rather not talk about them!"

Betty seemed determined to resume some semblance of her normal life. She resumed her golf dates with her girlfriends, and she and Bob were again spotted in the many nightspots of Las Vegas. Betty loved the gaming tables and would have played all night — or as long as the money lasted. She was still a poor gambler and an even poorer loser. When she had been married to Harry James, she had denied persistent rumours that she had lost a fortune at the tables. She maintained, "Show business is too much of a gamble in itself for me to get into any heavy games."

But she did. It was only after hours of coaxing and cajoling that Bob could pry her away from the tables. It led to many rows between them, sometimes culminating with Betty walking out on him. But it was all quickly made up and forgotten next day. Betty would chide him for being a "big spoilsport," although she knew he was right.

But all play and no work wasn't Betty's style, and soon after her return to Las Vegas she contacted her agent to announce she was ready to go back to work. "I want to get the bad taste of *Belle Starr* out of my mouth," she told him. When several weeks passed with no work on the horizon, she became a little uneasy. Was it really the end this time? She knew all too well that no one wanted to be associated with failure. And *Belle Starr* was a big failure, even though it wasn't entirely her fault.

Perhaps she shouldn't have been so hasty in refusing the Aldrich film. Maybe it was just the break she needed to get her name back in movies. Truthfully, she knew she couldn't have accepted the offer; she had been away from the film industry too long. What she really needed was a top show, geared to her particular talents. And Fate was about to step in again.

When her agent did call, it was to offer her the lead in a summer theatre company's production of *Born Yesterday*, a role created by the late, great Judy Holliday. Betty was anxious to return to the footlights, and the play was by now a classic in the American theatre. But it was a straight comedy, with no musical numbers to help her through the performance.

She mulled over the offer. It was a splendid play, but what she really had been hoping for was a revival of *Guys and Dolls* or a limited engagement of *Hello, Dolly!* She was worried that she might not have enough talent to carry a straight legitimate play, especially one pioneered by the highly-talented Miss Holliday.

With Bob's encouragement — "what would I do without him?" she would confide to friends — she accepted the deal. "At least I'll only have myself to blame if I flop this time," she quipped, only half kidding.

The company played to packed houses in Baltimore, Philadelphia, Maine, and several other areas on the East-coast circuit , finishing the tour in Illinois a week before Christmas. [153] The "dumb-blonde" role was tailor-made for Betty, and she was well-received wherever she appeared.

The success of the tour was just the tonic Betty needed. It was good to be part of show business again, she said. And it was even better to be identified with a hit — "albeit second-hand," she confided to friend Carol Burnett.

The summer theatre booking agents noted her financial returns for the tour, which were among the highest for the season. *Born Yesterday* was cheaper to stage than a musical of the magnitude of *Guys and Dolls*. They made a mental note to use Grable whenever possible.

Summer theatre was a growth industry in the United States, and Betty had gotten in at the beginning. In fact, when pal Dorothy Lamour decided to do a tour on the circuit, she sought Betty's advice on venues and directors. And Betty always recommended her favorite stage director, Don Arden.

New Year in Las Vegas was a happy time for Betty. She was reunited with her daughters and grandchildren. Later in the month she held a private party for several hundred show-business friends at the Riviera Hotel to celebrate her fortieth year in the business. The party went on into the wee small hours, and Betty was in there with the rest of the revellers. The "reborn" Grable didn't dance the night away to the big band sounds of the forties either — Betty was into disco dancing in a big way and she was thoroughly enjoying the experience.

"Forty years! Not bad for a no-talent chorus girl, huh?" she remarked as she danced with guest Andy Williams.

The year 1970 promised to be a busy one for Betty. Offers for summer theatre work were coming in thick and fast, and it was just a matter of getting the best deal. The upturn in her career delighted her. Was it really only seven short months ago that she was moping over the disaster of *Belle Starr*?

"Show business," she mused. "It can take you to the highest heights. And it can also break your heart!"

CHAPTER SIXTEEN

After more than a year's hiatus from television, the medium beckoned once again, and Betty joined the panel of "Hollywood Squares" for the new season. She won many new followers with her quick wit and breezy personality, although she admitted she didn't particularly enjoy television panel games.

As she had thought, 1970 was proving to be a very lucrative year for her. The Geritol vitamin company used pictures of Betty at various stages in her life, with the final picture showing her as she looked in the present day. The ad claimed that she kept her youthful looks and vitality by taking her daily "pill." She also did a newspaper layout for a national airline. She had once been approached to do a denture fixative ad, but the company backed off when they were informed that Betty's teeth were her own.

With old pals Jane Russell and Rhonda Fleming, she talked of getting an act together featuring the three of them — a blonde, a brunette, and a redhead — aiming to take it to the top nightclubs. But the idea fizzled out. A writer came up with the idea of having the three beauties make a pilot for a projected TV series, loosely based on the plot of *How To Marry a Millionaire*. The girls were to portray retired airline stewardesses, now divorced and living in New York. It would have been a sort of early forerunner of "The Golden Girls," but it never got past the talking stage.

Soon after her return from London, she had unwittingly hit the headlines — and gossip columns — when Rory Calhoun's estranged wife, Lita Baron, sued her husband for divorce, claiming that he had been unfaithful to her with Betty Grable and seventy-eight other women! Grable contacted her lawyer to see what could be done about her name being besmirched in this way.

It is possible, but highly unlikely, that Grable may have had a mild fling with Calhoun when they both worked on *Meet Me After the Show* and *How to Marry a Millionaire*. Betty claimed she never believed in adultery, and, in any case, during those years she was still deeply in love with Harry James. As far as the trip to Europe was concerned, Bob Remick was adamant that he was the only person to share Betty's bed. And he insisted that he and Betty had such a good, loving relationship that there was never a time when either of them "strayed." They were happy with each other.

She wanted to issue a denial, but her lawyer advised her to ignore the accusations, and let the matter die a natural death. She did, and the whole divorce business was soon forgotten. The Grable image of "wholesomeness" remained intact.

The next few months saw her off on a fresh tour with *Born Yesterday* as well as a variety of television appearances. She also undertook a short tour of *Hello, Dolly!* during 1971, playing Atlanta, Georgia and Toledo, Ohio.

Carol Burnett and Betty were great friends, and she was often asked to guest on the Burnett show. Betty almost always refused, saying she was too busy, but she did manage to put in a few guest spots. It was the same with Lucille Ball; Betty seemed to feel she was being done a "favor" when she was asked to appear on friends' shows, when in fact her talent and popularity were the big draw. One memorable slot when she did agree to appear in the "Carol Burnett Show" featured Betty singing "Hello, Dolly!" (for which she had to get special permission from David Merrick) and performing a few comedy routines with her hostess.

Her Chicago friend and fan, Mike Levitt, had been in and out of Betty's life quite regularly since her return from London. She had asked him to spend a holiday in Las Vegas, which he did. She treated him royally. She was very fond of him and once told him, "You know, Mikey, you are the only friend I have in the world."

Levitt said later:

I thought it was a very sad thing for her to say. She had many friends, but I really don't think she allowed herself to get close enough to too many people to regard them as friends. She had many show-business chums, but they were like workmates to her. Betty could, and often did, open her heart to complete strangers — once she found them to be genuine. Betty Ritz was different, but they were distanced from each other, through Ritz living in Acapulco.

Betty was always promising herself that she would drop in on her and spend some weeks in the Mexican resort. But there was always a show to do, a TV spectacular to shoot, or a new play to rehearse. And it always bugged Dorothy Lamour when Betty blew hot and cold with their long-time friendship. It was as if she was afraid to get too close to people, particularly her women friends. 154

Mike, a trained hairdresser, said that Betty had offered to set him up in business in Las Vegas. "It was very flattering, but the sort of friendship Betty wanted might have proved too smothering — and could have endangered the nice relationship we had. I was also very fond of Bob Remick. He was a regular guy."

Betty was asked to make a TV commercial for Geritol, and was given an all-expense-paid trip to New York for her and Bob. She insisted that Mike Levitt be included in the deal " . . . as my hairdresser." He was, and the entourage was given the red-carpet treatment in New York, including a suite at the Plaza Hotel, all expenses paid. On their first night in the city, Betty decided she would have an early night as she had to be up at 5 a.m. for the TV shooting schedule.

Mike Levitt remembered:

Betty thought it would be nice if we had dinner in the suite instead of going downstairs to dine. We all agreed but when Betty looked at the menu, she said: 'I don't care if the TV company is picking up the tab. The prices for room service are ridiculous.' So it was decided we would bring in some food —

chicken, cold cuts and salad (just like a picnic, Betty said). While Bob and I went out in search of an all-night delicatessen, Betty said she would mix the pre-dinner martinis.

By the time we returned, Betty had consumed quite a few martinis and was all set to party. We sat on the floor and ate our picnic. Betty was in fine form, laughing and joking. Suddenly she decided she wanted to go out on the town. She asked me to take her to a bar after Bob had refused to escort her. He wanted her to stay home and get some sleep before the commercial. Once Betty made up her mind, there was no stopping her. We left the hotel, and the doorman hailed a taxi to take us to a bar. Betty said she'd rather walk. A couple of blocks away we came on a piano bar. We went in and ordered a couple of vodka martinis.

As it happened, it turned out to be a gay bar and she was quickly recognized. Drinks were sent up to us, and Betty was soon deep in conversation with some ardent — and very excited — fans. They just couldn't believe their luck! The next thing I knew Betty was up at the piano, singing songs from her films. The fans loved it — and so did Betty. She was having a ball. When we first went into the bar [it] wasn't too busy, but once Betty started her 'act'. they seemed to empty out from all the other bars just to be with her.

The place was jumping — packed with guys who just wanted to shake the hand of Hollywood's most famous musical star. She was having the time of her life. And so were they — I hadn't realized till then just how revered she still was.

By now it was nearly 2 a.m. and I had promised Bob I would get her back to the hotel for her all-important sleep. I went over to the piano and reminded her of the lateness of the hour. She smiled at me, put her lips up to kiss me. I responded and as our lips met, she bit into my upper lip. God, it was painful. I have the scar to this day to remind me. [155]

After the lip-biting incident, Grable appeared to sober up and Mike got her back to the hotel without much trouble. But she still wasn't sleepy. She decided her hair was a mess. It was too dark for the commercial, and she asked Bob to go out to an all-night drug store for some bleaching agent and a platinum rinse. Bob obliged, knowing that to refuse Betty in her current mood was tempting fate. He returned shortly and Betty got to work on her hair. By the time she got into bed it was almost 4 a.m.. An hour later she was up, showered, and dressed, ready for the studio limousine at 6 a.m.

The first take of the commercial was perfect and was completed in less than an hour. Betty was pleased; they hadn't called her "one-take Betty" during her years at Twentieth for nothing. None of the crew could believe that their star had only had about an hour's sleep. She looked great.

Unfortunately, the sound engineer found a fault in the playback, and the scene had to be shot again. Filming went on all day, each take progressively worse than the last. Eventually the director abandoned filming. Betty returned to the hotel in a bad frame of mind. "She felt responsible, and nothing could get her out of this mood."

Recalled Mike:

> There was no party atmosphere in Betty's suite that night. She was in a deep depression. Any suggestions Bob and I came up with fell on deaf ears. Perhaps she was dog-tired at not having any rest the night before, but I think she was angry about the abandonment of the TV shoot. She was a perfectionist in her work, and she was irked that while she started off the filming in her usual professional manner, the technicalities of filming had let her down. [156]

Next day the trio parted at Kennedy Airport; Mike caught his flight to Chicago while Betty and Bob flew on to Las Vegas. She made Mike promise to come out and visit her soon. He promised he would.

There was talk of Betty taking over from Ruby Keeler in the revival of the hit musical *No, No Nanette*, on Broadway. Betty turned it down, but added that she would like to take the show into London. She said she wanted to make amends to her British fans, "Last time I left a bad taste in their mouths, I guess I owe it to them."

However, the producers had asked Alice Faye to head the London production, and she was considering the offer. The London opening of the show wasn't scheduled until the middle of the following year, so there was still a chance for Betty to appear in London should Alice refuse the part.

Shortly after she returned home, the vitamin pill sponsors called again. This time they would film in Los Angeles. In a pitch at projecting Betty as the world's most glamorous grandmother, they proposed that she appear in the commercial with her two daughters and five grandchildren. Betty agreed. The filming was done in two days, and it was an enormously successful television advertisement for the company.

Betty and Bob returned to Las Vegas. Mike Levitt joined them there for a long weekend, and Betty took him to see "The Dean Martin Show." During the performance, Dean Martin introduced Betty to the audience as ". . . one of the best loved stars of show business."

Betty had resumed her nightly rounds of the casinos, placing bets here and there, but seldom hitting a winning streak. She gave Mike a handful of chips and told him to try his luck. Mike Levitt was not a gambling man; when he did hit a winning streak, he quit while he was ahead, cashed in his chips, and came away with some $5000 dollars. Betty wasn't so lucky. By the time Bob managed to pry her away from the roulette table, she was down several thousand dollars.

At home later, Levitt saw that Betty was somewhat depressed, and, to cheer her up, he told her he had won around $5000 and attempted to present it to her. Betty turned on him. "When I give a friend some money to spend on the tables, I don't expect it to be returned to me — as though I was a pauper!" Levitt was about to protest, but could see that she was not to be trifled with. Levitt remembered:

She was so mad that she jumped up from her chair and headed straight for the bathroom where she proceeded to flush away the dollar bills I had just given her! Bob rushed in and managed to save most of the money. Betty went straight to her bedroom and locked the door. We never saw her again that night, but next morning she appeared her usual self and acted as though nothing untoward had happened. The incident of the previous night was never mentioned.

In January, 1971, Betty returned to Los Angeles to begin rehearsals for a CBS musical tribute to Tennessee Ernie Ford. The show was to be taped before a live audience the following month. Maureen O'Hara was the other big name guest, but most of the publicity went to Betty and old co-star Dick Haymes, reunited to sing a medley of songs from their hit films. The show was eventually aired a year later. Critics gave it only a lukewarm reception, with Grable and Haymes getting the most praise. Betty loved doing the show, and was delighted for her friend Dick, who was on the comeback trail.

By this time, Betty was reckoned to be the biggest draw on the summer stock circuit. For the summer of 1971, Betty was contracted by the Theatre Projects Company to appear in Neil Simon's *Plaza Suite*, but the deal fell through. Instead, Betty took to the road again with *Born Yesterday*, playing many cities in the Eastern States with the usual rave reviews. She had come to be identified with this role almost as closely as she had been with *Hello Dolly!* And she was pleased to be such a success in it — "no singing, no dancing . . . just a finely tuned acting performance," as one critic put it.

To please her fans, she still managed to show off her legs now and again. In one scene in which she emerged from her bedroom, she was usually covered up in a long negligée. But Betty often wore a black baby-doll see-through piece of lingerie, which showed her still-fabulous figure to great advantage. The audience loved it. [157]

In September, 1971, Betty signed a contract to do the show, *This is Show Business*, in her home town of St. Louis. It was produced by *Guys and Dolls* friend Ed Greenberg. *This Is Show Business* was presented at the city's Municipal Opera House. (Betty was posthumously awarded a place in the Municipal Opera House Hall of Fame.) The show, co-starring Dorothy Lamour, Don Ameche, Chita Rivera, Rudy Vallee, and Dennis Day, did good business, and Betty was well received as the home-town girl who made the big time. Unfortunately, she wasn't feeling too well at the time and one of her numbers had to be cut. But she did do a medley of her most famous songs and duetted "I Want to be Happy" with Dorothy Lamour.

She was still a name to be reckoned with, as this latest tour was proving, and she again came to the attention of the producers of *No, No Nanette*. The London version had long since been cast with British actress Dame Anna Neagle in the role. After much deliberation, Alice Faye had decided against a long West End run, much to the disappointment of her legions of fans.

The show's producers contacted Betty offering her the lead in the Australian national tour. She would open for a six-month run in Melbourne, then she would head the national tour of other cities for the next six months. The salary was fabulous and Betty accepted the deal. She was pleased with everyt aspect of the proposal — and she particularly looked forward to meeting her Australian and New Zealand fans at last. [158]

Many of them had booked flights to London to see her in *Belle Starr*, but the show had folded before their travel plans were completed. Several years earlier she had cancelled — at the last minute — a tour of Australia with her night club act. [159] Now she could make it up to them. She wrote to her two biggest "Down Under" fans, Chris Moor of Wellington, New Zealand, and Keith Raistrick of Melbourne, telling them of the forthcoming trip.

Before she could leave on her travels, though, Hollywood called again. This time it was the Academy of Motion Picture Arts and Sciences. They wanted her to be a presenter at the 1972 Awards presentation. She was told that a bungalow had been reserved for her at the Beverly Hills Hotel.

Betty called Mike Levitt and insisted that he come west for the awards ceremony. She refused to hang up until Mike agreed to accompany her and Bob. On arrival at the Beverly Hills Hotel, Betty was disappointed to find that the bungalows had been reallocated, owing to the large entourage of the Academy's guest of honor, Charlie Chaplin. There was nothing she could do but accept the sumptuous suite they offered her in the main hotel complex.

As Mike Levitt was helping Betty to unpack, the sound of sirens filtered into the suite. Mike went to the window to look. Betty asked, "What is it?" and Levitt replied, "It's only an ambulance."

Quick as a flash, Betty said, "Maybe old Charlie didn't make it after all. Call the desk and see if we can have his bungalow."

The evening was a great success for Betty. She gathered much attention as she stood in the foyer, elegantly dressed in a turquoise gown, set off by a deep suntan, with her blonde hair lovingly styled by Mike Levitt. It was to be her last television appearance before a nation-wide audience.

At the Academy dinner, Betty, Bob, and Mike shared a table with Jane Russell, Martha Raye, and Dorothy Lamour. The group was in high spirits, gossiping, reminiscing over old times, and generally having fun. Seated at the table next to them was actor Jack Nicholson. The blonde former pin-up queen appeared quite taken with Nicholson, and more than once whispered to Mike Levitt: "Is he looking at me?" Replied Levitt with a wry smile: "Honey, every red-blooded male in this room is looking at you. How could they miss you in that low-cut gown?" Betty giggled like a teenager.

Australian-born actor Peter Finch, in town for the remake of *Lost Horizon*, admitted to being a long-time Grable fan. He table-hopped until he reached her and introduced himself. Betty invited him to join them for drinks. The British-based actor, at one time a protégé of Sir Laurence Olivier, was an avid film buff, and he was in his element at such a star-studded occasion. Afterwards he told a journalist: "Imagine, sitting at a table with those Hollywood greats. I love Betty Grable. I find her very alive, warm and humorous. And sincere. She lived up to my every expectation. She is a beautiful and fascinating woman. What a girl." [160]

The evening was a great social success. Betty had fun meeting up with old friends. James Bacon, her long-time championing journalist-friend from the old days, reminisced: "Oh Betty, wasn't life just great in those days? Remember when you topped the box office polls for nine successive years?"

"*Ten* successive years!" Betty corrected him quietly. [161]

Robert Wagner and his wife, Natalie Wood, greeted her warmly. She had known Bob since his days as a young actor starting out at Twentieth Century-Fox, and Natalie (known as Hollywood's Child) had been on the studio payroll since she was a toddler. They chatted about old times, and Bob remarked: "How come we never made a picture together?" Betty laughed: "Honey, they couldn't have my old face up there on the screen with someone as young, fresh, and handsome as you."

They both laughed over the time Betty almost had him barred from the lot for staring at her, during his earlier years at the studio. Wagner well understood Betty's temperament and her problems at the studios in the early fifties. "A star like Grable was carrying the whole film and she was well aware of her responsibilities to her co-stars, crew, and the studio. It was an enormous responsibility. I know — I've been there!" [162]

Ann Miller passed by on her way to the powder room. "Hi, Betty!" she called out. Betty returned the friendly greeting. To Mike, she said: "Just look at that gown — straight out of M-G-M's wardrobe, I'll bet." Much as she loved Ann Miller, she always had a little jibe at her expense. Once, invited to the opening of a new nightclub, she was informed that Ann would also be present. Dryly, Betty quipped: "Honey, Ann would be at the opening of an envelope!"

A journalist asked her about her future plans. She told him: "I have paid so much money into the Motion Picture Relief Fund, I

suppose I could always live at one of their retirement homes —
alternatively, I am quite domesticated, and would make quite a
good live-in maid!"

She was in fine form. No one, least of all Grable herself, would
have believed the cruel turn fate had in store for her over the next
few weeks.

* * * * *

Cancer! After informing Betty's ex-husband and daughters, Bob
Remick contacted her agent. There was nothing to do but cancel
the Australian trip. The agent cabled the Williamson-Edgeley
theatre chain in Melbourne, and informed them that Betty was
pulling out of the show because of illness.

Apparently, the Australian management had doubts as to the
severity of Betty's ailment and checked with the hospital. Once
they were satisfied it was serious, Michael Edgeley, head of the
group, announced that"Miss Betty Grable is seriously ill. Her tour
of Australia has been cancelled. Her doctors have informed me
that the star is fighting for her life."[163]

As the story was picked up around the world, the Santa Monica
hospital switchboard was jammed with callers inquiring about
Betty's condition. Betty was furious with the scare story, and
emphasized to Bob and her manager that it should be played
down. A denial was issued by the hospital's chief physician,
stating that it was only an ulcer complaint and that the star would
be released from hospital in a day or two.

The truth was the cancer was inoperable. It was at the apex of
her lungs. Cobalt treatment was the only weapon they could use
to destroy the cancerous cells and, hopefully, stem the spread of
the disease.

Betty was released after a week, but stayed in Los Angeles for
several weeks, undergoing treatment as an outpatient. Her weight
increased slightly and she was feeling generally much better, so
she was allowed to go home to Las Vegas where outpatient
treatment would continue.

Betty lived quietly for the next few months, seldom venturing farther than her lovely garden where she spent many hours with Kato. One afternoon a stray wandered into the garden and (as it was a young bitch) quickly made friends with Kato. After making inquiries around the neighborhood, Betty reasonably assumed it had been abandoned, so she decided to adopt it. She named it Elsa after the lion cub in her favorite "animal" movie *Born Free*. Said Levitt, "It was typical of animal-lover Betty to take on the responsibility of another pet — as if she didn't have enough troubles of her own! But that was Betty, she loved animals."

Betty, and all those who loved her, hoped that her bout with cancer was no more than a temporary hold-up in her plans. Her second-time-around career had blossomed. Whereas she had once been known in Hollywood as the "Solid Gold Blonde," now dinner theatre producers were coining similar phrases about her recent successful tours. She had won many new fans and was desperately disappointed at having to call off the tour of Australia. She felt she had let her fans down again and wrote to several of them to apologize.

After a few more months, Betty felt practically normal. Recent hospital checks had shown that the cancer had abated. Her cancer was in remission.

Betty was relieved and delighted. She thought she had licked the "Big C" and was desperate to work again. She even spoke of doing a sponsored slot for the Cancer Crusade campaign. Still, she didn't give up smoking despite repeated warnings by her doctors.

She was considering an offer of cabaret work at the Riviera Hotel, scene of her most famous successes. But the doctors advised against it, saying that carrying a floorshow in her condition would be far too strenuous.

She attended Debbie Reynolds' new show, and when Debbie greeted her from the stage, the fans kept Betty signing autographs for nearly an hour. Later she hosted a party for Debbie and the cast at her Tropicana Road home. Betty had always liked Debbie, considering her her natural replacement in musical films during the early fifties. The stars and dancers attending were in great form and the party didn't break up until well after sun-up! 164

Betty commuted regularly to Los Angeles for medical checkups. Her condition didn't seem to be worsening, and she began to relax. She had fun at the New Year celebrations in Las Vegas, partying until dawn with Bob — and Harry James. Harry was always a star attraction in the gambling town over the festive season. Betty thoroughly enjoyed her rounds of night clubs and parties.

Early in January, she was asked to head a new cast of *Born Yesterday* in Jacksonville, Florida. It was a four-week engagement at the Alhambra Theatre, starting in early February. Betty accepted. She was playing for top rates and also a percentage of the gross. It was the best deal she had had in years.

Bob queried the wisdom of accepting an engagement so far from home. Betty assured him she had never felt more fit in her life and the couple flew to Florida. The dates for the show had been brought forward to January 24, and Betty began rehearsals almost as soon as she arrived, though by now she knew the part backwards. 165

Like Bob Remick, many would question the wisdom of Betty accepting work in her current state of health. The simple truth was that doctors' fees, hospital bills, and the high cost of medication had bitten deeply into her reserves. Financially, she had to keep on working. Unknown to Bob, she was still covering Harry's gambling debts, which were mounting daily. Besides, Betty maintained, work was the best therapy for her. It took her mind off her health problems.

The management of the Alhambra, Jacksonville, found the advance bookings so heavy that they asked Betty to extend her season by another two weeks to meet the demand for tickets. This was before the show even opened! She agreed, happy in the knowledge that she was still a big box-office draw. She found the cast easy to work with and very professional in their craft. It was another triumph; the critics loved her.

During one performance in early March, Betty complained of feeling unwell before the curtain went up, but she insisted on going on with the show. Afterwards, she managed to reach the dressing room before collapsing. A doctor was summoned immediately. Bob took the house physician aside and told him of the gravity of Betty's illness. He advised Bob to get Betty back into the hospital as soon as possible.

After a pain-killing injection and a good night's rest, Betty insisted on going on with the show. She reasoned that it would "leave the cast stranded until they find a replacement." They only had one more week to do, and she promised that she would head straight back to the Santa Monica hospital when the engagement was completed.

The next night Betty was back in front of the audiences, fortified by stronger painkillers. Once she was on stage she felt great, and to the audience she appeared completely at ease in the role of the famous dumb-blonde. But as soon as the curtain came down, the pain returned — and it got worse each day.

The heavy booking had continued and Betty was asked if she would extend her stay a further two weeks. A management spokesman said the demand was "unprecedented" in the theatre's history. Even in her last few months of life, Betty Grable was once again breaking box-office records.

This gave her a great boost just when she needed it. The theatre management was also delighted, but apparently they didn't realize the gravity of Betty's illness. The star agreed on condition that this would be the last extension to the run. She told the producers she had some "urgent business" to attend to in California — and it couldn't wait much longer.

During the artistically and financially successful eight-week Florida run (for which she was paid top money, thus helping replenish her dwindling funds), Betty received many letters and cards from her fans who had read of her latest setback. Betty answered all of the cards, reassuring her fans that she was "perfectly healthy."

The cast members, who had taken Betty into their hearts for her sheer professionalism and good natured cameraderie, were most disappointed that they couldn't express their thanks by throwing her a farewell party. But co-star Art Kassul presented Betty with a beautiful solid gold bracelet — "for the solid gold blonde," he joked. Betty was very touched by his gesture and promised she would co-star with him at a new Florida venue in summer. Sadly, Kassul knew that it wouldn't be possible. He realized just how ill his famous co-star really was. [166]

Betty and Bob flew back to Los Angeles and headed straight for St. John's Hospital. After surgery, the doctor told Bob, "The cancer is now in her stomach. While the treatment for her lungs was successful, the disease just decided to show up elsewhere. There is not much we can do for her at this stage, except alleviate the pain as much as possible, and let her die with dignity." [167]

Once again, the media was informed that Betty was suffering from a "recurrence of her stomach ulcer." This was at her insistence; she was determined not to cause any alarm among her friends. The get-well messages and flowers came flooding in from all over the world. She refused to see anyone outside of her immediate family.

Mike Levitt flew in from Chicago, and went straight to the hospital. He was shocked at her appearance. He said:

> She had become so thin, but she was in great spirits and seemed pleased to see me. Bob and her sister Marjorie were at the hospital for hours each day, and I was glad to be able to take my turn of sitting with Betty, giving them a well-earned break.
>
> She used to ask me to count the get-well cards each morning. 'How many today, Mikey,' she would ask. 'Nearly nine hundred,' I replied. One morning less than 700 cards were delivered to her room. "See how quickly they forget," she sighed jocularly, when she heard the final count. [168]

Levitt maintained that no matter how bad she was feeling her sense of humor never left her. He remembered that during her first hospital stay, Betty was walking from her room to the X-ray department. Said Mike:

> The short robe she was wearing was tied at the back, and on the way to X-ray it loosened. Betty grabbed at the robe trying to cover herself. The nursing assistant said: 'Don't worry, Mrs. James — nobody's looking.' Quick as a flash, Betty replied: 'Well, they used to!' [169]

Mike also recalled Marjorie telling Betty that she had seen *My Blue Heaven* on TV the previous evening. Marjorie admitted that she'd cried when she heard Betty singing the song over the opening credits. Quipped Betty: "That bad, huh?"

And the previous year when she was first admitted, a nurse escorted her to her private room. As Betty put down her overnight bag, the nurse asked: "May I help you with your lingerie, Mrs. James?" Said Betty later: "Lingerie? Who did she think I was — Joan Crawford?"

For no obvious reason, Betty was registered as Mrs. James for all her stays in hospital. It couldn't have been to hide her identity, for she was still instantly recognizable.

She ventured out into a corridor one day where she came upon two other women patients — "they stared at me as though I was a freak. I knew at that moment I was dying, and I didn't know how to handle it." [170]

A female journalist syndicated the story that Betty was "dying" in the hospital. The shock report reached newspapers all over the world and had many of her friends making plans to visit. Grable was angry and upset at the story and said it was unforgivable for a responsible journalist to put out such a story. She was also angry at Rex Reed's scare stories. Many of Betty's show business friends were also angry with the writer, and told him so.

Betty had rallied and appeared to be brighter and stronger — and in less pain. However, she was certainly not out of danger. The doctors told Bob that she would be very lucky if she lived another six months. Bob was heartbroken but he never told Betty this prognosis, always happy to see her in good spirits and planning for the future.

She was allowed home to Las Vegas with the strict instuctions that she was not allowed to work. Betty said she wouldn't. She was glad to be home with her two faithful dogs, who had been looked after by her friend and housekeeper, Dolores O'Reilly, and others.

Before her latest battle with cancer, she had felt so good that she had contacted the agents for the Australian production of *No, No Nanette* and offered to undertake a much shorter tour. But they found that because of the gravity of her illness she was now virtually uninsurable. On her recommendation, the part went to Cyd Charisse, who had been a regular visitor to Betty at the hospital. Grable always maintained that Cyd had much better legs!

The wasting disease had taken its toll on Betty's once-beautiful figure. Her weight was down to around eighty pounds by the time she returned to Las Vegas. She seldom went out and a nurse was hired to administer her medication. But the nurse, on her first home job, turned out to be somewhat inefficient, and Bob took on the task of seeing to Betty's daily needs single-handed.

She pleaded with him to take her to see Ann-Margret's new show. Ann-Margret, whom Betty had long admired, was staging her first show since her near-fatal fall the previous year. She had undergone extensive cosmetic surgery and Betty applauded the young star's bravery in returning to work so soon.

Bob relented. Betty fixed her hair and make-up and Bob helped her dress for the occasion. At the night club she was well-received by the audience, who gave her a standing ovation. Afterwards, she went backstage to congratulate Ann-Margret.

During the show, Bob noticed that Betty barely touched the vodka she had ordered. He remembered reading somewhere that champagne was well-known for its relief-giving properties for cancer sufferers. He ordered a magnum of the best. Betty jokingly chided him for his reckless spending, but she was thrilled that he was thinking only of her. On leaving the hotel, she was set upon by a group of out-of-town revellers, who were insistent on taking a picture of Hollywood's most famous blonde. Betty, never one to let her fans down, willingly obliged and stood for some minutes in the chilly desert air while they got their camera shots.

An evening in her honor organized by the Thalian Society, a group of actresses who held an annual ball in aid of the mentally handicapped, had to be cancelled. It would have been the first time Grable would have received any official recognition from the film and television industry. Bob felt sad that this honor had come too late for Betty to stand in the spotlight just once more, even for a few minutes. Betty was too ill to even regret missing the honor.

By now, she was so weak that she could barely venture out into her beloved garden. Bob fed her, bathed her, and gave her pain-killing shots twice daily. He was a tower of strength.

On the occasional evening when Betty was feeling brighter, Bob would carry her from her bedroom into the living room where she would lie on a sofa. They would watch television, and when she tired of that, Betty would leaf through the enormous scrapbooks on her career that her mother had compiled over the years. She would stop at a page which jogged her memory and relive some story about her heyday in Hollywood. Her memory was as sharp as ever when it came to talking about her lengthy career.

In San Francisco, Bob Johnson, a long-time fan of Betty's, read of her latest setback and decided to visit her in Las Vegas. He turned up one evening at her Tropicana Road home. Bob greeted him at the door, but did not invite him into the house. He said Betty was asleep on a sofa and he didn't want to disturb her. Instead, the two men sat in the patio area, and talked about Betty.

They spoke at length about her illness, but Bob Johnson cut the conversation short when he found Bob Remick was getting quite upset. Before leaving, he asked Bob if he would mind getting Betty to autograph some photographs and songsheets if she were at all up to it. Remick said he would do what he could.

Two weeks later, the mailman popped a package into Mr. Johnson's mailbox. Betty, who always considered her fans, had signed every picture and music sheet. But her handwriting looked very weak. [171]

Another superfan, Louis Sannino and his wife, Mary, who had met Betty a couple of years previously, received a letter dated June, 14, 1973. It said:

> It was a pleasure to receive your beautiful card and I thank you, most sincerely, for your friendly expression of concern about my health. I am feeling quite well now and I have no doubt that the prayers and good wishes of my friends everywhere helped much and I am most grateful. May this find you well and happy and looking forward to a pleasant summer. Sincerely, Betty Grable.

The card had been written only three weeks before she died. There would be no "pleasant summer" for Betty Grable.

Betty insisted that Bob telephone Mike Levitt and ask him to come out for the Independence Day holiday the following month. "Don't take no for an answer," she called to Bob as he went to the phone. [172]

Later that month, Betty took a turn for the worse. Bob couldn't arouse her from her slumber to feed her breakfast. He immediately telephoned her doctor, who arranged with St. John's Hospital in Santa Monica to expect her arrival.

Betty was far too weak to fly. The wasting disease had sapped all her strength and she was now weighing in at around sixty-five pounds. Bob decided to drive to Santa Monica and borrowed a motor home from a friend to make the long journey more comfortable for Betty. He called on another friend, who agreed to share the driving with him. Bob had also telephoned Betty's family to tell them of Betty's worsening condition.

They made the trip to Santa Monica in just over five hours. On arrival, the high-ceilinged motor home crashed into the canopy at the hospital's main entrance, damaging the roof of the vehicle. However, that was the least of Bob's problems. He would explain the accident and make good any damage once this latest crisis was over.

Betty was examined immediately upon arrival, while Bob sat nervously in the waiting area. He asked the doctor to do any surgery that might save her life.

Presently, the senior physician came to him. "Mr. Remick, I'm afraid it is too late. She is too far gone. Even if surgery were possible, there is no strength left in her body to cope with the physical shock. There is nothing we can do for her now except try to ease the pain, and let her die with dignity. I'm sorry."[173]

Bob wept at the news. He was in a state of shock. All there was left to do was pray for a miracle for his beloved Betty.

CHAPTER SEVENTEEN

The Independence Day holiday was approaching. Mike Levitt was in an uneasy mood in his North Lakeshore Drive apartment in Chicago. Bob Remick had telephoned him earlier in the week, informing him of Betty's latest hospitalization. Not wishing to alarm him, Bob said she had gone in for more tests and should be out in a few weeks. However, because of the circumstances the proposed holiday weekend visit had to be cancelled.

Levitt realized that Betty wouldn't want to worry anyone about her present condition, and Bob was only carrying out her wishes. But Mike could tell by Bob's somber tone on the telephone that Betty was very seriously ill. As the Fourth of July loomed nearer, Levitt's uneasiness increased. He picked up the phone, called the airport, and booked a flight leaving for Los Angeles within a couple of hours. It was June 29 — a few days before he had initially planned to visit Betty and Bob.

As he packed his travel bag, he lifted a dark blue suit from the closet. "I looked at it and wondered why I was packing it. But I just put it in the case, and headed for the airport." [174]

Betty's sister Marjorie, who was again not in the best of health herself, visited her every day. Bob spent about eighteen hours a day at the hospital, and Vicki and Jessica also attended their mother daily.

Betty Grable was heavily sedated to relieve the raging pain. But she never complained, drifting between periods of consciousness and deep coma-like sleep. When she was awake she was always pleased to have Bob and her family around her. At times she was lucid and talked about getting out of the hospital. Other times she would talk about her parents and other names from the past. Her happiest times in the hospital were when her older grandchildren were allowed to visit. She would make the effort to appear as much like her old self as possible. Visitors were kept to a minimum — only her immediate family was allowed to come and go as it pleased.

Others tried to visit, including many of her co-workers like Dan Dailey. Harry James who, like Betty, had an unreasonable fear of hospitals, never visited at all. Alice Faye telephoned her daily. Jackie Coogan also called. George Raft, on being told that Betty was dying, broke down in tears. He claimed he had never loved anyone else. Sadly, he was too ill and frail himself to visit his beloved Betty. Strangely enough, June Haver was a regular — and apparently welcome — visitor. Perhaps Betty was trying to make amends.

Most of her famous visitors, realizing how heavily sedated she was, just stood for a few moments by her bedside, and offered up a silent prayer for the woman who was once regarded as one of Hollywood's supreme beauties.

When Mike Levitt arrived at the hospital on July 1, Marjorie, Bob, and Jessica were by the bedside. Jessica called to her mother, "Look, Mother, look who's here. It's Mikey." Mike Levitt had always been accepted by Betty's family as more than a fan — as a true friend — ever since the day he had stood in her private railroad compartment as a tongue-tied twelve-year-old.

Betty's eyelids fluttered. She focused on the young man and held out her hand. "Oh, Mikey," she said in a voice that was almost a whisper, "you came. I knew you would come for the holiday."

Mike was shocked at Betty's appearance. "You know what a cute little nose she had. Well, she had lost so much weight that it stood out from the rest of her features. I was afraid that the shock would show on my face, but Betty seemed too far gone to notice. She was happy I was there and that was all that mattered."

One scandal-sheet newspaper had offered a local freelance photographer $5000 for a picture of Betty lying in her hospital bed. The photographer said: "No matter how much money I was offered, I just couldn't pull a job like that — not on anyone like Betty Grable, who had given so much happiness to millions of people through the years. I was disgusted at their proposal."[175]

Between visits on July 2, Bob called Marjorie and advised her to bring the family to the hospital immediately. "Betty is sinking fast," he told them. Bob and Mike Levitt took turns watching over Betty as she dozed fitfully. Occasionally she would open her eyes and call for Bob, reaching for his hand. Once she had found it, her eyes would close again and a look of peace would settle on her face.

The car taking Marjorie and the girls from Beverly Hills to Santa Monica seemed to take forever, considering the shortness of the journey. It was the start of the early evening rush hour, and traffic was building up on Wilshire and Santa Monica Boulevards. Eventually they reached the hospital to find Betty, heavily sedated against the raging pain, lying still — with Bob's hand in hers.

It didn't seem likely that Betty would ever regain consciousness. She appeared to be oblivious to all that was going on around her. A nurse stood at the foot of the bed, never for a moment taking her eyes off the once-beautiful blonde. Her training in dealing with terminally-ill patients told her that Betty was slipping away — her breathing was less labored and a look of tranquility had settled on the star's face.

She was about to turn to buzz the doctor, when Betty opened her eyes. She smiled weakly at everyone around her bedside, and clutched Bob's hand. She raised her head an inch or two from the pillows to look into his face. "Oh, Bob," she sighed, and lay back on the pillow, closing her eyes for the last time. Betty Grable was dead. She was fifty-six years old.

It was 5:15 p.m. on Monday, July 2.

The nurse fled from the room in tears, as Bob and Betty's family consoled each other. Before they left the hospital, the nurse who had been assigned to Betty approached Bob and apologized for her unprofessional behavior. She said, "I just couldn't watch that beautiful woman die. I had always been a fan of hers — and when the end came I just couldn't take it." [176] Typically, Betty was still getting through to her fans, even on her deathbed. She would have been highly amused by it all.

Harry James was physically sick when told the news of Betty's death. All he could see before him was a vision of the beautiful, fun-loving blonde who had shared the major part of his life and borne two of his children.

The next day, the world's front pages headlined the death of "Hollywood's most famous pin-up girl." Newspaper office libraries were searched for the over-the-shoulder pose that had cheered troops throughout World War II. Journalists on two hemispheres extolled the time they met Betty Grable, and most of them had a story to tell.

One Canadian journalist, staff writer Ken Robertson of the *Toronto Sun*, recalled:

> I only met her once — and that was for an all-too-brief hour — but word of Betty Grable's death struck me as the loss of a valued friend. The great thing about her, even greater than the famous legs and striking figure, was her enthusiasm for life and the people around her.
>
> Last year I was in Las Vegas with Toronto freelance writer Bill Gray covering the sod-turning of M-G-M's Grand Hotel, complete with current stars and starlets. All the glamour girls and guys were there — posing for pictures and fighting for the spotlit areas. And suddenly, standing right in front of me was Betty Grable. I came up with the only thing I could think of to say. 'Hi,' I said.
>
> 'Hi, it's nice to meet you,' she answered. And I thought — she really means it. She really does think it's nice. That was my first impression. After an hour-long chat with her at a table in a dimly lit corner of the huge circus tent, it was still the predominant one. She really was interested in our conversation. At first I was a bit tongue-tied. After all, this was the girl whose pictures were musts during my teenage years — the girl who was the very essence of all that was good in those golden days.

The Girl With the Million Dollar Legs

As we talked there at the little round table, interrupted countless times by admirers, she asked questions about Toronto, about the newspaper and about me. She talked of the importance of meaningful relationships with others and I caught a trace of loneliness, I thought. I recall her leaning toward me across the table as she spoke in a low voice. The dazzling smile was gone for a moment. There was only this quiet voice and blue eyes gazing into mine. 'I think you know what I mean,' she said, 'Life is good if it's shared — otherwise, well . . .' Then she said: 'My, we're really getting deep, aren't we? Let me get the drinks.'

When I offered to make the trip to the bar she reminded me that 'facts are facts. And the fact is that I'll get served much faster by the bartender, so it's only good sense for me to go,' she chuckled. That's how I came to be waited on by one of the finest ladies in showbusiness — and I'll never forget her.

In London, Alexander Walker of the *Evening Standard* paid tribute on behalf of her British fans:

Long before her death she had become a firmly established symbol of a less complicated, more innocent America where girls came in two varieties, soft or tough, and where wisecracks were as natural as chewing gum. Where showgirls made it to the top in one night, or even one song, where romance began backstage, where a girl might have her eye on a man's wallet, but usually found her way inevitably to his heart . . . and where four drawing-pins stuck in the corners of a pin-up girl's picture made the lonely serviceman's mascot as he fought the good, just war. All this was Betty Grable.

There was no sadness. There were only happy memories of a beautiful blonde, who set the world alight with her special brand of sex appeal, sincerity and — above all — her sense of humor.

CHAPTER EIGHTEEN

The holiday period was a sad time for Betty Grable's family and friends. Because of the Independence Day celebration, it was decided that Betty would be buried on Friday, July 5. Arrangements for the funeral service were made with Pierce Brothers of Beverly Hills, who had also carried out the services for Betty's mother and father. Her body, once released from the hospital, was placed in a little chapel which was soon filled with flowers sent by friends and fans.

Betty's daughters spent the next couple of days at Marjorie's home, receiving guests who had called to offer their condolences. Letters of sympathy poured in from all over the world.

Mike Levitt stayed on in Los Angeles for the funeral. One evening when he was alone in the funeral chapel, his mind filled with memories of the good times he had had with Betty, the door opened and in walked two middle-aged women. Assuming they were family friends, he greeted them and invited them to join him in a prayer for Betty. One of them produced a camera and asked Mike to open the top half of the casket so she could take a picture. He was horrified and said so. The ladies, quite unperturbed, repeated their request. When he had regained his composure, Mike told them that Betty's family had insisted the casket be closed at all times. With that, the women turned on their heels and left. [177]

Betty's daughters wanted the funeral to be a strictly private affair. They knew that their mother would have hated to be laid to rest in a typical "Hollywood style circus," as she had called the funerals of some of her contemporaries

Betty was buried after a simple but moving ceremony which

351

was conducted by Reverend Dr. Thomas R. Miller and Reverend Tally H. Jarrett at All Saints Episcopal Church in Beverly Hills. The church was packed with more than 800 people who had come to pay their last respects. Rev. Jarrett gave a moving eulogy, which said in part:

> Words have an emptiness at a time such as this. Many of you knew Betty far better than I — so you know even better than I how difficult it is to convey the thoughts we all have now.
>
> We have come here today to offer our prayers and thanksgiving to God for a life. This life we remember here is one who was precious to all of us — for I know I speak for all of us and millions who are not here that we loved Betty Grable. Betty was one of those who shined even in the darkness.
>
> She had many great gifts and talents and she used them. Her refreshing manner was infectious. She had a zest for life that made her one of the most popular women who ever lived. Well we remember her for her contributions to the morale of this land during some pretty dark days in World War Two. She kept up our spirits and made us proud to be Americans — she was America to all of us. Who didn't think of Betty yesterday as we celebrated our independence — and thank God for her?
>
> One of the wonderful things about God is that he shows us joy and happiness in life. Certainly Betty was one of His special helpers in that department — she gave so many so much of herself to the Glory and Praise of God . . . So thanks be to God for Betty Grable. [178]

Among the mourners were Harry James and Jackie Coogan, Dan Dailey, Alice Faye, Don Ameche, Cesar Romero, Dorothy Lamour, Mitzi Gaynor with husband Jack Bean, June Haver and Fred MacMurray, Hugh O'Brian, director George Seaton, Patsy Kelly, columnists Lee Graham and Robert Kendall, and singer Johnnie Ray.

The owner of Battista's Italian restaurant in Las Vegas — one of Betty's favorite eating places — also attended, and sang "On a

Clear Day" at the specific request of Betty's family. It had been one of Betty's favorite songs.

Betty's legions of fans, many of whom had traveled from all over the United States, Canada, and Great Britain, wept openly during the service. An unknown woman broke from the police cordon, calling at the flower-bedecked coffin: "We love you, Betty." (Could it have been the woman who called out the same sentiment during Betty's first night on Broadway as Dolly?)

Harry James, after a hurried goodbye to his daughters, left by a side exit and ran to a waiting car. No one will ever know what his feelings were that day; it would have been their thirtieth wedding anniversary. Another piece of music that had been played at the ceremony was "their" song, "I Had the Craziest Dream" from the film *Springtime in the Rockies,* during the making of which they had fallen in love. It was a fitting choice of music as Betty loved Harry James until the day she died.

Some weeks after her death, Harry said in an interview: "People who had known her and hadn't seen her in over twenty years came to pay their respects. Grooms from the race tracks, "little" people from the studios. They were all there. And you know it takes a very special person, a lady in the true sense, to inspire that." [179]

Hugh O'Brian, her co-star in *Guys and Dolls,* said: "I can think of nothing more fun than to keep right on playing *Guys and Dolls* with her in whatever Valhalla it is to which all good troupers go." [180]

Outside the church, a silent crowd of more than a thousand paid their last respects to one of the world's most popular women. None of the other stars attending the ceremony would speak to the press or television crews. It was too sad and private a time for them. Each of them had his own special memories of a very special lady.

And so Betty Grable, the girl who Eisenhower said "helped us win the war," was laid in her final resting place, beside her mother and father.

The epitaph of the woman who had become a legend in her lifetime could be summed up in her own words. "I had the best of both worlds. A family and a career. And millions of friends all over the world."

* * * * *

Shortly after Betty's death, Bob Remick vacated the house on Tropicana Road. It was sold to the Tropicana Hotel complex. He refused to talk about his life with her, and shunned anyone who came near him with questions.

Unfortunately, he mentioned in confidence to an English friend that Betty had not made a new will, and that he was out in the cold as far as her family was concerned. Bob's friend "leaked" the story to the *London Sunday Express*, which prominently displayed it as a gossip column item headed: "Betty Grable's Last Lover Gets Nothing." Remick was outraged when he read the story. He vowed he would never again talk about his relationship with Betty .

Anyone who knew Bob at all realized that he was not a gigolo. He geniunely loved Betty and wanted to marry her. In fact, most of their friends thought the couple actually had married in a secret ceremony in London in 1969.

According to Mike Levitt, Betty's last love spent his life savings making her last few pain-ridden months as comfortable and stress-free as possible. The bills for her hospitalization and medication had taken most of her own resources. Levitt reckoned she left only about $15,000, plus the house, and a few precious antiques.

Just before she flew to London, in 1969, she had made a new will to include the expected grandchild. Bob knew this, and he also knew he wasn't included in the document. Would a gigolo hang around a very sick woman when he knew there was nothing in it for him? No. Bob was too straight a person to have "hung on" to Betty, as some unkind critics put it, ". . . for mercenary reasons."

In 1974, Bob Remick broke his vow of silence and spoke to a magazine journalist.

Betty and I discussed marriage on several occasions, but I think she always carried a big torch for Harry James, and we eventually decided to let things be as they were for the eight years we had together. In the last few months of her life, she thought of writing another will. But you know how these things are. She never got around to doing it.

I have no regrets. She was a lovely, lovely person, and now I have to do my own thing, starting from scratch. I'm a croupier in a Las Vegas casino, and I like it rather well. [181]

For some years after her death, Bob kept up a regular correspondence with many of Betty's fans and supplied pictures to those who still requested them. Her fans liked Bob, and they never forgot that it was he, more than anyone else in Betty Grable's family, who tended to her every need when she was gravely ill.

Remick eventually married and started his own family — of course, with Kato and Elsa very much a part of the household until their deaths. Bob is now a gaming inspector in a major Las Vegas casino.

* * * * *

Harry James died of cancer on July 5, 1983 — exactly ten years to the day after Betty's funeral. He continued working right up until a few months before his death. He kept in touch with his daughters and grandchildren, but he was a lonely old man towards the end.

Just before his death he was invited to appear on a TV tribute to Frank Sinatra. He was affronted that he was relegated to only one number in the spectacular. Many show business insiders believe Sinatra was paying him off for his poor treatment of Betty. Frank was very fond of Betty and, despite his own dalliances, never approved of James cheating on such a beautiful person as Betty Grable.

* * * * *

In the mid-seventies, Betty's former studio Twentieth Century-Fox paid a glowing, if belated, tribute to its all-time box-office champion in their television series, "That's Hollywood." The episode, written and produced by Tony Thomas, was titled simply "Gorgeous Grable," and her fans loved it. Former co-star Cesar Romero's voice was used over clips from her films and newsreel items of her life.

The tribute opened with Betty's big dance number in *Down Argentine Way*. As the film rolled, the voiceover said, "Betty was as welcome as a cool breeze in summer."

Cesar was full of praise for Betty. He said:

> Betty was a delightful girl. She was everything America stood for in the 1940s and '50s. She was wholesome — the girl next door. The girl you wanted to take home to meet mother. She was always considerate of her co-workers — no tantrums, never late. She was a true professional. I loved working with her.

Towards the end of the program, Betty was quoted as saying that she never thought of herself as anything special. "Maybe so," added the voiceover, "but there certainly was magic about her."

In the last shot came the final tribute. "She will always be a symbol of American innocence in those simpler, less complicated times when we were all in love — with love."

In Britain, Channel Four television showed nine Betty Grable musicals over a thirteen-month period. Public reaction to the screenings — which constituted the first-ever tribute to the star on British TV — was very favorable. Later, in 1991, Channel Four featured a retrospective season of thirteen Grable films over a thirteen-week period.

The giant Hitachi Corporation used Betty's famous wartime pin-up pose to promote its Christmas gift advertising, claiming that their gifts were the best stocking-fillers since Betty Grable.

Another Grable accolade occurred in May, 1989, when Twentieth Century-Fox's CBS-Fox television subsidiary and Key Video released nine of her films for general sale. Sales of these films (with stereo digital sound) were phenomenal, outstripping Monroe's video releases. CBS-Fox, delighted with this success, released another batch of titles for sale worldwide. A year later they released five titles for sale in Britain and Europe.

The ultimate accolade to Betty Grable, and true recognition of her input to the war effort, was given by the American Movie Classics channel on Armistice Day (November 11), 1993, when they ran a 24-hour showing of her most famous films. As far as is known, no other movie actress has been so honored.

Obviously, Betty's fans have never forgotten her. There is still an active fan club in operation, which produces four magazines a year devoted to Betty and other stars of the thirties and forties. The most surprising aspect of the fan club is that many of the members were born long after Betty had left Hollywood. They know of their favorite star only through showings of her films on television.

A Japanese gentleman visits Betty's crypt every week with a bouquet of fresh red roses. He never talks to anyone and no one knows his identity, but his devotion is legendary. Many other fans have visited her crypt at least once, and many do so annually. [182]

On his annual pilgrimage to Hollywood, superfan/collector Keith Raistrick learned that the original painting of Betty from the film *That Lady in Ermine* was up for sale. The asking price was $45,000. [183]

And on a recent trip to Las Vegas, Richard C. Marohn, MD, of Chicago, visited the new Debbie Reynolds Hotel and Conference Center, where he viewed Grable's red velvet gown from the film *Beautiful Blonde from Bashful Bend*. Museum curator Randy Hendrickson told him that many of Betty's costumes will be on display when the museum is completed. [184]

The legend lives on.

AFTERWORD

Anyone who met Betty Grable could not fail to recognize her genuine warmth and lack of big-star pretense. The friends she made in movies and later in theatre work all bear this out.

Her predecessor at Twentieth Century-Fox, Alice Faye, was asked about her relationship with Betty. Many critics were quick to point out that they never worked together again after *Tin Pan Alley*. Said Miss Faye:

> We remained good friends up until her death. Whenever I was in Las Vegas, I always used to visit her and we enjoyed each other's company. All that talk of dissent and career jealousies is just a lot of nonsense.
>
> I suppose it was good publicity and it helped to sell theatre tickets, but it just wasn't true. Towards the end when Betty was in the hospital I talked to her every day on the phone.
>
> We had good times together. When Harry James and my husband Phil (Harris) opened in a show at the Frontier Hotel in Las Vegas, Betty and I threatened to give them some competition by opening our own show across the street! [185]

In a 1971 interview with writer and film historian Robert Kendall, Alice was asked if there were any truth to rumors of a feud between her and Grable. Miss Faye laughed, "Not a word of truth. Betty and I respect each other and hate this ridiculous rumor. As a matter of fact, when Phil threw a birthday party for me in Las Vegas a few weeks ago Betty and her boyfriend were the first ones there." [186]

A former wardrobe assistant at Twentieth Century-Fox during

the war years was quite frank when asked for his memories of Betty. He said:

> Although I was assigned to men's wardrobe, we frequently overlapped into women's which was strictly against union rules. I worked with Betty on several pictures. It was wartime and cigarettes and good coffee were in short supply — but I had a source. Betty knew this and curried my favor to keep her going on these precious items. We seldom mixed socially, but I worked with her every day on the set.
>
> I was somewhat flattered that she made eyes at me and treated me as a close friend, but was aware of the fact that she was an actress and was just putting on an act to keep me at her beck and call. From my point of view all I can say is she was no different in real life than anyone else I knew in those days.
>
> The only thing I observed at the time was that she appeared to be extremely vain. If a mirror was handy, Betty talked with you while looking at her reflection. Naturally she knew that she drew the attention of every male over 12 years and under 90. After all, wasn't she the pin-up of every GI? We who worked with her did not hold her in awe the way people who saw her on the screen did. She treated all her co-workers as friends. Nothing uppish or prudish about her. It was just a job to her and it was just a job to us. [187]

Others have said that her shy easygoing manner and seeming lack of ambition was a very calculated move on her part to get the best out of people. Pure speculation. How long could anyone of Grable's stature keep up such a front. She worked with some of the biggest names in show business — actors, producers, directors. One would have thought that before long, somebody would have spotted a chink in her so-called armor.

Admittedly, she was nobody's fool. When she believed that things were not quite right, especially during the shooting of her films (and particularly during the production of the disastrous

Belle Starr) she would say so, but she always made sure of her facts first. She was careful not to hurt anyone's feelings — that is any-one who didn't deserve it!

In her own words, "I can get good and mad when I think I am being rooked. And I can get very insulting when somebody tries to suck me in on a publicity stunt. I've had enough of those in my life. One more would make me gag." [188]

In a tribute to her memory cinema manager John Hickey, who had spent a lot of time with Betty during her stay in the English capital, organized a special film night at the Starlight Cinema. Twentieth Century-Fox loaned them *Pin Up Girl*, and the proceeds of the evening were donated to the Imperial Cancer Fund. A week or so before the event Mr. Hickey called at His Majesty's Theatre in London's West End, where Betty's friend and former co-star Lauren Bacall was playing in *Applause*, and invited her to attend the tribute. Owing to her busy schedule Miss Bacall had to decline, but she spoke very highly of Betty and how sad she had been when she read of her death. She presented Mr Hickey with a size-able check to ensure the success of the evening's fundraising. [189]

In a TV interview on Marilyn Monroe which screened in 1987, actress Celeste Holm said: "I'd like to dispel much of the myth about Marilyn and talk about the real person ... In her spare time Marilyn spent hours watching Betty Grable movies — that's what she did! And the result was if you look now at a Betty Grable movie, you will see that Marilyn Monroe was giving an imitation — of Grable!"

Jeanine Basinger, an Associate Professor on American Film History at Wesleyan University, championed Betty Grable. Of the star, she wrote:

> Betty Grable herself contributed to the myth that she was just an ordinary talent with extraordinary success ... the truth is that she had more than a little of everything it took and together it was more than enough.
>
> As a dancer she was skilled, well-trained, and capable of

executing difficult steps with lightness and precision. When she ripped through an athletic romp with Gwen Verdon in *Meet Me After the Show* Grable showed she could more than keep up. As a singer she had a pleasant — though admittedly small — voice, melodious and clear. But she knew how to sell a song. She was responsible for introducing many of the big hits of the forties, "My Heart Tells Me," "Kokomo, Indiana," "You Do," and "I'm Always Chasing Rainbows," to name a few.

As for acting, Grable wasn't equipped to perform serious drama. She knew this and wisely steered away from attempts to change her image. Although Grable considered herself an average-looking girl in a world of Hedy Lamarrs and Lana Turners, she was a standout in Technicolor. She glowed and her platinum hair, red lips and blue eyes made her an all-American dream girl. Other characters in her films always looked as if they had just wandered from a black-and-white low budget movie![190]

Betty Grable was an original. She was a role model for other stars following in her wake. She had often been described as Alice Faye's replacement, but that just wasn't true. Alice excelled in her roles during her years at Twentieth, exuding romance and pathos laced with a good helping of hit songs. [191]

Betty was the feisty gold-digger — tough, temperamental and turbulent . . . until Cupid's arrow struck. Although she and Rita Hayworth vied for top pin-up status during the forties, it was no contest. Rita was born to be a femme fatale, as she proved in her many successful films, whereas Betty was always the showgirl with a heart of gold. No matter how she started out at the beginning of a film, love always won in the end. She was basically a "good girl" — and her fans loved her for that.

APPENDIX

Filmography

HAPPY DAYS (1929) Fox. 87 minutes
Directed by Benjamin Stoloff.
Riverboat musical. Betty, in blackface, dances in the Fox chorus.
CAST: Warner Baxter, Frank Albertson, El Brendel, Walter Catlett, Charles Farrell, Janet Gaynor, Edmund Lowe, Dixie Lee, Victor McLaglan, Will Rogers.

LET'S GO PLACES (1929) Fox. 70 minutes
Directed by Frank Strayer.
Screenplay by William K. Wells, from a story by Andrew Bennison. Songs by Archie Gottler, Sidney Mitchell, Con Conrad, Cliff Friend, Jimmy Monaco, Johnny Burke, George Little. Camera: Conrad Wells.
A musical look at early Hollywood in a slight story of mistaken identity when a young singer arrives in the film capital and is mistaken for a famous operatic tenor. Betty again in the chorus.
CAST: Joseph Wagstaff, Lola Lane, Sharon Lynn, Frank Richardson, Walter Catlett, Dixie Lee, Charles Judeis, Ilka Chase, Larry Steers, Betty Grable.

FOX MOVIETONE FOLLIES (1930) Fox. 70 minutes
Directed by Benjamin Stoloff. Screenplay by William K. Wells. Songs by Jack Meskill, Con Conrad. Camera: L. W. O'Connell.
Romantic musical involving a playboy and his chorus girl friend.
CAST: El Brendel, Marjorie White, Frank Richardson, Noel Francis, William Collier, Jr., Mirian Seegar, Huntly Gordon, Paul Nicholson, Yolanda D'Avril, Betty Grable.

WHOOPEE (1930) Goldwyn-UA. Technicolor. 94 minutes
Produced by Samuel Goldwyn and Florenz Ziegfeld. Directed by Thornton Freeland Screenplay by William Conselman, based on the musical play by William Anthony Maguire, adapted from the play by Owen Davis. Songs: Walter Donaldson, Gus Kahn, Edward Eliscu and Nacio Herb Brown. Dance direction: Busby Berkeley. Camera: Lee Garmes, Ray Rennehan, Gregg Toland.
Sally Morgan, in a bid to get out of a loveless engagement, uses Cantor to escape, so she can marry her childhood sweetheart. Betty Grable's first major exposure when she sings and leads the dancing in the 'Cowboys' number. She is easily recognizable, and later appears, with some fine semi close-ups, as a bridesmaid

in the wedding scene.

CAST: Eddie Cantor, Sally Morgan, Paul Gregory, Jack Rutherford, Ethel Shutta, Spencer Charters, Chief Caupolican, Albert Hackett, Marian Marsh, Will H. Phibrick, Walter Law, Barbara Weeks, Betty Grable, The George Olsen Band.

KIKI (1931) Goldwyn-United Artists. 96 minutes

Produced by Joseph M. Schenck. Directed by Sam Taylor. Screenplay by Sam Taylor, based on the play by David Belasco. Dance director: Busby Berkeley. Camera: Karl Strauss.

Not too much action for Betty in this silly showbiz story about a showgirl in love with an impresario. Betty is said to have coached Mary Pickford in dance routines and stood in for her in long shots.

CAST: Mary Pickford, Reginald Denny, Joseph Cawthorn, Margaret Livingston, Phil Tead, Fred Walton, Betty Grable.

PALMY DAYS (1931) Goldwyn. 80 minutes

Produced by Samuel Goldwyn. Directed by A. Edward Sutherland. Screenplay by Eddie Cantor, based on a story by Cantor, Morrie Ryskind, David Freedman, Keene Thompson. Songs: Ballard Macdonald, Con Conrad, Cliff Friend, Eddie Cantor, Benny Davis, Harry Akst. Dance director: Busby Berkeley. Camera: Gregg Toland.

Amiable story set in a futuristic bakery. Cantor, in drag, is hiding from gangsters who plan a robbery. Betty is on screen early with a few lines to speak, then heads the chorus in a big production number.

CAST: Eddie Cantor, Charlotte Greenwood, Spencer Charters, Barbara Weeks, George Raft, Paul Page, Harry Wood, Charles Middleton, Betty Grable.

THE GREEKS HAD A WORD FOR THEM (1932) (a/k/a THREE BROADWAY GIRLS) Goldwyn-United Artists. 77 minutes

Produced by Samuel Goldwyn. Directed by Lowell Sherman. Screenplay by Sidney Howard, based on a play by Zoe Atkins. Camera: George Barnes.

Three smart girls, dressed in Chanel creations, set out to trap millionaire husbands in this sophisticated comedy. Betty appears briefly as a model.

CAST: Madge Evans, Joan Blondell, Ina Claire, David Manners, Lowell Sherman, Phillips Smalley, Sidney Bracey, Betty Grable

Remade as *Three Blind Mice* (1938), *Moon Over Miami* (1941), *Three Little Girls in Blue* (1946), *How To Marry a Millionaire* (1953).

THE KID FROM SPAIN (1932) Goldwyn-United Artists. 90 minutes

Produced by Samuel Goldwyn. Directed by Leo McCarey. Screenplay by William Anthony McGuire, Bert Kalmar, Harry Ruby. Songs: Bert Kalmar, Harry Ruby, Harry Akst. Musical director: Alfred Newman. Choreography: Busby Berkeley. Camera: Gregg Toland.

Youthful Betty Grable opens the film with a close-up shot that leads the Goldwyn Girls into the first number. In the remainder of this crazy comedy she is difficult to spot in the chorus.

CAST: Eddie Cantor, Lyda Roberti, Robert Young, Ruth Hall, John Miljan, Noah Beery, J. Carroll Naish, Robert O'Connor, Stanley Fields, Paul Porcasi, Walter

Walker, Ben Hendricks, Jr., Harry Gribbon, Theresa Maxwell Conover, The Goldwyn Girls - including Betty Grable, Jane Wyman (billed as Sarah Jane Fulks, her real name), Paulette Goddard, Toby Wing.

CHILD OF MANHATTAN (1932) Columbia. 91 minutes
Directed by Ed Buzzell. Screenplay by Gertrude Purcell, based on a play by Preston Sturges. Song: Elmer Colby, Maurice Abrahams. Camera: Ted Tetzlaff.
Betty's first film in which she is identified by a character name. The story centered on a dance-hall girl (Nancy Carroll) who gets pregnant, loses the baby, and leaves her husband, finding romance in Mexico. True love wins in the end.
CAST: Nancy Carroll, John Boles, Warburton Gamble, Clara Blandick, Jane Darwell, Gary Owen, Betty Grable, Luis Alberni, Jessie Ralph, Charles Jones, Tyler Brooke, Betty Kendall.

PROBATION (1932) Chesterfield. 60 minutes
Directed by Richard Thorpe. Screenplay by Edward T. Lowe, based on a story by Arthur Hoehl. Camera: M. A. Anderson.
Romance ensues when a high society dame takes on a probationer as her chauffeur. Disappointing drama with very little for Betty Grable to do.
CAST: Sally Blane, J. Farrel MacDonald, Eddie Phillips, Clara Kimball Young, Betty Grable, David Rollins, Mary Jane Irving, Matty Kemp, David Durand.

HOLD 'EM JAIL (1932) RKO. 69 minutes
Produced by David O. Selznick and Harry Joe Brown. Directed by Norman Taurog. Screenplay by S. J. Perelman, Walter De Leon, Eddie Welch. Musical director: Max Steiner. Camera: Len Smith.
Innocent jailbirds Wheeler and Woolsey involved with a prison football team. Betty plays the prison warden's daughter.
CAST: Bert Wheeler, Robert Woolsey, Betty Grable, Edgar Kennedy, Edna May Oliver, Roscoe Yates, Paul Hurst, Warren Hymer, Robert Armstrong, Jed Prouty, John Sheehan, Spencer Charters, Monty Banks.

CAVALCADE (1933) Fox. 109 minutes
Produced by Winfield Sheehan. Directed by Frank Lloyd. Screenplay by Sonya Levien, based on the play by Noel Coward. Songs: Noel Coward. Choreography: Sammy Lee. Camera: Ernest Palmer.
Betty is billed as "girl on a couch" in a scene towards the end of this saga of the Marryott family during the Great War. But her most ardent fan would find it hard to identify her. This film won three Oscars, and a best actress nomination for distinguished British actress Diana Wynyard.
CAST: Clive Brook, Diana Wynyard, Ursula Jeans, Herbert Mundin, Una O'Connor, Merle Tottenham, Irene Brown, Beryl Mercer, Frank Lawton, John Warburton, Margaret Lindsay, Tempe Piggott, Bill Bevan, Desmond Roberts, Frank Atkinson, Ann Shaw, Adele Crane, Stuart Hall, Mary Forbes, Lionel Belmore, C. Montague Shaw, Bonita Granville, Sheila McGill, Douglas Scott, Dickie Henderson, Jr., Claude King, Betty Grable, Brandon Hurst.

Filmography

SWEETHEART OF SIGMA CHI (1933) Monogram. 73 minutes

Directed by Edwin I. Marin. Screenplay by Frank L. Moss, based on the story by George Waggner. Songs: George Waggner, Ed Ward. Camera: Gilbert Warrenton. Dances staged by Eddie Prinz.

College capers as flirty Mary Carlisle falls for Buster Crabbe.

Betty appears with the Ted Fiorito Orchestra.

CAST: Mary Carlisle, Buster Crabbe, Charles Starrett, Florence Lake, Eddie Tambiyn, Sally Starr, Mary Blackford, Tom Dugan, Burr McIntosh, Major Goodsell, Grady Sutton, Purnell Pratt, Franklin Parker, Ted Fiorito and his Orchestra, with Leif Erickson, Betty Grable, Bill Carey, Muzzy Marcelino, The Three Midshipmen, and The Blue Keys.

MELODY CRUISE (1933) RKO. 76 minutes

Produced by Merian C. Cooper, associate Louis Brock. Directed by Mark Sandrich. Screenplay by Ben Holmes, Allen Rivkin, R. G. Wolfson. Songs: Will Jason, Val Burton. Camera: Bert Glennon. Musical director: Max Steiner.

Betty performs as a stewardess in this romantic comedy set on board a steamship.

CAST: Charles Ruggles, Phil Harris, Greta Nissen, Helen Mack, Chick Chandler, Jane Brewster, Shirley Chambers, Florence Roberts, Marjorie Gateson, Betty Grable.

WHAT PRICE INNOCENCE (1933) Columbia. 63 minutes

Directed by Willard Mack. Screenplay by Willard Mack. Camera: Joseph A. Valentine.

Early "teenage-problem" drama. Betty plays a girlfriend of a young woman (Jean Parker) who commits suicide when her love for an older man comes to an end.

CAST: Willard Mack, Minna Gombell, Jean Parker, Betty Grable, Bryant Washburn, Ben Alexander, Beatrice Banyard, Louise Beavers.

BY YOUR LEAVE (1934) RKO. 81 minutes

Produced by Pandro S. Berman. Directed by Lloyd Corrigan. Screenplay by Allan Scott, based on a play by Gladys Hurlbut. Camera: Nick Musuraca, Vernon Walker.

Girl-next-door Betty gets involved in trying to put some sparkle into Frank Morgan's love life.

CAST: Frank Morgan, Genevieve Tobin, Neil Hamilton, Marian Nixon, Glenn Anders, Neil Hamilton, Gene Lockhart, Margaret Hamilton, Betty Grable, Lona Andre, Charles Ray.

STUDENT TOUR (1934) M-G-M. 85 minutes

Directed by Charles Reisner. Screenplay by Philip Dunn, Ralph Spence, based on a story by George Seaton, Arthur Bloch, Samuel Marx. Songs: Nacio Herb Brown, Arthur Freed. Camera: Joseph A. Valentine.

Poor vehicle for the talented Jimmy Durante, cast as a rowing team coach. In a small role, Grable had some nice close-ups, a few smart lines of dialogue and performed "The Snake Dance."

Film debut of Nelson Eddy.

CAST: Jimmy Durante, Charles Butterworth, Maxine Doyle, Phil Regan, Florence McKinney, Douglas Fowley, Monte Blue, Betty Grable, Fay McKenzie, Bobby Gordon, Mary Loos, Pauline Brooks, Bruce Bennett, Nelson Eddy, Mischa Auer, Arthur Hoyt, Dave O'Brien, Dale Van Sickle, Joan Arlen, June Storey, Bryant Washburn, Dixie Dean, Mary Jane Irving, Maxine Nash, Edna May Jones, Clarice Wood, Eddie Hart, Helen Chan.

THE GAY DIVORCEE (1934) RKO. 107 minutes
Produced by Pandro S. Berman. Directed by Mark Sandrich. Screenplay by George Marion, Jr., Dorothy Yost, Edward Kaufman, based on the play, *The Gay Divorce,* by Dwight Taylor. Songs: Cole Porter, Mack Gordon, Harry Revel, Con Conrad, Herb Magidson. Choreography: Dave Gould, Hermes Pan. Camera: David Abel.
Major musical set in England concerning the romantic adventures of Astaire and Rogers (the divorcée of the title). Betty scored a big hit in the speciality number "Let's K-knock K-knees," with E. E. Horton. Grable's impact (and unmistakable star quality) must have worried Rogers when she saw the lively young blonde perform.
CAST: Fred Astaire, Ginger Rogers, Alice Brady, Edward Everett Horton, Erik Rhodes, Betty Grable, Charles Coleman, William Austin, Lillian Miles, George Davis, Alphonse Martell, E. E. Clive, Paul Porcasi, Charles Hall.

THE NITWITS (1935) RKO. 81 minutes
Produced by Lee Marcus. Directed by George Stevens. Screenplay by Fred Guiol, Al Boasberg, from a story by Stuart Palmer. Songs: L. Wolfe Gilbert, Felix Bernard, Dorothy Fields, Jimmy McHugh. Camera: Edward Cronjager.
Typical Wheeler and Woolsey fare, as they play cigar-stand owners in an office building where a killer is on the loose. Betty is arrested on suspicion . . . little is then seen of her until the climax.
CAST: Bert Wheeler, Robert Woolsey, Fred Keating, Betty Grable, Evelyn Brent, Erik Rhodes, Hale Hamilton, Charles Wilson, Arthur Aylesworth, Willie Best, Lew Kelley, Dorothy Granger.

OLD MAN RHYTHM (1935) RKO. 75 minutes
Produced by Zion Myers. Directed by Edward Ludwig. Screenplay by Sig Herzig, Ernest Pagano, based on a story by Lewis Gensler, Sig Herzig, Don Hartman. Songs: Lewis Gensler, Johnny Mercer. Choreography: Hermes Pan. Musical Director: Roy Webb. Camera: Nick Musuraca.
Another college epic with the popular Buddy Rogers enrolling in college. Betty sings with a quartet and does a "toe dance."
CAST: Charles "Buddy" Rogers, George Barbier, Barbara Kent, Grace Bradley, Betty Grable, Eric Blore, Erik Rhodes, John Arledge, Johnny Mercer, Donald Meek, Dave Chasen, Joy Hodges, Douglas Foley, Margaret Nearing, Ronald Graham, Sonny Lamont, William Carey, Lucille Ball, Marian Darling, Jane Hamilton, Maxine Jennings, Kay Sutton, Jack Thomas, Erich Von Stroheim, Jr., Carlyle Blackwell, Jr., Bryant Washburn, Jr., Claude Gillingwater, Jr..

COLLEGIATE (1936) Paramount. 81 minutes
Produced by Louis D. Lighton. Directed by Ralph Murray. Screenplay by Walter De

Leon, Francis Martin, based on a story by Alice Duer Miller. Songs: Mack Gordon, Harry Revel. Musical director: Georgie Stoll. Choreography: LeRoy Prinz. Camera: William Mellon.

More college capers as playboy Jack Oakie takes on the unlikely role of a college dean.

CAST: Joe Penner, Jack Oakie, Ned Sparks, Frances Langford, Betty Grable, Lynne Overman, Betty Jane Cooper, Mack Gordon, Harry Revel, Henry Kilker, Donald Gallagher, Albert Conti, Helen Brown, Ted Shea, Johnny Wrey, Bob Goodstein, Jack Crosby, Bob Crosby, Ruby Shaeffer, Jimmy Dime, Dorothy Jarvis, Nancy Emery, Katherine Hankin, Irene Bennett, Martha O'Driscoll, Edgar Dearing, Guy Usher, Marjorie Reynolds.

Remade as COLLEGE SWING (1938)

FOLLOW THE FLEET (1936) RKO. 110 minutes

Produced by Pandro S. Berman. Directed by Mark Sandrich. Screenplay by Dwight Taylor, based on the play, *Shore Leave,* by Hubert Osborne, Allan Scott. Songs: Irving Berlin. Musical director: Max Steiner. Choreography: Hermes Pan. Camera: David Abel.

Well-tried story of a Plain Jane (Harriet Hilliard) blossoming into a beauty. Astaire and Scott play sailors on shore leave, Ginger is a dance hall singer. Very little for Betty to do in this, but she looks *so* pretty.

CAST: Fred Astaire, Ginger Rogers, Randolph Scott, Harriet Hilliard, Astrid Allwyn, Ray Mayer, Harry Beresford, Addison Randall, Russell Hicks, Brooks Benedict, Lucille Ball, Betty Grable, Joy Hodges, Jennie Gray, Tony Martin, Maxine Jennings, Frank Jenks, Frank Mills, Edward Burns, Herbert Rawlinson, Jane Hamilton.

PIGSKIN PARADE (1936) 20th Century-Fox. 93 minutes

Produced by Bogart Rogers. Directed by David Butler. Screenplay by Harry Tugend, Jack Yellen, William Sonselman, based on a story by Arthur Sheekman, Nat Perrin, Mark Kelly. Songs: Sidney Mitchell, Lew Pollack. Musical director: David Buttolph. Camera: Arthur Miller.

Haley and Patsy Kelly play a married couple, who also happen to be college football coaches, who promote country hick Stuart Erwin, whose tactics take the team on to win the Yale Bowl. Grable gets to sing "It's Love I'm After," while Judy Garland steals the film with several numbers.

CAST: Stuart Erwin, Patsy Kelly, Jack Haley, Johnny Downs, Betty Grable, Arline Judge, Dixie Dunbar, Judy Garland, Tony Martin, Fred Kohler, Jr., Elisha Cook, Jr., Pat Flaherty, Jack Murphy, Dave Sharpe, Si Jenks, Jack Stoney, John Dilson, Ben Hall, Lynn Bari, Charles Wilson, Alan Ladd, Edward Le Saint, Jack Best, Maurice Cass, Douglas Wood, Charles Croker King.

Academy Awards: Nomination for Best Supporting Actor: Stuart Erwin.

DON'T TURN 'EM LOOSE (1936) RKO. 65 minutes

Produced by Robert Sisk. Directed by Ben Stoloff, Screenplay by Harry Segall, based on the story by Ferdinand Reyher. Camera: Jack MacKenzie.

Dull melodrama with Lewis Stone as principal of a high school, who kills his son, when he again goes off the rails while on parole.

CAST: Lewis Stone, James Gleason, Bruce Cabot, Betty Grable, Nella Walker, Louise Latimer, Grace Bradley, Frank M. Thomas, Maxine Jennings, Frank Jenks, Harry Jans, John Arledge, Addison Randall, Fern Emmett, Arthur Hoyt, Frenchy Durelle, Phillip Morris, Tommy Graham, Gordon Jones, John Ince.

THIS WAY PLEASE (1937) Paramount. 70 minutes
Produced by Mel Shauer. Directed by Robert Florey. Screenplay by Grant Garrett, Seena Owen, Howard J. Green, from a story by Maxwell Shane, Bill Thomas. Camera: Harry Fishbeck. Songs: Frederick Hollander, Sam Coslow, Al Siegal. Dance director: LeRoy Prinz. Musical director: Boris Morros.
Betty goes for an audition as a singer, but instead lands a job as a theatre usherette, where she falls for visiting movie star, Buddy Rogers. Grable performed well and had some good routines.
CAST: Charles "Buddy" Rogers, Mary Livingstone, Betty Grable, Ned Sparks, Jim and Marian Jordon (Fibber McGee and Molly), Porter Hall, Lee Bowman, Cecil Cunningham, Wally Vernon, Romo Vincent, Jerry Bergen, Rufe Davis.

THRILL OF A LIFETIME (1937) Paramount. 72 minutes
Produced by Fanchon. Directed by George Archainbaud. Screenplay by Seena Owen, Grant Garret, from their story. Camera: William Mellor. Songs: Frederick Hollander and Sam Caslow. Choreography: LeRoy Prinz, Carlos Romero. Musical director: Boris Morros.
Betty plays a lovesick secretary in love with her boss, who runs a love-nest camp. Wearing spectacles for most of the footage, Grable, with some help from Judy Canova, then changes her image. The boss then sees what he has been missing.
CAST: Judy Canova, Betty Grable, Larry "Buster" Crabbe, Dorothy Lamour, Johnny Downs, Ben Blue, Eleanor Whitney, Leif Erikson, The Fanchonettes, Howard Mitchell, Marie Burton, Tommy Wonder, Paula De Cardo, Norah Gale, Harriette Haddon, Lola Jensen, Gwen Kenyon, Billy Daniels, Frank Abel, Lee Bennett, Carlyle Blackwell, Jr., Bob Parrish, The Yacht Club Boys.

COLLEGE SWING (1938) Paramount. 86 minutes
Produced by Lewis Gensler. Directed by Raoul Walsh. Screenplay by Walter De Leon, Morrie Ryskind, Preston Sturges, based on a story by Tedd Lesser and Frederick Hazlitt Brennan. Camera: Victor Milner. Dances staged by LeRoy Prinz. Musical director: Boris Morros.
For Jack Oakie (Collegiate) read Gracie Allen, as the dizzy blonde becomes Dean. More polished, and funnier than the original. Betty, with husband Jackie Coogan, sings and dances to the title song.
CAST: George Burns, Gracie Allen, Martha Raye, Bob Hope, Edward Everett Horton, Florence George, Ben Blue, Betty Grable, Jackie Coogan, John Payne, Cecil Cunningham, Robert Cummings, Jerry Colonna, The Slate Brothers.

GIVE ME A SAILOR (1938) Paramount. 80 minutes
Produced by Jeff Lazarus. Directed by Elliott Nugent. Screenplay by Doris Anderson, Frank Butler, based on a play by Anne Nichols. Camera: Victor Milner. Songs: Leo Robin and Ralph Rainger. Choreography: LeRoy Prinz. Musical director: Boris Morros.

Martha Raye enters a national bake-a-cake competition but, thanks to a bungling photographer, she ends up the winner of a beautiful legs contest! Wacky romantic comedy. Betty gets to sing "What Goes on Here in My Heart," but her role is a strangely unsympathetic one.

CAST: Martha Raye, Bob Hope, Betty Grable, J. C. Nugent, Jack Whiting, Clarence Kolb, Nana Bryant, Emerson Treacy, Bonnie Jean Churchill, Kathleen Lockhart, Ralph Sanford, Edward Earle, Eddie Kane.

CAMPUS CONFESSIONS (1938) Paramount. 65 minutes

Produced by William Thomas. Directed by George Archainbaud. Screenplay by Lloyd Corrigan, Erwin Gelsey. Camera: Henry Sharp. Musical director: Boris Morros.

Betty, as a college newspaper reporter, takes the lead in this college basketball romance. Famed basketball star Hank Luisetti lends credence to the tale. Bright comedy.

CAST: Betty Grable, Eleanore Whitney, William Henry, Fritz Feld, John Arledge, Thurston Hall, Roy Gordon, Lane Chandler, Richard Denning, Matty Kemp, Sumner Getchell, Hank Luisetti.

MAN ABOUT TOWN (1939) Paramount. 86 minutes

Produced by Arthur Hornblow, Jr.. Directed by Mark Sandrich. Screenplay by Morrie Ryskind, from a story by Morrie Ryskind, Allan Scott and Zio Meyers. Camera: Ted Tatzlaff. Songs: Frank Loesser, Frederick Hollander, Matty Malneck, Leo Robin, Ralph Rainger. Choreography: Merriel Abbott, LeRoy Prinz. Musical director: Victor Young.

Betty was set for female lead in this Jack Benny comedy, but was replaced by Lamour when she was hospitalized for an appendectomy. However she was brought in for "Fidgety Joe," a bright specialty number.

CAST: Jack Benny, Dorothy Lamour, Edward Arnold, Binnie Barnes, Phil Harris, Eddie (Rochester) Anderson, Monty Woley, Isabel Jeans, Betty Grable, E. E. Clive, Leonard Mudie, Peggy Steward, Patti Sacks, Matty Malneck Orchestra, Merriel Abbott Dancers, Pina Troupe.

MILLION DOLLAR LEGS (1939) Paramount. 59 minutes

Directed by Nick Grinde. Screenplay by Lewis Foster, Richard English, based on a story by Lewis Foster. Camera: Harry Fischbeck.

Betty's final collegiate film — and her last for Paramount. The story refers to a college rowing team — and not the star's famous underpinnings. Jackie Coogan is also featured, as is 14-year-old Donald O'Connor.

CAST: Betty Grable, John Hartley, Donald O'Connor, Jackie Coogan, Larry Crabbe, Peter Lind Hayes, Dorothea Kent, Richard Denning, Phllip Warren, Edward Arnold, Thurston Hall, Roy Gordon, Matty Kemp, John Matthews, William Tracey, Ross Clark, Anthony March, Tom Dugan, Roger Laswell, George Anderson, William Holden.

THE DAY THE BOOKIES WEPT (1939) RKO. 64 minutes

Produced by Robert Sisk. Directed by Leslie Goodwin. Screenplay by Bert Granet, George Jeske, based on the novel *Crazy Over Pigeons*, by Daniel Fuchs. Camera:

Jack Mackenzie. Musical director: Arthur Morton
Joe Penner, Betty, and a horse named Hiccup! Penner buys an "alcoholic" horse for
his taxi driver syndicate. Betty, as a waitress, supplies the love interest.
CAST: Joe Penner, Betty Grable, Richard Lane, Tom Kennedy, Thurston Hall,
Bernadene Hays, Carol Hughes, William Wright, Prince Alert, Emory Parnell,
Vinton Haworth.

DOWN ARGENTINE WAY (1940) 20th Century-Fox. Technicolor. 94 minutes
Produced by Darryl F. Zanuck. Directed by Irving Cummings. Screenplay by
Darrrell Ware and Karl Tunberg. Camera: Leon Shamroy and Ray Rennahan.
Songs and lyrics by Harry Warren and Mack Gordon. Choreography: Nick
Castle. Musical director Emil Newman.
At last, the film that set Betty Grable's career aflight after ten years of waiting in the
wings. Slight storyline involving horses, racing, and breeders. Betty takes a trip
to Argentina to buy a racehorse and falls in love with Don Ameche. Also marked
the American film debut of colorful Carmen Miranda. Good support from
Charlotte Greenwood and Leonid Kinsky, and a great dance routine by the
Nicholas Brothers. Grable sang hit song, "Two Dreams Met," and led the
chorus in the title number.
CAST: Don Ameche, Betty Grable, Carmen Miranda, Charlotte Greenwood, J.
Carrol Naish, Henry Stephenson, Katharine Aldridge, Leonid Kinskey, Chris-
Pin Martin, Robert Conway, Gregory Gaye, Bobby Stone, Charles Judels,
Nicholas Brothers, Bando da Lua.

TIN PAN ALLEY (1940) 20th Century-Fox. 94 minutes
Produced by Darryl F. Zanuck. Directed by Walter Lang. Screenplay by Robert Ellis
and Helen Logan. Camera: Leon Shamroy. New Song ("You Say the Sweetest
Things, Baby") by Harry Warren and Mack Gordon. Choreography: Seymour
Felix. Musical director Alfred Newman.
Struggling song writers Harrigan and Calhoun (John Payne and Jack Oakie) use the
Blane Sisters (Alice Faye as Katie, and Betty Grable as Lily) to boost them to suc-
cess. Katie falls for Harrigan and joins their music publishing house while Lily
goes solo in London. After a falling-out, Katie follows her sister to England, but
all four are reunited there when the boys join the army. Fabulous old songs and
great performances by the principals. "The Sheikh of Araby" is a standout num-
ber for Grable and Faye.
CAST: Alice Faye, Betty Grable, John Payne, Jack Oakie, Allen Jenkins, Esther
Ralston, John Loder, Elisha Cook, Jr., Fred Keating, Billy Gilbert, Lionel Pape,
Ben Carter, Lillian Porter, Billy Bevan, Dewey Robinson, John Sheehan, George
Watts. Nicholas Brothers, Hal K. Dawson, Robert Emmett Keane. Specialities:
Princess Vanessa Ammoa, Roberts Brothers, Brian Sisters.
Remade as I'LL GET BY (1950) with June Haver, William Lundigan, Gloria De
Haven.

MOON OVER MIAMI (1941) 20th Century-Fox. Technicolor. 91 minutes
Produced by Harry Joe Brown. Directed by Walter Lang. Screenplay by Vincent
Lawrence and Brown Holmes, based on a story by Stephen Powys, adapted by

George Seaton. Camera: Leon Shamroy and Perevell Marley. Music and Lyrics by Leo Robin and Ralph Rainger. Choreography: Hermes Pan. Musical director: Alfred Newman.

A colorful musical set well ahead of its time, said most film critics of this bright musical remake of THREE BLIND MICE (1938).

Betty Grable and Carole Landis play sisters working as hash house waitresses in a Texas diner who come into a smaller-than-expected inheritance. With their aunt (Charlotte Greenwood) the three set off for Miami to catch at least one millionaire. Grable dallies between two wealthy suitors, Don Ameche and Robert Cummings, while Greenwood hits it off with waiter Jack Haley. However it is Landis who ends up with the real millionaire, while Betty settles for love. Some lively dance routines, especially when Betty joins the Condos Brothers for a fast tap routine, then accompanies choreographer Pan in the delightful "Conga to a Nursery Rhyme."

CAST: Don Ameche, Betty Grable, Robert Cummings, Carole Landis, Charlotte Greenwood, Jack Haley, Cobina Wright, Jr., George Lessey, Fortunio Bonanova, Robert Conway, The Condos Brothers, Robert Greig, Minor Watson, George Humbert, Spencer Charters, Lynn Roberts, Larry McGrath.

Remade as *Three Little Girls in Blue* (1946), *How To Marry a Millionaire* (1953)

A YANK IN THE RAF (1941) 20th Century-Fox. 98 minutes

Produced by Darryl F. Zanuck. Directed by Henry King. Screenplay by Darrel Ware and Karl Tunberg, based on a story by Melville Crossman (Zanuck's pen name). Camera: Leon Shamroy. Art direction: Richard Day, James Basevi. Songs: Leo Robin, Ralph Rainger. Musical director: Alfred Newman.

Based on the short story, "Eagle Squadron," written by Zanuck. This was the first major film dealing with World War II. Zanuck cast Grable in her first dramatic starring role opposite Tyrone Power who played a young pilot who joins the Royal Air Force and becomes a hero. Grable played his showgirl girlfriend and performed a couple of low-key song-and-dance routines. The film used actual aerial footage of early WW2 air battles, giving it a touch of authenticity. It was one of the most popular films of 1941 and did much to boost interest in and support for the British war effort.

CAST: Tyrone Power, Betty Grable, John Sutton, Reginald Gardiner, Donald Stuart, Norton Lowry, Richard Fraser, Ralph Byrd, Bruce Lester, Denis Green, Lester Matthews, Frederic Worlock, Lynn Roberts, Fortunio Bonanova, James Craven, Howard Davies.

I WAKE UP SCREAMING (a/k/a HOT SPOT) (1941) 20th Century-Fox. 81 minutes

Produced by Milton Sperling. Directed by H. Bruce Humberstone. Screenplay by Dwight Taylor, from a novel by Steve Fisher. Camera: Edward Cronjager. Musical director: Cyril J. Mockridge.

When an ambitious young girl (Carole Landis) is murdered, suspicion falls on her promoter boyfriend (Victor Mature). However, the dead girl's sister (Grable) thinks otherwise and helps Mature unmask the real killer. Good performances from the principals in this early "film noire," told in flashback, but they are all overshadowed by Laird Cregar, who plays the sinister detective investigating the case.

Appendix

CAST: Betty Grable, Victor Mature, Carole Landis, Laird Cregar, William Gargan, Alan Mowbray, Allyn Joslyn, Elisha Cook, Jr., Chick Chandler, Morris Ankrum, Frank Orth, Wade Boteler, Ralph Dunn, Brooks Benedict, Forbes Murray.
Remade in 1953 as *Vicki*, starring Jeanne Crain, Jean Peters, and Elliot Reed.

SONG OF THE ISLANDS (1942) 20th Century-Fox. Technicolor. 75 minutes
Producer William LeBaron. Directed by Walter Lang. Screenplay by Joseph Schrank, Robert Pirosh, Robert Ellis, Helen Logan. Camera: Ernest Palmer. Songs: Mack Gordon and Harry Warren. Choreography: Hermes Pan. Musical director: Alfred Newman.
Back to the musical genre for Grable in this lushly staged escapist nonsense. Betty plays a teacher returning from the mainland to her Hawaiian isle home, only to become romantically involved with cattle baron's son, Mature. Since the film was merely an excuse for the stars to show off their torsos, the mystery remains — why did it take four screenwriters to come up with this non-plot? However, it is all done in high style, with a sensational-looking Grable giving her all for the war effort in this morale-booster, which became a big box office hit. Most fans think this was the most beautiful "entrance" Grable ever made in one of her movies — being paddled across a lagoon, singing the title song. A colorful travelogue set to music!
CAST: Betty Grable, Victor Mature, Jack Oakie, Thomas Mitchell, George Barbier, Billy Gilbert, Hilo Hattie, Lillian Porter, Hal K. Dawson, Amy Cordone, Bruce Wong, Alex Polland, Harold Lishman, Harry Owens and his Royal Hawaiians.

FOOTLIGHT SERENADE (1942) 20th Century-Fox. 81 minutes.
Produced by William Le Baron. Directed by Gregory Ratoff. Screenplay by Robert Ellis, Helen Logan, Lynn Starling from the story, "Dynamite" by Fidel La Barba and Kenneth Earl. Camera: Lee Garmes. Songs: Leo Robin, Ralph Rainger. Choreography: Hermes Pan. Musical director: Charles Henderson.
Authentic-looking backstage settings, plus some great dancing by Grable, lift this routine musical out of the rut. Grable plays a chorus girl who gets lucky and wins the lead in a musical starring a conceited boxer. Grable secretly marries John Payne, a struggling performer who is also cast in the show, which causes all sorts of problems. Fine dance routines, with Hermes Pan making the perfect partner for Grable. Also features Jane Wyman in an early screen role.
CAST: John Payne, Betty Grable, Victor Mature, Jane Wyman, James Gleason, Phil Silvers, Cobina Wright, Jr., June Lang, Frank Orth, Mantan Moreland, Irving Bacon, Charles Tanne, George Dobbs, Sheila Ryan, Frank Coghlan, Jr., Harry Barris, Trudy Marhall, Don Wilson, John Dilson.

SPRINGTIME IN THE ROCKIES (1942) 20th Century-Fox. Technicolor. 90 minutes
Produced by Darryl F. Zanuck. Directed by Irvine Cummings. Screenplay by Walter Bullock, Ken Englund, from a story by Philip Wylie. Camera: Ernest Palmer. Songs: Mack Gordon, Harry Warren. Choreography: Hermes Pan. Musical director: Alfred Newman.
Canada's Lake Louise is the setting for this lush musical with a Rockies backdrop. Betty and John Payne play a couple of warring Broadway headliners. When Betty

takes off for Canada with love rival Cesar Romero, Payne follows, with Carmen Miranda (his secretary!) and E. E. Horton in tow. Fun-filled musical in a spectacular setting with Grable and Romero executing some fine ballroom-style dancing.

CAST: Betty Grable, John Payne, Carmen Miranda, Cesar Romero, Harry James and his Music Makers with Helen Forrest, Bando da Lua, Charlotte Greenwood, Edward Everett Horton, Frank Orth, Harry Hayden, Jackie Gleason, Trudy Marshall, Chick Chandler, Iron Eyes Cody, Bess Flowers.

CONEY ISLAND (1943) 20th Century-Fox. Technicolor. 96 minutes
Produced by William Perlberg. Directed by Walter Lang. Screenplay by George Seaton. Camera: Ernest Palmer. Songs: Leo Robin, Ralph Rainger. Choreography: Hermes Pan. Musical director: Alfred Newman.

Grable plays a diamond-in-the-rough saloon singer in her first costume musical, set in the turn-of-the century New York pleasure beach. Rival con men, Cesar Romero and George Montgomery, vie for her affections. Montgomery wins out when he helps Betty realize her full potential as an entertainer and become famous on Broadway. Great songs and dances in this highly entertaining musical which saw Grable move into the superstar league.

CAST: Betty Grable, George Montgomery, Cesar Romero, Charles Winninger, Phil Silvers, Matt Briggs, Paul Hurst, Frank Orth, Phyllis Kennedy, Carmen D'Antonio, Andrew Tombes, Harry Seymour, Hal K. Dawson, Bud Williams, Alec Craig, Herbert Ashley, James Lucas, Francis Sayles, Tene Ramey, Gus Reed, Delos Jewkos, George Grumlick.

Remade as *Wabash Avenue* (1950) with Grable in her original role, but with two new leading men, Victor Mature and Phil Silvers.

SWEET ROSIE O'GRADY (1943) 20th Century-Fox. Technicolor. 74 minutes
Produced by William Perlberg. Directed by Irving Cummings. Screenplay by Ken Englund, based on stories by Frederick Stephani, Walter R. Lipman, Edward Van Every. Camera: Ernest Palmer, A.S.C.. New songs: Mack Gordon, Harry Warren. Choreography: Hermes Pan. Musical numbers staged by Fanchon. Musical directors: Alfred Newman and Charles Henderson.

Grable remained in a "time warp" for her second successive costume musical. This time she plays a burlesque queen who goes "legit" in London as Madeleine Marlowe and becomes engaged to a duke, (Reginald Gardiner). On her "triumphant" return to New York, inquisitive Sam McGee (Robert Young), an investigative reporter for the Police Gazette, unmasks her as a phony. A witty musical, full of good humor and excellent singing and dancing, with Grable again looking competely at home in the period costume. "If you thought the nineties were gay, you should have seen the eighties!" ran the publicity blurb.

CAST: Betty Grable, Robert Young, Adolphe Menjou, Reginald Gardiner, Virginia Grey, Phil Regan, Sig Ruman, Alan Dinehart, Robert Cavanaugh, Frank Orth, Jonathan Hale, Stanley Clements, Byron Foulger, Lilyan Irene, Milton Parsons, Dorothy Vaughan, Hal K. Dawson, George Chandler, Charles Trowbridge, St. Brendan's Choir, Leo Diamond and His Solitaires.

Remade as *That Wonderful Urge* (1948) with Tyrone Power and Gene Tierney.

PIN UP GIRL (1944) 20th Century-Fox. Technicolor. 83 minutes

Produced by William Le Baron. Directed by H. Bruce Humberstone. Screenplay by Robert Ellis, Helen Logan, Earl Baldwin. Camera: Ernest Palmer. Songs: Mack Gordon, Jimmy Monaco. Choreography: Hermes Pan. Musical directors: Emil Newman and Charles Henderson.

Amusing tale as Grable plays a small-time entertainer with a big imagination. Her fibbing leads her into a romantic triangle with a returning war hero, but also brings her fame and fortune as a pin-up girl and top star. Weak story and cast, but Grable more than makes up for it with some good comedy touches and fine dancing, again partnered by Hermes Pan. The finale remains a real curio, with Betty leading a military march. The ending pleased no one, least of all Grable. However the picture was a runaway financial success. Her progressing pregnancy during the making of this film precluded her performing a fast tap routine with the Condos Brothers.

CAST: Betty Grable, John Harvey, Martha Raye, Joe E. Brown, Eugene Pallette, Dorothea Kent, Dave Willock, Roger Clark, Irving Bacon, Angela Blue, Mantan Moreland, J. Farrell MacDonald, Lillian Porter, Max Willenz, Charles Spivak and His Orchestra, Gloria Nord and Skating Vanities, the Condos Brothers.

FOUR JILLS IN A JEEP (1944) 20th Century-Fox. 89 minutes

Produced by Irving Starr. Directed by William A Seiter.

A true-life story of Carole Landis, Martha Raye, Kay Francis, and Mitzi Mayfair during their tours entertaining the troops in England and North Africa during WW2. Betty sings "Cuddle Up A Little Closer" in a guest spot.

CAST: Kay Francis, Carole Landis, Martha Raye, Mitzi Mayfair, John Harvey, Dick Haymes, Phil Silvers, Glenn Langan, George Jessel, Lester Matthews, Ralph Byrd, Miles Mander, Lester Dorr, Paul Harvey, Mary Servos. Guest stars: Alice Faye, Betty Grable, Carmen Miranda.

BILLY ROSE'S DIAMOND HORSESHOE (1945) 20th Century-Fox. Technicolor. 106 minutes

Produced by William Perlberg. Directed by George Seaton. Screenplay by George Seaton from a play by John Kenyon Nicholson. Camera: Ernest Palmer. Songs: Harry Warren and Mack Gordon. Choreography: Hermes Pan. Camera: Ernest Palmer. Musical direrctors: Alfred Newman, Charles Henderson.

Sumptuously staged musical depicting life at Billy Rose's famous New York nightclub. Showgirl Betty takes the offer of a mink coat to help out her girlfriend whose romance is suffering because of the arrival of her boyfriend's son (Dick Haymes). Grable sets out to lure Haymes away from the club and back to medical school. As usual, love wins in the end. Film introduced "The More I See You" and "I Wish I Knew," both of which became standards.

CAST: Betty Grable, Dick Haymes, William Gaxton, Beatrice Kay, Phil Silvers, Carmen Cavallero, Willie Solar, Margaret Dumont, Roy Benson, George Melford, Hal K. Dawson, Kenny Williams, Reed Hadley, Eddie Acuff, Edward Gargan, Ruth Rickaby, Dorothy Day, Julie London, Milton Kibbee, Bess Flowers, Paul Bakanas, Charles Coleman, Eric Wilton.

Filmography

THE DOLLY SISTERS (1945) 20th Century-Fox. Technicolor. 114 minutes.

Produced by George Jessel. Directed by Irving Cummings. Screenplay by John Larkin, Marian Spitzer. Camera: Ernest Palmer. Songs: Mack Gordon, James Monaco, Harry Revell. Choreography: Seymour Felix. Musical directors: Alfred Newman and Charles Henderson.

Highly fictional bio of the fabled Hungarian sisters who took America and Europe by storm. At times it feels like a remake of *Tin Pan Alley,* but Grable and June Haver perform admirably in this song-filled show. A strong favorite among Grable fans.

CAST: Betty Grable, John Payne, June Haver, S. Z .Sakall, Reginald Gardiner, Frank Latimore, Gene Sheldon, Sig Rumann, Trudy Marshall, Colette Lyons, Evan Thomas, Donna Jo Gribble, Robert Middlemass, Paul Hurst, Lester Allan, Frank Orth, J. Farrel MacDonald, Mae Marsh, George E. Stone.

DO YOU LOVE ME? (a/k/a *Kitten on the Keys*) (1946) 20th Century-Fox. Technicolor. 91 minutes

Produced by George Jessel. Directed by Gregory Ratoff. Screenplay by Robert Ellis and Helen Logan, based on a story by Bert Granet. Camera: Edward Cronjager. Songs: Charles Henderson, Harold Adamson, Harry James, Harry Ruby, Jimmy McHugh, Herbert Magidson, Matty Malneck. Choreography: Seymour Felix. Musical directors: Emil Newman and Charles Henderson.

Mildly amusing story of a dowdy dean of a music school (Maureen O'Hara) who falls for the charms of Harry James and his singer, Dick Haymes. Which one will she choose? To answer the question: Grable has a guest role as a James admirer!

CAST: Maureen O'Hara, Dick Haymes, Harry James, Reginald Gardiner, Richard Gaines, Stanley Prager, Harry James' Music Makers, B. S. Pully, Chick Chandler, Alma Kruger, Almira Sessions, Douglas Wood, Harlan Briggs, Julia Dean, Harry Hays Morgan, Lex Barker, Lillian Porter, Marjorie Jackson, Jack Scordi, Diane Ascher. Guest star: Betty Grable.

THE SHOCKING MISS PILGRIM (1947) 20th Century-Fox. Technicolor. 87 minutes.

Produced by William Perlberg. Directed by George Seaton. Screenplay by George Seaton, based on a story by Ernest and Frederica Maas. Camera: Leon Shamroy. Songs: George and Ira Gershwin. Choreography: Hermes Pan. Musical directors: Alfred Newman and Charles Henderson.

Charming performance by Grable in this equally charming story of the early Women's Lib movement. Betty plays a "typewriter" who arrives in Boston seeking employment. She succeeds and also manages to win her boss's love, via several lovely Gershwin tunes.

CAST: Betty Grable, Dick Haymes, Anne Revere, Allyn Joslyn, Gene Lockhart, Elizabeth Patterson, Elizabeth Risdon, Arthur Shields, Charles Kemper, Roy Roberts, Stanley Prager, Ed Laughton, Hal K. Dawson, Lillian Bronson, Raymond Largay, Constance Purdy, Mildred Stone, Pierre Watkin, Junius Matthews, Frank Dawson.

MOTHER WORE TIGHTS (1947) 20th Century-Fox. Technicolor. 107 minutes
Produced by Lamar Trotti. Directed by Walter Lang. Screenplay by Lamar Trotti, based on the book by Miriam Young. Camera: Harry Jackson. Songs: Mack Gordon, Joseph Myrow, Harry Warren, Gus Kahn. Choreography: Seymour Felix, Kenny Williams. Musical director: Alfred Newman.
First teaming of the Grable-Dailey dance team. The film was a resounding success for the new screen twosome. The story concerned a vaudeville couple and the problems they have bringing up their family. Another Grable favorite among fans. Great songs and dance routines. Betty is excellent in a role that has her age from a teenager to a grandma.
CAST: Betty Grable, Dan Dailey, Mona Freeman, Connie Marshall, Vanessa Brown, Robert Arthur, Sara Allgood, William Frawley, Ruth Nelson, Annabel Shaw, George Cleveland, Michael Dunne, Veda Ann Borg, Lee Patrick, Senor Wences, Maude Elburne, Kathleen Lockhart, Brad Slaven, George Davis, Lotte Stein, Antonio Filauri.
Academy Awards: Best scoring of a musical picture: Alfred Newman.
AA Nominations: Best song: "You Do." Best color cinematography.

THAT LADY IN ERMINE (1948) 20th Century-Fox. Technicolor. 88 minutes.
Produced and directed by Ernst Lubitsch. Co-directed by Otto Preminger. Screenplay by Samson Raphaelson, based on the operetta, *This Is The Moment*, by Rudolph Schanzer and Ernest Welisch. Camera: Leon Shamroy. Songs: Leo Robin, Rudolph Schanzer, Ernest Welisch. Choreography: Hermes Pan. Musical director: Alfred Newman.
Charming Ruritanian musical fantasy which has Grable in a dual role, wooed by romantic Hussar Douglas Fairbanks, Jr.. But the film turned out a disappointment despite some good songs and spectacular sets. Ernst Lubitsch died only eight days after the film went into production. It was completed by Otto Preminger.
CAST: Betty Grable, Douglas Fairbanks, Jr., Cesar Romero, Walter Abel, Reginald Gardiner, Harry Davenport, Virginia Campbell, Whit Bissell, Edmund MacDonald, David Bond, Harry Cording, Belle Mitchell, Mary Bear, Jack George, John Parrish, Mayo Newhall, Lester Allan, Duke York.
Academy Awards: Nomination for Best Song, "This Is The Moment."

WHEN MY BABY SMILES AT ME (1948) 20th Century-Fox. Technicolor. 98 minutes
Produced by George Jessel. Directed by Walter Lang. Screenplay by Lamar Trotti, from the play, *Burlesque* by George Manker Watters and Arthur Hopkins. Camera: Harry Jackson. Songs: Mack Gordon and Josef Myrow. Choreography: Seymour Felix. Musical director: Alfred Newman.
Life and times of a vaudeville couple. Dan Dailey gets a chance to go solo on Broadway. Wife Betty encourages him while she remains on the circuit. Women and booze become Dan's downfall, and it takes the loving Grable to get him back in harness. Tuneful musical.
CAST: Betty Grable, Dan Dailey, Jack Oakie, June Havoc, Richard Arlen, James Gleason, Vanita Wade, Kenny Williams, Jean Wallace, Patti Behrs, Robert Emmet

Keane, Jerry Maren, George Lewis, Tom Stevenson, Sam Bernard, Mauritz Hugo, Frank Scannell, J. Farrell MacDonald, Les Clark, Harry Seymour, Noel Neill, Lu Anne Jones, Joanne Dale, Dorothy Babb.

Academy Award nominations: Best Actor, Dan Dailey; Best Musical Score, Alfred Newman.

THE BEAUTIFUL BLONDE FROM BASHFUL BEND (1949) 20th Century-Fox. Technicolor. 77 minutes

Produced, directed, and written by Preston Sturges. Based on a story by Earl Fenton. Camera: Harry Jackson. Songs: Mack Gordon and Joseph Myrow, Don George, Lionel Newman. Musical director: Cyril Mockridge.

Farcical Western with Betty as the Beautiful Blonde sharpshooter who has problems with her lover, Cesar Romero. The only problem is that when she gets close enough to get a shot at him, the local judge gets in the way. The film suffered from heavy censorship and the final cut is unsatisfactory, though the cast, which includes many old-timers, works hard for the few laughs.

CAST: Betty Grable, Cesar Romero, Rudy Vallee, Olga San Juan, Sterling Holloway, Danny Jackson, Hugh Herbert, Margaret Hamilton, El Brendel, Porter Hall, Patti Behrs, Crisp-Pin Martin, Emory Parnell, Alan Bridge, J. Farrell MacDonald, Richard Hale, Georgia Caine, Marie Windsor, Mary Monica MacDonald.

WABASH AVENUE (1950) 20th Century-Fox. Technicolor. 92 minutes

Produced by William Perlberg. Directed by Henry Koster. Written by Charles Lederer and Harry Tugend. Camera: Arthur E. Arling. Songs: Mack Gordon, Joseph Myrow, Bert Kalmar, Joe Cooper. Choreography: Billy Daniel. Musical director: Lionel Newman.

Déjà vu Grable. Spirited remake of her earlier success, *Coney Island*, only this time the setting is the Chicago World's Fair, with two new leading men — Victor Mature and Phil Harris. Some good songs and lots of fancy dancing, with Betty partnered by new choreographer pal, Billy Daniel. Great fun!

CAST: Betty Grable, Victor Mature, Phil Harris, Reginald Gardiner, James Barton, Barry Kelley, Margaret Hamilton, Jacqueline Dalya, Robin Raymond, Hal K. Dawson, Colette Lyons, Charles Arnt, Dorothy Neumann, Alexander Pope, Billy Daniel, Henry Kulky.

Academy Awards Nomination: Best Song, "Wilhelmina."

MY BLUE HEAVEN (1950) 20th Century-Fox. Technicolor. 96 minutes

Produced by Sol C. Siegel. Directed by Henry Koster. Screenplay by Lamar Trotti, Claude Binyon, based on the story, "Storks Don't Bring Babies," by S. K. Lauren. Camera: Arthur E. Arling. Songs: Ralph Blane and Harold Arlen. Choreography: Billy Daniel and Seymour Felix. Musical director: Alfred Newman.

Grable and Dailey on their third outing together. This time they play a married couple with a successful radio program. After Betty suffers a miscarriage, they move into television. But Betty still wants to become a mother and gets involved in some shady adoption methods. Slight story, but some great dancing from the principals — and Mitzi Gaynor, making her screen debut.

CAST: Betty Grable, Dan Dailey, David Wayne, Jane Wyatt, Mitzi Gaynor, Una Merkel, Louise Beavers, Laura Pierpont, Don Hicks, Irving Fulton, Billy Daniel,

Larry Keating, Minerva Urecal, Mae Marsh, Noel Rayburn, Phylis Coates, Lois Hall, Frank Remley.

CALL ME MISTER (1951) 20th Century-Fox. Technicolor. 95 minutes

Produced by Fred Kohlmar. Directed by Lloyd Bacon. Screenplay by Albert E. Lewin and Burt Styler, suggested by the revue, *Call Me Mister*, by Harold J. Rome and Arnold M. Auerbach. Camera: Arthur E. Arling. Songs: Mack Gordon, Sammy Fain, Harold J. Rome, Frances Ash, Jerry Seelan, Earl K. Brent. Choreography: Busby Berkeley. Musical director: Alfred Newman.

Practically a remake of A YANK IN THE RAF, updated to coincide with the end of WW2. Since the original Broadway show was a revue, and therefore had no storyline, the scriptwriters simply rehashed YANK. Few songs remain from the original revue, but Betty is in fine dancing form, particularly with the Dunhill Trio.

This was the final film in the famous Grable-Dailey partnership.

CAST: Betty Grable, Dan Dailey, Danny Thomas, Dale Robertson, Benay Venuta, Richard Boone, Jeffrey Hunter, Frank Fontaine, Harry Von Zell, The Dunhill Trio (Lou Spencer, Art Stanley, Bob Roberts), Bobby Short, Dave Willock, Tommy Bond, Frank Clark, Jerry Paris, Fred Libby, Ken Christy, Russ Conway, Mack Williams, Maylia, Steve Clark, Robert Easton, John McKee, John McGuire, Jack Kelly, Paul Burke, Harry Lauter, Robert Stockwell.

MEET ME AFTER THE SHOW (1951) 20th Century-Fox. Technicolor. 86 minutes

Produced by George Jessel. Directed by Richard Sale. Screenplay by Richard Sale and Mary Loos, from a story by Erna Lazarus and W. Scott Darling. Camera: Arthur E. Arling, A.S.C.. Songs: Jules Styne and Leo Robin. Choreography: Jack Cole. Musical director: Lionel Newman.

First-rate Grable musical. Betty plays a Broadway star who fakes amnesia to get back at her wayward husband. She reverts to the honky-tonk entertainer she was before her husband "discovered" her and made her into a star. Good humored, with some splendid Jack Cole dance numbers — which suited Betty perfectly.

CAST: Betty Grable, Macdonald Carey, Eddie Albert, Rory Calhoun, Fred Clark, Lois Andrews, Irene Ryan, Steve Condos, Jerry Brandow, Arthur Walge, Edwin Max, Robert Nash, Don Kohler, Rodney Bell, Harry Antrim, Lvyess Bradley, Gwen Verdon, Max Wagner, Al Murphy, Jewel Rose, Carol Savage, Michael Darrin, Joe Haworth, Perc Launders, Billy Newell.

THE FARMER TAKES A WIFE (1953) 20th Century-Fox. Technicolor. 80 minutes

Produced by Frank P. Rosenberg. Directed by Henry Levin. Screenplay by Walter Bullock, based on the novel, *Rome Haul* by Walter D. Edmonds, and the play by Frank B. Elser. Camera: Arthur E. Arling, A.S.C.. Songs: Harold Arlen and Dorothy Fields. Choreography: Jack Cole. Musical directors: Lionel Newman and Cyril Mockridge.

Musical version of the 1935 film of the same name. Betty is a canal barge cook who, with the help of farmer Dale Robertson, rebuilds her father's derelict barge and wins the annual Erie Canal race. Meanwhile, love blossoms! Good songs, sung with verve. But the leg show is sadly missed.

CAST: Betty Grable, Dale Robertson, Thelma Ritter, Eddie Foy, Jr., John Carroll, Charlotte Austin, Kathleen Crowley, Merry Anders, Donna Lee Hickey, Noreen

Michaels, Ruth Hall, Mort Mills, Gwen Verdon, Gordon Nelson, Ed Hinton, Emile Meyer, Lee Phelps, Ted Jordan.

HOW TO MARRY A MILLIONAIRE (1953) 20th Century-Fox. Technicolor. CinemaScope. 95 minutes
Produced by Nunnally Johnson. Directed by Jean Negulesco. Screenplay by Nunnally Johnson, based on the plays, *The Greeks Had a Word For Them*, by Zoe Atkins, and *Loco* by Katherine Albert and Dale Eunson. Camera: Joe MacDonald. Musical directors: Alfred Newman and Cyril Mockridge. 20th Century-Fox Orchestra's Street Scene conducted by Alfred Newman.
The first film completed in the new CinemaScope process. An oft-told tale of girls on the lookout for millionaire husbands. Grable, Monroe, and Bacall descend on Manhattan in their search. Fast-moving comedy with a great performance from Grable, despite being up against formidable competition.
CAST: Betty Grable, Marilyn Monroe, Lauren Bacall, David Wayne, Rory Calhoun, Cameron Mitchell, Alex D'Arcy, Fred Clark, William Powell, George Dunn, Harry Carter, Tudor Owen, Percy Helton, Maurice Marsac, Emmett Vogan, Charlotte Austin, Merry Anders, Ruth Hall, Lida Thomas, Robert Adler, Hermine Sterler, Abney Mott, Rankin Mansfield, Ralph Reid, Jan Arvan, Ivis Goulding, Dayton Lummis, Van Des Autels, Eric Wilton, Ivan Triesault, Herbert Deans, George Saurel, Hope Lanid, Tom Greenway, Beryl McCutcheon, Jane Liddell, James F. Stone, Tom Martin.

THREE FOR THE SHOW (a/k/a *The Pleasure Is All Mine*) (1955) Columbia. Technicolor. CinemaScope. 93 minutes
Produced by Jonie Taps. Directed by H. C. Potter. Screenplay by Edward Hope and Leonard Stern, based on the play, *Too Many Husbands*, by W. Somerset Maugham. Songs: Hoagy Carmichael, George and Ira Gershwin, Gene Austin, Roy Bergere, Harold Adamson, Bob Russell, Lester Lee. Choreography: Jack Cole. Musical director: Morris Stoloff.
Exquisitely gowned by Jean Louis, Betty Grable returns to the musical genre in this marital mix-up when she marries Gower Champion, only to discover her first husband (Jack Lemmon) is alive and well. Merry mayhem ensues as Betty has to decide which one she will keep. Grable again benefits from the Jack Cole choreography, especially in the "How Come You Do Me Like You Do" number — showing her rival over at Fox (Monroe!) how a Latin rhythm number *should* be performed! Good performances, but a pity the script let the stars down.
CAST: Betty Grable, Marge and Gower Champion, Jack Lemmon, Myron McCormick, Paul Harvey, Robert Bice, Hal K. Dawson, Charlotte Lawrence, Gene Wesson, Willard Waterman, Aileen Carlyle, Rudy Lee, Eugene Borden.

HOW TO BE VERY, VERY POPULAR (1955) 20th Century-Fox. Color by De Luxe. CinemaScope. 89 minutes
Produced and directed by Nunnally Johnson. Screenplay by Nunnally Johnson, based on the play, *She Loves Me Not* by Howard Lindsay, from the novel by Edward Hope. Camera: Milton Krasner. Songs by Jule Styne, Sammy Cahn, Charles Calhoun. Choreography: Paul Godkin. Musical direction: Lionel Newman and Cyril Mockridge.

When two strippers witness a murder, they go on the lam — to a boys college! While the murderer hunts them, stripper Sheree North falls under the spell of an amateur hypnotist. Grable, more sensibly, falls for wealthy mature student Robert Cummings. This was Grable's final film. A rather sad ending to a glorious career. The cast couldn't be blamed; the principals performed above and beyond the call of the script.

CAST: Betty Grable, Sheree North, Bob Cummings, Charles Coburn, Tommy Noonan, Orson Bean, Fred Clark, Alice Pearce, Rhys Williams, Andrew Tombes, Noel Toy, Emory Parnell, Harry Carter, Jesslyn Fax, Jack Mather, Charlotte Austin, Michael Lally, Milton Parsons, Harry Seymour, Hank Mann, Leslie Parrish.

Filmography

FILM SHORTS

EX-SWEETIES (1931) Educational. produced by Mack Sennett. Betty's first appearance under the name of FRANCES DEAN.

CRASHING HOLLYWOOD (1931) Educational. Directed by William Goodrich (Fatty Arbuckle). Betty is again billed as Frances Dean.

ONCE A HERO (1931) Directed by William Goodrich. Billed as Frances Dean.

LADY! PLEASE! (1932) Educational. Directed by Del Lord. Billed as Frances Dean.

HOLLYWOOD LUCK (1932) Educational. Directed by William Goodrich. Billed as Frances Dean.

THE FLIRTY SLEEPWALKER (1932) Educational. Directed by Del Lord. Billed as Frances Dean.

HOLLYWOOD LIGHTS (1932) Educational. Directed by William Goodrich. Billed as Frances Dean.

OVER THE COUNTER (1932) M-G-M. Directed by Jack Cummings. Billed as Frances Dean.

AIR TONIC (1933) RKO. Directed by Sam White. Betty Grable appears with the Ted Fiorito Orchestra, along with Leif Erickson.

ELMER STEPS OUT (1934) Columbia. Directed by Jules White. With Frank Albertson, Betty Grable, and Gloria Warner.

SUSIE'S AFFAIRS (1934) Columbia. Directed by Archie Gottler. With Arthur Jarrett, Betty Grable, and Thelma White.

BUSINESS IS A PLEASURE (1934) Technicolor. Warner Bros. Directed by Eddie Cline. Betty Grable as a singing shopgirl.

THE SPIRIT OF '76 (1935) Astor. Directed by Leigh Jason. Betty Grable plays girlfriend of U. S. president (Walter King) in this futuristic look at America.

A NIGHT AT THE BILTMORE BOWL (1935) RKO. Directed by Alf Goulding. Betty Grable, with other new RKO talents including Lucille Ball, Joy Hodges, Edgar Kennedy, Anne Shirley, and Preston Foster in semi-documentary about nightlife at the Biltmore.

DRAWING RUMORS (1935) RKO. Directed by Ben Holmes. Betty Grable and Joey Ray in marital drama.

A QUIET FOURTH (1935) RKO. Directed by Fred Guiol. Betty Grable in Independence Day comedy romance. Very poor comedy!

SUNKIST STARS AT PALM SPRINGS (1936) M-G-M. Technicolor. Directed by Roy Rolland. Betty Grable's first screen appearance with new boyfriend, Jackie Coogan. Also features Johnny Weissmuller, Claire Trevor, Betty Furness (later to become Grable's stand in), Frances Langford, Buster Keaton, and Walter Huston.

HEDDA HOPPER'S HOLLYWOOD (1941) Paramount. Famed gossip columnist Hedda reminisces over her early Hollywood career. Betty is seen briefly entering the Mocambo nightclub with George Raft. Immediately behind the couple is gangster Bugsy Siegal.

ALL STAR BOND RALLY (1945) 20th Century-Fox. Directed by Michael Audley. Betty Grable's "I'll Be Marching to a Love Song"— the cut number from *Footlight Serenade* (1942) — is inserted into this War Bond promotional film. Also features Harry James, Bing Crosby, and Frank Sinatra. Hosted by Bob Hope.

HOLLYWOOD PARK (1946) 20th Century-Fox. Documentary about the Hollywood Park race track and the stars who frequented it. With Betty Grable, Harry James, Jackie Coogan, George Raft, and Darryl Zanuck.

HOLLYWOOD BOUND (1947) Astor. Compilation of Betty Grable's appearances under the name of Frances Dean. Distributors and theatre managers were urged to boycott this "exploitation" film.

Note: Various bibliographies dealing with the early films of Betty Grable/Frances Dean, credit her with a short entitled *Hips Hips Hooray* (1934), but on viewing this film recently I can find no evidence of Betty, and her name didn't appear in the credits.

DISCOGRAPHY

SOUND TRACK ALBUMS

(NOTE: Many of these albums are bootleg recordings and may not come up to the expected high standard or quality of modern recording techniques.)

THE GAY DIVORCEE/Swingtime: EMTC 101
Betty sings "Let's K-knock K-knees" with Edward Everett Horton.

PIGSKIN PARADE/Everybody Sing: Pilgrim 4000
Betty sings "The Balboa" with Judy Garland and others.

Flirtation Walk/She Loves Me Not/COLLEGIATE/Here Is My Heart: Caliban 6042

DOWN ARGENTINE WAY/TIN PAN ALLEY: Caliban 6003

TIN PAN ALLEY: Soundtrak STK 110

Rose of Washington Square/FOOTLIGHT SERENADE: Caliban 6002

SPRINGTIME IN THE ROCKIES (radio version): Pelican LP 128

SPRINGTIME IN THE ROCKIES/SWEET ROSIE O'GRADY: Sandy Hook SH 2009

CONEY ISLAND/MOON OVER MIAMI: Caliban 6001

PIN-UP GIRL/SONG OF THE ISLANDS: Caliban 6009

FOUR JILLS IN A JEEP: Hollywood Soundstage ST407

FOLLOW THE FLEET/A Damsel in Distress: Scarce Rarities SR-5505
(Betty, with Joy Hodges and Jennie Gray, backing Ginger Rogers in "Let Yourself Go" number)

DIAMOND HORSESHOE/Doris Day Performs: Caliban 6028

THE DOLLY SISTERS: Classic International Filmusicals CIF3010

MOTHER WORE TIGHTS/THE SHOCKING MISS PILGRIM: CIF 3008

WABASH AVENUE/Sing Baby, Sing: Caliban 6029

MY BLUE HEAVEN/You Were Meant for Me: Titania 503

CALL ME MISTER/Starlift: Titania 510

MEET ME AFTER THE SHOW/Painting the Clouds With Sunshine: Caliban 6012

THREE FOR THE SHOW (EP - 45rpm): Mercury EP-2-3283

THREE FOR THE SHOW 10" LP: Mercury MG25204.
You can hear Betty sing "Which One"; this version was cut from final film.

Mailcall Radio Show No. 122: Betty sings "My Heart Tells Me": Vintage Jazz Classics VCJ 1048 (CD)

Mailcall Radio Show No. 62: Betty sings "Sing Me a Song of the Islands": Vintage Jazz Classics VJC 1049 (CD)

Appendix

SOLO ALBUMS:

BETTY GRABLE RARE RECORDINGS 1930-1970: Sandy Hook SH 2014
Sound track numbers from several of Betty's early films plus radio recordings of
Academy Awards show, 1958, and TV recording of "Hello, Dolly."

BETTY GRABLE: 18 Previously Unreleased Performances from 1934 to 1960:
Star-Tone ST 219
   (includes "The Snake Dance"; (Rehearsal check from *Student Tour*); "Let's   K-
knock K-knees" (radio performance of *The Gay Divorcee*); "Delighted to Meet You";
"Is It Love or Infatuation?" (radio performance of *This Way Please*); "Fidgety Joe"
(radio performance of *Man About Town*); "I Can't Begin To Tell You" (Ruth Haag);
"Artificial Flowers"; medley: "Music Makers"; "I've Heard That Song Before"; James
Session; "You Made Me Love You"; "Ciribiribin" (with Perry Como and Harry
James); "Little Rock" (with Janis Page); Special Radio Performance, "I Wish That I
Could Shimmy Like My Sister Kate"; "Baby, Won't You Say You Love Me";
"Wilhelmina"; "May I Tempt You With a Big Red Rosy Apple?"; "Doing the Tango";
"Night Life"; "Lullaby of Broadway"; "I Refuse To Rock 'n' Roll"; "What Did I Do?"
(Bing Crosby radio broadcast).

COMPILATION ALBUMS

CHOICE CUTS, Vol 1: ST 500/1.
   Betty sings duet with Ben Gage (dubbing for Victor Mature) "Blue Shadows and
White Gardenias," cut number from *Song of the Islands*.

CALLING ALL STARS: Star Tone 203
Betty sings "Sweetheart Time" (from *Thrill of a Lifetime*) with Buster Crabbe.

CUT! Vol 1:   Out Take Records OTF-1
   Betty sings "I'll Be Marching to a Love Song," cut number from *Footlight
Serenade*.

CUT! Vol 3: Out Take Records OTF-3
   Betty sings "There's Something About Midnight," cut number from *That Lady
in Ermine*.

CLASSIC MOVIE MUSICALS OF SAMMY FAIN: Box Office JJA 19842
   Betty sings "I'm Gonna Love That Guy," and "I Just Can't Do Enough for You,
Baby" (with Dan Dailey) from *Call Me Mister*.

THE GERSHWINS IN HOLLYWOOD: Box Office JJA 19773
   Betty sings "I've Got a Crush On You" with Jack Lemmon, from *Three for the
Show*.

GOLDEN MOMENTS FROM THE SILVER SCREEN: Harmony Records
H30549
   Betty sings "I Can't Begin to Tell You" from *The Dolly Sisters*.

HOLLYWOOD STARS: Accord Records 129011 (CD)
Betty sings "Pan Americana Jubilee" (*Springtime in the Rockies*); "The Balboa" (*Pigskin Parade*). Radio programs compilation.

HOLLYWOOD STARS GO TO WAR: Vintage Jive Classics VJC1048 — (CD)
Betty sings "My Heart Tells Me" from *Sweet Rosie O'Grady*.

HOLLYWOOD STORY: Festival Album Double 214
Betty sings "My Heart Tells Me," from *Sweet Rosie O'Grady*.

HOLLYWOOD YEARS OF HARRY WARREN 1930-57: Box Office JJA 19791
Betty sings "Two Dreams Met" with Don Ameche, from *Down Argentine Way*; "Pan Americana Jubilee," finale from *Springtime in the Rockies*, with John Payne, Carmen Miranda, and Cesar Romero; "My Heart Tells Me" with Phil Regan (*Sweet Rosie O'Grady*); and "I Wish I Knew" (*Diamond Horseshoe*).

THE HOT CANARIES: CL 2534 (CD)
Betty sings "I Can't Begin to Tell You" from *The Dolly Sisters*.

I CAN'T BEGIN TO TELL YOU: Columbia, 1945 — deleted single from Betty (billed as Ruth Haag) Grable and Harry James.

LADIES OF BURLESQUE: Legends 1000/2
Betty sings "May I Tempt You With a Big Red Rosy Apple?" from *Wabash Avenue*.

THANKS FOR THE MEMORY: THE CLASSIC MOVIE MUSICALS OF RALPH RAINGER 1930-43: Box Office JJA 1981
Betty sings "Loveliness and Love" with Don Ameche (*Moon Over Miami*); "Hi-ya Love" and "Another Little Dream Won't Do Us Any Harm" (*A Yank in the RAF*) "I'm Still Crazy For You" (with John Payne) and "I Heard The Birdies Sing" (from *Footlight Serenade*); "Take it From There" and "Danger in a Dance" finale (*Coney Island*).

THOSE BOMBASTIC BLONDE BOMBSHELLS: Wallisrite Records BGMM42 (CD)
Compilation with Betty singing numbers from TV shows: "Doing the Tango"; "Ya Gotta Give the People Hoke" with Van Johnson and Sergio Franchi; "Digga Digga Do"; "The Band Played On"; "I'm Just Wild About Harry"; "One For My Baby"; "Baby, Won't You Please Come Home"; plus "My Hearts Tells Me" (*Sweet Rosie O'Grady*) and "Sweetheart Time" with Buster Crabbe (*Thrill of a Lifetime*).

THOSE SENSATIONAL SWINGING SIRENS OF THE SILVER SCREEN: Vintage Jazz Classics VJC 1002-2 (CD)
Betty sings "Hello, Dolly!" from Carol Burnett TV show, 1968

SOUNDTRACKS AND THEMES FROM GREAT MOVIES: Pye PLP 1009
Betty sings "I've Got a Crush on You" with Jack Lemmon from *Three for the Show*.

YOU MADE ME LOVE YOU — HARRY JAMES AND HIS MUSIC MAKERS: A 22656 (CD)
Many of Harry's hit recordings, plus Betty, as Ruth Haag, singing "I Can't Begin To Tell You."

WHITE CLIFFS OF DOVER: MCA Records WCK 35199 (CD)
Betty sings "I Can't Begin To Tell You" with the Harry James Orchestra.

TV APPEARANCES

SHOWER OF STARS (CBS) September, 1954.
Cast: Betty Grable, Mario Lanza, Harry James, Fred Clark, Marvin Kaplan.
Televised in color, Betty made her live TV debut in this 60-minute variety show with husband Harry, and Mario Lanza. She sang "I'm Just Wild About Harry," "Digga Digga Doo," "Baby, Won't You Please Come Home?" and "One For My Baby." She caused a minor sensation when she appeared on the show in a gold lamé dress which showed much more cleavage than she ever had in her films.

SHOWER OF STARS (CBS) November, 1954
Cast: Betty Grable, Ed Wynn, Harry James, Danny Thomas, guest appearance by Groucho Marx. Hosted by William Lundigan.
Betty clowned with Harry and Ed Wynn in a take-off on the Cinderella story, and sang "You're Just Too Marvelous," sitting atop a grand piano "played " by Ed Wynn. Quipped Wynn: "This is the first time a grand baby has sat on my baby grand!"

SHOWER OF STARS (CBS) June, 1955
Cast: Betty Grable, Dan Dailey, Harry James, Edgar Bergen, Red Skelton, Shirley MacLaine, Ethel Merman, Gene Nelson, Marilyn Maxwell, Jack Oakie, Tony Martin.
Betty sang and danced to "Swingin' The Muses" with Gene Nelson, making a welcome return to the small screen after she bowed out of a previous show because of an injured ankle. She was replaced on the earlier show by Shirley MacLaine.

THE BOB HOPE CHEVY SHOW (NBC) December, 1955.
Cast: Bob Hope, Betty Grable, James Mason, Joan Rhodes.
Betty joined Bob Hope in a number entitled "Hope and Grable," a parody on the stars to the tune of "Love and Marriage." Also featured British actor James Mason and English strongwoman Joan Rhodes.

CLEOPATRA COLLINS (NBC) March, 1956.
Cast: Betty Grable, Casey Adams, Rick Jason, Jack Kruschen, Louise Beavers, Michael Winkelman.
Cleo Collins (Grable), a former model and beauty queen, now happily married to Pete (Casey Adams), finds herself in trouble when an old boyfriend turns up, reminding a jealous Pete of his wife's glamorous past.
This was a pilot for a series to star Grable, but the option wasn't picked up.
FORD STAR THEATRE: TWENTIETH CENTURY (CBS) April, 1956.
Cast: Betty Grable, Orson Welles, Keenan Wynn, Ray Collins, Gage Clark, Olive

Sturgess, Lance Fuller, Roy Glenn. Produced by Arthur Schwartz. Directed by Paul Nickell.

Orson Welles played Oscar Jaffe in this TV adaptation of Ben Hecht's famous comedy, co-starring Betty Grable (previously filmed in 1934 starring John Barrymore and Carole Lombard).

Oscar is a bankrupt producer who tries to woo famous star Lily Garland (Grable) to his company and thus save his bacon. Much of the action takes place on the famous Chicago-Los Angeles Pullman.

Although most critics thought Betty too "wholesome" for the role, they admitted she showed promise as a comedy actress. However, they thought the teaming of Welles and Grable was bad casting.

THE BOB HOPE SHOW (NBC) June, 1956.
Cast: Bob Hope, Betty Grable, Dorothy Lamour, Jane Russell, Marilyn Maxwell, George Sanders, Ed Sullivan, Steve Allen.
Betty did a comedy routine with Hope, then joined Lamour, Maxwell, and Russell for a musical parody entitled "Taking A Chance on Hope."

THE DINAH SHORE CHEVY SHOW (NBC) November, 1956.
Betty joined Dinah in a number of scenes and together they dressed as flappers for a "Singin' in the Rain" number.

KTLA's 10th ANNIVERSARY SHOW (KTLA) January, 1957.
The Los Angeles TV station celebration broadcast of its 10th anniversary with many stars, including Betty and Harry James.

THE BOB HOPE SHOW (NBC), January, 1957.
Cast: Bob Hope, Betty Grable, Eddie Fisher, Rowan and Martin, Harry James.
Hope sold his soul to the Devil (Harry James) in order to become a big star. In this comedy routine, Betty played Marsha Mantrap, a caricature of a Hollywood blonde superstar. She also sang and danced to "Get Happy."

THE ED SULLIVAN SHOW (CBS) September, 1957.
Cast: Host Ed Sullivan, Betty Grable, Harry James, George Raft, Carol Channing, Jo Stafford, Joe Nemeth, Jack Dempsey.
Big production number featured Betty, with a lavish set, showed Betty performing "Put Your Arms Around Me, Honey" from *Coney Island*.

THE EDDIE FISHER SHOW (NBC) October, 1957.
Cast: Eddie Fisher, Betty Grable, George Gobel.
Grable sang numbers from *Guys and Dolls*, performed a duet with Fisher, and did some comedy with Fisher and Gobel.

THE I LOVE LUCY HOUR (CBS) February, 1958.
Cast: Lucille Ball, Desi Arnaz, Betty Grable, Harry James, Vivian Vance, and William Frawley.
Subtitled "Lucy Wins A Horse," the comedy revolved around Lucy's horse which she wanted to keep for little Ricky, much against Desi's wishes. Betty had her

moment when she performed "The Bayamo," a Latin number reminiscent of her Hollywood heyday musicals but, as usual, Lucy hogged the show.

THE JERRY LEWIS SHOW (NBC) February, 1958.
Cast: Jerry Lewis, Betty Grable, Sophie Tucker, Hans Conreid.
A poor show for Betty in this Las Vegas transmission. Her big number is spoiled by the antics of Lewis, who creates havoc trying to upstage Betty for laughs.

THE 30th ANNUAL ACADEMY AWARDS SHOW (NBC) March, 1958.
The opening production number of the annual show was a medley of Academy Award winning songs. Betty, accompanied by the Harry James Orchestra, sang "Lullaby of Broadway."

SHOWER OF STARS (CBS) April, 1958.
Cast: Jack Benny and Mary Livingstone, Betty Grable, Janis Paige, "Rochester" Anderson, Dennis Day, Don Wilson.
Betty returned to Shower show after a three-year absence. Her big number was "What Did I Do?" from her film *When My Baby Smiles at Me*. She also partnered Janis Paige in "Just Two Little Girls from Little Rock" from *Gentlemen Prefer Blondes*.

THE BOB HOPE BUICK SHOW (NBC) November, 1958.
Cast: Bob Hope, Betty Grable, Gloria Swanson, Randy Sparks, Wally Cox.
Same again with Betty singing and dancing, plus a couple of mildly amusing sketches with Hope.

THE DINAH SHORE CHEVY SHOW (NBC). Betty was Dinah's top guest in three shows within 12 months: March 1959, November 1959, and April 1960.
Other stars included Tony Randall, Ella Fitzgerald, Vic Damone, Jackie Cooper.

FORD STAR TIME (NBC) June, 1960.
Cast: George Burns, Jack Benny, Betty Grable, Bobby Darin, Polly Bergen.
Choreographed for the first time for TV by Hermes Pan, Betty did a sensational strip routine to "I Refuse To Rock 'n' Roll."

PERRY COMO'S KRAFT MUSIC HALL (NBC) December, 1960
Perry joined Betty and Harry James in a medley of old film favorites, including "I Had The Craziest Dream" from *Springtime in the Rockies*. Grable also sang "Artificial Flowers."

THE ANDY WILLIAMS SHOW (NBC) November, 1962.
Cast: Andy Williams, Betty Grable, Danny Kaye, The Osmonds, The New Christie Minstrels, Lawrence Welk.
Betty's big production number was "Night Life."
THE HOLLYWOOD PALACE (ABC) October, 1964.
Cast: Betty Grable, Harry James, Diahann Carroll, Smothers Brothers.
In addition to singing and dancing, plus a few comedy moments with the Smothers, Betty successfully hosted the show.

THE HOLLYWOOD PALACE (ABC) December, 1964.

Cast: Betty Grable, Van Johnson, Sergio Franchi, Paul Gilbert, Jackie Mason.

Host Van Johnson joined Betty and Sergio Franchi in "Ya Gotta Give the People Hoke."

CAROL BURNETT SHOW (CBS) February, 1968.

Cast: Carol Burnett, Betty Grable, Martha Raye, Harvey Korman, Lyle Waggoner, Vicki Lawrence.

Betty came back to big-time television after Broadway success with *Hello Dolly!* and sang the show's title number (after special permission from David Merrick) and also did a comedy number with Carol and Martha.

HOLLYWOOD SQUARES (NBC) September, October, November, 1969, and March, 1970.

Betty Grable appeared as a guest star on these programs. She was always very popular, but Betty didn't like the panel game format too much.

THOSE FABULOUS FORDIES (NBC) recorded in the spring of 1971, and transmitted February, 1972.

Starring Tennessee Ernie Ford, Betty Grable, Maureen O'Hara, Dick Haymes, Frank Gorshin.

In this Ernie Ford musical tribute, most of the attention was centered on Betty and Dick Haymes reprising songs they made famous in their films together, including "The More I See You." Betty also did a dance number. This was her last major appearance on television as a performer.

44th ANNUAL ACADEMY AWARDS SHOW (NBC).

In April, 1972, Betty accompanied Dick Haymes on stage as a co-presenter on the 44th Annual Academy Awards Show. The couple presented awards for Best Original Song Score.

Since her death, Betty has been featured in film clips of her movies (and newsreel footage) over the years.

She was prominent in the compilation "Fred Astaire Salutes the Fox Musicals" in 1974. Also for her old studio, she appeared in several installments of "That's Hollywood," a weekly thirty-minute 20th Century-Fox Television/ABC series which ran for several seasons. Jack Haley, Jr. was executive producer. It became a "must-watch" for all movie buffs and video copies are highly prized. Betty was prominent in episodes entitled "The Fox Blondes," "The Pin-Up Girls," "The Musicals," and even had her own "special" simply titled "Gorgeous Grable," a glowing tribute to her contribution to the musical cinema.

Although Betty made her true TV debut in SHOWER OF STARS (1954), she had earlier appeared in the audience of the Walter Winchell Show (1953), soon after completing *How To Marry a Millionaire*. She also was the mystery guest on "What's My Line?" (1965, 1967), Johnny Carson's "Tonight Show" (1965) and "The Merv Griffin Show" (1971). Major broadcasting executives all maintained that having Grable on their show helped to boost the ratings.

THEATRE DATES

TATTLE TALES (1932). A musical revue which opened in the Los Angeles area in December, 1932. Betty was featured in the Frank Fay starrer. In April, 1933, after several try-outs, the show moved to San Francisco. The show was already in trouble and Barbara Stanwyck, then married to Fay, joined the show to help boost ticket sales while Betty left the show in that city to join the Ted Fiorito Orchestra as a singer.

HOLLYWOOD SECRETS (1936). Betty joined Jackie Coogan in this tantalizingly titled variety show. The show opened in Baltimore, in December, 1935, and successfully toured several cities, closing at the Roxy Theater, New York in 1936.

TREASURE ISLAND MUSIC HALL, San Francisco, July 1939.
Betty was featured with Jack Haley on this prestigious vaudeville bill to help celebrate the San Francisco Golden Gate Exposition.

VAUDEVILLE (1939). Betty topped the bill in this variety show which opened in Washington, D. C., in August, 1939, and toured several cities, closing in Chicago in September.

DU BARRY WAS A LADY (1939). Betty landed a good role in this Merman-Lahr musical comedy which raised her stock immensely in the eyes of Hollywood. After try-outs in New Haven, Boston, and Philadelphia, the show arrived on Broadway on December 6, 1939. She received great notices and became a star overnight. Betty left the show in June, 1940, to return to Hollywood, replacing Alice Faye in *Down Argentine Way*.

VAUDEVILLE (1940). To help publicize *Down Argentine Way*, Betty made an appearance at the Chicago Theater for a two-week engagement.

VARIETY (1953). Chicago Theatre, November 27-December 3. Fresh from her triumph with *How To Marry a Millionaire* (which was also playing Chicago at the same time), Betty joined husband Harry James in a fast-moving revue in which she featured many of her movie song-and-dance routines. Also starred Billy Daniel, who choreographed.

GUYS AND DOLLS (1962). Dunes Hotel, Las Vegas, December, 1962. At last Betty got a chance to show how great she would have been as Miss Adelaide had she been chosen for the film version of this classic Damon Runyon tale. Reunited with Dan Dailey (who played Sky Masterton), the show was originally scheduled for a four-week run. Tickets sales went through the roof and the Hollywood couple played the venue for eight months.
Variety wrote, "Miss Grable has come out of semi-retirement and tackled something she has never done — a starring role on the musical comedy stage, and she's a delightful success. She plays the part as if it were written for her."
Guys and Dolls also played the Melodyland Theater, Anaheim, in September,

1963, on a limited engagement (Hugh O'Brian replaced Dan Dailey). In June, 1968, Grable revived the show for the Westbury Music Fair, New York, then moving on the following week to play the Shady Grove Music Fair.

In July, 1968, Betty was invited to play Miss Adelaide as guest star of the Honolulu Civic Light Opera Company in their semi-professional production of *Guys and Dolls*, at the Honolulu Theatre.

HIGH BUTTON SHOES (1964)
Betty was reunited with Dan Dailey in this revival of the modest Broadway show at the Melodyland Theatre, Anaheim, California. It opened on September 29 for a two-week run. Producers Sammy Lee and Danny Dare tried to find a backer who was willing to stage the show in Los Angeles, but were unsuccessful.

HELLO, DOLLY! (1965)
Betty was signed for the Las Vegas production of *Hello, Dolly!* after much persuasion.

In a pre-Vegas tour, Betty and her road company opened at the Tivoli Theatre, Chattanooga, Tennessee, on November 3. She also played Knoxville, Tennessee; Louisville, Kentucky; Columbus, Ohio; St. Paul, Minnesota; Omaha, Nebraska; closing in Denver, Colorado. On December 23, 1965, the company premièred at the Riviera Hotel, Las Vegas, where the show ran successfully for the next ten months.

A couple of weeks after closing in September, 1965, Betty took on the national tour with her company, playing many cities across the United States, including Chicago, San Antonio; Fort Worth; Kansas City; Fort Wayne; Charlotte, North Carolina, Scranton; Baltimore; and Wilmington, Delaware.

After a brief respite, Betty replaced Martha Raye in the Broadway version, opening at the St. James Theatre on June 12, 1967. She was an immediate success and once again found herself the toast of Broadway after an absence of almost twenty years. She remained on Broadway until December, 1967.

In 1971, Betty took a further short tour as Dolly, playing Chicago, Atlanta, and Toledo, Ohio.

BELLE STARR (1969). Betty made her European debut in a show "specially written for her" by Warren Douglas. Produced by Jerry Schaffer, Rory Calhoun, and Clarke Reynolds. Originally titled *The Piecefull Palace*. The show opened at the Alhambra, Glasgow, April 1, 1969, and then at the Palace Theatre, London, April 30, closing after twenty-one performances.

Although technically a try-out in Glasgow, the city treated it as a world première and turned out in force to pay homage to its favorite musical star. On opening night she took several curtain calls and made a short speech of thanks.

Most critics were kind, paying tribute to "Hollywood's Greatest Musical Star," as she was billed. Said Mamie Crichton of the *Daily Express* in her review headlined "Salute to Miss Grable," "Flowers and curtain calls, storms of applause and floods of nostalgia made Glasgow's salute to Betty Grable last night "the highlight of her whole career." These words in her short speech, charged with emotion, came after the rollicking première of *The Piecefull Palace* — one more glamorous night in the history of the Alhambra, soon to disappear."

Archie McCulloch of the *Glasgow Evening Citizen* remarked on how youthful

Grable looked and added,"I bet most of the ladies in the audience, many of whom were half her age, wished they could look half as good as Grable!"

Variety's Scottish correspondent Gordon Irving noted: "Betty Grable, on her European stage bow, comes over with all the attractive know-how of the longtime trouper."

BORN YESTERDAY (1969).

Betty quickly became the biggest draw on the Straw Hat Circuit with this Garson Kanin play. Betty played the role of dumb blonde Billie Dawn to perfection, becoming as closely identified with this role as she did with Miss Adelaide in *Guys and Dolls*. She made her debut in late 1969 and toured throughout the United States during 1970, 1972, and 1973.

THIS IS SHOW BUSINESS (1971).

Betty appeared with old chums Dorothy Lamour, Don Ameche, and Rudy Vallee in this variety show, part of St. Louis Civic Week. It was Betty's final appearance in her home town, and two of the numbers she was scheduled to perform had to be cut because she was already feeling ill. Other stars appearing: Chita Rivera and Dennis Day.

BORN YESTERDAY (1973).

Betty Grable's final engagement. Despite being very ill, Betty accepted the three-week engagement at the Alhambra Dinner Theatre in Jacksonville, Florida, opening on January 24. The show was such a success that it broke all existing records for the theatre. It was extended several times, finally closing on March 23. Betty Grable died just over three months later.

Betty Grable also played numerous nightclub and casino room venues before and after her film career. She was always very popular with Las Vegas patrons, but she was very proud of her appearance at the Latin Quarter, New York, in April, 1959, where she played her three-week engagement to a standing room only audience.

VIDEO AND LASERDISCS

WHOOPEE. Earliest video appearance as 14-year-old Betty leads the chorus in this amusing Goldwyn musical of 1930. Embassy 3076 and HBO 90748. In Technicolor.

THE GREEKS HAD A WORD FOR THEM (a/k/a *Three Broadway Girls*) Barr Films HMO 176V
CAVALCADE CBS/Fox 1809

DON'T TURN 'EM LOOSE. King Video

PROBATION (contained in video package entitled *The Worst of Hollywood Volume 3*) Silver Mine Video 610
HOLD 'EM JAIL Republic Home Video 0739

MELODY CRUISE Turner Home Entertainment 6089

OLD MAN RHYTHM King Video

Nostalgia Merchant NM 8015. UK *The Movie Greats Video Collection* VC 3046; Laser disc Image ID8303TU

THE NITWITS Laser disc Image Entertainment 6089

FOLLOW THE FLEET Turner Home Entertainment 2038; Laser Disc Image ID8303TU

THE DAY THE BOOKIES WEPT Blackhawk Video BV 416

DOWN ARGENTINE WAY Key Video 1718; Laser disc CBS/Fox 1741-80 (coupled with PIN UP GIRL)

TIN PAN ALLEY Fox Video 1818

MOON OVER MIAMI Key Video 1725; UK CBS/Fox 1725

I WAKE UP SCREAMING (a/k/a *Hot Spot*) Key Video 1720; UK CBS/Fox 1720

SONG OF THE ISLANDS Key Video 1722. Laser disc CBS/Fox 1742/80 (coupled with SPRINGTIME IN THE ROCKIES)

FOOTLIGHT SERENADE Key Video 1719

SPRINGTIME IN THE ROCKIES Key Video 1723; UK CBS/Fox 1723; Laser disc CBS/Fox 1742-80 (coupled with SONG OF THE ISLANDS)

PIN UP GIRL Key Video 1725; UK CBS/Fox 1721.
Laser disc CBS/Fox 1741-80 (coupled with DOWN ARGENTINE WAY)

BILLY ROSE'S DIAMOND HORSESHOE U. K. only CBS/Fox 1774

THE FARMER TAKES A WIFE Key Video 1724; Laser disc CBS/Fox 1808-80 (coupled with THE BEAUTIFUL BLONDE FROM BASHFUL BEND)
HOW TO MARRY A MILLIONAIRE CBS/Fox 1023; U. K. CBS/Fox Laser disc: CBS/Fox 1023-80
THREE FOR THE SHOW Laser: Pioneer PSE 91-15; VHS: Columbia Classics VBV 13205 (Australia and New Zealand only)

Television Shows in which Betty Grable is featured:

Bob Hope Five Hour Marathon. Shokus Video 416 B-VGoing Hollywood — The War Years. Warner Home Video

Gotta Dance, Gotta Sing. RKO 1010

Hedda Hopper's Hollywood (1946). Republic Home Video 5025

Hollywood Goes to War. Video Images 801
(with Betty singing cut number "I'll Be Marching to a Love Song" from *Footlight Serenade*).

Hollywood Home Movies. Maljack Productions

The Love Goddesses. Embassy 6002.
(Compilation film with Betty in scenes from her Paramount films.)

Magnificent Movie Musicals. Goodtimes Video 8094
(includes the theatrical trailer for *The Dolly Sisters*)

March of Time — Showbiz in the War Years. Embassy 1762

Movie Star Commercials and Important Messages. Liberty Home Video 059L
(rarity containing Betty's Playtex Girdle commercial)

Saturday Night at the Movies. Media Home Entertainment

Showbiz Goes to War. Video Late Show 220-1020

Shower of Stars — Volume 1. Classic Television

Shower of Stars — Volume 5. Classic Television

Endnotes

Note: In addition to my own conversations with Betty Grabl;e over a period of months, much of the dialogue in this book has been reproduced from primary and secondary sources such as conversations and correspondence with friends and associates of Betty Grable, as well as books, magazines, articles, journals, etc.

All dialogue cited is as close to what was said to me as I could make it. Many of the articles quoted came to me in the form of clippings or were located in private collections and scrapbooks and not attributed to their original sources. We have taken great care to correctly identify original source material whenever possible.

1. Mike Levitt to author, Chicago, 1980.
2. Marjorie Grable Arnold to author, Los Angeles, 1980.
3. Some biographers believe the family name was once Graßle, and had been changed by a careless immigration official on the family's arrival in America. The German character eszett which is the double "s" resembles the English character "ß" and probably was misread by an immigration official.
4. Marjorie Grable Arnold to author, Los Angeles, 1980.
5. Ibid.
6. Mike Levitt to author, Chicago, March, 1980 (repeating the story as told to him by Lillian Grable years ago).
7. Marjorie Grable Arnold to author, Los Angeles, 1980.
8. Ibid.
9. Ibid.
10. Ibid.
11. Mike Levitt to author, Chicago, 1980.
12. Marjorie Grable Arnold to author, Los Angeles, 1980.
13. Ibid.
14. Dolores Hope to author, Royal Concert Hall, Glasgow, Scotland, 1994.
15. Dick Haymes to author, Amsterdam, 1970.
16. *Life*, December 11, 1940.
17. *Notes on a Cowardly Lion,* 1988.
18. *Judy*, W. H. Allen Ltd., 1975.
19. Marjorie Grable Arnold to author, Los Angeles, 1980.
20. Ibid.
21. Vallee, "Grable Makes Good Again," *Silver Screen,* August, 1940.
22. Press Release from the Twentieth Century-Fox Publicity Department, August 1940.
23. Len Scumaci Collection. NOTE: This article was found in Len Scumaci's private collection of memorabilia. It had been removed from the original magazine with no publication date or author information included.
24. Len Scumaci Collection. (See Note in No. 23.)
25. In 1994, Fox Video released *Tin Pan Alley*, inserting the cut number, "Get Out and Get Under," which Alice Faye sings as a solo. No mention is made of her performing the number with Grable and Oakie, but the restored solo spot is a big bonus for Faye fans.
26 *Hollywood in the Forties,* Tantivy Press, London, A. S. Barnes and Co., 1968.
27 Len Scumaci Collection. (See Note in No. 23.)
28 *Zanuck: The Rise and Fall of Hollywood's Last Tycoon,* McGraw Hill, 1984.
29 *The Secret Life of Tyrone Power,* William Morrow, 1979.
30 *Cinema Manager,* 1940. (This was a United Kingdom trade publication distributed to cinema managers at the time.)

31 Twentieth Century-Fox Pressbook for *I Wake Up Screaming,* 1941. This particular quote is by Humberstone.

32 *Zanuck: The Rise and Fall of Hollywood's Last Tycoon,* McGraw Hill, 1984. While it was known as *I Wake Up Screaming* in the U. S., in Britain it remained *Hot Spot,* while in Latin American countries and Spain it was titled *Who Murdered Vicky?* In 1953 the film was remade as *Vicky* with Jeanne Crain in the Grable role and Jean Peters as Vicky.

33 "The Heartbreak Behind the Betty Grable - George Raft Parting," *Movieland,* June 1943. (This was widely quoted at the time.)

34 The James Family Album, (UK). (The James Family Album was a small-time UK fan club for Betty Grable and Harry James. The publication only lasted for about six issues. It was published and printed privately in the United Kingdom. These magazines are in the John Purdy Collection.).

35 Ibid.

36 Parsons, Louella, "The Heartbreak Behind the Betty Grable-George Raft Parting,", *Movieland,* June, 1943. (This was widely quoted at the time.).

37 "Betty's Tours of the Army Camps," *Silver Screen,* December, 1942.

38 Ibid.

39 Len Scumaci Collection. (See Note in No. 23.)

40 Ibid.

41 Twentieth Century-Fox Publicity Release, 1942 (widely quoted in newspapers at the time.).

42 Imperial War Museum, London, England, 1993. This quote was from a placard on display at the museum which featured the pin-up shot and the information that, "more than 10 million copies of this shot had been distributed" during the war years.

43 Unidentified newspaper clipping sent to Author by Jimmy Janisch of Burbank, California.

44 *The Heart of Hollywood,* David Smith, Ltd., 1945.

45 A widely publicized quote, seen many times in unattributed articles in various collections. The original source is unknown, but the quote itself was verified by Miss Grable to the author.

46 Dick Haymes to author, Amsterdam , 1970.

47 Len Scumaci Collection. (See Note in No. 23.) Other collectors also have this clipping, apparently culled from various fan magazines at the time.

48 Ibid.

49 Anonymous source to Bob Johnson, Related to author, Oakland, California, 1978.

50 Ibid.

51 Marjorie Grable Arnold to author, Los Angeles, 1980.

52 Unidentified magazine article sent to author.

53 Betty Ritz Baez, Acapulco, Mexico, 1980.

54 Dan Dailey to Len Scumaci, Chicago, 1976.

55 Ava Gardner to Pat Green, of Films and Filming, London.

56 Berch, Barbara, "Close-Up of Betty Grable," *Movieland,* May, 1943.

57 Len Scumai Collection. (See Note in No. 23.)

58 "Grable-James, the Enchanted Couple," *Photoplay,* March, 1945.

59 From the Pressbook for *That Lady in Ermine,* Twentieth Century-Fox, 1949. (For private distribution to exhibitors only.)

60 Ibid.

61 Publicity Release by Twentieth Century-Fox, 1949.

62 Mike Levitt to author, etc.

63 The James Family Album, United Kingdom, 1950.

64 Len Scumaci to author, Chicago, March, 1980. (This story surrounding the Oscar was widely circulated over the years.)

65 Len Scumaci to author, Chicago, March, 1980.

66 Maddox, "I'm a Betty Grable Fan, says Preston Sturges," *Motion Picture*, June, 1949.

67 Cesar Romero in correspondence with Richard Marohn MD, of Chicago, Illinois.

68 Maddox, "I'm a Betty Grable Fan, says Preston Sturges," *Motion Picture*, June, 1949.

69 Cesar Romero in correspondence with Richard Marohn MD, of Chicago, Illinois.

70 *Don't Say Yes Unitl I Finish Talking*, Doubleday, 1971.

71 "I'm Still Wild About Harry" interview with Betty Grable appeared in *Modern Screen*, September, 1949.

72 *A Director's Guild of American Oral History*, Scarecrow Press, 1987.

73 Anonymous source to Bob Johnston, Oakland, California, 1978.

74 *Marilyn Monroe*, W. H. Allan and Company, 1961.

75 Billy Daniel in conversation with and letters to Len Scumaci.

76 "Leg Surgery," (from an unidentified magazine clipping).

77 Parsons, Louella. (from her original syndicated column.) Also "The Truth About Those Grable Rumors", *Movie Stars Parade,* October, 1951.

78 Ibid.

79 Mitzi Gaynor to author, Valley Forge, Pennsylvania, 1978.

80 Len Scumaci Collection. (See Note in No. 23.)

81 *People Will Talk*, Aurum Press Ltd, 1986.

82 Maddox, "My Days With Grable, by Macdonald Carey," *Movies,* August, 1951.

83 Ibid.

84 "The Truth About Those Grable Rumors," *Movie Stars Parade*, October, 1951.

85 These quotes by Grable and Zanuck were widely used in various magazines and newspapers in 1951, at the time of Grable's suspension. 86 Ibid.

87 Harry James to author, Motherwell, Scotland, 1978.

88 Bette Davis to author, Isle of Mull, Scotland, September, 1972.

89 Twentieth Century-Fox Pressbook for *When My Baby Smiles At Me*. This quote is by director Walter Lang.

90 *Movie Life*. Article was from the Len Scumaci collection; date and author are unknown.

91 Hopper, Hedda. This item, from her column, was widely quoted at the time of the suspension in various newspapers and magazines.

92 Ibid

93 Ibid.

94 *The Letters of Nunnally Johnson*, Alfred A. Knopf, 1987.

95 *The Unabridged Marilyn*, Congdon and Weed, 1981.

96 Academy of Motion Picture Arts and Sciences, Los Angeles, California. The author got this Louis Berg quote from a clipping in their collection.

97 Betty Ritz Baez to Mike Levitt, Chicago, 1980.

98 Sam Lesner (Chicago critic) wrote this in the Chicago-American, November, 1953.

99 Mike Levitt to author, Chicago, 1980.

100 Parsons, Louella, from an interview with Betty Grable that was widely quoted in her syndicated column and in newspapers and magazines in 1953.

101 Jack Lemmon to author, New York, 1978.

102 Majdalany, Fred, *Sunday Pictorial Newspaper*, May 9, 1955.

103 Len Scumaci to Author, Chicago, March, 1980.

104 Unidentified magazine article. This article was sent to me by a Grable fan several years ago. Unfortunately, it came without publication or author data. However, I felt it gave such great insight into the early days of television and Betty Grable's involvement in it that I wanted to include it. I would be grateful if any reader could enlighten me as to the source of this article.

105 TV reviewer wrote this about the Bob Hope-Chevy Show in a San Francisco newspaper article sent to the author by Robert Johnson of Oakland, California. (author's byline missing).

106 Mike Levitt to author, Chicago, 1980.

107 Diana Dors to author, Glasgow, 1975.

108 Mike Levitt to author, Chicago, 1980.

109 Ibid.

110 Ibid.

111 Ibid.

112 George, *Ginger, Loretta and Irene Who?* , Simon and Schuster, 1976.

111 Mike Levitt to author, Chicago, 1980.

114 Ibid.

115 Ibid.

116 Len Scumaci to author, Chicago, March 1980.

117 Bob Remick to author, Glasgow, Scotland, 1969.

118 Savino, Guy (critic for a New York City newspaper). This quote by the usher was quoted in the critical review by Mr. Savino. Newspaper is unknown.

119 Ibid.

120 John Hickey to author, London, May, 1969.

121 Bob Isoz to author in correspondence with him September, 1988.

122 Ralph Dykstra, of St Louis, in letter to *Hollywood Studio Magazine*.

123 Bernie Freedman to author, Toronto, September, 1993.

124 Lengthy quote by Grable - The source of this article is unknown. It is from the Leonard Scumaci collection and unattributed.

125 Mike Levitt to author, Chicago, 1980.

126 Freddie Carpenter to author, Glasgow June, 1967.

127 Linda M Schreiber, to author, New York, 1967.

128 Warren Douglas to author, Glasgow, March,m 1969 .

129 Tom Jones to writer Billy Sloan, London, 1993.

130 Warren Douglas to author, Glasgow, March, 1969.

131 Davis, Ivor, in an interview with Betty Grable that took place upon her arrival in Great Britain, *London Daily Express*, February, 1969.

132 Frank Rainbow to author, Glasgow, March, 1969.

133 Betty's arrival in London was covered and quoted in every British newspaper of February 28, 1969.

134 Gordon Reed to author,. March, 1969.

135 Valerie Walsh to author, Glasgow, Scotland, March, 1969.

136 Aldo Triballi to author, London, May, 1969.

137 John Hickey to author, London, May 1969.

138 Willie Moran to author, Glasgow, April, 1969.

139 Dick Shane to author, Glasgow, Scotland, March, 1969.

140 John Wright to author, Glasgow, April, 1969.

141 Jack Card to author, Glasgow, April, 1969.

142 Gene Yusem to author, Glasgow, April, 1969.

143 Donald McMillan to author, Glasgow, April, 1969.

144 Bette Davis to author, Isle of Mull, Scotland, September, 1972.

145 Barbara Windsor to Mrs Cameron, London, May, 1969.

146 Warren Douglas to author, Jackson, Calif, December, 1978.

147 Bob Isoz to author in correspondence, September, 1988.

148 Aldo Triballi to author, London, May, 1969.

149 John Hickey to author, London, May 1969.

150 Blayne Barrington to author, Glasgow, Scotland, March, 1969.

151 Aldo Triballi to author, London, May 1969.

152 Press clipping sent to author by Bob Johnson of Oakland, California from an unidentified New York City newspaper. This was used in various publications following her death.

153 Millie De Palmer, Portland, Maine, in correspondence with author, 1991-92.

154 Mike Levitt to author, Chicago, 1980.

155 Ibid.

156 Ibid.

157 Len Scumaci, to author, Chicago, 1980.

158 Chris Moor, New Zealand, in correspondence with author, from 1978 to 1990.

159 Keith Raistrick to author, Manchester, 1988.

160 Mike Levitt to author, Chicago, 1980.

161 Mike Levitt to author, Chicago, 1980.

162 Robert Wagner to author, Glasgow, 1972.

163 This quote was from the Edgeley Theatre Group as quoted in an unidentified Australian newspaper. It was picked up by all the wire services and flashed around the world.

164 Mike Levitt to author, Chicago, 1980.

165 Len Scumaci to author, Chicago, 1980.

166 Ibid.

167 Mike Levitt to author, Chicago, 1980.

168 Ibid.

169 Ibid.

170 Ibid.

171 Bob Johnson, Oakland, Calif, to author December 1978.

172 Mike Levitt to author, Chicago, 1980.

173 Ibid.

174 Ibid.

175 Ibid.

176 Ibid.

177 Ibid.

178 Library, Academy of Motion Picture Arts and Sciences. This is from the text of Rev. Tally Jarrett's service and eulogy at Betty's funeral.

179 Ardmore, "The Men in Her Life Remember Her," *Photoplay*, October, 1973.

180 Ibid.

181 Bob Remick in correspondence with author. This quote was also noted in a unattributed magazine article in the John Purdy collection.

182 Keith Raistrick, to author, Manchester, 1989.

183 Ibid.

184 Richard C. Marohn, MD, Chicago, Illinois, to author in December, 1994.

185 Robert Kendall interview with Alice Faye, 1971.

186 Ibid.

187 Anonymous source to Robert Johnson, Oakland, Calif, 1978.

188 This quote was widely used in the 1940s - original source is unknown.

189 John Hickey to author, London, 1989.

190 Basinger, Jeanine, in an article on Betty Grable in *Close-Ups*, edited by Danny Peary, New York: Workman Publishing Inc., 1978.

191 In his excellent book, *The Films of Alice Faye*, W. Franklyn Mosier observed: ". . . Faye and Grable projected quite a different personality from the screen. *Down Argentine Way* was changed to fit the Grable temperament of a more extroverted blonde and to concentrate on her natural talents for dancing. In all fairness, one cannot claim that Monroe "replaced" Grable. Their styles were markedly different. Grable was bright, breezy, bold, and brash; Monroe was a smoldering sexpot, a unique personality - not essentially a singer like Faye, nor a dancer like Grable. Comparisons between the three are thus unwarranted and entirely unfair to any of the trio of ladies in question."

Bibliography

BOOKS

Arce, Hector. *The Secret Life of Tyrone Power*. New York: William Morrow and Co., 1979.
Cairn, James. *The Heart of Hollywood*. London: David Smith, Ltd. 1945.
Close-Ups. Edited by Danny Peary. New York: Workman Publishing, 1978.
Eells, George, *Ginger, Loretta, and Irene Who?* New York: Simon and Schuster, 1976.
Frank, Gerold. *Judy*. London: W.H. Allen, Ltd., 1975.
Gussow. *Don't Say Yes Until I Finish Talking*. New York: Doubleday, 1971.
Higham, Charles and Joel Greenberg. *Hollywood in the Forties*. London: Tantivy Press, 1968.
Johnson, Dorris and Ellen Leventhal. *The Letters of Nunnally Johnson*. New York: Alfred A. Knopf, 1987.
Kobal, John. *People Will Talk*. London: Aurum Press, Ltd., 1986
Koster, Henry. *A Director's Guild of American Oral History*. Metuchen, New Jersey: Scarecrow Press, Inc., 1987.
Mosley, Leonard. *Zanuck: The Rise and Fall of Hollywood's Last Tycoon*. New York: McGraw Hill, 1984
Riese, Randall and Neal Hitchens. *The Unabridged Marilyn*. London: Congdon and Weed, 1981.
Zotolow. *Marilyn Monroe*. London: W.H. Allen & Company, 1961.

MAGAZINE FEATURES ON BETTY GRABLE
These magazines, most of which are now rare collectors' items, proved a useful source of information on Miss Grable's career. Listed in chronological order.
The New Pearl Blonde, *Miss Modern*, February, 1938
Billion Dollar Ballyhoo, Betty Grable, *Look*, 21 June, 1938
Is Betty Grable to Blame for Her Marriage Headache? *Screen Guide*, April, 1939
Grable on Broadway, Du Barry was a Lady (cover picture) *Life*, 11 December, 1939
Betty Grable Comes to Broadway, by Edith Farrell, *National Police Gazette*, December, 1939
Grable Makes Good Again, by W L Vallee, *Silver Screen*, August, 1940
Down Argentine Way, *Movie Story*, August, 1940
She Laid an Egg, Then Boiled It, *PIC*, 15 October, 1940
Tin Pan Alley, *Lady*, November, 1940
Confessions of a Campus Cutie, *Modern Screen*, January, 1941
Tin Pan Alley, *Movie Story*, January, 1941
Father's Illness Made Her a Star, *Everybody's Weekly*, 22 March, 1941
Tin Pan Alley, *Film Weekly*, Australia, April, 1941
Look Out Ginger, Here Comes Grable, *Picturegoer and Film Weekly*, April, 1941
How I Keep My Figure, by Betty Grable, *Photoplay*, May 1941
The Boys All Go for Betty, by E Wilson, *Silver Screen*, July, 1941
The Grable-Raft Affair, *Modern Screen*, August, 1941
Life and Loves of Betty Grable, *Screenland*, August, 1941
Out on Two Limbs, by Kyle Crichton, *Look Magazine*, September, 1941
A Yank in the RAF, *Movie Story*, October, 1941
A Yank in the RAF, *Picturegoer*, 13 December, 1941
A Yank in the RAF, *Picture Show* (UK), 14 February, 1942
What Makes Betty Grable Run? *Photoplay*, May, 1942
The Follies of Betty Grable, by Leon Surmelian, *Movies*, June, 1942
Betty Grable's Bachelor Girl Hideaway, *Movie Stars Parade*, June, 1942
Hot Spot review, *Today's Cinema*, 1 June, 1942
Modern Screen Goes on a Date, *Modern Screen*, June, 1942
Servicemen's Sweetheart, *Screen Guide*, August, 1942
Betty, Behave! *Screenland*, August, 1942
Betty Grable Today, *Screen Guide*, 1942
Are Women Natural Born Feudists? (Grable and others) by M J Manners, *Silver Screen*, December, 1942
Betty's Tours of the Army Camps, *Silver Screen*, December, 1942
Footlight Serenade, *Daily Film Renter*, 3 February, 1943
Does Grable Need a Change? by Lionel Collier, *Picturegoer and Film Weekly*, 20 February, 1943
Footlight Serenade, *Photoplay*, 6 March, 1943
Footlight Serenade, *Picturegoer*, March, 1943

Bibliography

Close Up of Betty Grable, by Barbara Berch, *Movieland*, May, 1943
Letter from Liza to Betty Grable, *Silver Screen*, May, 1943
Her Legs are a Hollywood Landmark, *Life Magazine*, 7 June, 1943
Heartbreak Behind the Betty Grable-George Raft Parting, *Movieland*, June, 1943
Goodbye to Love, by May Driscoll, *Motion Picture*, June, 1943
The Champ Betty Grable, *Photoplay*, June, 1943
Grable Marries James, *Life Magazine*, 19 July, 1943
Vote for the Queen of the Pin-Up Girls, *Movie Stars Parade*, August, 1943
What About Betty Grable and Harry James? *Photoplay*, August, 1943
Coney Island, *The Cinema*, 1 September, 1943
Grable-James: Hollywood Said It Couldn't Happen, *Movies*, September, 1943
The Exclusive Story of the Grable-James Marriage, *Movieland*, September, 1943
The Love Story of Betty Grable and Harry James, *Modern Screen*, October, 1943
Betty Grable - an Autobiography, *Cosmopolitan*, October, 1943
End of Heartbreak, by John Drake, *Motion Picture*, October, 1943
Pin-Up Girl, *Movie Story*, December, 1943
Manual of Arms - and Legs! *Esquire Magazine*, December, 1943
The Most Looked-At Face of 1943, *Picture Post*, 8 January, 1944
Betty Grable: Her New Baby, *Life Magazine*, 8 May, 1944
Introducing Miss James, *Photoplay*, May, 1944
The Night Betty Grable's Baby Was Born, *Movieland*, June, 1944
Sweet Rosie O'Grady, *Screen Romance*, July, 1944
Grab-Bag on Grable, *Photoplay*, December, 1944
Christmas is Every Day, says Betty Grable, *Movie Stars Parade*, January, 1945
Hot Trumpeter, *Movies*, January, 1945
Jottings on James, *Screen Stars*, February, 1945
Grable-James, the Enchanted Couple, *Photoplay*, March, 1945
Grable's Baby is a Year Old, *Lady Magazine*, 19 March, 1945
What Grable and Mr James Argue About, *Photoplay*, July, 1945
If I Had a Second Chance, by Betty Grable, *Movieland*, September, 1945
Betty Grable's Secret Date, *Photoplay*, October, 194568
Betty Grable Defends Mrs Harry James, *Delight*, 1945
The Sisters They Call Dolly, by Bruce Woodhouse, *Illustrated*, 6 January, 1946
Happiness Inc, by Abigail Putnam, *Modern Screen*, February, 1946.
The Shocking Miss Grable, by Carl A Schroeder, *Screen Guide*, April, 1946
Betty and the Simple Life, *Silver Screen*, May, 1946
If You Were the Ranch Guest of Betty Grable, *Photoplay*, May, 1946
The Life Story of Betty Grable, *Picture Show*, May, 1946
Betty Grable, Pin-Up Girl, *Motion Picture*, May, 1946
The Song I Remember, *Photoplay*, June, 1946
Pin-Up Winner, *Screen Guide*, August, 1946
Mother Wore Tights, *Daily Film Renter*, 21 August, 1946
Saturday Off, by Howard Sharpe, *Modern Screen*, September, 1946
How Betty Grable Lives, by Parva Petersen, *Modern Screen*, September, 1946
Betty Grable, by Robin Coons, *Screen Guide*, September, 1946
It's Like This With Harry and Me, by Betty Grable, *Photoplay*, November, 1946
America's Favourite Blonde, *Screen Album*, January, 1947
It's the Darndest Thing, *Photoplay*, April, 1947
Betty at her Best, by Robert Scott, *Movieland*, May, 1947
Betty Grable and Dick Haymes, The Shocking Miss Pilgrim. *Picture Show*, 14 June, 1947
The Startling Truth About Betty Grable, by May Mann, *Movies*, 1947
Grable Grabs The Greenbacks, *Lady Magazine*, September, 1947
Mother Wore Tights, *Movie Story*, October, 1947
Grable Has a Grumble, *Picturegoer*, November, 1947
Betty Grable as a Mother, *Silver Screen*, December, 1947
Betty Grable...Our Cover Girl - and Why, by Sidney Skolsky, *Motion Picture*, December, 1947
They'll Remember Mama, *Photoplay*, January, 1948
Confessions of a Mother-in-law by Lillian Grable, *Modern Screen*, March, 1948
Rules for Wives, by Betty Grable, *Photoplay*, April, 1948

Illusions in Lace, *Movie Stars Parade*, April, 1948
The Role I Like Best, by Betty Grable, *Saturday Evening Post*, 10 April, 1948.
Inside Betty Grable's Trailer, by Aline Mosby, *National Police Gazette*, April, 1948
This is Myself by Betty Grable, *Movieland*, June, 1948
Living the Daydream, *Time Magazine*, 23 August, 1948
My Wife Betty, by Harry James, *Screen Guide*, September, 1948
That Lady in Ermine, *Screen Stories*, September, 1948
Thanks to My Dancing, by Betty Grable, *Hollywood Album*, December, 1948
Harry's Girl, by Lillian Grable, *Modern Screen*, December, 1948
When My Baby Smiles at Me, *Movie Story*, January, 1949
Betty Grable - Her Divided Heart, *Photoplay*, January, 1949
Should Betty Grable Wear Tights? by Marjorie Williams, *Picturegoer*, 1 January, 1949
The Grable Fable, by Virginia Lee, *Film Illustrated*, February, 1949
G is For Gorgeous, Glamorous Grable, by Crawford Dixon, *Screen Guide*, April, 1949
The Betty Grable I Know, by Adela Rogers St Johns, Movie *Stars Parade*, April, 1949
I'm a Betty Grable Fan, says Preston Sturges, by Ben Maddox, *Motion Picture*, June, 1949
The Beautiful Blonde from Beverly Hills, *TV Guide*, June, 1949
There is Nothing Like a Dame, by Richard Moore, *Motion Picture*, June, 1949
Her Legs Are Her Fortune, by Dan Fowler, *Look Magazine*, 16 August, 1949
Blonde Bonanza, *Photoplay*, September, 1949
I'm Still Wild About Harry, by Betty Grable, *Modern Screen*, September, 1949
Grable Goes to the Stable, *Picturegoer*, October, 1949
Betty Lets Her Hair Down, by Marie Brasselle, *Screenland*, 1949
Tinsel and Tears, *Screenland*, January, 1950
I Don't Run Betty's Life, by Lillian Grable, *Modern Screen*, February, 1950
I Danced My Way To Fame, Movie Stars *Parade*, March, 1950
La Dame au manteau d'hermine (That Lady in Ermine), *Mon Film* (France) 1 March, 1950
What Every Girl Should Know, *James Family Album*, April, 1950
The World's Most Popular Blonde, *Saturday Evening Post*, 15 April,
The Beautiful Blonde from Bashful Bend, *Picturegoer*, 22 April, 1950
The Beautiful Blonde from Bashful Bend, *Picture Show*, 29 April, 1950
I'm Sorry About Those Rumours, says Betty Grable, by Frances Lane, *Silver Screen*, May, 1950
Wabash Avenue, *Screen Stories*, May, 1950
The Betty Grable Fans Ask For, *Movie Play*, May, 1950
Betty Grable, *Screen Album*, Spring, 1950
I'm No Career Girl, says Betty Grable, *Movieland*, June, 1950
Wabash Avenue, by C. Emge, *Down Beat*, 2 June, 1950
Three Little Words, by William B Hartley, *Modern Screen*, July, 1950
She Bows to No-one, *Silver Screen*, August, 1950
Call Her Betty James, *Motion Picture*, August, 1950
Glorifying Grandma's Games, *Movie Pix*, September, 1950
Are Grable's Legs Worth $200,000 a year? *National Police Gazette*, September, 1950
Betty Grable, *Screen Guide*, September, 1950
My Blue Heaven, *Film Music Notes*, Sept/Oct, 1950
My Blue Heaven, *Metronome*, October, 1950
My Blue Heaven, *Movie Story*, October, 1950
Your Photoplay *Photo-plays*, November, 1950
The World's Most Popular Blonde, by Pete Martin, *Look*, 1950
Ten Years With Betty Grable, *Motion Picture*, 1950
Love, Laughter and Tears, by Adela Rogers St. Johns, *American Weekly*, 1950
The Legend of the Legs, by Fredda Dudley Bailing, *Screenland*, 1950
Mother Is a Glamor Girl, *Screen Guide*, March, 1951
Pin Up, *Photoplay*, April, 1951
Call Me Mister, *Screen Stories*, April, 1951
Does Mother Know Best? *Photoplay*, May, 1951
Call Me Mister, *Metronome*, May, 1951
Off Screen Betty, by Reba and Bonnie Churchill, *Silver Screen*, July, 1951
Harry and the Sleeping Beauties, *Hollywood Family Album*, July, 1951
My Days with Grable, by Macdonald Carey, as told to Ben Maddox, *Movies*, August, 1951

Is Grable Quitting? *Modern Screen,* August, 1951
Daughter Knows Best, *Movieland,* August, 1951
Betty Talks to Horses, by Don Allen, *Photoplay,* August, 1951
Betty Grable's Revealing Story, *Screen Stars,* August, 1951
Grable Has a Grumble, *Picturegoer,* September, 1951
There Is No Betty Grable, *Motion Picture,* October, 1951
The Truth About the Grable Rumors, *TV and Screen Guide,* October, 1951
The Truth About Those Grable Rumors, *Movie Stars Parade,* October, 1951
Meet Me After The Show, *Screen Stories,* November, 1951
Meet Me After The Show (cover and spread), *Picturegoer,* 8 December, 1951
Meet Me After The Show (cover and spread), *Picture Show,* 8 December, 1951
My Favourite Role, *Film Review,* 1951/52
Meet Me After the Show, *Metronome,* January, 1952
Betty Grable cover, *Modern Screen,* April, 1952
The Real Case of the Lucky Legs, by Lloyd Shearer, *Pageant Magazine,* May, 1952
Is The Grable Feud Hotter Than Ever? *Movieland,* May, 1952
Betty Grable and John Wayne - cover tribute - *Newsweek,* 16 June, 1952
Betty Takes a Bow, *Photoplay,* July, 1952
Why I Got Tired of It All, by Betty Grable, *Silver Screen,* August, 1952
Betty Grable cover, *Modern Screen,* December, 1952
Scrapbook of a Star - Betty Grable, *Screen Annual,* December 1952
               They Only Look at My Legs, *Picturegoer Annual,* December, 1952
Betty's Other Life, *Photoplay,* February, 1953
Betty Grable Fights Back, *Movie Stars Parade,* February, 1953
Is Grable Jealous of Monroe? *Motion Picture,* February, 1953
The Farmer Takes a Wife, *Screen Stories,* March, 1953
Does Grable Care? by Margaret Hinxman (editor) *Picturegoer,* 27 June, 1953
Is Betty Grable Gingham or Velvet, by Reba and Bonnie Churchill, *Screenland,* June, 1953
The Farmer Takes a Wife, *Picture Show,* 27 June, 1953
Hey, Rockette Running Out of Fuel, by Connie Schreider, *Screen Life,* July, 1953
Nice Goin', Mrs James, *Photoplay,* July, 1953
Why They Thought Grable Was Through, *Movieland,* August, 1953
How To Marry A Millionaire, *Picturegoer,* 2 August, 1953
How To Marry a Millionaire, and feature on *Cinemascope, Illustrated,* 2 August, 1953
The Farmer Takes A Wife, Grable Goes It Alone, *Metronome,* 9 September, 1953
Love Affair - Betty Grable-Harry James, by Julie Paul. *Motion Picture,* September, 1953
How To Marry a Millionaire. *Screen Stories,* November, 1953
Betty Grable cover, *Screen Album,* Winter, 1953
Caught in the Act, *Down Beat,* 4 December, 1953
Ten Year Double Feature, *Screen Annual,* December, 1953
Hollywood Life Stories - Betty Grable, Dell Publishing, 1953
Betty Grable's Movie Life in Pictures, *Movie Life,* January, 1954
How To Marry a Millionaire, color picture, *Photoplay,* January, 1954
How To Marry a Millionaire, *Picturegoer,* January, 1954
How To Marry a Millionare, *Picture Show,* January, 1954
How To Marry a Millionaire (story and critique), *Photoplay,* February, 1954
Miss Grable Steps Out, *Motion Screen,* March, 1954
The Gorgeous Gal With the Million Dollar Legs, *Parade Magazine,* 1954
Betty Grable portrait, *Saturday Evening Post,* 9 October, 1954
She Has What She Wants, by Jack Sydols, *Movie Fan,* 1954
Three For The Show, *Screen Stories,* February, 1955
Hollywood is looking for a new Betty Grable, *Hit Parade,* February, 1955
Three For The Show, *Photoplay,* May, 1955
The Return of Grable, by Reba and Bonnie Churchill, *Modern Screen,* March, 1955
Three For The Show, *Picturegoer,* 7 May, 1955
Three For The Show, *Picture Show,* 7 May, 1955
Betty Grable - She's Shy, by J W Richardson, *Movie Life,* July, 1955
Betty Grable for Guys and Dolls, *Picturegoer,* July, 1955
How To Be Very, Very Popular, *Parade,* July, 1955

Bibliography

How To Be Very, Very Popular, *Tid-Bits*, July, 1955
Spend a Day With Betty Grable, *Picturegoer Annual*, December, 1955
The Fun I Have With My Daughters, by Betty Grable, *Modern Screen*, August, 1956
Monroe Will Never Beat Grable, says Zanuck, *Picturegoer*, 23 February, 1957
The World's Most Famous Pin-Up, *Parade*, 1960
Those Fabulous Legs Are Dancing Again, *Reveille*, 1960
Betty was THE Blonde Bombshell, by Peter Noble, *The Viewer*, 17 August, 1963
Betty Grable, by Gene Ringold, *Screen Facts*, Fall, 1963
Birds Thou Never Were, by Helen Laurenson, *Nova Magazine*, Summer, 1969
Legend Revisited, by Barbara Ettore, *Chicago Today*, 9 December, 1969
The Legs That Helped Win World War 2, by Jane Ardmore, *Motion Picture*, May, 1971
Thanks for the Memory, by Alan Warner, *Films and Filming*, October, 1971
Her Legs Are Still A-1. by Ralph Bloom. *8 O'Clock*, 18 March, 1972
Pin Up Girls (Grable, Turner, Hayworth), *Cinema Scene*, 1973
The Pin Up Girl with the Luscious Legs, by Bill Collins, *TV Times*, (Australia), 5 October, 1974.
Pin Up Who Launched a Million Dreams, by Simon Wood, June, 1982
Girl With the Million Dollar Legs, *New Idea*, 17 February, 73.
The Girl With The Million Dollar Legs, by Robert Kendall, *Movie Classics*, December, 1973
Betty Grable Fights Back, *Movie Mirror*, July, 1973
Remembering Betty Grable, by Jeanine Basinger, *Film Fan Monthly*, July/August, 1973
Grable Remembered, by R Baker, *Films Illustrated*, August, 1973
Betty Grable (1916-1973) Filmography by J Girney, *Films in Review*, August, 1973
Betty Grable — In Memory, *Show Magazine*, September, 1973
Grable on Record, *Gramophone*, September, 1973
Betty Grable, by R. D. Richardson, *After Dark*, September, 1973
A Final Tribute to Betty Grable, by Robert Kendall, Hollywood *Studio Magazine*, September, 1973.
Death Reveals Betty Grable's Secret Love, *Modern Screen*, October, 1973
The Men in Her Life Remember Betty Grable, *Photoplay*, October, 1973
She Shined Even in Darkness, *Rona Barrett's Hollywood*, November, 1973
Betty Grable, *Screen World*, January, 1974
Betty Grable Letters, *Films in Review*, January, 1974
Betty Grable - Mother Knew Best, by Walter H Hogan, *Nostalgia Illustrated*, January, 1975
The Legs that Helped Win the War, *Headlines*, August, 1975.
Hollywood's Most Famous Photograph, by Chris Moor, *Hollywood Studio Magazine*, September, 1981
Screen Greats, Screen Stars Vol. 7, *Starlog Press*, 1983
Pin Up Girl, by John J. Croft, *Classic Images*, April, 1985
Gene Ringold. "Betty Grable: She Lived a Lot." *Hollywood Studio Magazine*. August, 1986.
Betty Grable color poster. *Hollywood Studio Magazine*. October, 1987.
"Pin Up Special." *Hollywood Studio Magazine*. December, 1988.
"Betty Grable, Superstar!" *Hollywood Studio Magazine*. March, 1988
"Hollywood's Greatest Pin-Up Girls." *Hollywood Studio Magazine*. December, 1988
"Bathing Beauties," *Hollywood Studio Magazine*. August, 1989.
"The Ups and Down of Betty Grable." by Eve Golden, *Classic Images*, January, 1992.
"Betty Grable — Star of the Month." by David Hofstede. *Hollywood Collectibles*. August, 1994.

Index

Index

Index

Index

Index

Photo Acknowledgements

The following photographs are from the collection of Bernie Freedman of Toronto:

Photo Section 1: 1-1, 1-3, 1-5, 1-6, 1-7, 1-8, 1-13, 1-17, 1-18, 1-20, 1-21, 1-22, 1-24,
Photo Section 2: 2-2, 2-3, 2-5, 2-8, 2-15, 2-20, 2-21,
Photo Section 3: 3-12, 3-15,
As well as the photos that appear on the following pages: x, 92, and 350

The following photographs are from the collection of John Purdy of Stockport:

Photo Section 1: 1-2, 1-9, 1-10, 1-12, 1-14, 1-15, 1-16, 1-19, 1-23,
Photo Section 2: 2-1, 2-4, 2-6, 2-7, 2-10, 2-11, 2-12, 2-13, 2-14, 2-16, 2-18, 2-19,
Photo Section 3: 3-2, 3-3, 3-4, 3-5, 3-6, 3-7, 3-8, 3 9, 3 10, 3-16, 3-19, 3-20, 3-22,
As well as the photos that appear on the following pages: iv, 72, 112, 186, 309, and 323

The following photographs are from the Author's collection:
Photo Section 1: 1-4, 1-11,
Photo Section 2: 2-9, 2-17,
Photo Section 3: 3-1, 3-11, 3-13, 3-14, 3-17, 3-18, 3-23.
As well as the photos that appear on the following pages: vi, 247, and 291

The photo numbered 3-21 is from the collection of Robert Kendall of Florida.

The photo seen on page 220 is from the Associated Press and is used with their permission.

IN ADDITION: All of the exquisitly executed original artwork in this volume was done by artist Bernie Freedman of Toronto, Canada. His beautiful renderings of Betty Grable are used in this book with his express permission as his legacy to her.

415

About the Author

Photo credit: Iain Barkley, Glasgow, Scotland

Author Tom McGee combines his "lifelong love affair with Betty Grable" with his career as a journalist to bring you this honest, lovingly written biography. A native and resident of Scotland, his career has taken him to many places, including a stint in Saudi Arabia.

Mr. McGee is the editor/publisher of *Betty Grable's Hollywood*, a movie buff/nostalgia magazine that comes out quarterly and deals with the stars of the thirties and forties. In addition, he has had numerous articles printed in magazines such as *Photoplay* (UK), *Picturegoer*, *TV Times* (UK), *Hollywood Then and Now*, and *Films and Filming*. He also assisted with research on the book, *The Trade Unionist and the Tycoon* by Allister Mackie. *The Girl with the Million Dollar Legs* is Tom's first full-length biography.

Now freelancing, Tom is very busy working on projects for various local newspapers, but still finds time to enjoy his other interests in cinema, theatre, gardening, and travel. He lives in Glasgow and enjoys long country walks with his dog, Lucky.